Yahoo Groups • Noah Plan
• bibleprincip

Truth Quest History - Book list
   Michelle Miller

All through the Ages - Book list
   Christine Miller

Haycock's Topical Bible ⇒ Encyclopedia of
                              Bible truth — $36 ⁴⁹/se

The Noah Plan Lessons
Kindergarten

Sheree Beale and Rosemarie Ricciardi

Carole Adams, Art Ricciardi, Martha Shirley, Barbara Keller
Contributing Editors

Governing Principle:

God's Principle of Individuality

The Principle Approach®

FOUNDATION FOR AMERICAN CHRISTIAN EDUCATION
Chesapeake, Virginia

The Noah Plan Lessons Kindergarten

Sheree Beale and Rosemarie Ricciardi

Carole Adams, Art Ricciardi, Martha Shirley, Barbara Keller
Contributing Editors

COPYRIGHT © AUGUST 2003
FOUNDATION FOR AMERICAN CHRISTIAN EDUCATION
ISBN 0-912498-29-3

PUBLISHED BY
FOUNDATION FOR AMERICAN CHRISTIAN EDUCATION
CHESAPEAKE, VIRGINIA
1-800-352-3223 • www.face.net

Catalogue and Mail Order Address
PO Box 9588, Chesapeake, VA 23321
800-352-3223 • www.face.net

Typography, technical editing:
Desta Garrett

Cover Design: Carol Phillips
Pictures used with permission:
Abacus—Activities for Learning, Hutchinson, Minnesota
StoneBridge Kindergarten Students

Acknowledgments

Verna Marie Hall, researcher and compiler of America's Christian history and co-founder of the Foundation for American Christian Education, believed in God's ability to restore our nation through educating a generation. She envisioned a shelf of curriculum guides to instill in American children the love of liberty, the love of their Christian history, and the grasp of the Biblical principles that give substance to their faith for life and learning.

Rosalie June Slater, author of the Principle Approach®, mentored hundreds of Christian teachers in discovering for themselves the love of learning and the liberty of Principle Approach teaching and learning. She taught us the principles inherent in the subjects of the curriculum and how they teach us the knowledge of God. We are indebted to Verna Hall and Rosalie Slater for the substance of this book.

The Noah Plan Lessons give in print for the first time the weekly lesson guides for the Principle Approach. Master teachers in the F.A.C.E. demonstration school contributed their time and talent over many years to this work. Sheree Beale is the master teacher who brings fresh manna from her classroom where she daily nurtures kindergartners. Sheree epitomizes the heart of the teacher for the child while making learning a joy as teacher-scholar. She is a living legend in her professional service.

The F.A.C.E. Noah Plan coordinating editor, Rosemarie Ricciardi, brings to this project many years experience at all primary grade levels. Her grasp of the Principle Approach and ability to teach it has blessed families and children for two decades. Rosemarie transformed the spirit and letter of Sheree's classroom into a book to be used by parents and teachers everywhere. Rosemarie coordinated the gifts and contributions of Martha Shirley, author of *the Noah Plan Reading Curriculum Guide* and the "Bible as Reader Program," Carole Adams, author of the *Noah Plan English Language Curriculum Guide,* Art Ricciardi, author of the *Noah Plan Mathematics Curriculum Guide,* and Barbara Keller, master teacher and assistant editor.

We at the Foundation for American Christian Education believe that the Deuteronomy 6 mandate to teach our children Biblical truth all day long "as they lie down and rise up" is not only possible but required of Christian parents and teachers everywhere. We offer *The Noah Plan Lessons: Kindergarten* as the tool of Principle Approach education. May the Lord Jesus Christ be glorified.

And thou shalt love the Lord thy God with all thine heart,
And with all thy soul, and with all thy might.
And these words, which I command thee this day, shall be in thine heart:
And thou shalt teach them diligently unto thy children,
And shalt talk of them when thou sittest in thine house,
And when thou walkest by the way,
and when thou liest down, and when thou risest up.

Where to Find What You Need for Kindergarten Noah Plan Lessons

Page Nos.

INTRODUCTION ix
The Noah Plan ix
The Principle Approach Vision for the Primary Grades xii
The Principle Approach Kindergarten xv

GETTING READY FOR KINDERGARTEN 1
Essential Books and Materials 3
Optional Supplementary Resources for each Quarter 4
Tools and Supplies for the Classroom 6
How This Book Is Organized 7
Steps for Beginning to Use the Noah Plan Lessons 8
A Proposed Schedule Teaching and Learning for Kindergarten 9
A Model Classroom Constitution and A Model Student Constitution 10
A Suggested Student Supply List 12
A Word Concerning Assessment in the Kinder "Garden" and Sample Report Card 13
Notebook Grading Sheet 16

QUARTER ONE 17
Mathematics Planning Sheet by Components 19
The Reading, Spelling, and English Weekly Routines 20
Reading and Phonemic Awareness Instruction Supplement 22
The Bible, Literature, History, Geography, and Science Lessons 26

QUARTER TWO 77
Mathematics Planning Sheet by Components 79
The Reading, Spelling and English Weekly Routines 80
Reading Vocabulary Instruction Supplement 82
The Bible, Literature, History, Geography, and Science Lessons 84

QUARTER THREE 133
Mathematics Planning Sheet by Components 135
The Reading, Spelling and English Weekly Routines 136
Reading Comprehension Instruction Strategies Supplement 138
The Bible, Literature, History, Geography, and Science Lessons 141

QUARTER FOUR 189
Mathematics Planning Sheet by Components 191
The Reading, Spelling, and English Weekly Routines.................................... 192
Reading Fluency Instruction Supplement 194
The Bible, Literature, History, Geography, and Science Lessons 196

SUPPLEMENTAL INFORMATION 243
Overviews of Kindergarten Subjects for Student Notebooks 245
Cultivating the Love of Learning in Kindergarten... 258
  Winnie-the-Pooh Tea Party 258
  Beatrix Potter Day 259
  Grandparents' Day 263
  Pioneer Day/*Little House in the Big Woods* Day 265
  The Kindergarten Field Studies 268
Kindergarten Mathematics... 269
Sample Teacher Lesson Plans and Actual Student Work for
  Bible as a Reader and English Lessons 282
Resources
  Alphabetical List of Books and Publishers 295
  Ordering Information 297

vii

The Noah Plan Lessons: Kindergarten

INTRODUCTION

You have in your hand the *Kindergarten Noah Plan Lessons.* The lessons are based upon a massive work of curriculum development in the Principle Approach® that occurred over a period of seventeen years as it was being implemented and 'tested' in the classroom. It is designed to enable the family and the teacher to practice the art and love of learning and to be *liberated* by its effects. *The Noah Plan* pedagogy takes schooling out of the mundane 'cookie cutter' mode and gives it transcendent and ennobling ends by fusing the American classical curriculum with the method of Biblical reasoning that makes the Word of God the basis of every subject.[1]

Please regard this edition of the *Kindergarten Noah Plan Lessons* as a work in progress—first fruits of a massive publishing project that will require many years of refinement. We invite you, the user, to make suggestions, tell us what works and what doesn't, and to contribute to the refinement of this book. You can reach us through the www.face.net web site, where you will also find a discussion board for posting questions and ideas. Sheree, Martha, Carole, Barbara, and Art, led by Rosemarie, are all master teachers whose first concern is that you, the teacher, be successful with this book.

The Qualities of The Noah Plan®

The Noah Plan Liberates the Educator. The Biblical principles of education and government form the Truth which, when known, "*shall make you free,*" (John 8:32) Jesus taught principles and provoked his hearers to think, reason, reflect, and respond from the heart. What really is a principle? It is the cause, source, or origin of any thing. God placed His glorious creation upon the bedrock of a set of governing principles. Those principles were demonstrated in the flesh-and-blood life of the person Christ. The Bible exposits recurring basic principles through every book, every story, every precept, and *every subject.* Principles are causative, primary, invisible but *foundational* to our thinking, our worldview, and our understanding. Principles cause an effect that is visible and secondary, external, but reflecting the internal. The effect of a Principle Approach education is "*the glorious liberty of the children of God.*" (Romans 8:21) In the classroom, that liberty quickens learning by inspiration, consecration, cultivation, and instruction.

The Noah Plan Creates a Rich Learning Environment. Real learning is a natural and satisfying activity for children and adults. God designed us to be learners, to be literate, and to embrace all knowledge, which is His provision for our wisdom. Knowledge also reflects its Creator, revealing the heart and nature of God. Thus, teaching and learning in a program based on the eternal, Biblical principles that appear in every subject is both satisfying and joyous. Too often education is reduced to practicing skills, regurgitating disconnected and isolated facts, or filling in the workbooks and moving on. This is a frail, sickly shadow of the feast our American Christian heritage offers us and our children. We have as a birthright the opportunity to study the Word of God freely in all its applications. Why aren't we learning to read using the Bible as a primary reader? In *The Noah Plan* we have the liberty to enjoy the best and greatest, all that is "*true, honest, just, pure, lovely, of good*

The Noah Plan Lessons Kindergarten © 2003 • Foundation for American Christian Education   ix *report, of virtue and praise.*" (Philippians 4:8) Why aren't we feasting on the great music, art, drama, and producing through education the great composers, painters, and writers to inspire the next generation? In *The Noah Plan* we suggest a rich, classical curriculum with diverse learning experiences to nurture the whole potential of the child—the spirit, the mind, the soul, and the body.

While we offer the complete curriculum as a display of Kindergarten subjects and lessons from which the teacher or parent may select what is applicable to the particular setting and needs, we urge the user to be sure to have a well-balanced program. School without art is an aberration. How can we pretend to teach the whole child if we ignore the aesthetic education of our children? Likewise, the teaching of modern and classical languages is a non-negotiable element of elementary and secondary education if we seriously intend to educate our children in an American classical approach.

Celebration is at the heart of the love of learning. We've included a section in the book with projects and special days for Kindergarten celebration of learning.

The Noah Plan Forms a Biblical Worldview in the Student.

Authentic Christian education rests upon teaching students to reason Biblically. Rosalie Slater in *Teaching and Learning America's Christian History: The Principle Approach,* contrasts methods and results:

Secular Methods and Goals

A. Creates a causative environment to which the student becomes responsive.

B. Conditions the student to look at the external social, economic, religious, and political climate before he determines how he will act.

C. Results in an individual who can 'discern the face of the sky' but cannot 'discern the signs of the times.'

Principle Approach Methods and Goals

A. Builds principles from God's Word into the thinking of the student, empowering him to subdue the environment rather than submit to it.

B. Teaches the student to look to the internal demands of conscience as causative of behavior and action and to see the external environment as effect.

C. Results in the student learning to subdue the earth for God's purpose and according to His will.

The Noah Plan Inculcates Biblical Reasoning in the Student. It provides the student with the advantage of an uncluttered, orderly mind, and insight into the connectedness of knowledge. The understanding of providential history gives the student a panoramic view from which to relate lessons from the past to **present** applications. It cultivates the spirit with a complete vision of life in God as the scripture ordains. No longer is the moral marrow—of who we are and what our purposes are—being schooled out of our children, because now we are reclaiming and restoring education's highest ends. The Principle Approach teaches us that the end of education is not just thinking or knowing but acting in accord with the truth of God's Word—true liberty.

The Nature of The Noah Plan®

To implement *The Noah Plan* successfully it is essential to understand its nature—its ideal, its potential, and its use as a model.

THE IDEAL. The Principle Approach was practiced in classrooms and home schools before *The Noah Plan* for decades. The Principle Approach can be taught directly using the "red books," the Webster's 1828 *Dictionary*, the Bible, and a good library. The ideal is that every individual teacher develops the specific curriculum for his/her own setting.

THE POTENTIAL. *The Noah Plan* offers a complete kindergarten through twelfth grade curriculum in twelve subjects as it is employed in the demonstration school. The nature of the Principle Approach dictates that *The Noah Plan* or any other model of Principle Approach curriculum be *an offering, not a mandate*. The teacher should select from it or use it as a guide from which to design an individual program for his/her class or family. The teacher who begins with *The Noah Plan* gets a "jump-start" in the Principle Approach for immediate help, which, over time, will give way to the teacher's own research and writing as he/she internalizes the methodology and is inspired to go beyond *The Noah Plan.* The potential is for the user to become a master teacher.

THE MODEL LESSONS. The lessons suggested here are the lessons developed in the demonstration school classrooms in each subject. They model the methodology that may be used to teach and learn any topic or subject. It is imperative that the user understand that the Principle Approach is a methodology not a curriculum. It is the method that liberates, inspires, cultivates, consecrates, and builds character.

The Christ 'His Story' of The Noah Plan®

The Foundation for American Christian Education first published the Principle Approach® in 1965 in *Teaching and Learning America's Christian History: The Principle Approach* as "America's historic Christian method of Biblical reasoning which makes the Truths of God's Word the basis of every subject in the school curriculum." Among the individuals and schools inspired by the original F.A.C.E. publications was a community of parents and teachers in Chesapeake, Virginia. There in 1980, StoneBridge School was established with the mission of implementing the philosophy, methodology, and curriculum governed by the Principle Approach and demonstrating its application in a K–12 curriculum.

Rosalie June Slater mentored many teachers and educational leaders in the decades that followed the publication of her monumental work. Carole Adams was one of those who looked to Verna Hall and Rosalie Slater for the pure stream of inspiration in Christian education. She became the founding head of StoneBridge School. Grade by grade, subject by subject, the curriculum developed through the efforts of dozens of teachers led by the original founding teachers. One of those, Elizabeth Youmans, became the lead editor of *The Noah Plan* after fifteen years of teaching and administrating in the school. Elizabeth wrote the *Noah Plan History/Geography Curriculum Guide.* Martha Shirley and Wendy Giancoli, two of the founding teachers, developed their own areas of the curriculum into the *Noah Plan Reading Curriculum Guide*, and the *StoneBridge Art Guide*, respectively. Carole Adams wrote the *Noah Plan English Language Curriculum Guide.* Meanwhile, Art Ricciardi, Principle Approach Curriculum Designer and Teacher Training Specialist, developed

The Noah Plan Lessons Kindergarten © 2003 • Foundation for American Christian Education

the mathematics curriculum and wrote the *Noah Plan Mathematics Curriculum Guide.*

Rosalie Slater produced the classical literature program for children selecting the classics and writing the teacher syllabus for each. She developed the junior high and high school literature programs which, along with the elementary, were edited for the *Noah Plan Literature Curriculum Guide.*

The Noah Plan publishing project was conceived and begun in 1995. The project now consists of the following publications:

- *The Noah Plan Program Notebook K–8* with *Self-Directed Seminar* and audio tapes

- *The Noah Plan Program Notebook 9–12* with *Self-Directed Seminar* and audio tapes

- Six *Noah Plan Curriculum Guides*—Literature, English, Reading, Mathematics, History/Geography, Art

The current publication project is *The Noah Plan Lessons,* grade-level weekly lesson guides to accompany *The Noah Plan* notebook and guides, edited by Rosemarie Ricciardi.

The Noah Plan Name-Sake

The Principle Approach curriculum was named *The Noah Plan* in reference to a phrase in the biography of Noah Webster by Rosalie Slater in the facsimile reprint of the 1828 *American Dictionary of the English Language,* page 13:

> These volumes [Noah Webster's textbooks] *republished again and again became the basis of an American system of education and their influence grew with the history of the young republic. . . . Wherever an individual wished to challenge his own ignorance or quench his thirst for knowledge, there, along with the Holy Bible and Shakespeare, were Noah Webster's* [books]. *Indeed if his Biblical name should have any significance to America it might be said that Noah's books were an ark in which the American Christian spirit rode the deluge of rising anti-Christian and anti-republican waters which threatened so often to inundate the nation.* [Emphasis added.]

The Foundation for American Christian Education presents a Principle Approach curriculum in the Noah Plan that purposes to preserve the American Christian spirit that it may continue to be the joy of many generations.

The Principle Approach Vision for The Primary Grades

The Principle Approach is reflective learning, thoughtfully done with careful research, reasoning, relating, and recording. The result is the formation of a character that gives honor to Christ and that operates from a Biblical worldview. This is a slow, line-upon-line process that begins with the small child and continues over the years of schooling until graduation to higher education. The primary grades are the seeding and germinating years for the good fruit to come.

SEEDS. In kindergarten the seeds must be planted—good seed and all the seeds. The seeds of all the academic areas are planted in kindergarten and first grade. The habits that are formed, the work

xii   The Noah Plan Lessons Kindergarten © 2003 • Foundation for American Christian Education skills, the attitudes, the interests, the strategies of learning—all form the basis of scholarship. Classroom management, stewardship of property, interpersonal relationships; daily habits of punctuality, accountability, and wholesome attitudes; standards of work held to a high level for penmanship, page headings, notebook work, verbal expression—all comprise the structure in which good character thrives. The teacher who insists upon and appreciates politeness and good manners, respect for parents and teachers, initiative and faithfulness, nurtures lifelong habits of successful living.

NURTURE. The primary grades provide the nurture to the new seedlings as they germinate and grow. They need the sun of the teacher's encouragement and praise, the water of the Word, the regulation of a well-governed classroom, the fertilizer of inspiration, the protection of high standards with swift, private correction, and the cultivation of a happy, positive, trusting relationship between teacher and child. In this environment, children master the basic literacy skills, the vocabulary of the subjects, and the rudiments of the notebook habit. They learn to reason by the use of symbols, by understanding internal to external, by using concrete images to represent abstract ideas. They memorize, recite, write, dramatize, and do guided projects.

THE CHRISTIAN IDEA OF THE CHILD.[2] Viewing children through the Christian idea of the child means affirming their wholeness and imparting a sense of their particular, individual purpose in God's providence. It means that we see them as able – able to learn, to grow, to self-govern, to reason at their level and with the correct mediation that the teacher is there to provide. The teacher must respect each child and the image of God within while fully realizing the God-ordained responsibility that teaching imposes. "Not many should become teachers, my brethren, for you know that we will be judged by a higher standard and with greater severity, thus we assume the greater accountability and the more condemnation." (James 3:1) The key word at primary level is *nurture*.

> nurture, n. [Fr. *Nourriture*, from *nourir*, to nourish.] That which nourishes; food; diet. 2. That which promotes growth; education; instruction. "Fathers, do not irritate and provoke your children to anger—do not exasperate them to resentment—but rear them [tenderly] in the training and discipline and the counsel and admonition of the Lord." (Ephesians 6:4)

THE LOVE OF LEARNING. The teacher should model the love of learning by her enthusiasm and genuine interest. This love of learning is contagious, giving the students inquisitive minds, a love of scholarship, fascination with God's creation in all its diversity, and the desire to master subjects. In primary school celebration is key. Special Days are held to celebrate areas of the curriculum—"Pioneer Day" when *Little House in the Big Woods* is completed, "Winnie-the-Pooh Tea Party," etc. These Special Days provide hands-on activities, games, foods unique to the occasion, and a monumental memory that reinforces the love of learning.

THE NOTEBOOK METHOD.[3] We plant the seeds of the notebook method in kindergarten and nurture them through the primary grades. In the primary grades, students see the notebook as a tool of scholarship used daily in the classroom under the teacher's careful direction.

1. The notebook teaches students excellent standards as they permanently record their thinking and learning with reflection and care, and as they create an individual expression of the subject.

2. The student work filed in the notebook is held to the standards of neatness, completeness, accuracy, and order.

The Noah Plan Lessons Kindergarten © 2003 • Foundation for American Christian Education

3. The notebook is *not* a filing cabinet to catch every piece of paper throughout the year. It *is* a permanent record of the year's work collecting the substance of the study of the subject.

4. The object is *not* to contain all the facts in the binder. The object *is* to make a record of the research, reasoning, and relating of the subject throughout the year.

5. Standards should include:

   - The teacher's requirements for the notebook order (tabs and dividers, title page, etc.)
   - The overview of the subjects contained in the notebook
   - The standard for neatness as prescribed by the teacher (the acceptable mode of making corrections; ruled lines where underlining or labeling maps is required; colored pencils used for illustration and maps, etc.)

THE REASON QUESTION. The Principle Approach is reflective learning. Questioning should require the student to think, analyze, connect ideas, observe, identify, discover, and articulate. In primary grades, class discussion, and, often, paraphrasing of ideas, result in a higher level of thinking. Speaking complete sentence answers to brief "essay" questions, and later in the year, writing answers in the notebook helps the student master the subject and compile a complete record of his learning.

THE CLASSROOM CONSTITUTION. The Principle Approach classroom provides a positive environment for learning and for the development of Christian character. The teacher is responsible to govern the classroom and to give account for its stewardship. While the standard is Christian character that reflects the operation of the Holy Spirit in the teacher's life, the teacher's unique spirit and character are mirrored in the classroom and in the pupils. "*A pupil is not above his teacher, but every one when he is fully taught will be like his teacher.*" (Luke 6:40) Classroom disciplines and order reflect the Biblical principles of education and government.

Good classroom governance eliminates the tension of policing and patrolling to which class discipline too often declines. The basics of good classroom governance include:

1. God is the source of all authority, law, and government as defined in His Word. Children must be taught the difference between being 'controlled' and learning to accept God's authority in their lives. This process requires love and patience on the part of the teacher and continuous reinforcement.

2. Christian self-government begins when the student, in obedience to God's Word, rules over his own spirit and chooses to submit to the authority of the teacher, God's representative in the classroom.

3. The classroom constitution is the document of 'law' by which each student agrees to be governed. The teacher writes the classroom constitution. It describes the behavior of a self-governed student by stating concrete rules and guidelines necessary for class order.

The classroom constitution should be taught at the beginning of the school year and signed by each student as a symbol of consent. A copy of the constitution should be placed in the front of the student notebook. A larger copy should be placed on the classroom wall for display throughout the year. The purposes of the constitution in the classroom may be summarized as follows:

1. Provides the structure of Christian government in the classroom.
2. Establishes the rules of order, the requirements, and the controls necessary to protect the life, liberty, and property of each student.
3. Forms the character of each child by inspiring internal control and conformance to Christian ideals.
4. Teaches the student the purpose and meaning of Christian self-government.
5. Articulates the seven principles of government and education in practical, visible ways.
6. Mirrors the character of the Christian constitutional republic for the student.
7. Provides for the development of Christian self-government individually for each child.

Discipline is the compass that directs the gifts and learning of each child. The teacher should thoroughly understand the authority vested in him or her to minister discipline. Research the words *authority, government, discipline* in the Webster's 1828 *Dictionary*.

THE SUBJECT OVERVIEWS. The overviews for each kindergarten subject are found after all of the weekly lessons: NPLK, 245–257. The overviews provide the purpose, principles, content, and resources of each subject. A copy of the overview is placed after the title page of the student's notebook to provide the student with the whole view of the year's work in the subject. It should be referred to as each new unit is introduced to show the student his progress through the subject and remind him of the whole purpose.

Kindergarten

Planting Seeds of All Learning

Kindergarten provides the initial step of formal schooling and, thus, becomes a vital instrument in the character development of the student. Academic and developmental needs are respected in the kindergarten program with a wholistic approach that meets the spiritual, mental, emotional, and physical needs of each child.

The seeds of academic mastery are planted through the introduction of the Bible, English, classics of literature and poetry, arithmetic, geography, history, science, French, and the arts. Introduction of these subjects produces a love of learning at an early age and combined with "Special Day" celebrations, makes learning come "alive." The Notebook Approach is modified for this age group. In kindergarten, children begin to identify the notebook as a tool of learning and grow in their ability to use it.

The careful instruction of receptive and expressive language skills and the creative teaching of written English lay a secure foundation for literacy. Motor exercise, coordination, directionality, auditory and visual discrimination, comprehension skills, interpretation, alertness to direction, spatial dominion, appreciation of words and language, number values, counting, measuring, sequencing, are all part of kindergarten skill building. The kindergarten classroom is organized to guide the child in developing Christian character and qualities conducive to learning success—organization and beginning study skills, accountability for classroom behavior, responsibility, diligence, industry, faithfulness, politeness and good manners. Kindergarten prepares children for the important primary step of their education.

The Principle Approach Vision for Kindergartners

In kindergarten, a positive and effective introduction to formal schooling is more important than achieving the "primer-level" basic literacy in reading, writing, and arithmetic. This can be accomplished when the teacher embraces *the Christian idea of the child,* and creates a classroom reflective of this noble ideal. As this spirit is upheld and ministered daily, the rich classical curriculum can be enjoyed without force-feeding or stress to teacher or child. In academics, the basics are practiced appropriately and the curriculum is celebrated. The mornings are given to Bible, arithmetic, reading, and English. In the afternoons, literature, history, geography, science, French, music, art, and physical education are enjoyed. As the year progresses, children are writing more frequently and producing their record of the subjects. The Principle Approach also has a "basic literacy" that must be learned, beginning in primary grades:

- The principle of the year is "God's Principle of Individuality." This principle is identified in all the subjects throughout the year.

- The Chain of Christianity which forms the basis of the history lessons is placed on a timeline on the wall and referred to continually to inculcate a sense of chronology and the connectedness of providential history.

- The globe and maps are used frequently to impart an understanding of geography in every subject to teach the student that geography is the stage upon which history is enacted.

- Art and music enrich all areas of the curriculum as well as being taught individually as a skill.

- The encouragement and practice of verbal expression enables the articulation of the subjects individually through discussion, oral presentations, recitations, drama, and oral reading.

- Writing includes the higher goal of learning to write paragraphs by students orally contributing as the teacher develops a paragraph on the board.

- The celebration of learning creates a positive atmosphere for scholarship and productivity.

- The study of French completes the language education of kindergartners, cultivating their language-learning abilities, establishing the sound system of a foreign language early, and expanding their understanding of how language works.

- The kindergarten notebook reflects the growing ownership of the subjects by keeping an orderly record throughout the year.
- The "reason question" is introduced and taught orally. This is a question that causes a thoughtful "essay answer" of complete sentences through which the student re-expresses the subject in his answer.

God's Principle of Individuality

The first Biblical principle of education is God's Principle of Individuality—the foundational assumption that every child is made in God's image, fallen in nature but by God's grace destined for immortality, gifted for a special purpose in God's providence, and of infinite individual value. In teaching and learning, reasoning from this point, we cannot think of children as generic raw material, to be stamped into the mold of curriculum and mass assembled into society.

Guided by God's Principle of Individuality, it is possible to maintain the sanctity and dignity of individually-created children while moving them through the grades or process steps to bring each one to the fullest expression of his individual value in Christ.

Certain goals and purposes govern grade levels or the ascending steps through which we "do" school. In the Principle Approach, the standards that are distinctly "internal" are priority. The Biblical view of the child requires that we teach the whole child as an *individual* created specifically by God unto good works and for His purposes. A lock-step system of grading is impractical. Rather, we look for the growth of character as the touchstone as we progress through the primary grades.

The model set here in the *Noah Plan Lessons* should be seen only as a point of reference for the individual teacher or parent. The goal is not to do as much as you can. The goal is to practice the *methodology* at the pace that is practical and effective in the particular application. How much of the curriculum you cover is a matter of individual need, practicality, and conscience.

The key word for Noah Plan users is Liberty!

---

[1] Slater, Rosalie J. *Teaching and Learning America's Christian History: The Principle Approach.* San Francisco: F.A.C.E., 1965.

[2] Adams, Carole. "The Christian Idea of the Child." Originally published in *The Journal of F.A.C.E.*, Vol. II, 1991; Revised and appended to the *Family and the Nation: Biblical Childhood*, Rosalie J. Slater. San Francisco: F.A.C.E., 2003.

[3] See *The Noah Plan Self-Directed Seminar*, F.A.C.E.

Benji W.

Getting Ready for Kindergarten

God's Principle of Individuality

Everything in God's universe is revelational of
God's infinity, God's diversity, God's individuality.
God creates distinct individuals.
God maintains the identity and individuality
of every thing which he created.

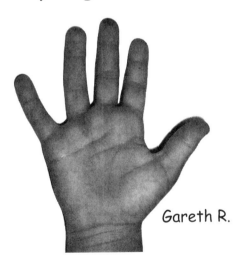

Gareth R.

STARTING WITH ME

*God made me special
Like no one you see,
God made me a witness
To His diversity.*

—Rosalie June Slater

Gareth R.

Essential Materials Needed for Use with The Noah Plan Kindergarten Lessons

Order Information for all Noah Plan Resources on pages 295–298

(Abbreviations for the following books are used within the text as listed here.)

1. The Noah Plan®—the complete Program for Kindergarten which includes:

   The Noah Plan Program Notebook (NPPN).

   The Noah Plan Self-Directed Seminar and Principle Approach Methods (NPSDS)*

   The Noah Plan Lessons for Kindergarten (NPLK)

   Six Noah Plan Curriculum Guides:

       The Noah Plan Mathematics Curriculum Guide (NPMG)

       The Noah Plan English Language Curriculum Guide (NPEG)

       The Noah Plan Reading Curriculum Guide (NPRG)

       The Noah Plan History-Geography Curriculum Guide (NPH&GG)

       The Noah Plan Literature Curriculum Guide (NPLG)

       The StoneBridge Art Guide (SAG)

       The Noah Plan Science Curriculum Guide (NPSG) (*under production*)

   American Dictionary of the English Language, Facsimile Edition, (Webster's 1828 *Dictionary*)

   Christian History of the Constitution, Vol. I: *Christian Self-Government* (CHOC)

   Teaching and Learning America's Christian History: The Principle Approach (T&L)

   Christian History of the American Revolution: Consider and Ponder (C&P)

2. Starter Kit (which includes *The Writing Road to Reading*® 2003 Edition)

3. Bible (King James Version) for memory work

4. *Family and the Nation: Biblical Childhood*, including "Christian Idea of the Child"

5. *Phonemic Awareness in Young Children: A Classroom Curriculum*

6. *The Early Reader's Bible*

7. The French Primer: *Premiers Pas de Français*.

8. The Kindergarten Classics:

   Winnie-the-Pooh, Peter Rabbit, Bambi, Little House in the Big Woods, Abraham Lincoln (d'Aulaire), *Tales of Shakespeare* (Lamb's), *Uncle Remus Stories, Aesop's Fables, A Child's Garden of Verses, Mother Goose and other nursery rhymes, lullabies, fairy tales*, children's poets and poetry

9. *RightStart Math*™ for Kindergarten

10. Globe, atlas, student atlas, wall map of the physical world, a classroom Christian history timeline

---

*Included in NPPN and also sold separately.

Optional Supplementary Resources by Quarters

We have used these books in the lesson plans; however, you are free to use comparable resources from your local library, old book stores, or other sources.

Concerning the supplementary readers for Bible as Reader: according to *The Writing Road to Reading,* by Romalda Spalding, it is recommended that after the student has mastered the 150 most commonly used words, reading can be from storybooks of interest to the child. Basal readers with a controlled vocabulary may or may not be used. The supplementary readers listed below are optional and other books may also be found listed in the Appendix of Spalding's book.

All Quarters

Bible:
- Dickson New Analytical Study Bible, KJV
- *Commentary on the Whole Bible*, Matthew Henry
- *International Bible Dictionary*, J. D. Douglas and Merrill C. Tenney
- *Children's Illustrated Bible*, Selina Hastings

Geography:
- *Beginning Geography*, K–2, Volumes 1–3

Science:
- Encyclopedia

Quarter 1

Bible as Reader:
- *Primary Phonics*, Educators Publishing Service (EPS)
  8361-G3C Set of ten storybooks (workbook optional)
  8551-G3C Set of ten storybooks (workbook optional)
  8362-G3C Set of ten storybooks (workbook optional)
  8573-G3C Set of ten storybooks (workbook optional)
  8574-G3C Set of ten storybooks (workbook optional)
- *Little Books 1–10*, Abeka
- *Little Owl Books*, Abeka
- *Basic Phonics Readers Set*, Abeka

Literature:
- Fairy tale books
- Lullaby books
- Poetry books of Christina Rossetti

History:
- Dog books
- *Fun with Snowflakes Stencils*, Paul E. Kennedy
- *Snowflake Bentley*, Jacqueline Briggs Martin

Science:
- Zoology books

Quarter 2

Bible as Reader:
- *Primary Phonics* (See quarter 1.)
- *Little Books 1–10*, Abeka
- *Little Owl Books*, Abeka
- *Basic Phonics Readers Set*, Abeka

Literature:
- Book of the Christmas story
- Animal tales written by Beatrix Potter
- *Peter Rabbit and Friends Cook Book*, Naia Bray-Moffatt, or *Peter Rabbit's Natural Foods Cookbook*, Arnold Dobrin
- *Divine and Moral Songs in Easy Language*, Isaac Watts
- Nursery rhyme books
- Poetry books of Isaac Watts
- Poetry books of Henry Wadsworth Longfellow

History:
- *3 in 1: (A Picture of God)*, Joanne Marxhausen
- *America's Providential History*, Mark A. Beliles & Steven K. McDowell
- *Plimoth Plantation Day Packet*, Elizabeth Youmans
- Teacher Guide: "Christopher Columbus, Christ-bearer to the New World"

Science:
- *Who Lives Here,* Dot & Sy Barlowe

Quarter 3

Bible as Reader:
- *Reading for Fun Enrichment Library*, Abeka
- *Big Owl Books*, Abeka
- *First Grade Readers*, Abeka

History:
- *A Children's Color Book of Jamestown in Virginia*, Priscilla Hunt
- *Admiral Christbearer Coloring Book*, William A. Roy, Jr.
- *America's Providential History*, Mark A. Beliles & Steven K. McDowell
- *Columbus*, Ingri & Edgar Parin d'Aulaire
- *George Washington*, Ingri & Edgar Parin d'Aulaire
- *Plimoth Plantation Day Packet*, Elizabeth Youmans
- *Squanto, Friend of the Pilgrims,* Clyde Robert Bulla
- *The Plimoth Plantation Coloring Book,* Carolyn Freeman Travers

Geography:
- Antarctica articles, *Journal of F.A.C.E.*, Volume I

Science:
- Books on anatomy for primary school children:
  - *Learning about My Body,*
  - *Me and My Body,* David Evans & Claudette Williams
  - *My First Body Book,* Chris & Melanie Rice
  - *My Five Senses,* Aliki Brandenberg
  - *The Skeleton Inside You,* Philip Balestrino
  - *What's Inside My Body,* Angela Royston

Quarter 4

Bible as Reader:
- *Reading for Fun Enrichment Library*, Abeka
- *Big Owl Books*, Abeka
- *First Grade Readers*, Abeka

Literature:
- *Little House in the Big Woods*, Laura Ingalls Wilder
- Teacher Guide: "Pilgrim-Pioneer Character Moving Westward" Rosalie J. Slater

History:
- George Washington's *Rules of Civility and Decent Behaviour*, in *George Washington: The Character and Influence of One Man*, Verna M. Hall.
- *Our National Symbols*, Linda Carlson Johnson
- *Rudiments of America's Christian History and Government: Student Handbook*, Rosalie J. Slater & Verna M. Hall

Science:
- Books about botany and leaves

Tools and Supplies for the Classroom

These items are used in *The Noah Plan Lessons: Kindergarten*, but are optional.

American and Christian flags
Bulletin board
Chalkboard/Whiteboard/Charts (to include chalk or markers)
Construction paper (variety of colors)
Crayons
Globe
Glue
Lined and unlined notebook paper
Magazines for cutting (*Ranger Rick*, *National Geographic*, etc.)
Overhead projector
The Noah Plan Map Maker's Kit (colored pencils, student atlas, ruler, map standard)
The Noah Plan Wall Timeline
Wall map of the world
Overhead projector

History
Leaf stencils
Pictures and artifacts related to colonial life
Pictures of English life in 1600s
Pictures of Patriots—George Washington
Pictures of United States symbols—*Declaration of Independence*, *U.S. Constitution*, Liberty Bell, Statue of Liberty, American Bald Eagle, Seal of the President, American Flag
Pictures, charts, and artifacts of life in Jamestown
Sand and seashells
Snowflakes stencils
Words and music to patriot songs

Geography
Books, magazines, artifacts, music, and food related to the seven continents
Pictures of the Solar System, universe, Earth

Literature
Music for Psalm 100
Pictures, music, clothing, foods, etc. of frontier life
Pictures of Shakespeare, the Globe Theater

Science
Animal bones
Beans seeds (lima, and others)
Cards for labeling
Celery or carnation
Clear glasses
Edible flowers (broccoli, cauliflower)
Food coloring
Items for touching, smelling, tasting, and hearing
Microscope
Pictures of the parts of plants, trees
Pictures of the skeletal, muscular, circulatory, respiratory, digestive, nervous systems
Pictures of worms, reptiles, echinoderms, mollusks, porifera, protozoa, coelenterates, arthropods, amphibians, reptiles, fish, birds, mammals
Potting soil
Prepared slides of one-celled animals, worms,
Root vegetables for tasting and rooting
Small peat or clay pots
Stethoscope
Wax or contact paper for preserving flowers
X-ray

How This Book Is Organized

The Noah Plan Lessons: Kindergarten employs the Principle Approach in teaching and learning all the subjects of the school curriculum. The teaching and learning of English and Reading depend strongly upon establishing instruction routines that are consistently practiced every day, every week. Routines establish the skill needed to bring the student toward mastery in these subjects. The teacher should use the weekly routines to guide the scheduling and practice of reading and English instruction.

Bible, History, Geography, Literature, and **Science** offer you Principle Approach lesson plans that can be taught age appropriately, at a comfortable pace for the home or school employing them, and probe into the nature and character of God by examining His creation diligently, meaningfully, yet enjoyably.

The teaching and learning of **Mathematics** requires the consistent use of the language and vocabulary of the subject, and the demonstration of principles applied practically to solve meaningful problems. The daily lessons plans provided by *RightStart*™ provide the mathematical content only. The author and editor of the mathematics curriculum section have provided you also with the quarterly planning charts and a teaching schedule that identify the governmental and subject principles for your usage, and the key individuals mathematics timeline, etc. that completes it as a study of mathematics using the Principle Approach.

The Noah Plan Lessons: Kindergarten is divided into the **Introduction** (The Noah Plan; The Principle Approach Vision for the Primary Grades; Kindergarten) and three sections:

Section 1	Section 2	Section 3
Getting Ready for Kindergarten	Entire Kindergarten Curriculum by Quarters	Supplemental Information

• Essential Materials
• Supplementary Resources
• Tools & Supplies
• Steps for Beginning to Use the Noah Plan Lessons
• Teaching Schedule
• Classroom & Student Constitutions
• Supply List
• Assessment
• Sample Grade Report
• Notebook Grading Sheet
	Mathematics:
	  • Component Charts
	  • Daily *RightStart*™ Lesson Plans
	
	Reading & English:
	  • Weekly Routines
	
	Bible, Literature, History, Geography, Science:
	  • Weekly Lesson Plans
		• Subject Overviews
		• Special Day Descriptions
		• Field Trips Description
		• Mathematics
		• Sample Teacher Lesson Plans
		• Sample Student Work
		• Resource List & Ordering Information

Steps for Beginning to Use the Noah Plan Lessons
How to Use the Book for a Successful Principle Approach Kindergarten

1. How do I get prepared?

- ⊙ Get a 3-ring binder to begin a teacher notebook.
- File your notes and assignments for your *Noah Plan Self-Directed Seminar* (NPSDS) behind a divider in the teacher notebook for future reference.
- ⊙ Complete the study of the NPSDS which will give you:
  - the background necessary to practice the Principle Approach philosophy,
  - the methodology and the curriculum,
  - the familiarity with the reference volumes as you complete your lessons.
  - Allow several weeks to complete this study.
- Make a page in the teacher notebook for recording your questions as you begin to use the *Noah Plan Lessons Kindergarten* (NPLK).

(Your questions will be answered as you progress through the materials.)

2. What do I need to collect and organize?

- Collect the essential materials, supplementary resources, and supplies you will need. (See pages 3–6, 9–12, 14–16)
- Put dividers in your teacher notebook for each subject you will be teaching.
- File your research and other collected information in your teacher notebook.
- Organize your classroom with the tools you will need to support your curriculum: Noah Plan Wall Timeline, map, globe, etc.
- Use the sample schedule or devise one that works well for you. The day should be orderly and comfortably paced.

3. What will help me to visualize the program?

- Read the Noah Plan subject overviews to get the whole picture for the entire curriculum. (NPLK, 245–257)
- Select any subject and read its lessons for one quarter to get a sense of the flow of instruction and student response moving toward personal ownership.
- Discover how all the Noah Plan books are cross-referenced.

4. What do I do next?

- Follow the directions for the beginning lessons of each subject in the NPLK.

    Bible/Bible as Reader, 26–27, 283–289

    Math, 19; 271–281

    Reading & English Routines, 20–25

    English, 290

    Literature, 28

    History, 29

    Geography, 30

    Science, 31

- Later you might see the need to set up separate notebooks for each subject.

8　　The Noah Plan Lessons Kindergarten © 2003 • Foundation for American Christian Education

Teaching Schedule for Kindergarten

Hours	Monday	Tuesday	Wednesday	Thursday	Friday
8:30–9:00	Bible	Bible	Bible	Chapel / Bible	Bible
9:00–9:30	Arithmetic*	Arithmetic	Arithmetic	Arithmetic	Arithmetic
9:30–10:00	Snack & Recess	Snack & Recess	Snack & Recess	Snack & Recess	Snack & Recess
10:00–12:15	Reading & English	Reading & English	Reading & English	Reading & English	Reading & English
12:15–1:00	Lunch & Physical Education	Lunch & Physical Education	Lunch & Physical Education	Lunch & Physical Education	Lunch & Physical Education
1:00–1:30	History	Science	History	Science	History
1:30–2:00	Literature	Geography	Literature	Geography	Literature
2:00–2:30	Rest & Tutorial Time	Rest & Tutorial Time	Rest & Tutorial Time	Rest & Tutorial Time	Rest & Tutorial Time
2:30–3:00	Music	French	Art	French	Music

*See the Sample Annual Teaching Schedule for Mathematics, NPLK, 276.

Kindergarten
Classroom Constitution

I. **Purpose and Goal**

Government is an arrangement for the general good. Rules and standards are meant to protect us and to help us become better people. A high standard of education and character pleasing to the Lord is our goal.

II. **Rules governing conduct while on school premises:**

"I will behave myself wisely in a perfect way." (Psalm 101:2)

"Let all things be done decently and in order." (I Corinthians 14:40)

DEPORTMENT: "the manner of acting in relation to the duties of life."
(*American Dictionary*, Noah Webster, 1828)

I am self-governed when:

1. I quickly obey my teacher and do what is asked of me.

2. I show respect to my teacher and friends by listening when they speak.

3. I speak kindly to my friends.

4. I am careful with all property—mine, the school's, and other's.

5. I am quiet and orderly when visiting any place outside my classroom.

III. **Agreements:**

A. As the teacher and example to each student, I agree to fulfill my responsibilities. I will regard each child individually and minister to his own personal needs and capabilities. If a child needs correction I will judge the method used by the child's knowledge, maturity, and patterns of behavior.

_____
Teacher's Signature

B. After reading and discussing the above constitution with my child, I agree to encourage my child to govern himself by these standards. If any question arises, I will contact the teacher immediately.

_____
Parent's Signature

C. After discussing the above constitution, I agree to serve God by governing myself by these classroom standards.

_____
Student's Signature

Kindergarten
Classroom Constitution
Student Notebook Copy

1. I will obey my teachers at all times.

2. I will respect my classmates at all times.

3. I will be a good steward of school property.

———————————————————————
Student's Signature

Suggested Student Supply List

The following supply list has been prepared with much consideration given to long term usefulness and durability. The development of neatness and organizational skills has also been considered. All supplies will be needed on the first day of school. Be sure to label all items and clothing, including each crayon or pencil, with permanent marker.

QUANTITY	ITEM
1	Bible—*Early Reader's Bible,* Thomas Nelson Publishers, 1993
2	Looseleaf notebooks—standard two-inch binders with 1½ -inch rings *(No trapper-keepers, please!)*
11	Notebook dividers with tabs
1	Packaged standard lined notebook paper (200 sheets). Please leave paper in package for shelf storage.
10	No. 2 pencils
1	Box crayons (at least 24)
1	Cardboard (or plastic) pencil box
1	Rest mat—kindergarten size (approximately 1" x 18" x 44"); please no oversized mats
1	Paint smock or large shirt
1	Lunch box
2	Plastic document protectors
1	*Primary Composition Notebook,* Spalding Education International, (602) 866-7801
1	Map Maker's Kit

NOTEBOOK SETUP

Please set up your student's notebooks as follows and bring them to school the first day:

#1 Notebook – Student Name

Label tabs on the dividers in the order given below (please print neatly):

1. Bible
2. Arithmetic
3. English
4. Literature

#2 Notebook – Student Name

Label tabs in the order given below (please print neatly):

1. History
2. Geography
3. Science
4. French
5. Art
6. Music
7. P.E.

A Word Concerning Assessment in the Kinder "Garden"

Milestones serve several purposes. They measure distance between two points. They measure progress in a journey. They serve as memorials to the evaluation of progress as the journey is made. Grading reports are the milestones of school life and are essential for these same reasons, but they often are a dread as much as a delight. It is especially difficult to grade our beginners who are so fresh on the path of academic life and for whom a grade at this age sometimes measures maturity. Respecting God's Principle of Individuality, we prioritize individual readiness in kindergarten and provide space and time for each child to naturally produce the bloom of mental, emotional, and physical "readiness." Our job is to nurture and cultivate what resides by the gift of God within each one through inspiration, consecration, and instruction. The natural rhythms of life have as many individual tempos as there are children.

We have chosen a system of grading in kindergarten that is most expressive of our priorities. Our kindergarten program is primarily the "sowing" stage of the whole education process—sowing the seeds of literacy, skill mastery, a broad academic foundation, Christian character, and Biblical reasoning. How is it possible to translate that into subjects and grades on a report card? It is comparable to the farmer attempting to predict his harvest on the basis of pounds of seeds planted. There are many variables. We must depend upon the vigilance of the teacher and her faithfulness to seed, water, re-seed, weed, re-seed and cultivate as she tends her kinder "garden." The report card then reports progress. On the report card (NPLK, 14–15), the assessment ✓ (check) indicates steady progress. It means "a moving forward in growth; increase; advance in knowledge, intellectual or moral improvement; proficiency." It comes from Latin, *pro* and *gradior*, to step or go. Occasionally an *SP* (for slow progress) indicates an area of concern. The ✓+ (check plus) for accelerated progress means that the child is working at a rate that exceeds steady progress. Steady progress is excellence evaluated individually. What is more excellent for any four or five-year-old than steady growth?

The word *deportment* has been chosen to cover all areas of behavior, self-conduct, work habits, and manners. *Deportment* is defined by Noah Webster, father of American Christian education, in his 1828 *Dictionary*, as "carriage; manner of acting in relation to the duties of life; behavior; demeanor; conduct; management." This word best describes the child's response to classroom and individual governing standards.

See sample **Grade Report** demonstrating assessment (set up to be xeroxed two-sided on one sheet of paper and folded), on the following two pages.

Kindergarten
Grade Report

Student: _____

Year: _____

Teacher: _____

Principal: _____

Date: _____

Promoted to Grade: _____

Comments by Quarter:

1. _____

2. _____

3. _____

4. _____

SOCIAL EMOTIONAL DEVELOPMENT	QTR 1	QTR 2	QTR 3	QTR 4
Demonstrates Courtesy				
Obeys quickly and cheerfully				
Responds well to correction				
Listens when others talk				
Works and plays well with others				
Is developing self-control				
Meets new situations with confidence				
Accepts responsibility				
Respects property				

WORK HABITS	QTR 1	QTR 2	QTR 3	QTR 4
Follows group direction				
Follows individual direction				
Usually completes a task				
Is careful to do his/her best work				
Works without disturbing others				
Participates willingly in most activities				

ATTENDANCE:	QTR 1	QTR 2	QTR 3	QTR 4	TOTAL
Days Present					
Days Absent					
Days Tardy					

SUBJECT	QTR 1	QTR 2	QTR 3	QTR 4	AVG
Bible					
Phonics					
Spelling					
Reading					
Literature					
Penmanship					
Arithmetic					
Science					
History					
Geography					
French					
P.E.					
Music					
Art					

GRADING SCALE:

SP Slow progress
✓ Steady progress
✓+ **Excellent progress**

Notebook Grading Sheet

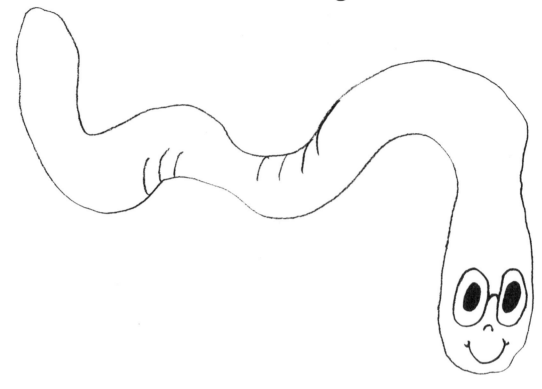

Your Notebook Shows:

_____

_____

_____

_____

_____

Quarter One

All through the Night

Sleep, my child, and peace attend thee
  All through the night,
Guardian angels God will send thee,
  All through the night.

Soft the drowsy hours are creeping
  Hill and vale in slumber sleeping,
I my loving vigil keeping,
  All through the night.

While the moon her watch is keeping,
  All through the night,
While the weary world is sleeping,
  All through the night.

O'er thy spirit gently stealing,
  Visions of delight revealing,
Breathes a pure and holy feeling,
  All through the night.

—Alfred Lord Tennyson

Gareth R.

John M.

Quarter One Planning Sheet for Teaching Mathematics by Components

Teacher: Mr. Ricciardi   **Grade Level:** K

"Eye hath not seen nor ear heard, neither have entered into the heart of man, the things which God hath prepared for them that love him." 1 Corinthians 2:9

Week	Foundations	Numbers	Numeration/Notation	Measurement	Operations	Problem Solving		Summary of Principles
1		See lesson plans for this entire week. NPLK, 277–281						The principles and leading ideas of mathematics are demonstrated in the lessons, and are continually clarified for the children as the year progresses.
2 RSL 1–4	CFG–symbols, CSG–consent, CSP–consent, GPI–infinity	Quantities 1–6, Ordinal numbers	Finger sets, Tallying, Tapping, Vocabulary	End–middle–end, Quadrilateral, Triangle	Addition, "+1 more" strategy, Changing quantities, Directionality—left/right, Subtraction	Constructing, Disagreeing agreeably, Drawing, Engineering, Games, Matching	Patterning, Practicing, Reciting, Sorting, Subitizing, Translating	**Governmental Principles**
3 RSL 5–8	CFG–drawing, GPI–order	Quantities 1–10	Finger sets, Reading abacus entries, Tallying, Tapping, Vocabulary	Linear measure, Time	Addition, Subtraction	Abacus entries, Constructing, Drawing, Ordering	Reciting, Sorting, Subitizing, Translating	*God's Principle of Individuality* (GPI) Mathematics measures 'how much.' Each number is a unique quantity.
4 RSL 9–11	CFG–matching, quantities, GPI–infinity, order	Quantities 1–10	Tallying, Tapping, Vocabulary	Geoboard, Lines, Planes, Rectangle, Square, Time	Addition, Subtraction	Abacus entries, Building, Drawing, Engineering, Memory game	Ordering, Patterning, Reciting, Translating	*Christian Self-Government* (CSG) Operations (+, −, ×, ÷) govern mathematics.
5 RSL 12–14	CFG–matching, quantities, GPI–infinity, order	Quantities 1–10, Even numbers, Odd numbers	Tallying, Taps, Writing numerals	Rectangle, Square	Addition, "+1 more" strategy, Multiplication by 2s, Subtraction	Abacus entries, Building, Engineering	Patterning, Reciting, Translating	*Christian Character* (AHCC) Mathematics demonstrates God's character. It is systematic, unchangeable, and orderly like God.
6 RSL 15–18	CFG–building, writing, GPI–infinity	Quantities 1–10, Even numbers, Odd numbers, Hundreds, Tens, Zero	Finger sets, Tallying, Vocabulary, Writing numerals	Equilateral triangle, Fractals, Hexagon, Rhombus	Addition, Multiplication by 2s, 10s	Abacus entries, Building, Engineering, Reciting, Subitizing, Translating		"*Conscience…Sacred Property*" (CSP) Mathematics enables the individual to Biblically care for property.
7 RSL 19–20	CFG–symbols, GPI–infinity	Quantities 1–10	Tallying, Writing numerals	Geoboard	Addition, Subtraction	Abacus entries, Constructing, Grouping, Patterning		*Christian Form of Government* (CFG) Quantity is represented in various ways. *Local Self-Government* (LSG) Christ's government is planted into the heart of the student as the student deals with the operations (government) and processes of mathematics.
8 RSL 21–23	AP–matching, CFG–writing, patterning, GPI–order	Place value, Quantities 1–10	Reading abacus entries, Symbols "+", Writing numerals	Circle	Addition, Multiplication by 10s, Subtraction	Abacus entries, Arranging, Games, Matching	Ordering, Partitioning, Practicing, Subitizing	*American Political Union* (APU) Numbers of like kind only may be added. **Subject Principles**
9 RSL 24–26	CFG–symbols, GPI–infinity	Quantities 1–10, Place value	Vocabulary	Money	Addition, Subtraction	Abacus entries, Comparing, Partitioning		*Associative Principle* (AP), NPMG, 104.
								See **Sample *Math Guide/Right-Start* Coordination, Lessons, & Annual Schedule, 269–281.**

The Noah Plan Lessons Kindergarten © 2003 • Foundation for American Christian Education

Quarter One—Weekly Routines for Reading and English

COMPONENT	Monday	Tuesday	Wednesday	Thursday	Friday
FOUNDATIONS	**Introduce** language as a gift from God, throughout the quarter, to learn that language is to help us communicate with Him and with each other. God uses language to communicate with us through His Word.				Look for opportunities to reinforce this idea in many lessons, NPEG, 47–49.
ORTHOGRAPHY Phonemic Awareness Instruction	**Administer** The Assessment Test, *Phonemic Awareness in Young Children,* 107–131. Determine instructional needs and begin training phonemic awareness skills. Teach "Suggested Kindergarten Schedule," *Phonemic Awareness in Young Children,* 137–141. **Introduce** phonograms and practice using the "Oral Phonogram Review Procedures" and "Written Phono-		gram Review Procedures," *The Writing Road to Reading,* 39–42. The "Suggested Kindergarten Schedule" provides for lessons to be implemented for approximately eight months. Examples of activities: 1) "Listening to Sounds" 2) "Poetry, Songs, Jingles" 3) "Rhyme Stories" 4) "Hiding the Alarm Clock."	**Introduce,** practice, extend, and revisit an activity. Repeat often to develop the ability to hear and manipulate phonemes, the smallest meaningful unit of speech. **Continue** oral and written phonogram review procedures.	
Penmanship		**Teach** correct lower case letter formation beginning with the clock circle and positions on the clock face as described in *The Writing Road to Reading,* 16–29.	**Teach** letter formation as new phonograms are introduced. *The Writing Road to Reading,* 16–29.	**Teach** letter formation as new phonograms are introduced.	
Spelling	**Wait to begin** *Spelling Dictation Procedures with the Extended Ayers List until **after** assessing mastery of 54 phonograms, The Writing Road to Reading, 43, 48–53.* • **Say** the whole word. • **Give** a short sentence. Student says each phonogram. Says again softly just before writing. Marks as needed. • **Monitor** student's writing, and signal for student to dictate the word for writing on the board. • **Write** word on the board from student dictation. • **Monitor** as student reads whole word as in normal conversation. Student reads all words for spelling (by sound or syllable). Reads all words for reading (as whole words). • **Assign** homework: Write first five words 3x and use in an oral sentence.	**Review** previously taught phonograms by dictating the sounds orally and having the student write the phonogram on lined paper. **Mix** and test between 8 and 16 phonograms after the initial introduction. **Review** previously learned phonograms by reading all words for spelling (by sound or syllable). Read all words for reading (as whole words). **Continue** *Spelling Dictation Procedure* with the next group of five words (see steps from Monday).	**Continue** *Spelling Dictation Procedure* with the next five words (see steps from Monday). **Read** spelling words orally. **Elicit** oral sentences from student. **Write** sentences from oral discussion on the chalkboard. (Student copies and may illustrate.) **Assign** homework: Write five words 3x and use in an oral sentence.	**Continue** to review previously learned phonograms by decoding (reading) and encoding (writing). **Continue** *Spelling Dictation Procedure.* Write the week's words in a practice test. **Assign** homework: Study for test.	**Continue** to review previously learned phonograms by decoding (reading) and encoding (writing). **Test** spelling words at the end of the week; do not require the markings for test, *Writing Road to Reading,* 85.

Quarter One—Weekly Routines for Reading and English (continued)

COMPONENT	Monday	Tuesday	Wednesday	Thursday	Friday
COMPOSITION	*In Kindergarten, formal composition writing begins in 4th quarter, but the foundations of composition writing are placed from the beginning by integrating an awareness of composing ideas throughout the subjects. After the first few weeks of school when the reading routines are established:*	**Introduce** composition—the composing of ideas in words, NPEG, 244. **Enjoy** in all subjects everyday picturesque, comical, rhyming, and rhythmic language sharing excellent models of vivid and effective writing.			**Cultivate** an appreciation of words and language through the enjoyment of them. **Create** opportunities daily for the child to relate, discuss, and present ideas in complete sentences and good order preparing to write sentences by mid-year, NPEG, 14-15.
SYNTAX	**Introduce** the structure of the English language and its parts wholistically by introducing the complete sentence rather than parts of speech.		**Practice** the sentence as a whole thought in daily speech.		**Demonstrate** the sentence by giving examples of complete thoughts in well-phrased sentences from the literature and Bible.
ETYMOLOGY	**Identify** syllables, NPRG, 111 **Build** into the student an understanding of syllables and the ability to hear and identify the syllables of any word.		**Teach** the precise meanings of words showing the student the dictionary and how to find precise meanings. **Enjoy** words that rhyme, describe, and many new words from Bible, literature, science, history, and geography. **Use** daily *Phonemic Awareness in Young Children,* 137–141.		
READING Phonetic Instruction	**Practice** phonograms using multi-sensory instruction—the Spalding Method, *The Writing Road to Reading,* 6, 39–42.		This practice can be done during the orthography segment.		
Oral Reading	**Assign** supplemental reader for home practice after mastery of single-letter phonograms is assessed, NPRG, 71. See suggested list of books in *Noah Plan Lessons Kindergarten,* NPLK, 3–5. **Check** progress daily as student reads aloud to teacher.		**Read** passages aloud to focus on comprehension rather than on decoding, *The Writing Road to Reading,* 133–141 and *McCall-Harby Test Lessons in Primary Reading* (in the Spalding Starter Kit for K–2). **Assign** supplemental reader for home practice. **Check** progress daily as student reads aloud to teacher.		**Read** aloud selected passages from the kindergarten literature curriculum, NPLG, 8–9.
Bible as Reader	**Read** passages from *The Early Reader's Bible* to correspond to Bible lessons in *Noah Plan Lessons Kindergarten* (NPLK). At the beginning of the year teacher reads aloud until child is able to read with assistance or independently, NPRG, 66–67, 96–97.		**Continue** passages from the *Early Reader's Bible.*		
Comprehension	**Teach** comprehension using suggestions in *The Writing Road to Reading,* 121–147 and *The Comprehension Connection,* 31–32. When student has learned to think and reason about ideas and information, use *McCall-Harby* book to teach student to answer literal		and inferential comprehension questions. *The Comprehension Connection* and *McCall-Harby* are in the Spalding Starter Kit for K–2. **Begin** explicit comprehension instruction as the student listens to the teacher read *McCall-Harby* narra-	tive, informative, and informative-narrative paragraphs, *The Writing Road to Reading,* 131–141. **Guide** comprehension planning and set goals using NPRG, 18–19, 92.	

Kindergarten Reading Instruction Supplement

INTRODUCTION

Martha B. Shirley

Four quarterly supplements for reading instruction have been compiled based upon the most recent research in reading instruction. The primary source is the National Reading Panel (NRP) report for 2000 and secondarily this author's classroom experiences and research. The supplementary pages include terminology that is presented in the "Weekly Routines for Reading and English" and teaching and learning methods and practices to implement the weekly planning of instruction. Biblical principles and leading ideas introduce each reading instruction supplement. The topics of the supplements are awareness, vocabulary, comprehension strategies, and fluency.

The National Reading Panel (NRP) reviewed more than 100,000 studies and identified effective practices that can help teachers and parents with methods and approaches that have worked well and caused reading improvement for large numbers of children. "Teachers can build their students' skills efficiently and effectively, with greater results than before. Most importantly, with targeted 'what works' instruction, the incidence of reading success should increase dramatically." (*Put Reading First,* iii)

The publication that resulted from the research is *Put Reading First: The Research Building Block for Teaching Children to Read.* It summarizes the findings of the National Reading Panel Report and provides analysis and discussion in major areas of reading instruction for kindergarten through grade three. The sixty-page publication can be downloaded by going to the National Institute for Literacy website at www.nifl.gov or ordered by mail, phone or e-mail by contacting National Institute for Literacy at ED Pubs, PO Box 1398, Jessup, MD 20794-1398, or by calling 1-800-228-8813, or by e-mailing EdPubOrders@aspensys.com.

Quarter One
Kindergarten Reading Instruction Supplement

PHONEMIC AWARENESS INSTRUCTION

PRINCIPLE AND LEADING IDEAS
God's Principle of Individuality:
- *Individual sounds (phonemes) make up spoken language.*
- *The sounds of speech (phonemes) are distinct from their meaning.*

Fact: Current research in beginning reading instruction has shown that phonemic awareness is a powerful predictor of success in learning to read. Adams (1990) tells us that children who cannot hear and manipulate the sounds in spoken words have an extremely difficult time learning how to decode; at least one out of five children depend critically on explicit instruction in phonemic awareness skills.

What is phonemic awareness? Phonemic awareness is the ability to notice, think about, and work with the individual sounds in spoken words. Before a child learns to read print, he needs to become aware of how the sounds in words work. He must understand that words are made up of speech sounds, or phonemes. A child who (1) can easily recognize words that begin alike, (2) can isolate the first or last sound in a word, (3) or combine or blend the separate sounds in a word to say the word will have an easier time learning to read and spell than a child who has few or none of these skills.

Phonemic awareness is not phonics. Phonemic awareness is working with spoken language to make words while phonics is understanding the relationship between letters and sounds in written language.

Why is phonemic awareness important? "Phoneme awareness is a prerequisite to learning phonics. Understanding that syllables are composed of speech sounds is critical for learning to read an alphabetic-phonic language because it is these specific speech sounds (phonemes) that letters represent. Without phonemic awareness, phonics would make no sense. Without an understanding of phonics, word recognition and spelling would depend on rote learning." (White, 1998.)

Phonemic awareness skills include the following:
- Hearing the separate words within a sentence
- Hearing the number of syllables within a word
- Recognition and creation of rhymes
- Listening for words that begin with the same sounds
- Blending of phonemes into words or syllables
- Substitution of phonemes within syllables/words
- Identification of beginning, middle, and final phonemes in words
- Segmentation of words/syllables into phonemes.

The beginning activities for phonemic awareness do not involve written letters (graphemes) or words and are therefore exclusive of phonics. White reminds us that later instruction and practice on phoneme awareness and phonics are complementary. *The most effective programs combine phonemic awareness and letter-sound relationships or beginning phonics.* "New words are always learned by studying the phonetic sounds of the spoken word. This distinguishes *The Spalding Method* from most other phonetic methods," (*The Writing Road to Reading*, 43).

When should instruction begin? Instruction is helpful to all students learning to read—preschoolers, kindergartners, first graders who are just starting to read and older, less able readers.

Which methods of instruction are most effective? In the beginning, activities in blending and segmenting words are most effective. Learning to blend phonemes with letters helps children read words. Learning to segment sound with letters helps them spell words. When a student is taught to manipulate phonemes by using the letters of the alphabet, instruction is most effective.

What materials are suggested?
- Alphabet letters (Choose foam or magnetic lower case letters which can be purchased in a toy store or a teacher store.)
- *Phonemic Awareness in Young Children: A Classroom Curriculum*, 137–141
- *The Writing Road to Reading: The Spalding Method for Teaching Speech, Spelling, Writing, and Reading.* 5th Revised Edition (2003)

References:

Adams, M. J. (1990). *Beginning to Read: Thinking and Learning About Print*, Cambridge, MA: MIT Press.

Put Reading First: The Research Building Blocks for Teaching Children to Read, September 2001. Copies available from National Institute for Literacy at ED Pubs, PO Box 1398, Jessup, MD 20794-1398. Phone 1-800-228-8813; Fax 301-430-1244. To download go to the National Institute for Literacy website at www.nifl.gov or send e-mail to EdPubOrders@aspensys.com.

White, Nancy (June 1998). *The Virginia Branch Newsletter*. International Dsylexia Association.

Teaching and Learning Phonemic Awareness

Effective phonemic awareness instruction teaches a student to notice, think about, and work with (manipulate) the individual sounds in spoken language. The broad term **Phonological Awareness** refers to a general appreciation of the sounds of speech as distinct from their meaning and includes phonemic awareness. In addition to phonemes, phonological awareness activities can involve work with rhymes, words, syllables, and onsets (beginning) and rimes (ending).

1. Develop the student's phonologically awareness—the sounds of language. He needs to understand how speech is represented by print.
    - Model and demonstrate how to break short sentences into individual words—use manipulatives (chips, cards, etc.) to represent words and importance of order to meaning.
    - Develop awareness of individual sounds in words by clapping out syllables.
    - Listen for and generate rhymes.
2. Develop phonemic awareness—words and syllables are comprised of a sequence of elementary speech sounds.
    - Focus on sounds of words not letters or spellings.
        T: How many sounds in the word **sun**?
        T: Let's try it together: /s/.../u/.../n/. How many? Good, three.
    - Focus attention and perception of isolated sounds.
        T: What is the first sound in **ham**?
        S: The first sound in **ham** is /h/.
    - Identify initial sounds and ending sounds
        T: What sound is the same sound in **sun, seal,** and **sat**?
        S: The first sound, /s/ is the same.
        T: What is the ending sound in **see, bee,** and **me**?
        S: The ending sound is /e/.
    - Blend phonemes into words.
        - Say initial sound, /m/ -ilk, /s/ -at.
        - Sound separate phonemes within words, /s/-/a/-/t/.
        - Say last sound, k- /it/.
    - Break up words into component sounds, *e.g.,*
        - /m/-oo/-/s/=moose
3. Use blending and segmenting activities to develop the relationship between sounds in words. Use the letters of the alphabet to demonstrate to the student the connection between the sound and the letter. Use foam shaped letters for more tactile awareness.
    a. Blending
        T: What word is /p/ /i/ /g/? Say the sound only.
        S: /p/ /i/ /g/ is **pig**.
        T: Now let's use our letters to "write" the sounds in **pig**.
        T: Spells **pig** with the letters.
        T Now we will read the word **pig**.
    a. Segmentation
        T: How many sounds are in **sun**?
        S: /s/ /u/ /n/. Three sounds.
        T: Let's "write" the sounds in **sun** using the letters.
        T: Runs hand under the whole word. "Now we're going to read **sun**."
    - Provide frequent, brief practice.

The Noah Plan Lessons Kindergarten © 2003 • Foundation for American Christian Education

Quarter One

TEACHING PLAN

Week One

Preparation	Lesson	Student Work	Accomplishments

Biblical Principle
The Bible is God's inspired written Word.
2 Timothy 3:16
 	
Leading Idea
The Bible is God's message to us for instruction and direction. It equips us to live for Him.
 	
Books
• Bible (King James for memory verses)
• Webster's 1828 *Dictionary*
• NPSDS, Notebook chapter
 	
Supplies
• Bible Overview (NPLK, 249)
• Notebook Grading Sheet (NPLK, 16)
• Unlined notebook page to include:
  • the title "Bible" for the student to write or trace
  • a space for the student to draw and color a picture of the Bible for his title page
 	
BAR—Bible as Reader (continued on page 27)
	Establish at the beginning of the day a time for praise, prayer, and teaching spiritual truth. (This routine will take place at the start of each day.)
	Teach the notebook standard of form. NPSDS, notebook chapter
	• **Discuss** the purpose of the notebook.
	• **Assist** the student in setting up his notebook.
	• **Distribute** and discuss the purpose of the Notebook Grading Sheet.
	• **Reinforce** daily the notebook standard of form.
	Distribute and discuss the Bible overview.
	Introduce the memory verse. Genesis 1:1
	• **Read** aloud and discuss the memory verse.
	• **Define** unfamiliar vocabulary.
	• **Discuss** God as Creator of all that exists.
	• **Practice** daily the memory verse with the student for his recitation on Friday.
	Guide the student to the Biblical Principle from the Leading Idea by reading aloud 2 Timothy 3:16.
	• **Discuss** the definition and origin of the Bible.
	• **Discuss** the purpose of the Bible.
	  · It teaches us what is true.
	  · It corrects our mistakes.
	  · It gives instructions and directions for our lives.
	  · It trains us to do what is right.
	  · It equips us to live for Him.
	• **Discuss** how the Bible is our guide for life.
	Discuss the divisions of the Bible:
	• The Old Testament—tells how God carried out His plan.
	• The New Testament—tells about the fulfillment of God's plan in Jesus Christ.
	Give a brief history of the English Bible.
	
	**BAR—Bible as Reader Lesson
	& Notebook Work**
	(continued on page 27)
		Listen as the teacher establishes the routine for each day.
		
		Listen to and follow directions from the teacher on setting up your notebook.
		• **Discuss** the purpose of the notebook and grading sheet.
		
		Discuss the Bible overview.
		Listen as the teacher reads aloud and discusses the memory verse.
		• **Discuss** unfamiliar vocabulary.
		• **Discuss** God as Creator of all that exists.
		• **Practice** and learn the memory verse for recitation on Friday.
		
		Discuss the definition and origin of the Bible.
		Identify the purpose of the Bible.
		
		Participate in a discussion about how the Bible is your guide to life.
		Discuss the divisions of the Bible.
		
		Listen as the teacher gives a brief history of the English Bible.
		
		**BAR—Bible as Reader Student
		& Notebook Work**
		(continued on page 27)
			• To receive the Bible as God's inspired Word
			• To understand the Bible is our guide for life
			• To learn new vocabulary
			• To learn and recite the memory verse
			• To complete and file notebook work

The Noah Plan Lessons Kindergarten © 2003 • Foundation for American Christian Education

Week One   Quarter One

TEACHING PLAN

Preparation	Lesson	Student Work	Accomplishments	✓
BAR—Bible As Reader Books • Dickson New Analytical Study Bible, 11–20	*Notebook Work* **Distribute** unlined paper for the student to write or trace the title and to draw and color a picture of the Bible. **BAR—Bible As Reader** Introduction to the English Bible "History of the English Bible" (See Weekly Routines for Reading and English.)	*Notebook Work* **Write** or trace the title and draw and color the picture of the Bible on the notebook page. **BAR—Bible As Reader** (See Weekly Routines for Reading and English.)		

BIBLE (continued)

Week One   **TEACHING PLAN**   **Quarter One**

Preparation	Lesson	Student Work	Accomplishments	✓
Biblical Principle The Bible is the inspired Word of God. 2 Timothy 3:16	**Teach** the notebook standard of form. (NPSDS, Notebook chapter) • **Assist** the student in setting up his notebook. (Keep the notebook simple. The teacher or parent can set up the student's notebook.)	**Listen** as the teacher explains the notebook standard of form. **Follow** the directions given by the teacher on setting up your notebook.	• To learn the note-book standard of form • To name a work of literature	
Leading Idea The Bible is the source and seedbed of all literature.	• **Reinforce** daily the notebook standard of form. **Distribute** and explain the literature overview. **Define** and discuss literature as learning through books. **Discuss** the purpose of literature:	**Listen** as the teacher explains the literature overview. **Listen** as the teacher defines and discusses literature.	• To identify Psalms as poetry • To know God better, to love Him more, and to walk in His ways	
Books • Bible (King James) • Webster's 1828 *Dictionary* • NPSDS, Notebook chapter • NPLG, 3, 8–9, 70–71, 73, 84–87	• To instruct and encourage us—Romans 15:4 • To become wiser in God's Ways—Proverbs 1:5 **Discuss** the qualities of literature. • Literature stirs up our imagination. • Literature helps us to recognize and love beauty. **Share** your favorite works of literature.	**Listen** as the teacher reads aloud Romans 15:4 and Proverbs 1:5 and discusses the purposes of literature. **Discuss** the qualities of literature. **Listen** as the teacher shares his favorite works of literature. **Name** your favorite works of literature.	• To praise God cheerfully for His greatness and for His power • To complete and file notebook work	
Supplies • Literature Overview (NPLK, 250) • Three-ring binder • Notebook paper • Dividers with tabs	**Encourage** the student to share his favorite works of literature. **Read** aloud 2 Timothy 3:16 and discuss how the Bible is a model of all the best literature because it is the inspired Word of God. **Define** psalms: poems; prayers to God; Praise songs to God **Identify** the book of Psalms as poetry by reading several selections that reflect poetry. (This is the literary type that you will be studying.) **Discuss** how the book of Psalms illustrates the Principle of Unity with Diversity. NPLG, 73	**Listen** as the teacher reads aloud 2 Timothy 3:16 and discusses the Bible as a model for all literature. **Listen** as the teacher defines psalm and identifies the book of Psalms as poetry. **Reason** aloud and answer questions. • Why is the Bible the model for all literature?		
	• The Psalms, almost all written by David, reflect his unique experience and character. • The Psalms, God's Book, reveals aspects of His nature and character. • It is this unity with diversity that identifies God's Principle of Individuality. *Notebook Work* **Instruct** the student in filing the overview behind the title page.	• What literary type is the book of Psalms? • How do the Psalms illustrate God's Principle of Individuality and Unity with Diversity? *Notebook Work* **File** the overview behind the title page.		

LITERATURE

28   The Noah Plan Lessons Kindergarten © 2003 • Foundation for American Christian Education

Quarter One

TEACHING PLAN

Week One

HISTORY

Preparation	Lesson	Student Work	Accomplishments	✓
Biblical Principle Christian Self-Government **Leading Idea** Mankind must be governed. Romans 13:1–3 **Books** • Bible (King James) • Webster's 1828 Dictionary • NPH&GG, 8–9, 47–50 • T&L, 184–188 • NPSDS, Notebook chapter **Supplies** • History Overview (NPLK, 251) • Enlarged classroom constitution for display (NPLK, 10) • Copy of student constitution for notebook (NPLK, 11)	**Teach** the notebook standard of form. (NPSDS, Notebook chapter) • **Assist** the student in setting up his notebook. (Keep the notebook simple. The teacher or parent can set up the student's notebook.) • **Reinforce** daily the notebook standard of form. **Distribute** and briefly explain the history overview. (This gives the student the whole view of the year's work.) **Guide** the student to the Biblical Principle from the Leading Idea. • **Read** aloud and paraphrase for the student Romans 13:1–3 and discuss the purpose and need for government. (To protect those who are obeying the law from those who are not obeying the law.) • **Define** and discuss the purpose of a constitution. (A constitution is a set of rules for people to live happily in a home, school, church, etc.) • **Define** Christian self-government. (When you accept Jesus as your Lord and Savior, you allow Him to govern you. He tells you how to act. Therefore, Christian self-government is allowing Jesus to govern your life.) • **Discuss** the application of Christian self-government in the classroom. (T&L, 186–188) • **Sign** the classroom and student's constitution (teacher and student) to represent the voluntary consent of the governed by the stated rules of conduct. *Notebook Work* **Create** a classroom/home school constitution (one large for classroom display, and one for insertion into the student's notebook). *CREATE FAMILY VERSION W STUDENTS / TYPE OUT 15/6N*	**Follow** the directions the teacher gives to set up your notebook. **Listen** as the teacher explains the history overview. **Listen** as the teacher reads aloud Romans 13:1–3 and participate in a discussion of the purpose and need for government. **Restate** the definition of constitution in your own words and participate in a discussion about the purpose of the constitution. (SHEET) **Restate** the definition of Christian self-government in your own words and participate in a discussion about the rules for classroom deportment. (SHEET) **Consent** to be governed by these rules by signing the constitution for classroom display and for your *Notebook Work* **File** your copy of the constitution behind the title page. **File** the history overview behind the constitution.	• To understand government is ordained by God • To understand the purpose and need for government • To understand the purpose of a constitution • To apply Christian self-government in the classroom • To voluntarily consent to sign the constitution • To complete and file notebook work	

The Noah Plan Lessons Kindergarten © 2003 • Foundation for American Christian Education

Week One   **TEACHING PLAN**   **Quarter One**

GEOGRAPHY

Preparation	Lesson	Student Work	Accomplishments	✓
Biblical Principle "In the beginning, God created the heaven and the earth." Genesis 1:1	**Teach** the notebook standard of form. NPSDS, Notebook chapter • **Assist** the student in setting up his notebook. (Keep the notebook simple. The teacher or the parent can set up the student's notebook.)	**Listen** to and follow the directions from the teacher on setting up your notebook.	• To set up the notebook • To restate the definition of geography	
Leading Idea God made everything. **Books** • Bible (King James) • Webster's 1828 *Dictionary* • NPSDS, Notebook chapter • NPH&GG, 125–128, 137–139, 171 • T&L, 141–153, 156–157	• **Reinforce** daily the notebook standard of form. **Distribute** and explain the overview. **Introduce** geography. • **Define** geography as the study of the Earth God has made. • **Lay** the Biblical foundation for geography. · **Define** Creation. · **State** geography begins with Creation. · **Define** Creator. · **Read** aloud and discuss the supporting foundational scriptures. Genesis 1; John 1:1–3; Hebrews 11:3; Nehemiah 9:6	**Listen** as the teacher explains the purpose of the geography overview. **Listen** as the teacher introduces the definition of geography and restate in your own words the definition of geography. **Listen** as the teacher reads aloud the supporting scriptures that lay the Biblical foundation for geography. • **Listen** as the teacher defines Creation and Creator. • **Participate** in a discussion of God as the Creator of all things. • **Participate** in a discussion of how God created the world out of nothing.	• To learn to listen attentively • To learn to follow directions • To know God as the Creator of the heavens and the Earth • To complete and file notebook work	
Supplies • Large wall map of the world and a globe with topographical and political features (needed for every lesson) • Prepared notebook page • Geography Overview (NPLK, 252) • The Noah Plan Map Makers' Kit, F.A.C.E., contains: colored pencils, ruler, map standard, and student atlas	• **Tell** a simple account of the Creation story. · **Discuss** how God created the world out of nothing. · **Establish** God as Creator of all that was created. *Notebook Work* **Distribute** the prepared notebook page for the student to write or trace the title and to color the picture. Prepared notebook page to include: • the title "Geography" for the student to write or trace • a picture of a map or globe for the student to color • a scripture that states the Biblical Principle (Example: Genesis 1:1) **Instruct** the student to file the overview behind the title page.	**Listen** as the teacher tells a simplified account of the Creation story. *Notebook Work* **Write** or trace the title and scripture on the notebook page and color the picture. **File** the overview behind the title page.	*Sample Title Page* Geography The earth is the Lord's. Psalm 24:1	

30   The Noah Plan Lessons Kindergarten © 2003 • Foundation for American Christian Education

Week One **Quarter One**

TEACHING PLAN

	Preparation	Lesson	Student Work	Accomplishments
SCIENCE	**Biblical Principle** "In the beginning God created the heaven and the earth." Genesis 1:1 **Leading Idea** The study of science reveals the character of God. **Books** • Bible (King James) • Webster's 1828 *Dictionary* • NPSDS, Notebook chapter **Supplies** • Science Overview (NPLK, 253) • Prepared notebook page to include: · the title "Science" for the student to write or trace · a space for the student to draw or color a picture related to science	**Teach** the notebook standard of form. NPSDS, Notebook chapter • **Assist** the student in setting up his notebook. (Keep the notebook simple. The teacher or parent can set up the student's notebook.) • **Reinforce** daily the notebook standard of form. **Guide** the student to the Biblical Principle from the Leading idea by introducing the student to science. • **Define** science as: The expression of God's creative power; the study of God's orderly world. • **Ask** the student to restate the definition of science in his own words. • **Read** aloud Genesis 1:1 and discuss the Biblical foundation of science. · Science began from the very mouth of God when He spoke all things into existence in six days. · The character of God is revealed during the first week of Creation: He is orderly; He is powerful; He is infinite, etc. **Engage** the student in a discussion on the importance of studying science by reading aloud the scriptures and discussing each point with the student: • Gen. 1:28—To use and care for every living thing God gave us • Gen. 3:9—To help us make good use of our time and possessions • Prov. 6:6 & Matt. 6:28—To learn about God and His ways. • 1 Tim. 1:4—To learn what is true about God's world • To help mankind—Example: a farmer learns the best time to plant his crops. • To appreciate, praise, honor, and glorify God, the Creator **Discuss** and give examples of the ways that proper stewardship of scientific knowledge has helped mankind: • Prevention, treatment, and cure of diseases • Cultivation of disease resistant plants • Modern machines, etc. *Notebook Work* **Distribute** the notebook page for the student to write or trace the title and to draw or color the picture related to science. **Instruct** the student to file the science overview behind the title page.	**Listen** as the teacher explains the notebook standard of form. **Participate** and follow the directions given by the teacher on setting up your notebook. **Listen** as the teacher defines science. **Restate** the definition of science in your own words. **Listen** as the teacher reads aloud Genesis 1:1 and participate in a discussion about the Biblical foundation of science. **Listen** as the teacher reads the scriptures and participate in a discussion about why it is important to study science. **Participate** in a discussion on the ways that proper stewardship of scientific knowledge has helped mankind. • Prevention, treatment, and cure of diseases • Cultivation of disease resistant plants • Modern machines, etc. *Notebook Work* **Write** or trace the title on the notebook page and draw or color a picture related to science. **File** the science overview behind the title page.	• To learn the importance of keeping a notebook • To learn the definition of science • To discuss the purpose of science and its benefits to man • To develop new vocabulary • To complete and file notebook work

The Noah Plan Lessons Kindergarten © 2003 • Foundation for American Christian Education

Quarter One

TEACHING PLAN

Week Two

BIBLE

Preparation	Lesson	Student Work	Accomplishments

Biblical Principle
Jesus is the promised Savior.
 	
Leading Idea
God showed He loved us by sending Jesus.
 	
Books
• Bible (KJ)
• Webster's 1828 *Dictionary*
 	
Supplies
• Notebook page to include:
  • the title "Loving God" for the student to write or trace
  • a space for the student to draw and color a picture of a way to show his love to God
 	
BAR
• *Early Reader's Bible*, 283–305
• NPRG
	Introduce the memory verse. Luke 2:11
	• **Read** aloud and discuss the memory verse.
	• **Define** unfamiliar vocabulary.
	• **Practice** daily the memory verse with the student for his recitation on Friday.
	Guide the student to the Biblical Principle from the Leading Idea by discussing the birth of Jesus:
	• He was the promised Savior.
	• He came to love us.
	• He came to save us from our sins and bring eternal life.
	Encourage the student to think of ways he can show his love to God.
	
	Notebook Work
	Distribute the prepared notebook page for the student to write or trace the title and to draw and color the picture of loving God.
	
	BAR
	"Jesus Came to Love Us"
	"Angels Sing to Shepherds"
	"The Wise Men Give Their Best"
	(See Weekly Routines for Reading and English.)
		Listen as the teacher reads aloud and discusses the memory verse.
		• **Discuss** unfamiliar vocabulary.
		• **Practice** and learn the memory verse for recitation on Friday.
		Discuss the birth of Jesus and the reasons for His coming to the Earth.
		
		Share ways you can show God you love Him.
		
		Notebook Work
		Write or trace the title on the notebook page and draw and color the picture of loving God.
		
		BAR
		(See Weekly Routines for Reading and English.)
			• To learn and recite the memory verse
			• To learn new vocabulary
			• To understand Jesus came to Earth to bring eternal life
			• To show God you love him
			• To tell others the good news about Jesus
			• To complete and file notebook page

32   The Noah Plan Lessons Kindergarten © 2003 • Foundation for American Christian Education

TEACHING PLAN

Quarter One

Week Two

LITERATURE

Preparation	Lesson	Student Work	Accomplishments

Biblical Principle
Living by God's Word brings liberty.
 	
Leading Idea
A heart yielded to God produces praise, worship, and thanksgiving.
 	
Books
• Bible (KJ)
• Webster's 1828 Dictionary
• NPLG, 8–9, 73–76
 	
Supplies
• Melody—music for Psalm 100
• Notebook page to include:
  • the title "King David" for student to write or trace
  • a space for the student to draw or color a picture
	Read aloud Psalm 100.
	
	Assist the student in memorizing Psalm 100. **Put** Psalm 100 to music and sing together.
	
	Discuss the individuality of the author, King David.
	• Greatest king of Israel
	• Ancestor of Jesus
	• Described by God as "a man who will obey" (1 Samuel 13:14)
	• A shepherd
	• A poet
	• A giant killer
	Guide the student to the Biblical Principle from the Leading Idea.
	
	• **Define** theme, praise and thanksgiving, *worship*.
	• **Discuss** the themes of Psalm 100—praise, worship, and thanksgiving.
	• **Ask** leading questions about the themes.
	
	Discuss how a yielded heart to God produces praise, worship, and thanksgiving in an individual.
	
	Notebook Work
	Distribute the notebook page for the student to write or trace the title and draw and color a picture of David praising God.
		Listen as the teacher reads aloud Psalm 100.
		• **Practice** and learn Psalm 100.
		• **Sing** Psalm 100.
		
		Listen as the teacher introduces the individuality of the author David and how God inspired him.
		
		Listen as the teacher defines themes, praise, worship, and thanksgiving.
		
		Identify praise, worship, and thanksgiving as the themes of Psalms 100.
		Reason and relate aloud:
		• What do these themes reveal to you about David's character?
		• What do these themes reveal about the nature and character of God?
		Discuss how a yielded heart to God produces praise, worship, and thanksgiving in an individual.
		
		Notebook Work
		Write or trace the title and draw and color a picture of David praising God.
			• To learn new vocabulary
			• To identify the theme of Psalm 100
			• To sing Psalm 100
			• To begin to understand that a yielded heart to God brings liberty
			• To complete and file notebook work

The Noah Plan Lessons Kindergarten © 2003 • Foundation for American Christian Education

Week Two

TEACHING PLAN

Quarter One

HISTORY

Preparation	Lesson	Student Work	Accomplishments	✓
Biblical Principle Remember God, His Ways, and His Word. **Leading Idea** God provides, prepares, and protects individuals in His Story. **Books** • Bible (KJ) • Webster's 1828 *Dictionary* • NPH&GG, 8–9, 42–46, 51–59, 78–79 • NPSDS, Providential History, Links & Timeline **Supplies** • Notebook page to include: • the title "His Story" for the student to write or trace • history-related pictures (cross, Bible, Pilgrims, etc.) for the student to color • Colored pencils	**Guide** the student to the Biblical Principle from the Leading Idea in an age appropriate manner. • **Introduce** and define history as Christ, His Story. • **Discuss** and explain the Biblical foundation of history (NPH&GG, 44–45): • To learn about God's work in men and nations • To learn about God's purpose in our nation • To recognize God's plan for us and our responsibility to carry out that plan • **Read** aloud and paraphrase for the student Nehemiah 9:6. • **Define** and discuss providential history. • God provides for every detail of His story. • God calls individuals and nations to forward His Story. • God prepares and protects individuals in His Story. • **Share** a personal example of God's Providential Hand in your life as a model for the student. • **Guide** the student to restate the definition of history and providence and to share a personal example of God's Providential Hand in his life. *Notebook Work* **Distribute** the prepared notebook page for the student to write or trace the title and to color the pictures.	**Listen** as the teacher defines history. **Listen** as the teacher explains the Biblical foundation of history. **Listen** as the teacher reads aloud Nehemiah 9:6 and defines and discusses the Pprovidential view of history. **Listen** as the teacher talks of God's Providential Hand in his life. **Restate** in your own words the definition of history and providence. **Share** a personal example of God's Providential Hand in your life. *Notebook Work* **Write** or trace the title on the notebook page and color the pictures. 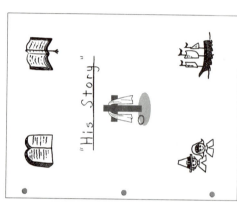	• To restate definitions of history and providence • To understand God provides, prepares, and protects each individual • To complete and file notebook work	

34 The Noah Plan Lessons Kindergarten © 2003 • Foundation for American Christian Education

Quarter One

TEACHING PLAN

Week Two

GEOGRAPHY

Preparation	Lesson	Student Work	Accomplishments	✓

Biblical Principle
God made the world and everything in it. Acts 17:24
 	
Leading Idea
The Earth is one small part of the universe.
 	
Books
• Bible (KJ)
• Webster's 1828 *Dictionary*
• T&L, 141–153, 156–157
• NPH&GG, 128, 137–139, 164–165
 	
Supplies
• Unlined notebook page with the title "The Earth in the Universe" for the student to write or trace
• Picture of the universe for display
• Picture of the Solar System for display
• Picture of the Solar System for the student to color
• Colored pencils
	Introduce the Earth in its universal setting.
	• **Define** and discuss the universe as everything God has made.
	• **Guide** the student to name some of the things that make up the universe: the heavens, the Earth, and all of God's Creation (the sun, moon, stars, man, animals, plants, etc.). Genesis 1:14–27
	• **Read** aloud Acts 17:24 and Proverbs 8:27–30 and discuss how the Earth is one small part of the universe. (You may want to paraphrase these verses for the student's understanding.)
	
	Discuss the Earth in the Solar System.
	• **Define** and discuss the Solar System as the sun, moon, stars, and planets. Genesis 1:14–18
	• **Show** the student a picture of the Solar System to include all nine known planets.
	  · **Discuss** the Solar System is a part of the universe.
	  · **Discuss** the Earth is one of nine planets in the Solar System.
	• **Discuss** the Earth's movements.
	  · Revolution—The Earth travels around the sun. This gives us one year.
	  · Rotation—The Earth spins around like a top. This gives us day and night.
	
	Demonstrate revolution and rotation by moving and spinning at the same time around the student. (The student represents the Sun and the teacher represents the Earth moving and spinning around the Sun.)
	
	GEOGRAPHY—Lesson
	(continued on page 36)
		Listen as the teacher defines universe.
		
		Name some of the things that make up the universe.
		
		Listen as the teacher reads aloud Acts 17:24 and Proverbs 8:27–30.
		• **Discuss** how the Earth is one small part of the universe.
		• **Discuss** God as the Creator of the universe.
		
		Listen as the teacher introduces the Solar System.
		• **Participate** in a discussion about the Solar System and the things that make up the Solar System.
		• **View** a picture of the Solar System with its planets in the universe.
		  · **Discuss** the Solar System as part of the universe.
		  · **Discuss** the Earth is one of the nine planets in the Solar System.
		
		Listen as the teacher explains the revolution and rotation of the Earth.
		• **Discuss** the Earth's moving around the sun, which produces one year.
		• **Discuss** the Earth's spinning around like a top as it moves around the Sun, which produces day and night.
		• **Participate** in a demonstration that shows the revolution and rotation of the Earth.
		
		GEOGRAPHY—Student Work
		(continued on page 36)
			• To begin to understand the vastness of the universe
			• To begin to understand the greatness of God
			• To learn to listen attentively
			• To understand revolution and rotation
			• To learn about the Earth in the Solar System
			• To understand the Earth is one of nine planets
			• To complete and file notebook work	

The Noah Plan Lessons Kindergarten © 2003 • Foundation for American Christian Education   35

Week Two　　　　　　　　　**TEACHING PLAN**　　　　　　　　　　Quarter One

Preparation	Lesson	Student Work	Accomplishments	✓
	• **Read** aloud and paraphrase Acts 17:28 for the student and discuss Jesus being in the center of your lives. *Notebook Work* **Distribute** the prepared notebook page for the student to write or trace the title. • **Instruct** the student to draw dots all over the page. • **Instruct** the student to circle one of the dots to represent the Earth in the universe. • **Write** on the board the word Earth for the student to copy next to the circled dot. (This is an expression of God's Principle of Individuality, Representation, and Unity with Diversity.) **Distribute** a picture of the Solar System with all nine planets and instruct the student to color the picture of the Earth green.	• **Listen** as the teacher reads aloud Acts 17:28 and discusses Jesus being in the center of your life. *Notebook Work* **Write** or trace the title on the unlined notebook page. • **Cover** the unlined notebook page with dots to represent the universe. • **Circle** one dot to represent the Earth. • **Label** the dot Earth. **Color** the Earth green on the picture of the Solar System.		

GEOGRAPHY (continued)

36　　　The Noah Plan Lessons Kindergarten © 2003 • Foundation for American Christian Education

Week Two · Quarter One

TEACHING PLAN

Preparation	Lesson	Student Work	Accomplishments	✓

Biblical Principle "Come now, and let us reason together. . . ." Isaiah 1:18
 	
Leading Idea God is orderly and systematic. (1 Corinthians 14:40)
 	
Books
• Bible (KJ)
• Webster's 1828 *Dictionary*
• Science books (Library)
 	
Supplies
• Notebook page to include:
  · the title "Scientific Method"
  · a space for the student to record notes and draw pictures of his experiment using the scientific method
• Two paper airplanes, one with a paper clip attached
	Guide the student to Biblical Principle from Leading Idea.
	• **Read** 1 Corinthians 14:40 and discuss the Leading Idea with the student:
	  · God is orderly.
	  · God is systematic, having a regular method or order.
	• **Define** the scientific method to the student:
	  · As a way a scientist thinks about problems and solving them
	  · As a method used by man to discover God's order
	• **Engage** the student in an experiment as you explain and demonstrate the following simplified version of the scientific method:
	  · **State** the problem or ask a question about what you are interested in finding out. (Show the student a feather and a baseball and ask which one would fall faster to the ground.)
	  · **Make** an educated guess about what you think will happen. (The baseball will fall faster.)
	  · **Test** your solution to the problem to see if it is correct. (Demonstrate by dropping the feather and the baseball at the same time.)
	  · **State** why you think the experiment happened the way it did. (The baseball is heavier than the feather, therefore the weight causes it to fall faster.)
	Guide the student in conducting an experiment using the scientific method using the scientific method the next class meeting. (This experiment will be done by the student. Only guide him when necessary.)
	• **Ask** the student to review the steps to the scientific method.
	• **Give** the student the two airplanes to test the length of flight.
	
	Science
	Lesson & Notebook Work
	(continued on page 38)
		Listen as the teacher reads aloud 1 Corinthians 14:40 and discusses God is a God of order and is systematic.
		
		Participate in a discussion as the teacher defines the scientific method.
		
		Participate in the experiment as the teacher explains and demonstrates the scientific method.
		• **State** the problem.
		
		• **Make** an educated guess about what you think will happen.
		• **Test** your solution to the problem to see if it is correct.
		
		• **State** why you think the experiment happened the way it did.
		
		Review the steps to the scientific method.
		
		Science
		Student & Notebook Work
		(continued on page 38)
			• To learn God is orderly and systematic
			• To learn and apply the scientific method
			• To identify the cause and effect of an experiment
			• To observe and tell what happens during an experiment
			• To participate in a demonstration on how to use the scientific method
			• To complete and file notebook work	

SCIENCE

The Noah Plan Lessons Kindergarten © 2003 • Foundation for American Christian Education   37

TEACHING PLAN

Quarter One

Week Two

Preparation	Lesson	Student Work	Accomplishments	✓
	• **Instruct** the student to follow the scientific method to conduct the experiment: · **Verbally** state the problem. · **Make** a guess about what you think will happen. · **Test** the solution to the problem to see if it is correct. · **State** why you think the experiment happened the way it did. **Read** aloud Isaiah 1:18 and reason and discuss how the scientific method relates to the Biblical Principle. **Introduce** and discuss briefly the science overview. (This gives the student the whole picture of what he will be studying for the school year.) *Notebook Work* **Distribute** the prepared notebook page for the student to write or trace the title. • **Model** on the board the notes for the student to copy. • **Instruct** the student to draw pictures of his experiment using the scientific method.	**Follow** the scientific method to conduct your experiment: · **Verbally** state the problem. · **Make** a guess about what you think will happen. · **Test** the solution to see if it correct. · **State** why you think the experiment happened the way it did. **Listen** as the teacher reads aloud Isaiah 1:18 and reason and discuss how the scientific method is a way for man to discover God's order. **Listen** as the teacher explains and discusses the science overview. *Notebook Work* **Write** or trace the title on the notebook page, record notes, and draw pictures of your experiment using the scientific method.		

SCIENCE (continued)

38   The Noah Plan Lessons Kindergarten © 2003 • Foundation for American Christian Education

Quarter One

TEACHING PLAN

Week Three

	Preparation	Lesson	Student Work	Accomplishments	✔

BIBLE	**Bible Principle**
	"Train up a child in the way he should go. . . ."
	Proverbs 22:6
	
	Leading Idea
	Jesus' early home training prepared Him to serve God.
	
	Books
	• Bible (KJ)
	• Webster's 1828 Dictionary
	• *The Family and the Nation: Biblical Childhood*, Rosalie J. Slater, F.A.C.E.
	
	Supplies
	• Notebook page to include:
	  • the title "Jesus' Childhood" for the student to write or trace
	  • a space for the student to draw and color a picture of Jesus with his parents or in the carpenter shop
	
	BAR
	• *Early Reader's Bible*, 307–313
	• NPRG
		Bible Principle
		Introduce the memory verse. Psalm 119:33
		• **Read** aloud and discuss the memory verse.
		• **Define** unfamiliar vocabulary.
		• **Practice** daily the memory verse with the student for his recitation on Friday.
		
		Guide the student to the Biblical Principle from the Leading Idea.
		• **Read** and discuss Proverbs 22:6.
		
		• **Discuss** what Jesus learned from His mother and father:
		  • Private prayer
		  • Giving thanks before and after each meal
		  • Obedience to God's laws
		  • Compassion
		  • Love for one another
		  • Study and love for the Holy Scriptures
		• **Discuss** what Jesus learned in school:
		  • Study, wisdom, and understanding of the Holy Scriptures.
		• **Discuss** what Jesus learned in the carpenter shop:
		  • Diligence
		  • Steadfastness
		  • Patience
		  • Work produces joy
		
		Notebook Work
		Distribute the prepared notebook page for the student to write or trace and to draw and color the picture.
		
		BAR
		The Hebrew home
		Jesus' training from his parents, school, and his work in the carpenter shop
		"Jesus' Happy Family"
		(See Weekly Routines for Reading and English.)
			Listen as the teacher reads aloud and discusses the memory verse.
			• **Discuss** unfamiliar vocabulary.
			• **Practice** and learn the memory verse for recitation on Friday.
			
			Listen as the teacher reads aloud and discusses Proverbs 22:6.
			• **Participate** in a discussion on what Jesus learned from His mother and father.
			
			• **Participate** in a discussion on what He learned in school.
			
			• **Participate** in a discussion on what He learned in the carpenter shop.
			
			Notebook Work
			Write or trace the title on the notebook page and draw and color the picture.
			
			BAR
			(See Weekly Routines for Reading and English.)
				• To learn and recite the memory verse
				• To learn new vocabulary
				• To obey your parents
				• To study the scriptures
				• To be diligent in your work
				• To help others in your family
				• To complete and file notebook work	

The Noah Plan Lessons Kindergarten © 2003 • Foundation for American Christian Education

Week Three

TEACHING PLAN

Quarter One

Literature

Preparation	Lesson	Student Work	Accomplishments
Biblical Principle "The preparations of the heart in man, and the answer of the tongue, is from the Lord." Proverbs 16:1 **Leading Idea** As the mother sings the lullaby, she gives love, security, warmth, shelter, and protection. She communicates her love for speech and language and prepares the child's heart and mind to receive God's communications. **Books** • Bible (KJ) • Webster's 1828 *Dictionary* • NPLG, 8–9, 88–91 • Lullaby books and tapes with words to "Away in a Manger" and "All through the Night" **Supplies** • Prepared notebook page for each lullaby • Classroom world map • Student atlas	**Guide** the student to the Biblical Principle from the Leading Idea. • **Read** aloud and discuss Proverbs 16:1. • **Define** the term lullaby and related terms such as lull, hush, and cuddle. • **Teach** lullabies as the first form of literature communicated to a baby. **Teach** words and melody to "Away in a Manger" and "All through the Night." **Identify** and discuss the literary elements of each lullaby such as theme, examples of imagery, rhyme, and personification. **Teach** how the individuality of a nation or time period and its identifying features can be seen in the literature it produces through the authors. • **Locate** nations on the classroom world map and in the student's atlas. • **Discuss** the individuality of the authors and their countries of origin. *Notebook Work* **Distribute** the prepared notebook pages for the student to write or trace the titles and to color the pictures. Notebook page for each lullaby to include: • the title for the student to write or trace • the words of the lullaby • a picture or space for the student to illustrate and color	**Listen** as the teacher reads aloud and discusses Proverbs 16:1. **Listen** as the teacher discusses the term lullaby and related terms. **Participate** in a discussion about lullabies: • What do they communicate? • How are they presented to the baby? **Learn** words and melody to "Away in a Manger" & "All through the Night." **Give** examples of rhyme, personification, imagery, etc. **Locate** nations on the classroom world map and in your student atlas. **Participate** in a discussion on the individuality of the authors and their countries of origin. *Notebook Work* **Write** or trace the titles on the notebook pages and color the pictures. _Away in a Manger_ Away in a manger, no crib for a bed, The little Lord Jesus laid down His sweet head; The stars in the heavens looked down where He lay, The little Lord Jesus asleep in the hay.	• To sing "Away in a Manger" and "All through the Night" • To love God and receive God's Word • To complete and file notebook work

The Noah Plan Lessons Kindergarten © 2003 • Foundation for American Christian Education

Quarter One

TEACHING PLAN

Week Three

HISTORY

Preparation	Lesson	Student Work	Accomplishments
Biblical Principle God launches events through individuals and nations for His purposes. **Leading Idea** The Chain of Christianity is the westward move of Christianity and liberty. **Books** • Bible (KJ) • NPH&GG, 8–9, 73–82, Appendix 339 for additional books on Creation • T&L, 158–159 • NPSDS, Providential History, Links & Timeline **Supplies** • Chalkboard • Prepared notebook page • Christian history timeline for classroom display (The Noah Plan Wall Timeline, F.A.C.E.) • Colored pencils	**Prepare**, display, and introduce the classroom Christian history timeline and discuss the first link on the Chain of Christianity—Creation. • **Read aloud** Genesis 1. • **Discuss** God as Creator by identifying His nature & character. • He is loving. • He is infinite. • He is orderly, etc. • **Discuss** God as Creator by identifying man as God's property. • Man is created in God's image. • Man is God's property by right of Creation. **Introduce** the Chain of Christianity and its westward move through individuals and nations using the prepared classroom Christian history timeline. • **Define** Chain of Christianity as a record of how God uses men and nations to move the Gospel westward and give examples. • God preserved Moses to be the deliverer of the Israelites from Egypt, to be the first historian, and to be the first lawgiver. • Paul carried the Gospel westward to Europe after having a vision. (Acts 16) • Columbus (Christbearer) carried the Gospel to the New World. • Squanto was providentially preserved and prepared to help the Pilgrims survive in the New World. • **Share** with the student the ways God has used you to spread the Gospel. • **Ask** the student to share ways God can use him to spread the Gospel. *Notebook Work* **Distribute** the prepared notebook page for the student to write or trace the title and to color each key link on the Christian history timeline as you encounter it in your history study. Prepared notebook page to include: • a simplified Christian history timeline with the title "Christian History Timeline" for the student to write or trace • the key links (dates and pictures only) for the student to color (NPH&GG, 78–79)	**Listen** as the teacher introduces the Christian history timeline, reads aloud Genesis 1, and introduces the Creation Link. • **Identify** God's nature and character. • **Discuss** man is made in the image of God. • **Discuss** man is God's property by right of Creation. **Listen** as the teacher introduces the Chain of Christianity and its westward move. • **Define** Chain of Christianity. • **Listen** as the teacher gives examples of how God uses men and nations to move the Gospel westward. • **Listen** as the teacher shares the ways God has used him to spread the Gospel. • **Ask** the student to share ways God can use him to spread the Gospel. *Notebook Work* **Write** or trace the title on the Christian history timeline notebook page and color the picture representing Creation	• To learn key vocabulary • To recognize the Sovereignty of God • To recognize God has a plan for each individual and nation • To complete and file notebook work

The Noah Plan Lessons Kindergarten © 2003 • Foundation for American Christian Education

41

TEACHING PLAN

Week Three Quarter One

GEOGRAPHY

Preparation	Lesson	Student Work	Accomplishments
Biblical Principle God has a plan for everything He created. **Leading Idea** God made the Earth with a distinct individuality for man to carry out His plan. **Books** • Bible (KJV) • Webster's 1828 *Dictionary* • NPH&GG, 128, 166 • T&L, 141–153, 156–157 **Supplies** • World map and globe • *Beginning Geography*, K–2 (referred to as EMBG in the future), Jo Ellen Moore. Monterey, CA: Evan-Moor, 1991–93: • *Volume 1: How To Use a Map* (1:1,3); • *Volume 2: Land Forms and Bodies of Water;* • *Volume 3: Continents and Oceans,* • Colored pencils	**Show** a picture of the Earth from space and discuss the shape of the Earth being like a big ball. Isaiah 40:22 **Introduce** the map and the globe. • **Show** a map and a globe and discuss how maps and globes are used to study the Earth. • **Lead** a discussion about the similarities and difference in maps and globes: • A map is a flat picture of the Earth. • A globe is a round model that gives us a picture of the Earth. **Discuss** the purpose of the Earth (Acts 17:24–28): • It is a place God created for man to live and to learn about Him. *Notebook Work* **Distribute** EMBG, Volume 1:1,3 of the map and globe for the student to color.	**Listen** as the teacher reads aloud Isaiah 40:22. • **View** a picture of the Earth. • **Describe** its shape. **View** a map and a globe as the teacher explains their purpose, similarities, and differences. **Listen** as the teacher reads aloud Acts 17:24–28 and participate in a discussion about the purpose of the Earth. *Notebook Work* **Color** the pictures of the map and globe.	• To recognize the individuality of the Earth • To articulate the purpose of the Earth • To discover the similarities and differences between a map and globe • To complete and file notebook work

42 The Noah Plan Lessons Kindergarten © 2003 • Foundation for American Christian Education

Week Three Quarter One

TEACHING PLAN

	Preparation	Lesson	Student Work	Accomplishments	✓

SCIENCE	**Biblical Principle**
	"In the beginning God created the heaven and the earth." Genesis 1:1
	
	Leading Idea
	All things were created by God.
	
	Books
	• Bible (KJ)
	• Webster's 1828 *Dictionary*
	• Science books (Library)
	
	Supplies
	• Magnets of all sizes and shapes
	• Objects for the student to play with which are metal and non-metal
	• Piece of glass
	• Iron filings
	• Bar magnet
	• Prepared notebook page to include:
	  • the title "Magnets" for the student to write or trace
	  • a T-chart with the titles "Attracted" on the left and "Not Attracted" on the right for the student to write or trace
		Science in the kindergarten curriculum is introduced through the days of Creation.
		Guide the student to the Biblical Principle from the Leading Idea.
		• **Read** aloud Genesis 1:1 and establish the idea that the science of physics was created by God on Day 1.
		
		• **Define** physics as the things God has created and how they operate.
		• **Discuss** the study of physics can include such subjects as light, heat, sound, magnets, and simple machines, etc.
		Distribute the magnets and small objects for the student to discover through play that:
		• Magnets have an invisible power that can push or pull.
		• There are some things that are attracted to magnets and some are not.
		• The things that are attracted to the magnets are metal.
		Ask the student to share his observations about magnets.
		
		Define a magnet as an object which can attract certain metals.
		Engage the student in the demonstration of how a magnet works.
		• **Place** a bar magnet under a piece of glass.
		• **Sprinkle** iron filings over the surface of the glass.
		• **Observe** the pull of the metal filings around the ends of the bar magnet.
		Engage the student in identifying the everyday uses of a magnet.
		Discuss and relate magnets to the invisible power of God.
		
		Notebook Work
		Distribute the prepared notebook page and model on the board the objects that are attracted and not attracted to magnets for the student to record.
			Listen as the teacher reads aloud Genesis 1:1 and establishes the idea that the science of physics was created by God on Day 1.
			Listen as the teacher defines physics and discusses subjects included in physics.
			
			Experiment, observe, and discover the characteristics of magnets by playing with them and other objects given to you by the teacher.
			
			Share your observations with the teacher.
			Listen as the teacher gives a definition of a magnet.
			Participate in the demonstration of how a magnet works.
			
			Identify the everyday uses of a magnet.
			Participate in a discussion and relate magnets to the invisible power of God.
			
			Notebook Work
			Write or trace the title on the notebook page and record the notes modeled on the board by the teacher.
				• To learn the Biblical foundation of physics
				• To make observations
				• To compare and classify objects
				• To conduct simple experiments
				• To draw conclusions about magnets
				• To complete and file notebook work	

The Noah Plan Lessons Kindergarten © 2003 • Foundation for American Christian Education   43

TEACHING PLAN

Quarter One

Week Four

Preparation	Lesson	Student Work	Accomplishments	✓
Biblical Principle Jesus always obeyed God, His father.	**Introduce** the memory verse. "Obey them that have rule over you. . . ." Hebrews 13:17 • **Read** aloud and discuss the memory verse.	**Listen** as the teacher reads aloud and discusses the memory verse.	• To learn and recite the memory verse • To learn new vocabulary	
Leading Idea Jesus is our model of how to please God.	• **Define** unfamiliar vocabulary. • **Discuss** the importance of obeying those who have authority over you. • **Identify** some of the people who have authority over you.	• **Discuss** unfamiliar vocabulary. • **Discuss** the importance of obeying those in authority over you. • **Identify** those who are in authority over you.	• To obey your parents and those in authority over you • To model your life after Jesus • To complete and file notebook work	
Books • Bible (KJ) • Webster's 1828 Dictionary • *The Family and the Nation: Biblical Childhood*, Rosalie J. Slater, F.A.C.E.	• **Practice** daily the memory verse with the student for his recitation on Friday. Guide the student to the Biblical Principle from the Leading Idea.	• **Practice** and learn the memory verse for recitation on Friday.		
Supplies • Notebook page to include: · the title "Jesus' Baptism" for the student to write or trace · a space for the student to draw and color the picture	• **Read** aloud Matthew 3:13–17. • **Define** baptism. • **Discuss** Jesus' submission to His Father's will to be baptized. • **Discuss** Jesus as our model of how to please God. · He was always obedient. · He always prayed. · He was humble. · He was compassionate. · He was loving. · He was patient, etc. • **Encourage** the student to share ways of how he can please God.	**Listen** as the teacher reads aloud Matthew 3:13–17, defines baptism, and discusses Jesus' submission to His Father's will to be baptized. **Discuss** Jesus as our model of how to please God. **Share** ways you can please God.		
	Notebook Work **Distribute** the prepared notebook page for the student to write or trace the title and to draw and color the picture showing a way to please God.	*Notebook Work* **Write** or trace the title on the notebook page and draw and color the picture.		
BAR • *Early Reader's Bible*, 314–321 • NPRG	**BAR** "Jesus Pleases God" (See Weekly Routines for Reading and English.)	**BAR** (See Weekly Routines for Reading and English.)		

TEACHING PLAN

Week Four
Quarter One

	Preparation	Lesson	Student Work	Accomplishments	✓
LITERATURE	**Biblical Principle** "The preparations of the heart in man, and the answer of the tongue, is from the Lord." Proverbs 16:1 **Leading Idea** As the mother sings the lullaby, she gives love, security, warmth, shelter, and protection. She communicates her love for speech and language and prepares the child's heart and mind to receive God's communications. **Books** • Bible (KJ) • NPLG, 8–9, 88–91 • Lullaby books and tapes with words to the lullabies listed **Supplies** • Notebook pages for each lullaby to include: • the title for the student to write or trace • the words of the lullaby • a picture or space for the student to illustrate and color • Colored pencils • Classroom world map • Student Atlas	**Review** the Biblical Principle and the Leading Idea. **Review** the definitions of lullaby and its related terms. **Teach** words and melody for "Sweet and Low," "Lullaby of an Infant Chief," "Bye, Baby Night is Come," and "Sleep, Baby, Sleep." **Identify** and discuss the literary elements of each lullaby such as theme, personification, imagery, and rhyme. **Teach** how the individuality of a nation or time period and its identifying features can be seen in the literature it produces through its authors. • **Locate** the nation of origin on the classroom world map and in the student atlas. • **Discuss** the individuality of the authors and their countries of origin. *Notebook Work* **Distribute** the prepared notebook pages for the student to write or trace the titles and to color the pictures. Notebook page for each lullaby to include: • the title for the student to write or trace • the words of the lullaby • a picture or space for the student to illustrate and color	**Participate** in a review of the Biblical Principle and Leading Idea. **Participate** in a review of the definition of lullaby and its related terms. **Learn** and sing words and melody for each lullaby. **Give** examples of the literary elements such as theme, personification, imagery, and rhyme from each lullaby. **Listen** as the teacher talks about the individuality of a nation. • **Locate** the nation of origin on the classroom world map and in your atlas. • **Discuss** the individuality of the author, the nation, and the time period of each lullaby. *Notebook Work* **Write** or trace the titles on the notebook pages and color the pictures.	• To sing "Sweet and Low," "Lullaby of an Infant Chief," "Bye, Baby Night is Come," and "Sleep, Baby, Sleep." • To love God and receive God's Word • To complete and file notebook work *Style*	

The Noah Plan Lessons Kindergarten © 2003 • Foundation for American Christian Education

Week Four

HISTORY

TEACHING PLAN

Quarter One

Preparation	Lesson	Student Work	Accomplishments
Biblical Principle God's Principle of Individuality **Leading Idea** Man is a witness to God's diversity. **Books** • Bible (KJ) • Webster's 1828 *Dictionary* • NPH&GG, 8–9, 75–79 • T&L, 155–156, 230–231 **Supplies** • Notebook page #1 to include: • the title "What Shows That I Am 'Me'?" for the student to write or trace • a T-chart (comparison chart) • Notebook page #2 to include: • the title "Starting with Me" by Rosalie J. Slater for the student to write or trace • the words to the poem • a space for student's self-portrait	**Review** the Creation Link on the Christian history timeline. **Introduce** and explain God's Principle of Individuality. • **Define** principle (things that are true) and individuality (the things that make something different from another.) • **Define** God's Principle of Individuality as God created all things unique (different) and for a purpose and He takes care of all the things He has created. • **Discuss** examples of how God's Principle of Individuality can be seen in the outward and inward identification of each person. • **Lead** the student to corporately create a T-chart (comparison/contrast chart) to represent those differences as you write it on the board. (T&L, 155) **Read** aloud "Starting With Me." • **Define** and discuss the meaning of witness and diversity. • **Review** and discuss with the student all the ways God made him special (height, weight, hair and eye color, etc.) • **Practice** the poem with the student for his recitation. **Read** aloud and discuss the poem "I Am God's Property." (This poem is taught and memorized in third quarter. See NPH&GG, 9) *Notebook Work* **Distribute** the prepared notebook page #1: • for the student to write or trace the title • for the student to record the T-chart to represent the outward and inward identifications of each person's individuality as you model it on the board. **Distribute** the prepared notebook page #2 for the student to write or trace the title and to draw a self-portrait	**Participate** in the Creation Link review. **Listen** as the teacher introduces God's Principle of Individuality through definitions of key terms and examples of unique external physical features and internal qualities as a means of identification. **Review** ways that God's Principle of Individuality can be seen internally and externally in each individual. **Participate** in creating a T-chart to represent those differences as the teacher writes it on the board. **Listen** as the teacher reads aloud the poem "Starting with Me." • **Define** and discuss the meaning of witness and diversity. • **Review** and discuss all the ways God made you special (height, weight, hair and eye color, etc.). • **Practice** and learn the poem for recitation. **Listen** as the teacher reads aloud and discusses the poem "I Am God's Property." *Notebook Work* **Write** or trace the title on notebook page #1 and record the T-chart modeled on the board by the teacher. **Write** or trace the title on notebook page #2 and draw a self-portrait.	• To review God's Principle of Individuality and the Creation Link • To recite the poem "Starting with Me" • To draw a self-portrait • To chart examples of Christian individuality • To complete and file notebook work

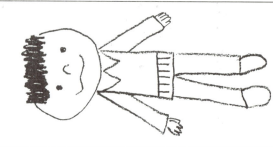

The Noah Plan Lessons Kindergarten © 2003 • Foundation for American Christian Education

TEACHING PLAN

Week Four   **Quarter One**

GEOGRAPHY

Preparation	Lesson	Student Work	Accomplishments	✓
Biblical Principle God created each part of the Earth. Genesis 1:9–10 **Leading Idea** The Earth is divided into three main parts. **Books** • Bible (KJ) • Webster's 1828 *Dictionary* • NPH&GG, 128, 173–174 • T&L, 141–153, 156–157 **Supplies** • Classroom world map containing the seven continents and the four oceans labeled • Unlined notebook page including: • the title "The Three Main Parts of the Earth" for the student to write or trace • a picture of a scene containing water, land, and atmosphere for the student to color • Colored pencils	**Introduce** and discuss the three main divisions or elements of the Earth's surface: • Atmosphere • **Define** atmosphere as the air that surrounds us and the air we breathe. • **Read** aloud Genesis 1:6–8 and discuss the creation of the atmosphere. It is necessary for breathing. • Water • **Define** water as the liquid part of the Earth. It is most necessary for living beings. • **Read** aloud Genesis 1:9 and discuss the gathering of the waters. • Land • **Define** land as the solid part of the Earth. It is the place upon which man carries out God's plan. • **Read** aloud Genesis 1:10 and discuss God made the land for people to live on. **Identify** the four great oceans and the seven continents on the classroom world map. *Notebook Work* **Distribute** the prepared notebook page for the student to write or trace the title and to color the picture.	**Listen** as the teacher introduces the three main parts of the Earth and participate in the discussion. • **Listen** as the teacher reads the scriptures that support the three main parts of the Earth. • **Listen** as the teacher defines the terms atmosphere, water, and land. **Identify** the four great oceans and the seven continents on the classroom world map. *Notebook Work* **Write** or trace the title on the notebook page and color the picture.	• To recognize the three divisions of the Earth • To recognize the purpose of the three divisions • To identify the four great oceans and the seven continents on a world map • To complete and file notebook work	

The Noah Plan Lessons Kindergarten © 2003 • Foundation for American Christian Education

Week Four

Quarter One

TEACHING PLAN

	Preparation	Lesson	Student Work	Accomplishments	✓
SCIENCE	**Biblical Principle** "I wisdom dwell with prudence, and find out knowledge or witty inventions." Proverbs 8:12 **Leading Idea** God gives man creativity to develop tools that help him work. **Books** • Bible (KJ) • Webster's 1828 *Dictionary* • Science books (Library) **Supplies** • Pictures of simple machines • A stack of 6–7 heavy books • A seesaw • Notebook page to include: • the title "Simple Machines" for the student to write or trace • a space for the student to draw pictures of simple machines	**Review** and discuss the study of physics and magnets. **Continue** the study of physics by guiding the student to the Biblical Principle from the Leading Idea. • **Read** aloud Proverbs 8:12 and discuss how God gives man creativity to develop tools that help him to do his work. • **Introduce** and discuss simple machines as a part of physics. · Simple machines make work easier for man. · Simple machines do not have a motor. · The power to operate a simple machine is supplied by man. • **Display** pictures and discuss examples of simple machines: · Lever—seesaw, wheelbarrow, oars · Pulley—a crane · Wheels and axles—egg beater · Wedge—axe · Inclined plane—a ramp • **Engage** the student in several demonstrations that show how simple machines aid man. · **Use** a nut cracker to open a walnut · **Move** a heavy box by using a handcart. · **Use** a pulley to lift a bucket of rocks. • **Guide** the student in conducting an experiment to see how a lever helps man. · **Ask** the student to lift the stack of books. · **Ask** the student to place the books on one end of a seesaw and push down on the other end. What happened? · **Ask** the student to move the books closer to the center of the seesaw and push down on the other end. What happened? · **Ask** which way was easier to lift the books? · **Guide** the student in drawing the conclusions that: the lever makes it easier to lift the books and the closer the books are to the center point the easier it is to lift them. *Notebook Work* **Distribute** the notebook page for the student to write or trace the title and draw pictures of simple machines.	**Review** and discuss the study of physics and magnets. **Listen** as the teacher reads aloud Proverbs 8:12 and discusses how God gives man creativity to develop tools. **Listen** as the teacher introduces and discusses simple machines are a part of physics and what makes a simple machine. **Observe** the pictures and listen as the teacher discusses examples of simple machines. **Participate** in demonstrations that show how simple machines aid man. **Follow** the teacher's instructions in conducting an experiment to see how a lever helps man. · **Lift** the stack of books. · **Place** the books on one end of a seesaw and push down on the other end. What happened? · **Move** the books closer to the center of the seesaw and push down on the other end. What happened? · **Which** way of lifting the books was easier? · **Draw** conclusions about the use of the lever. *Notebook Work* **Write** or trace the title on the distributed notebook page and draw pictures of the simple machines in the space provided.	• To review the study of physics and magnets • To apply scripture to the study of physics • To learn about simple machines • To use simple machines • To apply the scientific method to learn about simple machines • To complete and file notebook work	

48   The Noah Plan Lessons Kindergarten © 2003 • Foundation for American Christian Education

TEACHING PLAN

Week Five — **Quarter One**

Preparation

Bible Principle
God wants us to bless others with all He gives us.

Leading idea
Jesus' power was revealed because the boy was willing to share his lunch. (Stewardship)

Books
- Bible (KJ)
- Webster's 1828 Dictionary
- T&L, 230–231

Supplies
Notebook page to include:
- the title "Blessing Others" for the student to write or trace
- a space for the student to draw and color a picture of how he can bless others with his talents

BAR
- *Early Reader's Bible*, 371–377
- NPRG

Lesson

Introduce the memory verse.
"... For unto whomsoever much is given, of him shall be much required...." Luke 12:48
- **Read** aloud and discuss the memory verse.
- **Define** unfamiliar vocabulary.
- **Practice** daily the memory verse with the student for his recitation on Friday.

Guide the student to the Biblical Principle from the Leading Idea.

- **Paraphrase** and discuss the Parable of the Talents—Matthew 25:14–30.
- **Define** parable and talents.
- **Discuss** the Principle of Stewardship—God has given us responsibilities over all His property.
- **Discuss** what God has entrusted in our care. (T&L, 230–231)
  - Our body
  - Our conscience
  - Our talents
- **Discuss** how we can bless others with our talents.

Notebook Work
Distribute the prepared notebook page for the student to write or trace the title and to draw and color the picture of how he can bless others with his talents.

BAR
"A Boy Shares His Lunch"
(See Weekly Routines for Reading and English.)

Student Work

Listen as the teacher reads aloud and discusses the memory verse.
- **Discuss** unfamiliar vocabulary.
- **Practice** and learn the memory verse for recitation on Friday.

Listen as the teacher tells the Parable of the Talents.
- **Discuss** the definition of talents and parable.
- **Discuss** the Principle of Stewardship.
- **Discuss** what God has entrusted in your care.
- **Share** ways you can bless others with your talents.

Notebook Work
Write or trace the title and draw and color the picture of how you can bless others with your talents.

BAR
(See Weekly Routines for Reading and English.)

Accomplishments

- To learn and recite the memory verse
- To learn new vocabulary
- To understand the Principle of Stewardship
- To recognize the importance of using your talents wisely
- To complete and file notebook work

The Noah Plan Lessons Kindergarten © 2003 • Foundation for American Christian Education

Week Five   **TEACHING PLAN**   Quarter One

LITERATURE

Preparation	Lesson	Student Work	Accomplishments	✓
Biblical Principle "The preparations of the heart in man, and the answer of the tongue, is from the Lord." Proverbs 16:1 **Leading Idea** As the mother sings the lullaby, she gives love, security, warmth, shelter, and protection. She communicates her love for speech and language and prepares the child's heart and mind to receive God's communications. **Books** • Bible (KJ) • NPLG, 8–9, 88–91 • Lullaby books and tapes with words to the lullabies listed **Supplies** • Prepared notebook pages for each lullaby • Classroom world map • Student atlas	**Review** the Biblical Principle and Leading Idea. **Read** aloud Proverbs 16:1 **Continue** to review the definitions of lullaby and related terms. **Review** and sing lullabies previously taught. **Introduce** words and melody for "Hush, Little Baby," "Twinkle, Twinkle, Little Star," and "Rock-a-Bye-Baby." **Identify** and discuss the literary elements of each lullaby. **Teach** how the individuality of a nation or time period and its identifying features can be seen in the literature it produces through its authors. • **Locate** the nation of origin on the classroom world map and in the student atlas. • **Discuss** the individuality of the authors and their countries of origin. *Notebook work* **Distribute** the prepared notebook pages for the student to write or trace the titles and to color the pictures. Prepared notebook pages for each lullaby to include: • the title for the student to write or trace • the words of the lullaby • a picture or space for the student to illustrate and to color	**Participate** in a review of the Biblical Principle and Leading Idea. **Listen** as the teacher reads aloud Proverbs 16:1. **Review** the definition of the term lullaby and related terms. **Review** and sing lullabies previously taught. **Learn** words and melody to "Hush, Little Baby," "Twinkle, Twinkle, Little Star," and "Rock-a-Bye-Baby." **Give** examples of rhyme, personification, imagery, etc. **Locate** the nation of origin on the classroom world map and in your student atlas. **Discuss** the individuality of the authors and their countries of origin. *Notebook work* **Write** or trace the title on the notebook page and color the picture.	• To sing "Hush, Little Baby," "Twinkle, Twinkle, Little Star," and "Rock-a-Bye-Baby" • To love God and receive God's Word • To complete and file notebook work	

50   The Noah Plan Lessons Kindergarten © 2003 • Foundation for American Christian Education

TEACHING PLAN

Week Five · Quarter One

HISTORY

Preparation	Lesson	Student Work	Accomplishments

Biblical Principle
God's Principle of Individuality is seen in leaves.
 	
Leading Idea
Leaves are an expression of God's design.
 	
Books
• Bible (KJ)
• Webster's 1828 *Dictionary*
• NPH&GG, 8–9
• T&L, 155–156, 230–231
 	
Supplies
• Notebook page to include:
  • the title "God's Principle of Individuality in Leaves" for the student to write or trace
  • a space for the leaf rubbings
• Various types of real leaves or paper cut outs of several types of leaves for classification
• Leaf stencils
• Unlined paper
• Glue
	Continue the study of the Creation Link and God's Principle of Individuality.
	• **Review** by asking the student to recite the poem "Starting with Me."
	• **Review** the poem "I Am God's Property."
	Discuss God as Creator by identifying God's Principle of Individuality in His Creation.
	• **Read** aloud selections from Genesis 1.
	
	• **Define** design.
	• **Show** several variations of leaves.
	
	• **Lead** a discussion of how God's Principle of Individuality is seen in nature in the design of leaves.
	
	Present and play a classification game in which leaves are sorted by design/type (oak, maple, etc.).
	
	Demonstrate and assist the student to complete several variations of leaf rubbings.
	Examine and compare the leaf designs with the student.
	
	Notebook Work
	Distribute the prepared notebook page for the student to write or trace the title.
	• **Assist** the student in cutting out his leaf rubbings.
	• **Assist** the student in gluing the leaf rubbings onto the notebook page.
		Review the Creation Link and God's Principle of Individuality by reciting the poem "Starting with Me."
		
		Review "I Am God's Property."
		Listen as the teacher reads aloud selections from Genesis 1 and identifies God's Principle of Individuality in His Creation.
		• **Define** design.
		• **Examine** several variations of leaves.
		• **Discuss** how God's Principle of Individuality in nature can be seen in the design of leaves.
		Explore God's Principle of Individuality in the designs of leaves.
		• **Classify** leaves according to shape or type in a game.
		• **Complete** leaf rubbings with a variety of leaves.
		• **Compare** the designs of the leaves.
		
		Notebook Work
		Write or trace the title on the notebook page.
		• **Cut** leaf rubbings out.
		• **Glue** the leaf rubbings onto the notebook page.
			• To review and recite the poem "Starting with Me"
			• To review the poem "I Am God's Property"
			• To classify leaves
			• To recognize God's Individuality is everywhere
			• To make leaf rubbings
			• To complete and file notebook work

The Noah Plan Lessons Kindergarten © 2003 • Foundation for American Christian Education

TEACHING PLAN

Week Five **Quarter One**

GEOGRAPHY

Preparation	Lesson	Student Work	Accomplishments	✓
Biblical Principle Jesus directs our paths. Proverbs 3:6 **Leading Idea** The North Pole, the South Pole, and the equator are used to determine positions on the globe and to help us understand the climate of the Earth. **Books** • Bible (KJ) • NPH&GG, 128, 166–168 **Supplies** • World map and globe • EMBG, Volume 1:4	**Introduce** the North Pole, the South Pole, and the equator. • **Locate** the North Pole and the South Pole on the globe and describe their climates. · They are very cold. · They have six months of daylight followed by six months of darkness. · The coldest climate is near the poles. • **Locate** the equator on the globe and describe it. · It is an imaginary line (make-believe) that circles around the Earth and divides the Earth into two equal parts. · The hottest climate is near the equator. • **Show** and explain to the student that the areas between the poles and the equator have summer, autumn, winter, and spring. • **Teach** and demonstrate the position of N-S-E-W on a map. *Notebook Work* **Distribute** EMBG, Volume 1:4 and assist the student in placing the directions correctly on the map.	**Observe** as the teacher locates the North Pole, South Pole, and equator on the globe. **Listen** as the teacher describes the North Pole, South Pole, and equator. **Observe** and listen to the teacher explain the seasons between the poles and the equator. **Participate** in a discussion about directions (N-S-E-W). *Notebook Work* **Glue** the positions (N-S-E-W) in their correct place on the map.	• To locate directions, the two poles, and the equator on a globe • To articulate the differences between the two poles and the equator • To complete and file notebook work	

52   The Noah Plan Lessons Kindergarten © 2003 • Foundation for American Christian Education

TEACHING PLAN

Week Five   **Quarter One**

	Preparation	Lesson	Student Work	Accomplishments	✓

SCIENCE	**Biblical Principles**
	• God's Principle of Individuality
	• "Through faith we understand that the worlds were framed by the word of God, so that things which are seen were not made of things which do appear." Hebrews 11:3
	
	Leading Idea
	God created all things both seen and unseen.
	
	Books
	• Bible (KJ)
	• Webster's 1828 *Dictionary*
	• Science books (Library)
	
	Supplies
	• Koolaid packet
	• A clear glass
	• Water
	• A notebook page to include:
	  • The title "Chemistry" for the student to write or trace
	  • A space for the student to draw and color the pictures of the experiment
		Introduce the lesson by engaging the student in an experiment using the scientific method.
		• **State** the problem. (What will happen if you pour a packet of Koolaid into a clear glass of water without stirring?)
		• **Make** an educated guess about what you think will happen.
		• **Test** your solution to the problem to see if it is correct. (Allow the student to pour the powder into the water without mixing and observe the changes in the water over time.)
		• **State** the next day why you think the experiment happened the way it did. (After the water has mixed significantly, ask the student to state what happened.)
		Tell the children what they have been doing is a part of science called chemistry.
		• **Read** aloud Genesis 1:1 and establish the idea that the science of chemistry was created by God on Day 1 of Creation.
		
		• **Define** chemistry as the science of what things are made of and the changes that take place with them.
		  • Chemistry is the name given to the study of things.
		  • Chemists are people who study how things are made and what they are made of.
		• **Discuss** how the study of chemistry is important because it affects our lives in many ways.
		  • It provides us with many new products such as plastics, cellophane, medicines, nylons, etc.
		  • It answers questions we ask about our world, for example why iron gets rusty, how wood burns, etc.
		• **Discuss** how God's Principle of Individuality is related to the Koolaid experiment. (The taking of two individual things and combining them made something new.)
		Review the Koolaid experiment on the next day with the student.
		• **Observe** the results of the experiment.
		
		<center>**SCIENCE—**
		Lesson & Notebook Work
		(continued on page 54)</center>
			Participate in the experiment using the scientific method as instructed by the teacher.
			• **State** the problem.
			• **Make** an educated guess about what you think will happen.
			• **Test** your solution to the problem to see if it is correct.
			• **State** why you think the experiment happened the way it did the next day.
			
			Listen as the teacher identifies the type of science you have been doing.
			• **Listen** as the teacher reads aloud Genesis 1:1 and establishes the idea that the science of chemistry was created on Day 1 of creation.
			• **Listen** as the teacher defines and explains the science of chemistry.
			
			Participate in a discussion on the effect chemistry has on your life.
			
			Participate in the discussion on how God's Principle of Individuality is related to the experiment.
			Review together the experiment conducted on Day 1.
			Observe the results of the experiment.
			
			<center>**SCIENCE—**
			Student & Notebook Work
			(continued on page 54)</center>
				• To dissolve a powder into a liquid
				• To see Biblical Principles demonstrated
				• To observe and tell what happens during an experiment
				• To participate in a demonstration using the scientific method
				• To complete and file notebook work	

The Noah Plan Lessons Kindergarten © 2003 • Foundation for American Christian Education   53

TEACHING PLAN

Week Five   **Quarter One**

Preparation	Lesson	Student Work	Accomplishments	✓
	Explain to the student what happened to cause the Koolaid to mix. • When the power dissolves, it breaks apart into smaller parts called molecules. • Water also has small parts called molecules. • Molecules move. • This causes the Koolaid and water to mix. • **Ask** the student why the experiment happened the way it did.	**Listen** as the teacher explains what causes the Koolaid to mix. **Draw** a conclusion about why the experiment happened the way it did.		
	Read aloud Hebrews 11:3 to the students. **Engage** the student in a discussion relating the results of the experiment to Hebrews 11:3. • The children were able to see that the invisible water molecules move. • The unseen things of God were made to be seen for the student.	**Listen** as the teacher reads aloud Hebrews 11:3. **Participate** in a discussion relating the results of the experiment to Hebrews 11:3: • What did you learn about water molecules? • What did you learn about God and His Creation?		
	Notebook Work **Distribute** the prepared notebook page for the student to write or trace the title and to draw and to color the pictures.	*Notebook Work* **Write** or trace the title on the notebook page and draw and color the pictures.		

SCIENCE (continued)

The Noah Plan Lessons Kindergarten © 2003 • Foundation for American Christian Education

Quarter One

TEACHING PLAN

Week Six

	Preparation	Lesson	Student Work	Accomplishments	✓

BIBLE	**Biblical Principle**
	God wants us to be like Him and help those in need.
	
	Leading Ideas
	• The Samaritan treated the poor man with love.
	• Jesus helped the poor man in his need.
	
	Books
	• Bible (KJ)
	• Webster's 1828 *Dictionary*
	
	Supplies
	• Notebook page to include:
	  • the title "The Good Samaritan" for the student to write or trace
	  • a space for the student to draw and color a picture of the Good Samaritan helping the wounded man
	
	BAR
	• Luke 10:25–37
	• *Early Reader's Bible*, 419–425
	• NPRG
		Introduce the memory verse. ". . . Thou shalt love thy neighbor as thy self." Matthew 19:19
		• **Read** aloud and discuss the memory verse.
		• **Define** unfamiliar vocabulary.
		• **Practice** daily the memory verse with the student for his recitation on Friday.
		Guide the student to the Biblical Principle from the Leading Idea.
		• **Tell** the Parable of the Good Samaritan.
		• **Explain** the term Samaritan.
		• **Identify** the characters in the story.
		• **Discuss** which character pleased God by loving his neighbor as himself.
		• **Discuss** the ways the Samaritan showed his love to the man in need.
		• **Encourage** the student to share ways he can show love to the needy.
		
		Notebook Work
		Distribute the prepared notebook page for the student to write or trace the title and to draw and color a picture of the Samaritan helping the wounded man.
		
		BAR
		"Jesus Tells the Parable of the Good Samaritan"
		"A Man Who Wanted to See" (Content differs but the principle is the same.)
		(See Weekly Routines for Reading and English.)
			Listen as the teacher reads aloud and discusses the memory verse.
			• **Discuss** unfamiliar vocabulary.
			• **Practice** and learn the memory verse for recitation on Friday.
			Listen as the teacher tells the Parable of the Good Samaritan.
			• **Discuss** the term Samaritan.
			• **Identify** the characters in the story.
			• **Discuss** which character pleased God by loving his neighbor as himself.
			• **Discuss** the ways the Samaritan showed his love to the man in need.
			• **Share** ways you can show love to the needy.
			
			Notebook Work
			Write or trace the title on the notebook page and draw and color a picture of the Samaritan helping the wounded man.
			
			BAR
			(See Weekly Routines for Reading and English.)
				• To learn and recite the memory verse
				• To learn new vocabulary
				• To help people who need you
				• To apply Matthew 19:19
				• To complete and file notebook work	

The Noah Plan Lessons Kindergarten © 2003 • Foundation for American Christian Education

TEACHING PLAN

Quarter One

Week Six

LITERATURE

Preparation

Biblical Principles
- God's Principle of Individuality
- Unity with Diversity.

Leading Idea
The contribution of character and ideals of American thought are expressed in the individuality and the diversity of the writer's work.

Books
- Bible (KJ)
- Webster's 1828 *Dictionary*
- NPLG, 8–9, 108–123
- NPEG, 2220–234,
- books containing biographies of poets
- Poetry book containing selections by Christina Rossetti

Supplies
- Notebook page to include:
  - the poet's name
  - a picture of the poet
  - the words to "Holy Innocents"
- Colored pencils

Lesson

Guide a discussion of the Biblical Principle and Leading Idea.

Define and identify the qualities of poetry highlighting rhyme and rhythm.

Introduce poet Christina Rossetti by discussing her life and contribution on the Chain of Christianity. NPEG, 223

Read aloud several selections of her poetry.

Model and lead the student to identify examples of rhythm and rhyme in her poetry.

Read aloud "Holy Innocents."

Practice the poem with the student for oral recitation.

Notebook Work
Distribute the prepared notebook page for the student to color the picture of the poet.

Student Work

Participate in a discussion of the Biblical Principles and Leading Idea.

Define rhythm and rhyme as literary (poetic) elements.

Participate in a discussion about Christina Rossetti's contribution on the Chain of Christianity.

Identify examples of rhythm and rhyme in Christina Rossetti 's poetry selections that are read aloud.

Listen as the teacher reads aloud "Holy Innocents."

Practice and memorize the poem for oral recitation.

Notebook Work
Color the picture of the poet.

Accomplishments

- To identify examples of rhythm and rhyme
- To recite the poem "Holy Innocents"
- To know God better
- To love God more
- To walk in His Ways
- To recognize each individual has a function in God's plan and chooses to execute it or not
- To complete and file notebook work

The Noah Plan Lessons Kindergarten © 2003 • Foundation for American Christian Education

Quarter One

TEACHING PLAN

Week Six

Preparation	Lesson	Student Work	Accomplishments

Biblical Principle
God's Principle of Individuality
 	
Leading Idea
Seashells are an expression of God's diversity.
 	
Books
• Bible (KJ)
• Webster's 1828 *Dictionary*
• NPH&GG, 8–9
• T&L, 156
 	
Supplies
• Notebook page to include:
  · the title "God's Principle of Individuality in Seashells" for the student to write or trace the title
  · a space for the student to draw a beach scene and to glue sand and seashells
• Assorted seashells (various types and sizes)
• Sand
• Colored pencils
	Continue the study of the Creation Link.
	Review how "God's Principle of Individuality" in nature can be seen in the design of leaves.
	
	• **Introduce** how God's Principle of Individuality in nature can also be seen in the diversity of seashells.
	  · **Define** diversity.
	  · **Lead** an activity in which the student examines many shells and observes how many different types exist as well as how shells of the same type vary.
	
	Notebook Work
	Distribute the prepared notebook page for the student to write or trace the title.
	• **Instruct** the student to draw on the notebook page a simple beach scene.
	• **Instruct** the student to glue sand and small shells to the beach scene.
		Review how God's Principle of Individuality can be seen in nature through the design of leaves by comparing the leaf rubbings and prints that were mounted on notebook pages in the previous lesson.
		
		Listen as the teacher defines diversity.
		
		Participate in an activity in which a variety of shells are examined to observe their diversity.
		
		Notebook Work
		Write or trace the title on the notebook page.
		• **Draw** and color a beach scene.
		• **Glue** sand and small shells to the beach area.
			• To compare leaf rubbings
			• To observe diversity in shells
			• To complete and file notebook work

HISTORY

The Noah Plan Lessons Kindergarten © 2003 • Foundation for American Christian Education

57

Week Six

TEACHING PLAN

Quarter One

Preparation	Lesson	Student Work	Accomplishments	✓

Biblical Principle "Let all things be done decently and in order." 1 Corinthians 14:40
 	
 Leading Idea A map represents the character of God.
 	
 Books
 • Bible (KJ)
 • Webster's 1828 *Dictionary*
 • NPH&GG, 128, 148–149
 	
 Supplies
 • Simplify the map in NPH&GG, 147; or
 • Use EMBG, Volume 2:1 or 7 or Volume 3:1.
 • Student atlas
 • Map standard
 • Colored pencils
 • Overhead projector for modeling if available
	Introduce the student atlas.
	
	 • **Discuss** its purpose.
	 • **Identify** several features of the atlas as the student looks through the book.
	
	 Teach and demonstrate the map standard for physical maps using a simple world map.
	 • **Teach** the coloring of the map.
	   · Shade continents green.
	   · Distinguish shorelines with blue "caterpillar hairs." (NPH&GG, 149)
	
	 Guide the student to the Biblical Principle from the Leading Idea by pointing out God's character as seen in the map standard:
	 • Order
	 • Individuality/diversity
	 • Accuracy
	
	 Notebook Work
	 Distribute and instruct the student to use the map standard to complete the simple world map. (EMBG, Volume 2:1 or 7 or Volume 3:1)
		Listen as the teacher introduces and explains the student atlas.
		 • **Discuss** its purpose.
		 • **Observe** selected features of the atlas as your teacher identifies it for you.
		
		 Listen as the teacher explains the map standard.
		 Observe the teacher modeling the map standard on a simple world map.
		
		 Reason about the Biblical Principle from the Leading Idea by answering the reason question:
		 • How does a map represent the character of God?
		
		 Notebook Work
		 Color the simple world map according to the map standard for physical maps.
		 • Shade continents green.
		 • Distinguish shorelines with blue "caterpillar hairs."
			• To learn the purpose and use of an atlas
			 • To complete a simple world map according to the map standard
			 • To identify God's character
			 • To complete and file notebook work	

GEOGRAPHY

TEACHING PLAN

Week Six Quarter One

SCIENCE

Preparation	Lesson	Student Work	Accomplishments	✓
Biblical Principle God's Principle of Design **Leading Idea** The things created by God can be changed into different forms. **Books** • Bible (KJ) • Webster's 1828 *Dictionary* • Science books (Library) **Supplies** • Solids, liquids, gases for the student to observe and classify • Hot plate, pan, water • Notebook page to include: · The title "Three Forms of Matter" for the student to write or trace · A three-column chart with subheadings—solid, liquid, gas	**Discuss** the Biblical Principle and Leading Idea. **Review** the definition of chemistry. **Define** matter as the name scientists give for the things God made. **Show** and discuss the three forms of matter: • Solid—definite shape and volume (examples—a book, a desk, a shoe, etc.) • Liquid—definite volume which takes the shape of its container (example—water, juice, milk, etc.) • Gas—takes the shape and volume of the container (examples—air, helium, etc.) **Ask** the student to look around the classroom and identify different forms of matter. **Display** various items for the student to classify into one of the three forms of matter. **Discuss** and demonstrate how matter can be changed into another form. • Liquid to a solid—freeze water, make Popsicles • Solid to a liquid—let ice cubes melt, ice cream melts, etc. • Liquid to a gas—boil water to observe steam **Relate** God's Principle of Design to the various forms of matter from the Leading Idea. *Notebook Work* **Distribute** the prepared notebook page for the student to write or trace the title and to record the classification of the different types of matter.	**Participate** in a discussion of the Biblical Principle and Leading Idea. **Participate** in a review of chemistry. **Listen** as the teacher defines matter. **Observe** and participate in a discussion about the three forms of matter. **Look** around the classroom and identify forms of matter. **Classify** various items into one of the three forms of matter. **Observe** and participate in a discussion on how matter can be changed into another form. *Notebook Work* **Write** or trace the title on the notebook page and record the classification of the different types of matter under the appropriate subheadings.	• To review the definition of chemistry • To learn that matter is everything God has created • To learn the three forms of matter • To identify and classify different forms of matter • To apply the Biblical Principle to the three forms of matter • To complete and file notebook work	

The Noah Plan Lessons Kindergarten © 2003 • Foundation for American Christian Education   59

TEACHING PLAN

Week Seven Quarter One

Preparation	Lesson	Student Work	Accomplishments	✔

Biblical Principle
Jesus cares for us.
 	
Leading Idea
The shepherd helped the lost sheep.
 	
Books
• Bible (KJV)
• Webster's 1828 *Dictionary*
 	
Supplies
• Notebook page to include:
  · the title "The Lost Sheep" for the student to write or trace
  · a space for the student to draw and color a picture of a shepherd helping the lost sheep
	Introduce the memory verse.
	"He shall feed his flock like a shepherd. . . ." Isaiah 40:11
	• **Read** aloud and discuss the memory verse.
	• **Define** unfamiliar vocabulary.
	• **Practice** daily the memory verse with the student for his recitation on Friday.
	Guide the student to the Biblical Principle from the Leading Idea.
	• **Read** aloud the Parable of the Lost Sheep. Luke 15:3–7
	
	• **Identify** the responsibilities of the shepherd.
	  · He protects the sheep.
	  · He feeds the sheep.
	  · He gives them water.
	  · He gives rest to the sheep.
	• **Discuss** how the shepherd felt when he found the lost sheep.
	• **Read** aloud John 10:11 and discuss Jesus as our Good Shepherd. John 10:11
	• **Apply** this parable to how God feels when a person turns away from sin.
	
	Notebook Work
	Distribute the prepared notebook page for the student to write or trace the title and to draw and color the picture of the shepherd helping the lost sheep.
		Listen as the teacher reads aloud and discusses the memory verse.
		
		• **Discuss** unfamiliar vocabulary.
		• **Practice** and learn the memory verse for recitation on Friday.
		
		Listen as the teacher reads aloud the Parable of the Lost Sheep.
		• **Identify** the responsibilities of the shepherd.
		
		• **Discuss** how the shepherd felt when he found the lost sheep.
		• **Listen** as the teacher reads aloud John 10:11 and discusses Jesus as our Good Shepherd.
		• **Apply** this parable to how God feels when a person turns away from sin.
		
		Notebook Work
		Write or trace the title on the notebook page and draw and color a picture of a shepherd helping the lost sheep.
			• To learn and recite the memory verse
			• To learn new vocabulary
			• To know Jesus as our Good Shepherd
			• To complete and file notebook work	

BAR • *Early Reader's Bible*, 403–409 • NPRG	**BAR** "The Good Shepherd" (See Weekly Routines for Reading and English.)	**BAR** (See Weekly Routines for Reading and English.)		

Week Seven

Quarter One

TEACHING PLAN

Preparation	Lesson	Student Work	Accomplishments	✓
Biblical Principle Our actions result in consequences. Genesis 3:11–19 **Leading Idea** Fairy tales are a type of literature used to teach our children right from wrong. **Books** • Bible (KJ) • NPLG, 8–9, 100–104 • Fairy tale books **Supplies** • Classroom world map • Student atlas • Notebook page to include: • the title of the fairy tale for the student to write or trace • a space for the student to draw or color a picture or a picture for the student to color	**Guide** the student to the Biblical Principle from the Leading Idea. • **Read aloud** Genesis 3:11–19 and discuss how each individual is responsible for his own actions. **Introduce** fairy tales as a type of literature. • **Describe** the qualities of a fairy tale. NPLG, 100–104 • **Read** aloud "The Princess and the Pea," and "Jack and the Beanstalk." • **Discuss** the individuality of the authors and their country of origin. • **Locate** the author's country of origin on the classroom world map and in the student atlas. • **Discuss** with the student how to discern the actions of the characters and the conflict between good and evil. *Notebook Work* **Distribute** the prepared notebook page for the student to write or trace the title of the fairy tale and to draw or color the picture.	**Listen** as the teacher reads aloud Genesis 3:11–19 and participate in a discussion of how each individual is responsible for his own actions. **Listen** as the teacher introduces fairy tales as a type of literature. **Name** several qualities of a fairy tale. **Listen** as the teacher reads aloud "The Princess and the Pea," and "Jack and the Beanstalk." **Identify** aspects of the story that represent the individuality of the country of origin. **Locate** the country of origin on the classroom world map and in your student atlas. **Reason** aloud whether a character and his actions represent good or evil. *Notebook Work* **Write** or trace the title on the notebook page and draw or color the picture. 	• To name qualities of a fairy tale • To recognize each individual is responsible for his own actions • To develop the ability to discern between good and evil • To recognize the individuality of nations • To complete and file notebook work	

LITERATURE

The Noah Plan Lessons Kindergarten © 2003 • Foundation for American Christian Education

Week Seven **TEACHING PLAN** Quarter One

	Preparation	Lesson	Student Work	Accomplishments	✓

HISTORY	**Biblical Principle**
	God's Principle of Individuality
	
	Leading Idea
	Snowflakes are an expression of God's symmetry.
	
	Books
	• Bible (KJV)
	• Webster's 1828 Dictionary
	• NPH&GG, 8–9
	• *Snowflake Bentley*, Jacqueline Briggs (or book with magnified pictures of snowflakes)
	• *Fun with Snowflakes Stencils*, Paul E. Kennedy
	
	Supplies
	• Snowflake cutouts
	• Notebook page (light blue) to include:
	  • the title "God's Principle of Individuality in Snowflakes" for the student to write or trace
	  • a space for the student to glue the snowflake cut outs
		Review how the design of leaves and the diversity of shells are examples of God's Principle of Individuality in nature. **Introduce** how snowflakes are also an example of God's Principle of Individuality.
		
		• **Present** biographical information about *Snowflake Bentley*.
		
		• **Read** aloud *Snowflake Bentley*.
		
		• **Define** symmetrical (balanced; same on each side).
		
		• **Discuss** all snowflakes have six points and are symmetrical but no two snowflakes are alike.
		
		• **Show** pictures of magnified snowflakes.
		
		• **Pre-fold** and cut snowflakes of various designs and distribute them to the student to be unfolded and compared.
		
		Notebook Work
		Distribute the prepared notebook (light blue) for the student to write or trace the title and glue the snowflake cut outs.
			Participate in a review by naming the characteristics of leaves and shells that illustrate God's Principle of Individuality in nature.
			
			Listen as the teacher introduces *Snowflake Bentley*.
			
			Listen as the teacher reads aloud *Snowflake Bentley*.
			
			Listen as the teacher defines symmetrical.
			
			Participate in a discussion about snowflakes and identify the characteristics of a snowflake that demonstrate God's Principle of Individuality.
			
			Make observations about snowflakes by looking at pictures of magnified snowflakes.
			
			Unfold and compare the pre-cut snowflakes:
			• **Observe** symmetry.
			• **Count** the points.
			• **Compare** the design of each one.
			
			Notebook Work
			Write or trace the title and glue pre-cut snowflakes on notebook page.
				• To review God's Principle of Individuality in leaves and shells
				
				• To identify God's Principle of Individuality in snowflakes
				
				• To compare snowflakes
				
				• To create snowflake designs
				
				• To complete and file notebook work	

TEACHING PLAN

Week Seven   Quarter One

Preparation	Lesson	Student Work	Accomplishments	✓

Biblical Principle
God gathered the waters into seas or oceans. Genesis 1:9–10
 	
Leading Idea
God set boundaries for the seas or oceans. Jeremiah 5:22
 	
Books
• Bible (KJ)
• Webster's 1828 *Dictionary*
• NPH&GG, 128, 148–149, 173–174
 	
Supplies
• Simple world map with oceans labeled
• EMBG, Volume 2:1
• Student atlas
• Colored pencils
• Overhead projector to model work if available
	Introduce the waters of the Earth.
	• **Read** aloud Genesis 1:9–10 and discuss how mighty our God is to gather the waters into one place.
	• **Discuss** 70% of the Earth is covered with water. (Demonstrate the percentage with a circle graph.)
	
	• **Name** the four major oceans as you locate them on a globe and classroom world map.
	
	• **Instruct** and guide the student to locate the four oceans in his atlas.
	
	• **Discuss** the individuality of the four oceans:
	  • Pacific-largest and deepest
	  • Atlantic-second largest and most heavily traveled
	  • Indian-warmest
	  • Arctic-smallest and coldest
	
	Notebook Work
	Distribute the EMBG, Volume 2:1 map and model the coloring of the oceans blue. (This is an exception to the map standard.)
		Listen as the teacher reads aloud Genesis 1:9–10 and discusses how mighty our God is.
		Participate in a discussion about how much of the Earth is covered by water.
		Listen and observe as the teacher names and locates the four major oceans on the globe and classroom world map.
		Follow the instructions and guidelines of your teacher as you locate the four oceans in your atlas.
		Listen as the teacher describes the individuality of the four major oceans.
		
		Notebook Work
		Color the oceans on the world map blue.
			• To recognize God's greatness
			• To locate the four oceans on a globe and world map
			• To use an atlas to locate the four oceans
			• To name the four oceans
			• To recognize the individuality of the four oceans
			• To complete and file notebook work	

GEOGRAPHY

The Noah Plan Lessons Kindergarten © 2003 • Foundation for American Christian Education

Week Seven Quarter One

TEACHING PLAN

Preparation	Lesson	Student Work	Accomplishments
Biblical Principle God controls the weather. 1 Samuel 12:16–19	**Continue** to teach science according to the days of Creation. **Introduce** meteorology.	**Listen** as the teacher introduces and defines meteorology.	• To learn the definition of meteorology • To understand the term weather
Leading Idea Weather is always changing, but Jesus never changes. Hebrews 13:8	• It is the study of the air and weather. • It was created on the second day of Creation. **Read** aloud 1 Samuel 12:16–19 and discuss the weather is under God's control.	**Listen** as the teacher reads aloud 1 Samuel 12:16–19 and discusses weather being under God's control. **Participate** in a discussion about weather.	• To learn how to record data • To make and evaluate a hypothesis • To learn what the Bible says about weather
Books • Bible (KJ) • Webster's 1828 *Dictionary* • Weather books (Library) • Encyclopedia	**Discuss** weather: • Weather is what is happening in the air. • Weather keeps changing. • Weather changes from hour to hour and from day to day. • Weather may be hot and dry, cold and wet, calm and sunny, or windy and rainy. **Take** the student outside each day (weather permitting) to observe the weather. • **Ask** questions that would make the student more observant:	**Observe** the weather conditions outdoors and answer the questions the teacher asks about the weather.	• To learn Jesus is the same yesterday, today, and tomorrow • To recognize Jesus' faithfulness • To complete and file notebook work
Supplies • Notebook page to include: • the title "The Weather" for the student to write or trace • a space divided into four quadrants for the student to write or trace the title of the weather condition and to draw and color pictures representing the weather: · sunny · rainy · snowy · windy	· Is it sunny? How do you know? · How does it feel on a sunny day? · Is it cloudy? How do you know? · How do you feel on a windy day? · How is a rainy day different from a windy day? • **Assist** the student in keeping a daily classroom weather chart by having the student draw or glue a picture representing the weather on the calendar. • **Ask** the student to make a hypothesis (make a guess) by asking him to predict what the weather will be like based upon the previous day's weather. **Discuss** what the Bible says about the weather by reading aloud the scripture verses. • Rain—a sign of God's goodness (Jeremiah 14:22) • Snow—productive of good (Isaiah 55:10) • Clouds—Israel's guidance (Exodus 13:21–22) • Temperature—describes God's thoughts on being luke-warm (Revelation 3:14–16)	**Record** the daily weather conditions on a classroom calendar by drawing or gluing pictures on the calendar. **Make** a hypothesis on the next day's weather based upon the previous day's weather and check your hypothesis (guess) the next day. **Listen** as the teacher reads aloud the scripture verses pertaining to weather.	
	Science— Lesson & Notebook Work (continued on page 65)	**Science— Student & Notebook Work** (continued on page 65)	

64 The Noah Plan Lessons Kindergarten © 2003 • Foundation for American Christian Education

Week Seven

Quarter One

TEACHING PLAN

Preparation	Lesson	Student Work	Accomplishments	✓
	Guide the student to the Biblical Principle from the Leading Idea. • **Read** aloud Hebrews 13:8 and discuss how Jesus unlike the weather never changes and how faithful He is to keep His promises. • **Ask** the student for a time when Jesus was faithful to him. *Notebook Work* **Distribute** the prepared notebook page for the student to write or trace the title and to draw and color the pictures representing the four weather conditions. *Optional* **Distribute** the prepared notebook page for the student to write or trace the title and to cut and glue pictures from magazines representing the four weather conditions.	**Listen** as the teacher reads aloud Hebrews 13:8. • **Discuss** how Jesus unlike weather never changes and how He is faithful to keep His promises. • **Share** a time when Jesus was faithful to you. *Notebook Work* **Write** or trace the title on the notebook page and draw and color the pictures representing the four weather conditions. *Optional* **Write** or trace the title on the notebook page and cut and glue pictures from magazines representing the four weather conditions.		

SCIENCE (continued)

The Noah Plan Lessons Kindergarten © 2003 • Foundation for American Christian Education

Week Eight

TEACHING PLAN

Quarter One

Preparation	Lesson	Student Work	Accomplishments	✓
Biblical Principle Jesus overcame death and He lives.	**Introduce** the memory verse. "I am he that liveth, and was dead. . . ." Revelation 1:18	**Listen** as the teacher reads aloud and discusses the memory verse.	• To learn and recite the memory verse	
Leading Idea Mary sees the risen Christ.	• **Read** aloud and discuss the memory verse. • **Define** unfamiliar vocabulary. • **Practice** daily the memory verse with the student for his recitation on Friday.	• **Discuss** unfamiliar vocabulary. • **Practice** and learn the memory verse for recitation on Friday.	• To learn new vocabulary • To share the message of Jesus' victory • To complete and file notebook work	
Books • Bible (KJ) • Webster's 1828 *Dictionary*	**Guide** the student to the Biblical Principle from the Leading Idea. • **Tell** the story of Jesus' resurrection. Matthew 28	**Listen** as the teacher tells the story of Jesus' resurrection.		
Supplies • Notebook page to include: • the title "Jesus' Resurrection" for the student to write or trace • a space for the student to draw and color a picture of Jesus' Resurrection	• **Define** resurrection. • **Discuss** the significance of the resurrection. • It established Jesus as the true King. • It shows Jesus' power over evil. • It shows that Jesus is all-powerful. • **Share** the effect Jesus' resurrection made on you.	**Discuss** the term resurrection. **Discuss** the significance of Jesus' resurrection. **Listen** as the teacher shares the effect of Jesus' resurrection on his/ her life. **Discuss** the effect Jesus' resurrection had on your life.		
	• **Encourage** the student to share the effect Jesus' resurrection made on him.			
	Notebook Work **Distribute** the prepared notebook page for the student to write or trace the title and to draw and color a picture of Jesus' resurrection.	*Notebook Work* **Write** or trace the title on the notebook page and draw and color a picture of Jesus' resurrection.		
BAR • *Early Reader's Bible,* 459–465 • NPRG	**BAR** "Jesus Is Alive Again!" (See Weekly Routines for Reading and English.)	**BAR** (See Weekly Routines for Reading and English.)		

Week Eight

Quarter One

TEACHING PLAN

Preparation	Lesson	Student Work	Accomplishments	✓
Biblical Principle Our actions result in consequences. Genesis 3:11–19	**Review** the Biblical Principle and Leading Idea.	**Participate** in a review of the Biblical Principle and Leading Idea.	• To learn about the individualities of nations	
Leading Idea Fairy tales are a type of literature used to teach our children right from wrong.	**Review** the qualities of a fairy tale and the definition of theme.	**Participate** in a review of the qualities of a fairy tale and the definition of theme.	• To review the qualities of a fairy tale	
Books • Bible (KJ) • NPLG, 8–9, 100–104 • Fairy tale books	**Review** the themes of the "Princess and the Pea" and "Jack in the Beanstalk." **Read** aloud "Brave Little Tailor," "Bremen Town Musicians," and "Red Riding Hood."	**Participate** in a review of the themes of "The Princess and the Pea," and "Jack and the Beanstalk." **Listen** as teacher reads aloud the new fairy tales.	• To review the definition of theme • To recognize the individuality of a character can be seen through his actions	
Supplies • Classroom world map • Student atlas • Notebook page to include: • the title of the fairy tale for the student to write or trace • a space for the student to draw or color a picture or a picture for the student to color	• **Locate** the country of origins of the authors on the classroom world map and in the student's atlas. • **Discuss** the individuality of the authors and their country of origin. • **Lead** a discussion about the actions of the characters and the conflict between good and evil.	• **Locate** the country of origins of the authors on the classroom world map and in your atlas. • **Discuss** the individuality of the authors and their country of origin. • **Identify** the elements of good and evil in the characters and their actions.	• To develop the ability to discern between good and evil • To complete and file notebook work	
	Notebook Work **Distribute** the prepared notebook page for the student to write or trace the title of the fairy tale and to draw or color the picture.	*Notebook Work* **Write** or trace the title on the notebook page and draw or color the picture.		

LITERATURE

The Noah Plan Lessons Kindergarten © 2003 • Foundation for American Christian Education
67

Week Eight

TEACHING PLAN

Quarter One

HISTORY

Preparation	Lesson	Student Work	Accomplishments	✓
Biblical Principle God's Principle of Individuality	**Review** how the design of leaves, the diversity of shells, and the symmetry of snowflakes are examples of God's Principle of Individuality in nature.	**Review** by naming several characteristics of leaves, shells, and snowflakes that illustrate God's Principle of Individuality in nature.	• To review God's Principle of Individuality in leaves, shells, and snowflakes	
Leading Idea Distinct breeds of dogs are an expression of God's variety.	**Introduce** how distinct breeds of dogs are examples of God's variety (many kinds; types).	**View** pictures of different breeds of dogs and identify how their unique features make them suited for various purposes.	• To identify various breeds of dogs and their purposes	
Books • Bible (KJ) • NPH&GG, 8–9 • Dog books	• **Show** pictures of different breeds of dogs and identify their unique features.		• To recognize God's Principle of Individuality in dogs	
	• **Discuss** how the unique features of different breeds suit them for various purposes.	**Make** visual comparisons as the teacher shows pictures of different breeds of dogs.	• To create a mural on the bulletin board	
Supplies • Large piece of paper or poster board for mural	**Assign** the student to bring pictures of his dog or cut out pictures of dogs from magazines and assist the student in creating a mural on the bulletin board.	**Bring** pictures of your dog or cut out pictures from a magazine and participate in creating a mural on the bulletin board.	• To complete and file notebook work	
• Notebook page to include: • the title "God's Principle of Individuality in Dogs" for the student to write or trace • a simple outline of a dog for the student to color	*Notebook Work* **Distribute** the prepared notebook page for the student to write or trace the title and to color the dog to represent his favorite breed.	*Notebook Work* **Write** or trace the title and color the dog picture on the notebook page to represent a distinct breed (your favorite breed).		
• Magazines with pictures of dogs for the student to cut • Bulletin board to display dog mural • Colored pencils				

68   The Noah Plan Lessons Kindergarten © 2003 • Foundation for American Christian Education

Week Eight

Quarter One

TEACHING PLAN

	Preparation	Lesson	Student Work	Accomplishments	✓
GEOGRAPHY	**Biblical Principle** God created the dry land. Genesis 1:9 **Leading Idea** Each continent has a distinct and unique personality. **Books** • Bible (KJ) • NPH&GG, 128, 172–173 • T&L, 141–153, 156–157 **Supplies** • World map or globe • EMBG, Volume 2:7 • Overhead projector if available • Student atlas • Colored pencils	**Guide** the student to the Biblical Principle from the Leading Idea as you introduce the landmasses of the Earth. • **Read aloud** Genesis 1:9 and discuss God created dry land on the third day of Creation. • **Name** and locate the seven large landmasses (continents) of the Earth on the classroom world map and in the student atlas. • **Tell** the student that the landmasses are called continents. • **Help** the student pronounce the name of each continent as you point to it. • **Discuss** the shape and size of each continent. • **Review** and discuss the arrangement of the continents as they pertain to the equator. • There are three continents in the north above the equator and four in the South below the equator. • Each northern continent loosely connects to a southern continent: · North and South America · Europe and Africa · Asia and Australia · Exception—Antarctica • **Reason** with the student from the information studied thus far that God created each continent with a distinct and unique personality. *Notebook Work* **Distribute** and instruct the student in completing EMBG, Volume 2:7. **Use** an overhead projector to model the coloring.	**Listen** as the teacher reads aloud Genesis 1:9 and discusses the creation of dry land. **Listen** and observe as the teacher names and locates the seven large landmasses of the Earth on a classroom world map and in your atlas. **Learn** continent is another name for the seven large landmasses. **Practice** and learn the names of the continents. **Observe** and discuss the shape and size of each continent. **Review** the position of the equator and discuss the arrangement of the continents as they pertain to it. • **Learn** the three pairs of continents. **Reason** from this week's study that God created each continent with a distinct and unique personality. *Notebook Work* **Color** the map according to your teacher's directions.	• To learn God created land on the third day of Creation • To learn new vocabulary • To name and locate the seven continents • To recognize each continent by shape and size • To complete and file notebook work	

The Noah Plan Lessons Kindergarten © 2003 • Foundation for American Christian Education

Week Eight · TEACHING PLAN · Quarter One

SCIENCE	Preparation	Lesson	Student Work	Accomplishments	✓
	Biblical Principle God has provided an orderly world—an orderly sequence of days, seasons, and years. Genesis 1:14 **Leading Idea** God guarantees the seasons. Genesis 8:22 **Books** • Bible (KJ) • Webster's 1828 *Dictionary* • Weather books (Library) • Encyclopedia **Supplies** • Four pictures of the same scene during different seasons • Notebook page to include: · the title "My Favorite Season" for the student to write or trace · a space for the student to write a sentence about his favorite season · a space for the student to draw and color a picture about his favorite season	**Introduce** the seasons. • **Give** the student four pictures of the same scene during different seasons to study. • **Ask** the student questions about the pictures: · When do you think these pictures were taken? Why? · How did it feel outside when these pictures were taken? How do you know? · What are some similarities and/or differences between the pictures? **Guide** the student to the Biblical Principle from the Leading Idea. • **Read** aloud Genesis 1:14 and Genesis 8:22 and discuss the following with the student: · Each year the Earth goes through changes. · These changes are called seasons. · There are four seasons: autumn, winter, spring, and summer. · The weather varies with each season. • **Show** the seasonal pictures and identify with the student the similarities and/or differences between the seasons: · Type of weather · Type of clothing · Type of activities · Holidays · How the trees look · Effect on animal and plant life • **Discuss** how God's Principle of Individuality can be seen in the seasons. *Notebook Work* **Distribute** the prepared notebook page for the student to write or trace the title, write a sentence about his favorite season, and to draw and color a picture of his favorite season.	**Study** the four pictures of the same scene during different seasons. **Reason** and relate from the study of the four seasonal pictures and answer questions about the pictures: • When do you think these pictures were taken? Why? • How did it feel outside when these pictures were taken? How do you know? • What are some similarities and/or differences between the pictures? **Listen** as the teacher reads aloud Genesis 1:14 and Genesis 8:22 and discusses the following: • Each year the Earth goes through changes. • These changes are called seasons. • There are four seasons—autumn, winter, spring, and summer. • The weather varies with each season. • **View** the seasonal pictures and identify the similarities and/or differences between the seasons: · Type of weather · Type of clothing · Type of activities · Holidays · How the trees look · Effect on animal and plant life **Participate** in a discussion about how God's Principle of Individuality can be seen in the seasons. *Notebook Work* **Write** or trace the title on the notebook page, write a sentence about your favorite season, and draw and color a picture of your favorite season.	• To understand the characteristics of the four seasons • To reason and relate from the scriptures • To understand the seasons are guaranteed by God • To complete and file notebook work	

Week Nine   **TEACHING PLAN**   Quarter One

BIBLE

Preparation	Lesson	Student Work	Accomplishments	✓

Biblical Principle
Man is the steward of the Earth.
 	
Leading Idea
The Holy Land is the place where Jesus ministered to man on Earth.
 	
Books
• Bible (KJ)
• Webster's 1828 *Dictionary*
 	
Supplies
• Classroom wall map of the Holy Land
• A simplified map of the Holy Land to include:
  • the title "The Holy Land" for the student to write or trace
  • horizontal lines for the student to label Bethlehem, Jerusalem, Sea of Galilee, and River Jordan
 	
BAR
Map Work
	Introduce the memory verse.
	"…replenish the earth, and subdue it: and have dominion…."
	Genesis 1:28
	• **Read** aloud and discuss the memory verse.
	• **Define** unfamiliar vocabulary.
	• **Practice** daily the memory verse with the student for his recitation on Friday.
	Guide the student to the Biblical Principle from the Leading Idea.
	• **Define** steward.
	• **Discuss** how we can be good stewards of the Earth.
	• **Show** the map of the Holy Land to the student and locate Bethlehem, Jerusalem, Sea of Galilee, and River Jordan on the classroom world map.
	
	Notebook Work
	Distribute the prepared map of the Holy Land for the student:
	• to write or trace the title
	• to label Bethlehem, Jerusalem, Sea of Galilee, and River Jordan, and
	• to color the map according to the map standard.
	
	BAR
	Map locations—Bethlehem, Jerusalem, Sea of Galilee, and River Jordan.
	Vocabulary: rivers, mountains, sea, etc.
	(See Weekly Routines for Reading and English.)
		Listen as the teacher reads aloud and discusses the memory verse.
		
		• **Discuss** unfamiliar vocabulary.
		• **Practice** and learn the memory verse for recitation on Friday.
		
		Discuss the definition of steward.
		Discuss ways you can be a good steward of the Earth.
		View the classroom map of the Holy Land and observe as your teacher points out Bethlehem, Jerusalem, Sea of Galilee, and River Jordan.
		
		Notebook Work
		Write or trace the title on the map.
		Label Bethlehem, Jerusalem, Sea of Galilee, and River Jordan on the map.
		Color the map according to the map standard.
		
		BAR
		(See Weekly Routines for Reading and English.)
			• To learn and recite the memory verse
			• To learn new vocabulary
			• To replenish, subdue and have dominion over the Earth
			• To become acquainted with the Holy Land at the time of Jesus
			• To complete and file notebook work	

The Noah Plan Lessons Kindergarten © 2003 • Foundation for American Christian Education   71

Week Nine   TEACHING PLAN   Quarter One

Preparation	Lesson	Student Work	Accomplishments
Biblical Principle Our actions result in consequences. Genesis 3:11–19 **Leading Idea** Fairy tales are a type of literature used to teach our children right from wrong. **Books** • Bible (KJ) • NPLG, 8–9, 100–104 • Fairy tale books **Supplies** • Classroom world map • Student atlas • Notebook page to include: • the title of the fairy tale for the student to write or trace • a space for the student to draw or color a picture or a picture for the student to color	**Review** the Biblical Principle and Leading Idea. **Review** the theme of " Brave Little Tailor," "Bremen Town Musicians," and "Red Riding Hood." **Read** aloud "Emperor's New Clothes" and "The Frog Prince." • **Locate** the country of origins of the authors on the classroom world map and in the student's atlas. • **Discuss** the individuality of the authors and their country of origin. • **Lead** a discussion about the actions of the characters and the conflict between good and evil. *Notebook Work* **Distribute** the prepared notebook page for the student to write or trace the title of the fairy tale and to draw or color the picture.	**Participate** in a review of the Biblical Principle and Leading Idea. **Participate** in a review of the theme of "Brave Little Tailor," "Bremen Town Musicians," and "Red Riding Hood." **Listen** as teacher reads aloud the new fairy tales. • **Locate** the country of origins of the authors on the classroom world map and in the your atlas. • **Discuss** the individuality of the authors and their country of origin. • **Identify** elements of good and evil in the characters and their actions. *Notebook Work* **Write** or trace the title on the notebook page and draw or color the picture.	• To learn about the individuality of nations • To recognize the individuality of a character can be seen through his actions • To develop the ability to discern between good and evil • To identify elements of good and evil • To complete and file notebook work

LITERATURE

72   The Noah Plan Lessons Kindergarten © 2003 • Foundation for American Christian Education

TEACHING PLAN

Week Nine
Quarter One

Preparation	Lesson	Student Work	Accomplishments	✓
Biblical Principle God's Principle of Individuality **Leading Idea** God has a plan and purpose for everything He created. **Books** • Bible (KJ) • NPH&GG, 8–9 • T&L, 66, 141–153, 156 **Supplies** • Classroom world map • Notebook pages from previous lessons or other visuals for use in presentation	**Review** how the design of leaves, the diversity of shells, the symmetry of snowflakes, and the distinct breeds of dogs illustrate God's Principle of Individuality in nature. **Introduce** how the Earth was shaped to fit God's purpose and His plan is an example of God's individuality. • **Display** the classroom world map and compare the individualities in each continent (shape, size, and physical features). • **Identify** and locate the continents of history and nature. (Each continent along with map work will be studied in detail in geography class.) **Prepare** the student to give an oral and visual presentation (for Grandparent's Day, parents, and others) using his notebook headings for oral presentation and his notebook pages for visuals.	**Review** the Creation Link by recalling the characteristics of leaves, shells, snowflakes, and dogs that illustrate how God's Principle of Individuality is seen in nature. **Listen** as the teacher introduces and discusses the Earth and its continents as examples of God's Principle of Individuality. • **View** each continent on the classroom world map. • **Compare** their individuality. • **Observe** and learn the location of the continents of history and nature. **Prepare** to give an oral and visual presentation (for parents, grandparents or others) using your notebook headings for oral presentation and notebook pages for visuals. (See "Grandparents' Day," NPLK, 263.)	• To recognize God's Principle of Individuality in nature • To present an oral and visual review of God's Principle of Individuality	

HISTORY

The Noah Plan Lessons Kindergarten © 2003 • Foundation for American Christian Education

Week Nine | **TEACHING PLAN** | **Quarter One** | ✓

GEOGRAPHY

Preparation	Lesson	Student Work	Accomplishments

Biblical Principle
God created the topography of the Earth. Job 28:9–11
 	
Leading Idea
God uniquely designed mountains, deserts, and plains for man for His purpose.
 	
Books
• Bible (KJ)
• Webster's 1828 *Dictionary*
• NPH&GG, 128, 141, 175–177
• T&L, 141–153, 156–157
• CHOC I, 4–5
 	
Supplies
• Simple world map of the continents
• EMBG, Volume 1:14
• Pictures of mountains, deserts, and plains
• Student atlas
• Map standard
• Colored pencils
	Discuss the Biblical Principle and the Leading Idea.
	
	Introduce the topography of the continents.
	• **Read** aloud Genesis 1:9 and discuss the topography of the continents (mountains, deserts, plains) were also created on the third day of Creation.
	• **Define** mountains.
	  • Discuss the purpose of mountains:
	    · Boundaries: Numbers 34:7, 8
	    · Habitation of God: Psalm 68:15–16
	    · Refuge: Matthew 24:16
	    · Place of prayer: Matthew 14:23
	• **Define** deserts.
	  • Discuss the purpose of deserts:
	    · Home for John the Baptist: Luke 1:80
	    · Quiet place for Jesus: Mark 6:31
	    · A place of wilderness: Isaiah 48:21
	• **Define** plains.
	  • Discuss the purpose of plains:
	    · Great for farming
	    · Cities easily built on plains
	• **Identify** on the classroom world map the major mountains, deserts, and plains of the continents.
	
	Review the definition of the Chain of Christianity. (NPH&GG, 76)
	
	GEOGRAPHY—
	Lesson & Notebook Work
	(continued on page 75)
		Participate in a discussion of the Biblical Principle and Leading Idea.
		Listen as the teacher reads aloud Genesis 1:9 and discusses the creation of dry land and its topography.
		
		Learn the definition of mountains, deserts, and plains.
		• **Listen** as the teacher reads aloud the scriptures as they pertain to the topography of the continents.
		• **Discuss** the purpose of each.
		
		• **Listen** and observe as the teacher identifies the major mountains, deserts, and plains of each continent on the classroom world map.
		Review the definition of Chain of Christianity.
		
		GEOGRAPHY—
		Student Notebook Work
		(continued on page 75)
			• To learn about the topography of the continents
			• To learn new vocabulary
			• To learn the westward move of Christianity
			• To complete and file notebook work

Week Nine   Quarter One

TEACHING PLAN

Preparation	Lesson	Student Work	Accomplishments	✓
	Discuss how Christianity took a westward move starting with Asia, developing in Europe, and having its greatest effect in America:	**Listen** to and discuss the role of Asia, Europe, and America in the spreading of the Gospel westward.		
	• Asia			
	• It is the home of Christianity.			
	• It is where God placed the first man and woman.			
	• God's story (His story) began here.			
	• Europe			
	• Man learned more about God here.			
	• America			
	• This is where God placed us.			
	• It is a place of freedom to serve God.			
	Locate and identify Asia, Europe, and America on the classroom world map and in the student's atlas.	**Locate** Asia, Europe, and America on the classroom world map and in the your atlas.		
	Notebook Work	*Notebook Work*		
	Distribute a simple world map (EMBG, Volume 1:14) and model the coloring of the mountains, deserts, and plains according to the map standard. NPH&GG, 149	**Color** the mountains, deserts, and plains of each continent on the world map according to the map standard.		

GEOGRAPHY (continued)

The Noah Plan Lessons Kindergarten © 2003 • Foundation for American Christian Education   75

Week Nine

Quarter One

TEACHING PLAN

	Preparation	Lesson	Student Work	Accomplishments	✓
SCIENCE	**Biblical Principle** Seasons demonstrate God's goodness and providence. Acts 14:17 **Leading Idea** Why are the seasons on Earth? **Books** • Bible (KJ) • Webster's 1828 *Dictionary* • Weather books (library) • Encyclopedia **Supplies** • Flashlight • Globe mounted on a stand • Notebook page to include: • the title "The Seasons" for the student to write or trace • a space divided into four sections for students to draw and color a picture of what each season represents to them	**Review** the four seasons. • **Ask** the student to name the four seasons. • **Ask** the student to name some of their individual characteristics. **Discuss** and explain to the student that the seasons of the year depend on the amount of sunlight reaching the Earth. • **Explain** and demonstrate how the Earth's tilt as it moves around the Sun causes the change of seasons. • **Hold** the flashlight toward the globe. • **Place** the globe (Earth) close enough to the flashlight so that the flashlight illuminates part of the globe. • **Put** a large "X" on the Northern Hemisphere. • **Spin** the globe and ask the student to notice how the light hits the Northern Hemisphere. · Winter—the Northern Hemisphere tilts away from the Sun. · Summer—the Northern Hemisphere tilts toward the Sun. · Spring is between winter and summer. · Autumn is between summer and winter. · During spring and autumn time the North and South Poles receive the same amount of sunshine. **Guide** the student to the Biblical Principle from the Leading Idea: • **Read** Acts 14:17 and discuss the seasons demonstrate God's goodness. • He shows kindness by giving you rain. • He gives you crops in their seasons. • He provides you with plenty of food. • He fills your hearts with joy. *Notebook Work* **Distribute** the prepared notebook page for the student to write or trace the title and to draw and color a picture of what each season represents to them.	**Review** the names of the four seasons and give examples of the unique characteristics of each season. **Listen** as the teacher discusses and explains that the four seasons depend upon the amount of light reaching the Earth. • **Identify** on the board the sequence of the seasons (winter, spring, summer, autumn). **Participate** in a demonstration of how the tilt of the Earth as it moves around the sun causes the change of seasons. • **Observe** how the light hits the Northern Hemisphere. • Winter—the Northern Hemisphere tilts away from the Sun. • Summer—the Northern Hemisphere tilts toward the Sun. • Spring—between winter and summer. • Autumn—between summer and winter. • During spring and autumn time the North and South Poles receive the same amount of sunshine. **Listen** as the teacher reads aloud Acts 14:17 and participate in a discussion on how the seasons demonstrate God's goodness. *Notebook Work* **Write** or trace the title and draw and color a picture of what each season represents to you.	• To learn the causes of the four seasons through investigation • To observe and record observations about the seasons • To complete and file notebook work	

76 The Noah Plan Lessons Kindergarten © 2003 • Foundation for American Christian Education

Quarter Two

Hickory, dickory, dock,
The mouse ran up the clock;
The clock struck one,
The mouse ran down,
Hickory, dickory, dock.

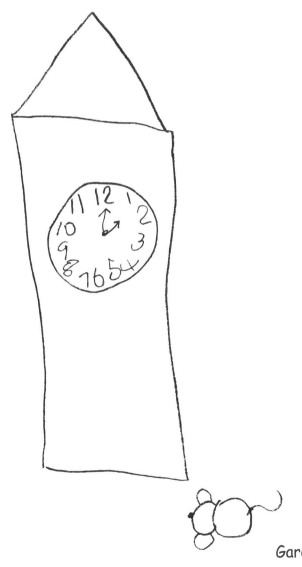

Gareth R.

Esther D.

Quarter Two Planning Sheet for Teaching Mathematics by Components

Teacher: Mr. Ricciardi   Grade Level: K

"Eye hath not seen nor ear heard, neither have entered into the heart of man, the things which God hath prepared for them that love him." 1 Corinthians 2:9

Week	Foundations	Numbers	Numeration/Notation	Measurement	Operations	Problem Solving	Summary of Principles
1 RSL 27–28	AHCC–Noah GPI–numbers PS–folding CFG–naming	Even numbers Half Ones Place value Tens	Reading abacus entries Reading calendar date Vocabulary	Ellipses Geoboard Hexagon Money Parallel lines Quadrilateral Rectangle Rhombus Square Time Triangle	Addition Multiplication by 2s	Abacus entries Arranging Drawing Engineering Folding Patterning Practicing Visualizing	The principles and leading ideas of mathematics are demonstrated in the lessons, and are continually clarified for the children as the year progresses. **Governmental Principles** **God's Principle of Individuality** (GPI) Mathematics measures 'how much.' Each number is a unique quantity. **Christian Self-Government** (CSG) Operations (+, -, x, ÷) govern mathematics. **Christian Character** (AHCC) Mathematics demonstrates God's character. It is systematic, unchangeable, and orderly like God. **"Conscience…Sacred Property"** (CSP) Mathematics enables the individual to Biblically care for property. **Christian Form of Government** (CFG) Quantity is represented in various ways. **Local Self-Government** (LSG) Christ's government is planted into the heart of the student as the student deals with the operations (government) and processes of mathematics. **American Political Union** (APU) Numbers of like kind only may be added. **Subject Principles** **Associative Principle** (AP), NPMG, 104 **Principle of Symmetry** (PS), NPMG, 139 **Distributive Principle** (DP), NPMG, 104, 113 See **Sample Math Guide/Right-Start Coordination, Lessons, & Annual Schedule**, 269–281.
2 RSL 29–30	AHCC–Noah CSP–estimating GPI–quantities CFG–reflection	Quantities 1–10 Place value	Reading abacus entries Vocabulary	Money Time	Addition Directionality—opposite Subtraction	Abacus entries Arranging Engineering Visualizing Estimating Patterning Subitizing	
3 RSL 31–32	AHCC–Noah APU–matching AP–matching CSP–consent DP–division GPI–coins CFG–representation, coins	Even numbers Odd numbers Place value Quantities 1s, 5s, 10s Sum	Finger sets Reading abacus entries Tallying Vocabulary	Circles Money Octagon Pentagon Semi-circle Time Trapezoid	Addition Division	Abacus entries Matching Practicing Translating	

4
RSL
33–35
	AHCC–Noah
	APU–associating
	AP–matching
	GPI–infinity, order
	CFG–representation,
	  patterning
		Even numbers
		Odd numbers
		Place value
		Quantities
		  1s, 5s, 10s
			Reading abacus entries
			Reading and writing
			  equations
			Symbols (+, =)
			Tallying
			Vocabulary–dozen
				Between
				Charting
				Money
				Time
					Addition—grouping,
					"+1 more" strategy
					Multiplication by 5s
						Abacus entries
						Completing equations
						Finding coins
						Matching
						Musical patterns
						Practicing
						Patterning
						Visualizing	

5 RSL 35–36	AHCC–Noah DP–partitioning GPI–quantities CFG–reading entries	Quantities 1–10 Sum	Reading abacus entries Writing equations Tallying Vocabulary	Time	Addition Subtraction	Abacus entries Partitioning Practicing Subitizing	
6 RSL 37–38	AHCC–Noah GPI–order CFG–reading entries	Place value Quantities 1–10	Reading abacus entries Tallying Vocabulary Writing equations	Middle Time	Addition Subtraction	Abacus entries Arranging Completing equations Practicing Subitizing	
7 RSL 38–39	AHCC–Noah APU–partners DP–partitioning GPI–quantities CFG–symbols	Place value Quantities 1–10	Reading abacus entries Tallying Vocabulary	Time	Addition Subtraction	Abacus entries Completing equations Partitioning Patterning Practicing	
8 RSL 40–41	DP–partitioning GPI–quantities	Place value Quantities 1–10 Sum	Reading abacus entries Writing equations	Time	Addition Subtraction	Completing equations Games Partitioning	
9 RSL 42–43	GPI–numbers DP–partitioning CFG–reading entries	Even numbers Odd numbers Ones, Tens Place value	Reading abacus entries		Addition Subtraction	Abacus entries Arranging Engineering	

The Noah Plan Lessons Kindergarten © 2003 • Foundation for American Christian Education

Quarter Two—Weekly Routines for Reading and English

COMPONENT	Monday	Tuesday	Wednesday	Thursday	Friday
FOUNDATIONS	Introduce language as a gift from God, throughout the quarter, to learn that language is to help us com-		municate with Him and with each other. God uses language to communicate with us through His Word.	Look for opportunities to reinforce this idea in many lessons, NPEG, 47–49.	
ORTHOGRAPHY Phonemic Awareness Instruction	Continue "Suggested Kindergarten Schedule," *Phonemic Awareness in Young Children*, 137–141. Adjust the pace of introducing the activities according to the strengths and needs of the student. Continue introduction of phonograms and practice		using the "Oral Phonogram Review Procedures" and "Written Phonogram Review Procedures," *The Writing Road to Reading*, 39–42. Practice to develop mastery of phonograms 1–54. Observe your student carefully to determine the	level of interest and understanding of each phonemic awareness activity. Do not hesitate to repeat the previous activities often as new ones are introduced. Continue oral and written phonogram review procedures.	
Penmanship	Be Sure the lower-case letters are well learned before introducing all the capital letters. Exception is first letters in student's name.		Introduce capital letter formation, *The Writing Road to Reading*, 29–30.	Teach letter formation as new phonograms are introduced.	
Spelling	Begin the Extended Ayers List, *The Writing Road to Reading*, 252–262. Refer to Scope and Sequence objectives in *The Writing Road to Reading*, 444. Mix and test between 8 and 16 phonograms after the initial introduction. Administer the Morrison-McCall Spelling Scale Test to determine the student's progress at the beginning of the quarter, *Spalding Spelling Assessment Manual*, 19. See "Spelling Assessment Procedures," in *Spalding Spelling Assessment Manual*, 7–13. Assign homework: Write first five words 3x and use in an oral sentence.		Continue *Spelling Dictation Procedure* with the next five words, *The Writing Road to Reading*, 49–53. Read spelling words orally. Elicit oral sentences from student. Write sentences from oral discussion on the chalkboard. (Student copies and may illustrate.) Assign homework: Write five words 3x and use in an oral sentence.	Continue to review previously learned phonograms by decoding (reading) and encoding (writing). Continue *Spelling Dictation Procedure* with the next five words Write the week's words in a practice test. Assign homework: Study for test.	Continue to review previously learned phonograms by decoding (reading) and encoding (writing). Test spelling words at the end of the week; do not require the markings for test, *Writing Road to Reading*, 85.
COMPOSITION	Continue to plant the seeds of good writing and speaking; lead the student to choose vivid and 'telling' words in place of "nice," "pretty," "good," etc; always require the student to use a complete sentence; create activities that cause the student to ob-		serve, notice, describe, and ask questions. Create opportunities daily for the child to relate, discuss, and present ideas in complete sentences and good order preparing to write sentences by mid-year, NPEG, 14–15.	Allow the student to retell, imagine, make lists of related ideas, and collect ideas about a subject. Practice making sentences and paragraphs orally together and then independently.	

80   The Noah Plan Lessons Kindergarten © 2003 • Foundation for American Christian Education

Quarter Two—Weekly Routines for Reading and English (continued)

COMPONENT	Monday	Tuesday	Wednesday	Thursday	Friday
SYNTAX	**Encourage** the use of complete sentences in daily speaking and now in writing.		**Demonstrate** the sentence by giving examples of complete thoughts in well-phrased sentences from the literature and Bible.		**Introduce** simple initial capitalization and end punctuation.
ETYMOLOGY	**Teach** the precise meaning of words. Show the dictionary and read the definition aloud to impart precise meaning. **Build** into the student an understanding of syllables		and the ability to identify the syllables of any word, NPRG, 111. **Enjoy** words that rhyme, describe, and many new words from Bible, literature, science, history, and geography.		**Use** daily *Phonemic Awareness in Young Children*, 137–141.
READING Phonetic instruction	**Practice** phonograms using multi-sensory instruction—the Spalding Method, *The Writing Road to Reading*, 6, 39–42.		This practice can be done during the orthography segment.		
Oral Reading	**Provide** opportunities for student-adult reading, helping word recognition and providing feedback. **Read** aloud spelling words from the board and also from the *cahier* (spelling notebook). **Read** *McCall-Harby* (1965) passages aloud and teach the names for the elements: character, setting, and event, so that student is able to identify these elements in other stories read aloud. **Assign** oral reading homework in supplementary readers (home readers) to be returned daily, NPRG, 71. See suggested list of books in NPLK.		**Read** passages aloud to focus on comprehension rather than on decoding. See *McCall-Harby Test Lessons in Primary Reading* (in the Spalding Starter Kit for K–2). **Assign** supplemental reader for home practice, NPRG, 71. **Check** progress as student reads aloud to teacher.		**Read** aloud selected passages from the kindergarten literature curriculum, NPLG, 8–9.
Bible as Reader	**Read** passages from *The Early Reader's Bible* to correspond to Bible lessons in *Noah Plan Lessons Kindergarten* (NPLK). For oral reading methods, see NPRG, 66, 97. At the beginning of the year teacher reads aloud until child is able to read with assistance or independently, NPRG, 66–67, 96–97.		**Continue** passages from *The Early Reader's Bible*.		
Comprehension	**Continue** to teach comprehension using • Identification of passage structure • Application of five mental actions, *Writing Road to Reading*, 121–147. **Use** the *McCall-Harby Test Lessons in Primary Reading* (1965) to teach passage structure and the con-		scious use of the mental actions. Use of the booklet passages develops comprehension skills because the lessons are short, interesting to children, and provide for explicit teaching and testing comprehension. **Learning** the elements of the three basic types of text		structure enables students to channel their concentration appropriately. Comprehension is enhanced when a student is taught to apply the five mental actions. **Consult** the "Reading Skills Chart" to guide quarterly planning and to set goals, NPRG, 19.

The Noah Plan Lessons Kindergarten © 2003 • Foundation for American Christian Education

Quarter Two
Kindergarten Reading Instruction Supplement

VOCABULARY INSTRUCTION

> PRINCIPLE AND LEADING IDEAS
> *The Principle of Christian Self-Government:*
> - *There is order in language, in sentences, and in words.*
> - *Rules of propriety govern the way language works.*
> - *My command of English helps me be self-governed in all areas of my life.*
>
> **Conscience Is the Most Sacred of All Property:**
> - *God gave me a property in my ability to speak, read, and write.*
> - *Exercising my gifts makes me a good steward, accountable to God.*
> - *I use my gift of language to serve God's glory and to keep a good conscience.*

Fact: What does research tell us about vocabulary instruction? Research reveals that (1) most vocabulary is learned indirectly, and (2) some vocabulary must be taught directly.

What are the ways of teaching and learning vocabulary? "Children learn the meanings of most words indirectly, through **everyday experiences with oral and written language.**" *(Put Reading First,* 35) The quality and quantity of their conversations with others and adults will have an impact on the word meanings they learn. Secondly, when **reading aloud to children** make clear the meanings of unfamiliar words and at the end of the passage engage the child in conversation about the passage. Help make connections to previous learning and experience. The third way children learn indirectly is by **reading extensively on their own**. "The more children read on their own, the more words they encounter and the more word meanings they learn." *(Put Reading First,* 35) God's word instructs parents to "teach them (God's word) to your children, talking about them when you sit at home and when you walk along the road, when you lie down and when you get up." Deuteronomy 11:19

Indirect or informal instruction should be balanced with direct instruction, especially to learn difficult words and concepts not part of a young child's everyday conversation and experience. "Direct instruction of vocabulary relevant to a given text leads to a better reading comprehension." *(Put Reading First,* 36) Recently when I was teaching the story of Gideon to second graders, it was necessary to **check their understanding** of the setting— Gideon was threshing wheat in a winepress. Not your typical work in a winepress! Direct instruction should also include teaching students word-learning strategies. We used the **dictionary** to check the meaning of threshing. We looked at the word winepress to figure out the meaning by looking at the **word parts**—and then we used the **context** to determine why Gideon would be in a winepress threshing wheat rather than in a field—he needed protection from the marauding Midianites.

Why is vocabulary important? Teaching beginning readers through their oral vocabulary helps them make sense of the words they see in print. As Christians we desire our children to make sense of the Bible and its truths. We extend the oral vocabulary and reading vocabulary through indirect

The Noah Plan Lessons Kindergarten © 2003 • Foundation for American Christian Education

and direct instruction. The reader must know what most of the words mean before he can understand what he is reading. Clarifying and enriching the meaning of known words enables a higher level of thinking and comprehending.

When should instruction begin? Instruction begins by reading aloud to children early and often. The single most important activity for building the knowledge required for eventual success in reading is reading aloud to children. This is especially so during the preschool years. (*Becoming a Nation of Readers*) Once the child is able to read himself, switch to having the child read for 15 minutes, followed by the parent or adult reading to the child for 15 minutes. Regular practice of easy readers develops the child's decoding ability. It is important for the parent or teacher to continue reading from books above the child's reading level in order to expand his background knowledge and enjoyment of literature. (*Straight Talk about Reading*)

Which methods of instruction are most effective? Vocabulary can be developed (1) **indirectly**, when the student engages in daily oral language, listens to adults read to him, and reads extensively on his own; and (2) **directly**, when a student is explicitly taught both individual words and word learning strategies. (*Put Reading First*)

What materials are suggested?

Slater, Rosalie June. *A Family Program for Reading Aloud,* 2nd Edition. F.A.C.E.
Andersen, Richard C., and et al. (1984). *Becoming a Nation of Readers: The Report of the Commission on Reading,* Champaign, IL: Center for the Study of Reading.
Bible on student's reading level.
Hall, Susan L. and Moats, Louisa C. (1999). *Straight Talk about Reading,* Chicago, IL: Contemporary books
Literature classics from private or public libraries.
Put Reading First: The Research Building Blocks for Teaching Children to Read, September 2001.
Copies available from National Institute for Literacy at ED Pubs, PO Box 1398, Jessup, MD 20794-1398. Phone 1-800-228-8813; Fax 301-430-1244. To download go to the National Institute for Literacy website at www.nifl.gov.
The Writing Road to Reading: The Spalding Method for Teaching Speech, Spelling, Writing, and Reading, 5th Edition (2003).

TEACHING PLAN

Quarter Two

Week One

Preparation	Lesson	Student Work	Accomplishments
BIBLE			

Biblical Principle
God is Creator of all things.
 	
Leading Idea
God created man and good things for him.
 	
Books
• Bible (KJ)
• Webster's 1828 *Dictionary*
 	
Supplies
• Unlined notebook page to include:
  • the title "Creation" for the student to write or trace
  • a space for the student to draw and color the pictures of the Creation story
 	
BAR—Bible As Reader
Books
• *Early Reader's Bible*, 3–9
• NPRG
	Introduce the memory verse. ". . . for thou hast created all things, and for thy pleasure they are and were created." Revelation 4:11
	• **Read** aloud and discuss the memory verse.
	
	• **Define** unfamiliar vocabulary.
	• **Practice** daily the memory verse with the student for his recitation on Friday.
	Guide the student to Biblical Principle from the Leading Idea.
	• **Read** the Creation story. Genesis 1:1–31
	
	• **Identify** the distinct categories created by God and man as one of these categories.
	
	• **Discuss** how man was made in the image of God. (This made him distinct from all of the animals and plants. Genesis 1:26; 2:25)
	• **Discuss** how God made all things for man to enjoy.
	
	Notebook Work
	Distribute the prepared unlined paper for the student to write or trace the title and to draw and color the Creation story.
	
	BAR—Bible As Reader
	"God Made Many Things" (See Weekly Routines for Reading and English.)
		Listen as the teacher reads aloud and discusses the memory verse.
		• **Discuss** unfamiliar vocabulary.
		• **Practice** and learn the memory verse for recitation on Friday.
		
		Listen as the teacher reads aloud the Creation story.
		• **Identify** the distinct categories created by God and man as one of these categories.
		• **Discuss** how man was made in the image of God.
		
		• **Discuss** how God made all things for man to enjoy.
		
		Notebook Work
		Write or trace the title and draw and color the pictures of the Creation story.
		
		BAR—Bible As Reader (See Weekly Routines for Reading and English.)
			• To learn and recite the memory verse
			• To learn new vocabulary
			• To thank God for His Creation
			• To understand man is distinct from all other Creations
			• To complete and file notebook work

The Noah Plan Lessons Kindergarten © 2003 • Foundation for American Christian Education

Quarter Two

TEACHING PLAN

Week One

Preparation	Lesson	Student Work	Accomplishments	✓

Biblical Principle
Language is a gift from God.
 	
Leading Idea
Mother Goose is a part of our English heritage that helps develop memory, imagination, and speech.
 	
Books
• Bible (KJ)
• Webster's 1828 *Dictionary*
• NPLG, 8–9, 92–99
• Nursery rhyme books
 	
Supplies
• Notebook pages for each nursery rhyme to include:
  · the title for the student to write or trace
  · the words to the nursery rhyme
  · a picture or space for the student to illustrate and color
• Colored pencils
	Present the history of Mother Goose and the nursery rhymes.
	• **Discuss** their place in the heritage of oral language.
	• **Use** the nursery rhymes to enlarge the student's vocabulary, to encourage the cultivation of imagination, and to teach literary elements.
	Review the definition of rhythm.
	• **Lead** the student to identify examples of this literary element in selected nursery rhymes ("A Dillar, a Dollar," "Baa, Baa, Black Sheep," "The Lion and the Unicorn," etc.).
	• **Lead** the student to clap the rhythm as he recites these rhymes aloud.
	Define humor.
	• **Instruct** the student to identify examples of this literary element in selected nursery rhymes ("Solomon Grundy," "Barber, Barber," "Hey Diddle, Diddle," etc.).
	• **Lead** the student to recite these rhymes.
	• **Sequence** the action of "Hey Diddle, Diddle."
	
	Reason and conclude with the student that language is a gift from God.
	
	Notebook Work
	Distribute the prepared notebook pages for the student to write or trace the titles and color the pictures.
		Listen as the teacher presents the history of Mother Goose and the nursery rhymes and their place in the heritage of oral language.
		
		Review the definition of rhythm.
		• **Identify** examples of this literary element as the teacher reads aloud selected nursery rhymes.
		
		• **Clap** the rhythm of selected nursery rhymes as the teacher leads oral recitations.
		• **Identify** things that are funny or *non*-sense as the teacher reads aloud selected nursery rhymes containing the literary element of humor.
		• **Recite** selected nursery rhymes.
		Sequence the action of "Hey Diddle, Diddle."
		
		Reason that language is a gift from God.
		
		Notebook Work
		Write or trace the titles on the notebook pages and color the pictures.
			• To recite nursery rhymes
			• To identify literary elements
			• To develop imaginative thinking and literacy
			• To develop a love for your English heritage
			• To create a love for God and His handiwork
			• To develop a trained and organized mind
			• To increase acquaintance with nursery rhymes
			• To develop the individual's ability to measure by God's Word what is true and what is untrue and therefore *non*-sense
			• To complete and file the notebook work	

LITERATURE

The Noah Plan Lessons Kindergarten © 2003 • Foundation for American Christian Education   85

Week One

TEACHING PLAN

Quarter Two

HISTORY

Preparation	Lesson	Student Work	Accomplishments	✓
Biblical Principle God launches events through individuals for His purposes.	**Review** the Creation Link on the Chain of Christianity. **Introduce** Moses.	**Review** by locating the Creation Link on the Chain of Christianity.	• To locate Egypt on the map	
Leading Idea God providentially preserved and prepared Moses to be Israel's deliverer from slavery, the first lawgiver, and the first historian.	• **Locate** Moses and the Law Link on the classroom Christian history timeline.	**Locate** Moses and the Law Link on the classroom Christian history timeline.	• To learn about God's purpose for Moses • To learn new vocabulary • To relate personal examples of God's providence and protection • To complete and file notebook work	
	• **Locate** Egypt on the classroom world map.	**Locate** Egypt on the classroom world map.		
	• **Tell** a simplified version of the Moses story.	**Listen** as the teacher tells the story of Moses.		
	• **Review** protection and discuss God's protection of Moses during infancy. Exodus 2:1–25	**Define** protection and providence in your own words.		
	• **Review** providence and discuss how God provided and prepared Moses for leadership. Exodus 3:1–4:31	**Participate** in a classroom discussion about the individuality of Moses and give specific examples of God's protection, preparation, and providence in Moses' life based on the information that has been presented in class.		
Books • Bible (KJ) • Webster's 1828 Dictionary • NPH&GG, 8–9, 51–53, 73–82, Appendix 339 for additional books on Moses and the Law • NPSDS, Providential History, Links & Timeline • T&L, 158	• **Identify** Moses as the deliverer of Israel from slavery, lawgiver, and historian.	**Identify** Moses as the deliverer of Israel from slavery, the first lawgiver, and the first historian.		
	• **Share** ways God has shown providence or protection in your life.	**Listen** as the teacher shares personal examples of God's providence and protection in his life.		
	• **Ask** the student to share ways God has shown providence or protection in his life.	**Relate** personal examples of how God has shown His providence or protection in your life.		
Supplies • Christian history timeline for classroom display (The Noah Plan Wall Timeline, F.A.C.E.) • Classroom world map • Prepared notebook page	*Notebook Work* **Instruct** the student to find the Christian history timeline that was filed behind the title page and to color the picture that represents Moses—the Law. **Distribute** the prepared notebook page for the student to write or trace the title and to color the picture of Moses. Prepared notebook page to include: • the title "Moses—Lawgiver and Historian" for the student to write or trace • a picture of Moses for the student to color	*Notebook Work* **Locate** and color the picture of Moses on your Christian history timeline. **Write** or trace the title on the notebook page and color the picture of Moses.		

86   The Noah Plan Lessons Kindergarten © 2003 • Foundation for American Christian Education

Quarter Two

TEACHING PLAN

Week One

Preparation	Lesson	Student Work	Accomplishments	✓
Biblical Principle Each continent was created uniquely to fit God's plan. Psalm 115:16	**Discuss** the idea that God's Principle of Individuality can be seen in the unique characteristics and function of each continent. **Guide** the student to the Biblical Principle from the Leading Idea.	**Listen** as the teacher presents the idea that God's Principle of Individuality can be seen in the unique characteristics and functions of each continent.	• To reason and relate knowledge of Asia to God's Principle of Individuality • To locate Asia on a world map, globe, and atlas • To complete and file notebook work	
Leading Idea The nature and character of God are revealed in the continent of Asia.	• **Introduce** the continent of Asia as the "continent of origins or beginnings." • **Discuss** the great diversity of its physical features (topography). • **Discuss** the great contrast in climate. • **Identify** its location in relation to the other continents on the classroom world map, globe, and in the student's atlas. • **Identify** and discuss how Asia reveals God's nature and character.	**Listen** as the teacher introduces the continent of Asia (the continent of origins or beginnings). • **Discuss** the great diversity of its physical features. • **Discuss** its great contrast in climate. • **Identify** its location in relation to the other continents on the classroom world map, globe, and in your atlas. **Identify** and discuss how Asia reveals God's nature and character.		
Books • Bible (KJ) • Webster's 1828 *Dictionary* • NPH&GG, 128, 141, 188–193 • T&L, 141–153, 156–157 • CHOC I, 3–5				
Supplies • World map and globe • EMBG, Volume 3:5 • Books and magazines containing pictures of Asia for viewing • Student atlas • Colored pencils	*Notebook Work* **Distribute** EMBG, Volume 3:5 and instruct the student in completing the page.	*Notebook Work* **Color** and complete the notebook page.		

GEOGRAPHY

The Noah Plan Lessons Kindergarten © 2003 • Foundation for American Christian Education

Week One TEACHING PLAN Quarter Two

	Preparation	Lesson	Student Work	Accomplishments	✓
SCIENCE	**Biblical Principle** • God's Principle of Individuality • Unity with Diversity **Leading Idea** The distinguishing characteristics of the ocean reveal God's individuality and diversity. **Books** • Bible (KJ) • Webster's 1828 *Dictionary* • Science books (Library) **Supplies** • Pictures of sea animals, sea plants, landforms of the ocean *Optional* • Microscope **SCIENCE—** *Notebook pages* (continued on page 89)	**Continue** to teach science according to the days of Creation. **Guide** the student to the Biblical Principle from the Leading Idea by introducing the student to oceanography. • **Define** oceanography as the study the ocean. • **Lay** the Biblical foundation for oceanography by reading aloud Genesis 1:7,10 and by discussing that God divided the waters on the second day of Creation. **Introduce** the individuality of the ocean: • **Sea animals:** · **Present** visual examples of sea animals (starfish, crabs, whales, dolphins, sponges, jellyfish, etc.) · **Discuss** distinguishing characteristics of the sea animals. · **Explain** how God's Principles of Individuality and Unity with Diversity can be seen in the animals of the ocean. • **Sea plants:** · **Present** visual examples of sea plants (algae, seaweed, etc.) · **Discuss** distinguishing characteristics of the sea plants. · **Explain** how God's Principles of Individuality and Unity with Diversity can be seen in the sea plants. **SCIENCE—** *Lesson & Notebook Work* (continued on page 89)	**Listen** as the teacher defines oceanography. **Listen** as the teacher reads aloud the scriptures that lay the Biblical foundation for oceanography and discusses that God divided the waters on the third day of Creation. **Listen** as your teacher introduces and presents visual examples of sea animals. **Name** some of the distinguishing characteristics of sea animals. **Relate** these characteristics to God's Principles of Individuality and Unity with Diversity as seen in the animals of the ocean. **Listen** as your teacher introduces and presents visual examples of sea plants. **Name** some of the distinguishing characteristics of sea plants. **Relate** these characteristics to God's Principles of Individuality and Unity with Diversity as seen in the plants of the ocean. **SCIENCE—** *Student & Notebook Work* (continued on page 89)	• To learn the Biblical foundation of oceanography • To identify various sea animals, sea plants, and land forms • To apply the Biblical Principles to oceanography • To complete and file notebook work	

88 The Noah Plan Lessons Kindergarten © 2003 • Foundation for American Christian Education

Week One   **TEACHING PLAN**   Quarter Two

Preparation	Lesson	Student Work	Accomplishments	✓
•Notebook page to include: • the title "Sea Animals" for the student to write or trace • a space for the student to draw pictures of sea animals • Notebook page to include: • the title "Sea Plants" for the student to write or trace • a space for the student to draw sea plants • Notebook page to include: • the title "Land-forms of the Ocean" for the student to write or trace • a space for the student to draw the landforms	• **Land** beneath the ocean: • **Present** visual examples of landforms beneath the ocean (hills, mountains, trenches, valleys, etc.) • **Discuss** distinguishing characteristics. • **Explain** how God's Principles of Individuality and Unity with Diversity can be seen in the distinguishing characteristics of the landforms. *Notebook Work* **Distribute** the notebook pages for the student to write or trace the titles and to draw sea animals, sea plants, and landforms.	**Listen** as your teacher introduces and presents visual examples of landforms underneath the ocean. **Name** some distinguishing characteristics of each landform. **Relate** these characteristics to God's Principles of Individuality and Unity with Diversity as seen in the landforms of the ocean. *Notebook Work* **Write** or trace the titles on the notebook pages and draw the sea animals, sea plants, and landforms.		

SCIENCE (continued)

The Noah Plan Lessons Kindergarten © 2003 • Foundation for American Christian Education   89

Week Two

Quarter Two

TEACHING PLAN

Preparation	Lesson	Student Work	Accomplishments	✓
Biblical Principle Disobedience is sin and separates us from God. **Leading Idea** Adam and Eve were sinful when they chose to disobey God. **Books** • Bible (KJ) • Webster's 1828 *Dictionary* **Supplies** • Notebook page to include: • the title "Adam and Eve" for the student to write or trace • a space for the student to draw and color a picture of Adam and Eve **BAR** • *Early Reader's Bible*, 11–17 • NPRG	**Introduce** the memory verse. Romans 5:19 • **Read** aloud and discuss the memory verse. • **Define** unfamiliar vocabulary. • **Practice** daily the memory verse with the student for his recitation on Friday. **Guide** the student to the Biblical Principle from the Leading Idea. • **Define** sin as disobeying God's law. • **Tell** the story of the fall of man and the first sin. • Why did Adam and Eve have to leave the Garden of Eden? • What are some of the consequences that happened because of their sin? • **Discuss** how God feels about sin. • **Discuss** the effect of sinful choices on people's lives. **Discuss** how God promised a Savior to bring people back to Him and to give them eternal life. *Notebook Work* **Distribute** the prepared notebook page for the student to write or trace the title and to draw and color the picture of Adam and Eve. **BAR** "Something Bad, Something Sad" (See Weekly Routines for Reading and English.)	**Listen** as the teacher reads aloud and discusses the memory verse. • **Discuss** unfamiliar vocabulary. • **Practice** and learn the memory verse for recitation on Friday. **Listen** as the teacher defines sin. **Listen** as the teacher tells the story of the fall of man and the first sin. **Answer** reason questions about the fall of man and the first sin. • Why did Adam and Eve have to leave the Garden of Eden? • What are some of the consequences that happened because of their sin? • **Discuss** how God feels about sin. • **Discuss** the effect of sinful choices on people's lives. **Discuss** why God promised a Savior. *Notebook Work* **Write** or trace the title on the notebook page and draw and color the picture of Adam and Eve. **BAR** (See Weekly Routines for Reading and English.)	• To learn and recite the memory verse • To learn new vocabulary • To understand disobedience is sin • To understand sin separates us from God • To understand Jesus came to Earth to bring eternal life • To complete and file notebook page	

BIBLE

90 The Noah Plan Lessons Kindergarten © 2003 • Foundation for American Christian Education

Week Two

Quarter Two

TEACHING PLAN

	Preparation	Lesson	Student Work	Accomplishments	✓
LITERATURE	**Biblical Principle** Language is a gift from God. **Leading Idea** Mother Goose is a part of our English heritage that helps develop memory, imagination, and speech. **Books** • Bible (KJ) • Webster's 1828 *Dictionary* • NPLG, 8–9, 92–99 • Nursery rhyme books **Supplies** • Notebook pages for each nursery rhyme to include: • the title for the student to write or trace • the words to the nursery rhyme • a picture or space for the student to illustrate and color • Colored pencils	**Review** the Biblical Principle and Leading Idea. **Review** the history of Mother Goose. **Recite** and review with the student previously introduced nursery rhymes by clapping the rhythm or identifying humorous elements. **Define** alliteration. • **Instruct** the student to identify examples of this literary element as you read aloud selected nursery rhymes ("Peter Piper," "Sing a Song of Sixpence," etc.). **Define** action and drama. • **Read** aloud "Little Miss Muffet." • **Provide** props for the student to act it out emphasizing the conflict and the emotion. **Define** rhyme. • **Instruct** the student to identify rhyming words as you read aloud selected nursery rhymes ("Humpty, Dumpty," "Jack and Jill," etc.). *Notebook Work* **Distribute** the prepared notebook pages for the student to write or trace the titles and color the pictures. *Additional suggestions* **Sequence** reproducible pictures of the action in "Little Miss Muffet" for the student to color **Build** the wall for Humpty Dumpty. **Cut** out and glue a picture of Humpty Dumpty on the wall.	**Participate** in a discussion of the Biblical Principle and Leading Idea. **Recall** interesting facts related to the history of Mother Goose. **Review** the literary elements and the nursery rhymes presented in the last lesson by clapping the rhythm or by identifying humorous elements as you recite them. **Listen** to the definition of alliteration. **Identify** the sound that is repeated as the teacher reads aloud the nursery rhymes illustrating this literary element. **Listen** to the definition of action and drama. **Participate** in a re-enactment of the action of the nursery rhymes illustrating this literary element. **Listen** to the definition of rhyme. **Identify** the rhyming words as the teacher reads aloud the nursery rhymes illustrating this literary element. *Notebook Work* **Write** or trace the titles on the notebook pages and color the pictures.	• To review the history of Mother Goose • To review the literary elements of previously introduced nursery rhymes • To identify literary elements • To complete and file notebook work	

The Noah Plan Lessons Kindergarten © 2003 • Foundation for American Christian Education

91

Week Two · Quarter Two

TEACHING PLAN

Preparation	Lesson	Student Work	Accomplishments

Biblical Principle
"But before faith came, we were under the law…the law was our schoolmaster to bring us unto Christ.…"
Galatians 3:23–24
 	
Leading Idea
The Ten Commandments points us to Christ.
 	
Books
• Bible (KJ)
• Webster's 1828 *Dictionary*
• NPH&GG, 8–9, 78
• T&L, 158
 	
Supplies
• Notebook page to include:
  · the title "The Ten Commandments" for the student to write or trace
  · a simplified picture of the Ten Commandments on tablets of stone for the student to color
• Colored pencils
	Introduce The Ten Commandments.
	• **Define** and discuss the term commandment.
	• **Read** aloud Galatians 3:23–24 and discuss the purpose of the Ten Commandments. (They showed us how much we need Jesus in our lives.)
	
	Read aloud the Ten Commandments and discuss the influence they have on the individual by asking:
	• What do they show us about God's character and His goodness?
	• What effect do they have on the individual? (There are consequences for those who disobey God's law.)
	Identify the first five books of the Bible that were written by Moses—Pentateuch.
	
	Notebook Work
	Distribute the prepared notebook page for the student to write or trace the title and to color the picture.
		Define and discuss the term commandment.
		Listen as the teacher reads aloud Galatians 3:23–24 and discusses the purpose of the Ten Commandments.
		Listen as the teacher reads aloud the commandments and participate in the discussion of their influence on the individual.
		
		Recognize and recite the names of the first five books of the Bible that were written by Moses.
		
		Notebook Work
		Write or trace the title on the notebook page and color the picture.
			• To know the purpose of the Ten Commandments
			• To recite the names of the first five books of the Bible
			• To recognize a need for Christ
			• To complete and file notebook work

HISTORY

Week Two

Quarter Two

TEACHING PLAN

	Preparation	Lesson	Student Work	Accomplishments	✓
GEOGRAPHY	**Biblical Principle** God created each continent distinct to fit His purpose and His plan. Psalm 115:16 **Leading Idea** The nature and character of God are revealed in the continent of Asia. **Books** • Bible (KJ) • NPH&GG, 28, 141, 188–193 • T&L, 141–153, 156–157 • CHOC I, 3 **Supplies** • World map and globe • Student atlas • Books and magazines containing pictures of Asia for viewing • Sources of Asian music, language or culture • Items of interest related to Asia • Old magazines (*National Geographic, Ranger Rick,* etc.) for cutting	**Review** Asia's place on the Chain of Christianity. • **Ask** the student to locate Asia on a world map, globe, and in his atlas. • **Answer** questions about Asia's unique physical characteristics. • **Recall** why Asia is considered the "continent of origins or beginnings." **Continue** to guide the student to the Biblical Principle from the Leading Idea by introducing interesting facts about Asia that demonstrate the individuality of its culture, its plants, and its animals. **Display** pictures or artifacts related to Asian culture, plants, and animals. **Prepare** and serve native foods, learn about interesting customs, listen to native music, or learn words of a native language. *Notebook Work* **Instruct** the student to find and cut pictures from magazines pertaining to Asia to be used in next week's lesson. **Instruct** the student to save these pictures in an envelope and put it into the pocket of his geography notebook.	**Review** with the teacher by: • **Locating** Asia on the classroom world map, globe, and in your atlas • **Answering** questions about Asia's unique physical characteristics • **Recalling** why Asia is called the "continent of origins or beginnings" **Listen** as the teacher presents interesting facts about the culture, plants, and animals of Asia. **View** (or bring and share) interesting items related to the culture, plants, or animals of Asia. **Sample** native foods, listen to native music, learn about interesting customs, or learn words of a native language. *Notebook Work* **Cut** pictures related to the topography, people, plant and animal life of Asia. • **Put** the pictures into an envelope. • **Place** the envelope into the pocket of your geography notebook.	• To locate Asia on a world map, globe, and atlas • To learn about the individuality of Asia • To continue to learn more about the character and nature of God in His Creations • To learn new words or songs • To sample native foods • To complete and file notebook work	

The Noah Plan Lessons Kindergarten © 2003 • Foundation for American Christian Education

93

Week Two

TEACHING PLAN

Quarter Two

Preparation	Lesson	Student Work	Accomplishments	✓
Biblical Principles • God's Principle of Individuality • Unity with Diversity **Leading Idea** The oceans reveal God's love of individuality and diversity. **Books** • Bible (KJ) • Webster's 1828 *Dictionary* • Science books (Library) **Supplies** • Glass bowl • Salt • Water	**Review** the Biblical Principles and Leading Idea. **Review** the individuality of the sea animals, sea plants, and the landforms beneath the ocean by asking leading questions. **Continue** studying the individuality of the ocean: • **Chemistry** of the ocean: sodium and chlorine · **Discuss** distinguishing characteristics of these two elements. · **Explain** how these two elements when combined form salt. · **Explain** how rainwater washes salt and other minerals into the ocean and makes the ocean salty. · **Conduct** an experiment that shows the student the salt in ocean water. · **Dissolve** a small amount of salt in a bowl of water. · **Place** the uncovered glass bowl in the sun. · **Note** the water evaporating. · **Discuss** how this demonstrates how salt and other minerals are in the ocean water. · **Discuss** how fresh water has some minerals in it. • **Explain** how God's Principles of Individuality and Unity with Diversity can be seen in the chemistry of the ocean through the distinguishing characteristics of the elements. • **Movement** of the ocean: tides, waves, and currents · **Define** the terms. · **Present** visual examples of each. · **Discuss** distinguishing characteristics. · **Ask** the student to relate these terms to experiences he may have had. · **Explain** God's Principle of Individuality and Unity with Diversity can be seen in the distinguishing characteristics of the movements of the ocean.	**Participate** in a review of the Biblical Principles and Leading Idea. **Participate** in a review of the individuality of sea animals, sea plants, and landforms. **Listen** as the teacher continues the study of the individuality of the ocean by introducing the chemistry of the ocean. **Participate** in a discussion that identifies the distinguishing characteristics of sodium and chlorine. **Listen** as the teacher explains how sodium and chlorine when combined form salt. **Listen** as the teacher explains how salt and chlorine make the water salty. **Participate** and follow the teacher's directions as she conducts the experiment. **Participate** in a discussion on how the chemistry of the ocean demonstrates God's Principles of Individuality and Unity with Diversity. **Listen** as the teacher introduces the movement of the ocean and defines tides, waves, and currents. **Observe** and discuss the distinguishing characteristics of—tides, waves, and currents. **Relate** your experience with tides, waves, and currents. **Participate** in a discussion relating the Biblical Principles to the observations of the movements of the ocean.	• To review the Biblical Principles and Leading Idea • To review the individuality of the sea animals, sea plants, and landforms of the ocean • To learn the chemistry of the ocean • To learn how the ocean became salty • To observe and tell what happens during an experiment	

SCIENCE

Quarter Two

TEACHING PLAN

Week Three

Preparation	Lesson	Student Work	Accomplishments
Bible Principle Obedience brings blessings. **Leading Idea** Noah obeyed God and He wants us to obey Him. **Books** • Bible (KJ) • Webster's 1828 Dictionary • *The Family and the Nation: Biblical Childhood*, Rosalie J. Slater, F.A.C.E. **Supplies** • Notebook page to include: 　• the title "Noah and the Flood" for the student to write or trace 　• a space for the student to draw and color a picture of Noah and the Ark **BAR** • *Early Reader's Bible*, 18–25 • NPRG	**Introduce** the memory verse. "Blessed are they that do his commandments. . . ." Revelation 22:14 • **Read** aloud and discuss the memory verse. • **Define** unfamiliar vocabulary. • **Practice** daily the memory verse with the student for his recitation on Friday. **Guide** the student to the Biblical Principle from the Leading Idea. • **Tell** the story of Noah and the flood. • **Discuss** why God was angry with the people. 　• They were wicked and sinful. • **Discuss** why God chose Noah to build the ark. 　• He and his family were kind and loving. • **Discuss** the covenant (promise) made to Noah after the flood. 　• God would never destroy the whole Earth again with a flood. • **Read** aloud Genesis 6:22 and discuss the things Noah did in obedience to God's command. • **Discuss** choosing to obey God results in enjoying His blessings. **Remind** the student that God promised a Savior to bring people back to Him and to give them eternal life and how Noah was part of this plan. *Notebook Work* **Distribute** the prepared notebook page for the student to write or trace and to draw and color the picture of Noah and the Ark. **BAR** "Noah Makes a Big Boat" (See Weekly Routines for Reading and English.) (See sample lesson, NPLK, 282–286.)	**Listen** as the teacher reads aloud and discusses the memory verse. • **Discuss** unfamiliar vocabulary. • **Practice** and learn the memory verse for recitation on Friday. **Listen** as the teacher tells you the story of Noah and the Flood. • **Answer** reason questions about the story. 　• Why was God angry with the people? 　• Why did God choose Noah to build the ark? 　• What was God's promise to Noah after the flood? • **Listen** as the teacher reads aloud Genesis 6:22 and participate in a discussion that Noah did everything that God commanded. • **Discuss** choosing to obey God results in enjoying His blessings. **Discuss** God's promise of a Savior to bring people back to Him and to give them eternal life and how Noah was part of this plan. *Notebook Work* **Write** or trace the title on the notebook page and draw and color the picture. **BAR** (See Weekly Routines for Reading and English.)	• To learn and recite the memory verse • To learn new vocabulary • To follow and obey God's commandments • To obey your parents and those in authority over you • To understand there are consequences to disobedience • To have hope in Jesus as our promised Savior • To complete and file notebook work

The Noah Plan Lessons Kindergarten © 2003 • Foundation for American Christian Education

Week Three

TEACHING PLAN

Quarter Two

LITERATURE

Preparation	Lesson	Student Work	Accomplishments	✓

Biblical Principles
• God's Principle of Individuality
• Unity with Diversity
 	
Leading Idea
Teaching literature is teaching character and teaching life.
(Slater, NPLG, 135)
 	
Books
• Bible (KJ)
• *Winnie-the-Pooh*, A. A. Milne
• Biographical information about A. A. Milne (Library) NPLG, 100–103, 135–138
 	
Supplies
• Prepared notebook pages
• Classroom world map and globe
• Student atlas
• Colored pencils
	Discuss the Biblical Principles and the Leading Idea.
	
	Introduce *Winnie-the-Pooh* by A. A. Milne.
	Present a brief biography of the author and his place on the Christian history timeline.
	
	Locate England on the classroom world map, globe, and in the student's atlas.
	Introduce and summarize the elements of a classic.
	Encourage the student to appreciate Milne's unique literary style and to listen for the setting and characters as you begin to read aloud the story (a section during each daily lesson).
	
	Notebook Work
	Distribute the prepared notebook page for the student to write or trace the character's name and to color the picture.
	• Notebook page to include:
	  • the title "Winnie-the-Pooh" and author of the book for the student to write or trace
	  • a picture from the book for the student to color
	• Notebook pages for each character to include:
	  • the character's name for the student to write or trace
	  • a picture or space for the student to illustrate and to color
		Participate in a discussion of the Biblical Principles and Leading Idea.
		Listen as the teacher introduces *Winnie-the-Pooh*, presents A. A. Milne's unique individuality through a brief biography, and locates his place on the Christian history timeline.
		Locate England on the classroom world map, globe, and student atlas.
		Discuss the elements of a classic and appreciate A. A. Milne's unique style of writing as you listen for descriptions of the setting and characters when the teacher reads aloud a section of the story during each daily lesson.
		
		Notebook Work:
		Write or trace the title on the notebook page and color the picture.
		Write or trace the character's name on the notebook page and color the picture.
		File the character pages behind the title page *Winnie-the-Pooh*.

			• To learn about A. A. Milne and his style of writing
			• To name the setting
			• To identify and describe characters
			• To enjoy the story, *Winnie-the-Pooh*
			• To complete and file notebook work	

Quarter Two

TEACHING PLAN

Week Three

	Preparation	Lesson	Student Work	Accomplishments	✓
HISTORY	**Biblical Principle** God instructed his people to build an altar. Exodus 17:14–16 **Leading Idea** Memorials keep us from forgetting. **Books** • Bible (KJ) • NPH&GG, 8–9, 284–291 • T&L, 178, 271–273 • *Plimoth Plantation Day Packet*, F.A.C.E	**Celebrate** Thanksgiving by recognizing the contribution that the Pilgrims made in the establishment of our country. • **Read** a primary level account of the Pilgrims and the Plimoth Colony. • **Identify** the reason for the Thanksgiving celebration. (God had answered the Pilgrim's prayers that saved them from a famine.) • **Plan** a special celebration, "Plimoth Plantation Day," highlighting the Pilgrim character. (The *"Plimoth Plantation Day Packet,* F.A.C.E. is a valuable resource for celebrating this special day.) **(NOTE:** A more in-depth study of the Pilgrim story will be done during the third quarter.) *Notebook Work* **Select** several activities described in the *Plimoth Plantation Day Packet.*	**Celebrate** Thanksgiving by learning about the contribution made by the Pilgrims in the establishment of our country. **Listen** as the teacher reads aloud an account of the Pilgrim story and identifies the reason for their Thanksgiving celebration. **Participate** in a special celebration highlighting the Pilgrim character. *Notebook Work* **Follow** the instructions given by your teacher.	• To recognize God's providential purpose for the Pilgrims • To celebrate Thanksgiving • To complete and file notebook work	

The Noah Plan Lessons Kindergarten © 2003 • Foundation for American Christian Education

Week Three   **TEACHING PLAN**   Quarter Two

	Preparation	Lesson	Student Work	Accomplishments	✓
GEOGRAPHY	**Biblical Principle** God created each continent distinct to fit His purpose and His plan. Psalm 115:16 **Leading Idea** The nature and character of God are revealed in the continent of Asia. **Books** • Bible (KJ) • NPH&GG, 128, 148–149, 226–227 • T&L, 141–153, 156–157 **Supplies** • Notebook page to include: • the title "Asia's Individuality" for the student to write or trace • a space to glue pictures of Asia • Simple outline map of Asia (Use maps from NPH&GG, 226–227 as a guide.) • Map standard • Colored pencils • Overhead projector if available	**Continue** to guide the student to the Biblical Principle from the Leading Idea by reviewing and discussing the individuality of Asia and by asking the student to recall topographical features, plants, and animals that are native to Asia. *Notebook Work* **Provide** a simple outline map of Asia and model on an overhead projector, chalkboard, etc. the map standard for physical maps. NPH&GG, 148–149 **Distribute** the prepared notebook page for the student to write or trace the title and instruct the student to glue onto it the pictures of Asia saved from last week's lesson. OR **Save** these pictures for a group project in the fourth quarter.	**Review** by naming unique topographical features of Asia and by naming plants and animals that are native to Asia. **Discuss** God's nature and character seen in Asia. *Notebook Work* **Color** the map of Asia according to the map standard for physical maps. **Write** or trace the title on the notebook page and glue the pictures related to Asia from last week's lesson onto it. OR **Save** these pictures for a group project in the fourth quarter. Asia	• To continue to learn more about the character and nature of God in His Creations • To complete and file notebook	

98   The Noah Plan Lessons Kindergarten © 2003 • Foundation for American Christian Education

Quarter Two

TEACHING PLAN

Week Three

SCIENCE

Preparation	Lesson	Student Work	Accomplishments

Biblical Principle
The Principle of Stewardship or Conservation.
Genesis 1:26–28
 	
Leading Idea
Wise use of our natural resources brings glory to God.
 	
Books
• Bible (KJ)
• Webster's 1828 *Dictionary*
• Science books (Library)
 	
Supplies
• Pictures of some of the types of food contained in the ocean
• Notebook page to include:
  • the title "Good Stewardship" for the student to write or trace
  • a space for the student to draw a picture of being a good steward of God's gifts
	Introduce the student to the conservation of natural resources as it pertains to oceanography.
	
	• **Define** the terms:
	  • Stewardship or Conservation—the wise use of natural resources
	  • Natural resources—the material gifts God has given us to use
	• **Discuss** with the student ways to be good stewards of God's material gifts as it pertains to oceanography.
	  • Do not pollute the waters—do not dump plastic bags, aluminum cans, poisonous chemicals, sewage, etc. into rivers, lakes, or the ocean.
	  • Farming the seas—breed fish and shellfish in underwater farms.
	• **Discuss** that the ocean provides people with many different kinds of food.
	• **Present** visual examples of some of the foods from the ocean.
	  • Fishes: sardines, tunas, sharks, herrings
	  • Crustaceans (Shellfish): shrimp, crabs, and lobsters
	  • Mollusks: clams, oysters, squids
	  • Algae: red, brown, and green seaweed
	  • Mammals: body oils, furs, and sometimes used as food (whales, seals, walruses)
	  • Reptiles: sea turtles
	• **Identify** the useful medicines that come from the ocean.
	  • Chemicals from seaweed help destroy viruses which cause cold sores.
	  • Chemicals from sponges are used to treat throat infections.
	  • Glue from barnacles is used by dentists to glue teeth in place.
	
	SCIENCE—
	Lesson & Notebook Work
	(continued on page 100)
		Listen as the teacher introduces the Principle of Stewardship or Conservation by reading aloud and discussing Genesis 1:26–28.
		
		Listen as the teacher defines the terms: stewardship or conservation and natural resources.
		
		Participate in a discussion on ways to be a good steward of God's material gifts as it pertains to oceanography.
		
		Participate in a discussion on how the ocean provides food for people.
		
		View visuals of some of foods found in the ocean.
		
		Listen as the teacher identifies the useful medicines that come from the ocean.
		
		SCIENCE—
		Student & Notebook Work
		(continued on page 100)
			• To learn new vocabulary—stewardship, conservation, natural resources
			• To learn about the natural resources God gave man and how to take care of them
			• To learn the provision of food God gave man from the ocean
			• To relate scripture to the Biblical Principles
			• To complete and file notebook work

The Noah Plan Lessons Kindergarten © 2003 • Foundation for American Christian Education   99

Week Three

Quarter Two

TEACHING PLAN

Preparation	Lesson	Student Work	Accomplishments	✓
	Read aloud Deuteronomy 24:19–22 and ask the student to relate this scripture to the Principle of Stewardship or Conservation. • It brings glory to God because His material gifts are not wasted. • It brings glory to God because we are helping those in need. *Notebook Work* **Distribute** the notebook page for the student to write or trace the title and to draw a picture of him being a good steward of God's gifts.	**Listen** as the teacher reads aloud Deuteronomy 24:19–22 and relate this scripture to the Principle of Stewardship or Conservation. *Notebook Work* **Write** or trace the title on the notebook page and draw a picture of you being a good steward of God's gifts.		

SCIENCE (continued)

100   The Noah Plan Lessons Kindergarten © 2003 • Foundation for American Christian Education

Quarter Two

TEACHING PLAN

Week Four

	Preparation	Lesson	Student Work	Accomplishments	✓

BIBLE	**Biblical Principle**
	God always keeps His promises.
	
	Leading Idea
	God kept His promise to Abraham.
	
	Books
	• Bible (KJ)
	• Webster's 1828 Dictionary
	• *The Family and the Nation: Biblical Childhood*, Rosalie J. Slater, F.A.C.E.
	
	Supplies
	• Notebook page to include:
	  • the title "Abraham" for the student to write or trace
	  • a space for the student to draw and color a picture of Abraham
	
	BAR
	• *Early Reader's Bible*, 34–41
	• NPRG
		Introduce the memory verse: "For all the promises of God in him are yea, and in him Amen. . . ." 2 Corinthians 1:20
		• **Read** aloud and discuss the memory verse.
		
		• **Define** unfamiliar vocabulary.
		• **Practice** daily the memory verse with the student for his recitation on Friday.
		Review the importance of obeying God from the story of Noah.
		Guide the student to the Biblical Principle from the Leading Idea.
		• **Tell** the story of Abraham.
		• **Discuss** the reasons why God choose Abraham to set His plan of redemption (the promised savior) in motion?
		  • His faith pleased God.
		  • He was obedient.
		• **Discuss** how God promised to bless Abraham and make him great.
		• **Discuss** Abraham's response to God's request?
		• **Discuss** how God keeps His promises to us.
		
		Notebook Work:
		Distribute the prepared notebook page for the student to write or trace the title and to draw and color the picture of Abraham.
		
		BAR
		"A Promise for Abraham"
		(See Weekly Routines for Reading and English.)
			Listen as the teacher reads aloud and discusses the memory verse.
			• **Discuss** unfamiliar vocabulary.
			• **Practice** and learn the memory verse for recitation on Friday.
			Review the importance of obeying God from the story of Noah.
			Listen as the teacher tells the story of Abraham, reason orally, and answer questions about the Leading Idea:
			• Why did God choose Abraham to set His plan of redemption (the promised savior) in motion?
			
			• What promise did God make to Abraham?
			• Did Abraham believe God's promise?
			• How does God keep His promises to us?
			
			Notebook Work
			Write or trace the title on the notebook page and draw and color the picture.
			
			BAR
			(See Weekly Routines for Reading and English.)
				• To learn and recite the memory verse
				• To learn new vocabulary
				• To obey God and His commandments
				• To believe God keeps His promises
				• To complete and file notebook work	

The Noah Plan Lessons Kindergarten © 2003 • Foundation for American Christian Education — 101

Week Four   TEACHING PLAN   Quarter Two

Preparation	Lesson	Student Work	Accomplishments	✓
Biblical Principles • God's Principle of Individuality • Unity with Diversity	**Review** the Biblical Principles and the Leading Idea.	**Participate** in a discussion of the Biblical Principles and Leading Idea.	• To review A. A. Milne's individuality as an author	
Leading Idea Teaching literature is teaching character and teaching life. (Slater, NPLG, 135)	**Review** A. A. Milne and the characters that were encountered in prior readings of *Winnie-the-Pooh* by asking the student: • To recall interesting aspects of Milne's individuality • To name internal and external qualities of various characters.	**Participate** in a review of A. A. Milne's individuality as an author. **Name** internal and external qualities of each character that has been previously encountered in the story.	• To identify and describe the characters • To complete and file notebook work	
Books • Bible (KJ) • NPLG, 8–9 • *Winnie-the-Pooh*, A. A. Milne	**Continue** to read aloud *Winnie-the-Pooh* until the story is completed. **Lead** the student to identify each character.	**Enjoy** and appreciate the story and the author's style as the teacher continues to read aloud a section each day. **Identify** new characters as they		
Supplies • Notebook pages for each character to include: • the character's name for the student to write or trace • a picture or space for the student to illustrate and to color • Colored pencils	**Give** descriptions of that character by naming internal and external qualities. *Notebook Work* **Distribute** the prepared character pages for the student to write or trace the names and to color the pictures.	appear in the story and describe the character by naming internal and external qualities. *Notebook Work* **Write** or trace the character's names on the notebook pages and color the pictures.		

LITERATURE

102   The Noah Plan Lessons Kindergarten © 2003 • Foundation for American Christian Education

Week Four | Quarter Two

TEACHING PLAN

HISTORY

Preparation

Biblical Principle
Jesus is our Savior.

Leading Idea
Jesus brings Christian self-government.

Books
- Bible (KJ)
- NPH&GG, 8–9, 78, Appendix 339 for additional books on Jesus, the Focal Point of History.
- NPSDS, Providential History, Links
- T&L, 159
- *America's Providential History*, Mark Beliles and Stephen McDowell, 24–29
- *3 in 1: (A Picture of God)*, Joanne Marxhausen

Supplies
- Christian history timeline for classroom display (The Noah Plan Wall Timeline, F.A.C.E.)
- Notebook page to include:
  · the title "Jesus, the Focal Point of History" for the student to write or trace
  · a picture of Jesus for the student to color
- Colored pencils

Lesson

Review by leading an oral review of the Ten Commandments:
- Their place as the second link on the Christian history timeline
- Their effect on government and the individual

Introduce Jesus Christ as the focal (main) point of history and the third link on the Chain of Christianity. (The birth of Christ and God's purpose for His coming to Earth will be taught in Bible class at Christmas time.)
- **Locate** with the student the third link on the Christian history timeline.
- **Read aloud** the book *3 in 1: (A Picture of God)* and lead a discussion about the character of Christ.
  · He is fully God.
  · He is fully man.

Lead a discussion on the eternal effects Jesus had on history.
- He made a way for Christian self-government.
- Man is able to govern himself according to God's Word.

Introduce the Gospel as God's Word and discuss the acceptance of the Gospel brings internal liberty.

Notebook Work

Instruct the student to find the Christian history timeline that was filed behind the title page in his notebook and to color the picture that represents Jesus the Focal Point of History.

Distribute the prepared notebook page for the student to write or trace the title and to color the picture of Jesus.

Student Work

Review orally by finding the Ten Commandments on the classroom Christian history timeline.
- **Identify** them as the second link.
- **Recall** orally the effect they have had on government and the individual.

Listen as the teacher introduces Jesus Christ as the focal point of history.

Locate the third link on the classroom Christian history timeline.

Listen as the teacher reads aloud the book *3 in 1: (A Picture of God)* and participate in a classroom discussion about the character of Christ.

Listen as the teacher discusses the eternal effects Jesus has had on history.
- **Discuss** how the heart of the individual is changed as a result of the Gospel.
- **Discuss** how God's Law is written on the heart and enables the individual to be internally self-governed.

Listen as the teacher introduces the Gospel as God's Word and discusses acceptance of the Gospel brings internal liberty.

Notebook Work

Locate and color the third link on your Christian history timeline.
Write or trace the title on the notebook page and color the picture of Jesus.

Accomplishments

- To review the Ten Commandments and their effect on government and the individual
- To locate the third link on the Christian history timeline
- To reason orally about the effect of the Gospel on the individual
- To recognize and acknowledge Jesus as the Savior
- To complete and file notebook work

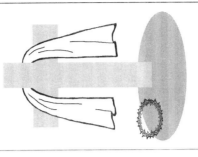

The Noah Plan Lessons Kindergarten © 2003 • Foundation for American Christian Education

Week Four

Quarter Two

TEACHING PLAN

Preparation	Lesson	Student Work	Accomplishments	✓
Biblical Principle God created each continent distinct to fit His purpose and His plan. Psalm 115:16 **Leading Idea** The nature and character of God are revealed in the continent of Europe. **Books** • Bible (KJ) • NPH&GG, 128, 141, 212–218 • T&L, 141–153, 156–157 • CHOC I, 3–4 **Supplies** • World map and globe • Student atlas • Colored pencils • EMBG, Volume 3:6	**Locate** Europe on the classroom world map and globe. **Assist** the student in locating Europe in his atlas. **Guide** the student to the Biblical Principle from the Leading Idea. • **Introduce** Europe as the "continent of development." • **Present** unique physical features that contribute to its function. • **Lead** an oral discussion about why Europe is considered the "continent of development." *Notebook Work* **Distribute** EMBG, Volume 3:6 and instruct the student in completing the page.	**Observe** the teacher as she locates Europe on the classroom world map and globe. **Locate** Europe in your atlas. **Listen** as the teacher introduces the continent of Europe and presents the unique physical features that contribute to its function. **Participate** in a discussion and reason orally about the continent of Europe: • What are some of the unique physical characteristics that helped support development and contributed to the westward movement of the gospel? *Notebook Work* **Color** and complete the notebook page.	• To locate Europe on a world map, globe, and atlas • To learn about the individuality of Europe • To continue to learn more about the character and nature of God in His Creations • To complete and file notebook work	

GEOGRAPHY

104   The Noah Plan Lessons Kindergarten © 2003 • Foundation for American Christian Education

Quarter Two

TEACHING PLAN

Week Four

SCIENCE

	Preparation	Lesson	Student Work	Accomplishments	✓
	Biblical Principle ". . . let the dry land appear: . . . And God called the dry *land* Earth. . . ." Genesis 1:9 **Leading Idea** God created the Earth on the third day. **Books** • Bible (KJ) • Webster's 1828 *Dictionary* • Science books (Library) **Supplies** • Onion, orange, peach, etc. • Knife • A large chart or overhead projector and transparency • Globe • Notebook page to include: • the title "The Layers of the Earth" for the student to write or trace • a picture of a cross-section of the Earth for the student to label	**Continue** to teach science according to the days of Creation. **Introduce** geology. • **Define** geology as the study of the Earth and its parts. • **Lay** the Biblical foundation for geology by reading aloud Genesis 1:1, 9–10 and by discussing God formed the Earth on the third day of Creation to provide a place for man to live. **Display** a globe and discuss these facts about the Earth: • It is a sphere (Isaiah 40:22). • It is surrounded by air (atmosphere). • More than half of the Earth is covered with water. **Introduce** the layers of the Earth by slicing in half different foods that have a sphere shape (onion, orange, peach, etc.) • **Guide** the student in examining the layers of the food. • **Explain** that the Earth has invisible layers that have been made visible by instruments. • **Display** a large picture (or use an overhead and transparency) showing a cross section of the layers of the Earth (crust, mantle, outer core, inner core). **Apply** God's Principles of Individuality and Unity with Diversity to the study of geology. *Notebook Work* **Distribute** the prepared notebook page for the student to write or trace the title and to label the layers of the Earth.	**Listen** as the teacher defines geology. **Listen** as the teacher reads aloud Genesis 1:1, 9–10 and discusses the Biblical foundation of geology. **View** a globe as the teacher discusses distinguishing characteristics about the Earth. **Listen** and observe as the teacher introduces the layers of the Earth. **Examine** the layers of food. **Listen** as the teacher explains the Earth has invisible layers that have been made visible by instruments. **View** the large picture showing a cross section of the layers of the Earth. **Relate** God's Principles of Individuality and Unity with Diversity to the study of geology. *Notebook Work* **Write** or trace the title on the notebook page and label the layers of the Earth.	• To define geology • To learn about the Biblical foundation of the Earth • To learn about the characteristics of the Earth and its parts • To apply Biblical principles to geology • To complete and file notebook work	

The Noah Plan Lessons Kindergarten © 2003 • Foundation for American Christian Education

105

Week Five   **TEACHING PLAN**   **Quarter Two**

BIBLE

Preparation	Lesson	Student Work	Accomplishments

Bible Principle
God directs those who love Him.
 	
Leading idea
God directed Jacob through his dream.
 	
Books
• Bible (KJ)
• Webster's 1828 *Dictionary*
 	
Supplies
• Notebook page to include:
  • the title "Jacob and His Dream" for the student to write or trace
  • a space for the student to draw and to color the picture of Jacob
 	
BAR
• *Early Reader's Bible,* 42–49
• NPRG
	Introduce the memory verse.
	"... The steps of a good man are ordered by the Lord. . . ." Psalm 37:23
	• **Read** aloud and discuss the memory verse.
	
	• **Define** unfamiliar vocabulary.
	• **Practice** daily the memory verse with the student for his recitation on Friday.
	Guide the student to the Biblical Principle from the Leading Idea.
	• **Tell** briefly the story of Jacob and Esau.
	• **Explain** briefly the events that lead to Jacob's dream.
	• **Discuss** the following:
	  • things Jacob saw in his dream,
	  • the promise God made to Jacob,
	  • the promise Jacob made to God.
	
	Notebook Work
	Distribute the prepared notebook page for the student to write or trace the title and to draw and color a picture of Jacob.
	
	BAR
	"Jacob Sees a Ladder"
	(See Weekly Routines for Reading and English.)
		Listen as the teacher reads aloud and discusses the memory verse.
		• **Discuss** unfamiliar vocabulary.
		• **Practice** and learn the memory verse for recitation on Friday.
		
		Listen as the teacher tells the story of Jacob and Esau.
		• **Discuss** the events that lead to Jacob's dream.
		• **Identify** the things Jacob saw in his dream.
		• **Discuss** the promise God made to Jacob.
		• **Discuss** the promise Jacob made to God.
		
		Notebook Work
		Write or trace the title and draw and color the picture of Jacob.
		
		BAR
		(See Weekly Routines for Reading and English.)
			• To learn and recite the memory verse
			• To learn new vocabulary
			• To understand God directs those who love Him
			• To understand God will use our dreams to talk to us
			• To complete and file notebook work

106   The Noah Plan Lessons Kindergarten © 2003 • Foundation for American Christian Education

Week Five

TEACHING PLAN

Quarter Two

	Preparation	Lesson	Student Work	Accomplishments	✓

LITERATURE	**Biblical Principles**
	• God's Principle of Individuality
	• Unity with Diversity
	
	Leading Idea
	Every poem is an expression of an individual's life, his gifts, and his faith.
	
	Books
	• Bible (KJ)
	• NPLG, 8–9, 108–123
	• Poetry books containing Longfellow's poetry
	• *Divine and Moral Songs for Children*, Isaac Watts
	
	Supplies
	• Biographical information for Longfellow and Watts
	• Notebook pages to include:
	  · the poet's name
	  · a picture of the poet
	  · the words to a selection of his poetry
	  · a picture or space for the student to illustrate and to color
	• Colored pencils
		Guide the student to the Biblical Principles from the Leading Idea.
		• **Introduce** the poet Henry Wadsworth Longfellow, his life, and his place on the Chain of Christianity.
		
		• **Instruct** the student to identify the literary elements such as rhythm, alliteration, and rhyme as you read aloud several selections of his poetry.
		
		• **Lead** a discussion about his poetic style.
		
		• **Introduce** Issac Watts, his biography, and his poetry using the suggestions above and focusing on the moral lessons.
		
		Notebook Work:
		Distribute the prepared notebook pages for the student to color.
			Participate in a discussion of the Biblical Principles and Leading Idea.
			Participate in a discussion about Henry Wadsworth Longfellow's life and his contribution on the Chain of Christianity.
			Listen as teacher reads aloud several of his poems and identifies literary elements such as rhythm, alliteration, and rhyme.
			Participate in a discussion about the author's poetic style.
			Participate in a discussion about the life of Isaac Watts, and his poetry focusing on the moral lessons.
			
			Notebook Work
			Color the notebook pages.
				• To learn about Henry Wadsworth Longfellow and Isaac Watts
				• To identify literary elements in poetry selections
				• To complete and file notebook work	

The Noah Plan Lessons Kindergarten © 2003 • Foundation for American Christian Education

TEACHING PLAN

Week Five Quarter Two

Preparation	Lesson	Student Work	Accomplishments	✓
Biblical Principle God launches events through individuals He has providentially called and prepared.	**Review** the effect that Jesus and the Gospel had on the heart of the individual. (Man is able to govern himself according to God's Word—Christian Self-Government.)	**Participate** in a review of the effect that Jesus and the Gospel had on the heart of the individual.	• To recognize each individual has a purpose in God's plan • To recognize God has a plan for everyone who receives Him into their heart • To recognize the need for the Savior • To complete and file notebook work	
Leading Idea The Gospel goes westward with Paul.	**Introduce** the Apostle Paul and the Christian Church as the fourth link on the Christian history timeline. • **Locate** with the student the fourth link on the classroom Christian history timeline.	**Locate** the fourth link on the classroom Christian history timeline.		
Books • Bible (KJ) • NPH&GG, 8–9, 70–71, Appendix 339 for additional books on Paul and the Christian Church • T&L, 159 • NPSDS, Providential History, Links	• **Present** background information about Paul. · Born Saul of Tarsus · Gifted apostle · Old Testament scholar · New Testament writer · Carried the Gospel westward • **Read** aloud Acts 9 and discuss Paul's conversion from persecutor to preacher. • **Ask** the student reason questions about Paul's conversion. · Why did Paul go to Damascus? · Who did Paul meet on the way to Damascus? · How did Paul's encounter change his life?	**Listen** as the teacher presents background information about Paul. **Listen** as the teacher tells the story of Paul's conversion. (Acts 9) **Answer** orally the reason questions about Paul's conversion. • Why did Paul go to Damascus? • Who did Paul meet on the way to Damascus? • How did Paul's encounter change his life?		
Supplies • Notebook page to include: · the title "Paul and the Christian Church" for the student to write or trace · a picture of Paul for the student to color • Colored pencils	• **Discuss** how God used Ananias to help Paul. Acts 9:17 *Notebook Work* **Instruct** the student to find the fourth link and color the representative picture on his individual Christian history timeline. **Distribute** the prepared notebook page for the student to write or trace the title and to color the picture of Paul.	**Discuss** how God used Ananias to help Paul. *Notebook Work* **Locate** and color the fourth link on your Christian history timeline. **Write** or trace the title on the notebook page and color the picture of Paul.		

HISTORY

108 The Noah Plan Lessons Kindergarten © 2003 • Foundation for American Christian Education

Quarter Two

TEACHING PLAN

Week Five

	Preparation	Lesson	Student Work	Accomplishments	✓
GEOGRAPHY	**Biblical Principle** God created each continent distinct to fit His purpose and His plan. Psalm 115:16 **Leading Idea** The nature and character of God are revealed in the continent of Europe. **Books** • Bible (KJ) • NPH&GG, 212–218 • T&L, 141–153, 156–157 **Supplies** • World map and globe • Student atlas • Books and magazines containing pictures of Europe for viewing • Sources of European music, language, and culture • Items of interest related to Europe • Old magazines (*National Geographic, Ranger Rick,* etc.) for cutting	**Continue** to guide the student to the Biblical Principle from the Leading Idea. • **Review** Europe's place on the Chain of Christianity and it's unique physical characteristics. • **Ask** the student to locate Europe on the classroom world map, globe, and in the student's atlas. **Lead** a discussion about interesting facts that demonstrate the individuality of Europe. • **Discuss** its many races. • **Discuss** its plant and animal life. • **Display** pictures or artifacts related to European culture, plants, and animals. • **Prepare** and serve foods or learn words of a native language or song. *Notebook Work* **Instruct** the student to find and cut pictures from magazines pertaining to Europe to be used in next week's lesson. **Instruct** the student to save these pictures in an envelope and put it into the pocket of his geography notebook.	**Participate** in an oral review of Europe's characteristics and function. **Locate** Europe on a world map, globe, and in your atlas. **Listen** as the teacher presents information about unique features of Europe and participate in a classroom discussion about the individuality of European culture, plants, and animals. **View** (or bring and share) interesting items related to the culture, plants, or animals of Europe. **Sample** native foods, listen to native music, learn about interesting customs, or learn words of a native language. *Notebook Work* **Cut** pictures related to the topography, people, plants and animals of Europe. • **Put** the pictures into an envelope. • **Place** the envelope into the pocket of your geography notebook.	• To locate Europe on a world map, globe, and atlas • To continue to learn more about the character and nature of God in His Creations • To sample native foods and learn words of a native language or song • To complete and file notebook work	

The Noah Plan Lessons Kindergarten © 2003 • Foundation for American Christian Education

Week Five　　　　　　　　　**TEACHING PLAN**　　　　　　　　　**Quarter Two**

	Preparation	Lesson	Student Work	Accomplishments
SCIENCE	**Biblical Principles** • God's Principle of Individuality • Unity with Diversity **Leading Idea** The Earth's crust is made up of three types of rocks. **Books** • Bible (KJ) • Webster's 1828 *Dictionary* • Science books (Library) **Supplies** • Pictures of the three types of rocks for display or samples of the rocks • Pictures of the three types of rocks for gluing • Notebook page to include: 　• the title "The Three Types of Rocks" for the student to write or trace 　• a space to glue and label pictures of the three types of rocks	**Review** the layers of the Earth and the definition of geology. **Introduce** the three types of rock that form the Earth's crust. • **Sedimentary** rocks (scrap rocks) are made when bits of matter settle together in layers and harden. (Show pictures of how this happens.) 　• Examples: sandstone, coal, shale, halite or rock salt, etc. 　• Uses: as building stones, in making of cement, bricks, and glass • **Igneous** rocks (fiery rocks) are formed by volcanoes. 　• Examples: granite, mica, pumice, quartz, obsidian, etc. 　• Uses: building stone, monuments, paving roads, dental powder, hand cleaners, gems • **Metamorphic** rocks (remade rocks) are formed when sedimentary and igneous rocks are changed by heat and pressure. 　• Example: slate, marble, quartzite, etc. 　• Uses: ornamental stone for monuments and table tops, roofing, chalkboards • **Present** visual examples of the three types of rock. • **Discuss** the distinguishing characteristics of each type of rock. • **Explain** how God's Principles of Individuality and Unity with Diversity can be seen in the Earth through the distinguishing characteristics of each rock form. *Notebook Work* **Distribute** the prepared notebook page for the student to write or trace the title and to glue and label the pictures.	**Review** with your teacher the layers of the Earth and the definition of geology. **Listen** and observe as the teacher introduces the three types of rocks that form the Earth's crust through visuals and participate in the discussion. **Participate** in a discussion by identifying the distinguishing characteristics of each type of rock. **Reason** and relate how rocks demonstrate the Principles of Individuality and Unity with Diversity. *Notebook Work* **Write** or trace the title on the notebook page and glue and label the pictures	• To learn about the characteristics of the three types of rocks in the Earth's crust • To examine different types of rocks • To relate God's Principles of Individuality and Unity with Diversity to rocks • To complete and file notebook work

110　　　The Noah Plan Lessons Kindergarten © 2003 • Foundation for American Christian Education

Quarter Two

TEACHING PLAN

Week Six

	Preparation	Lesson	Student Work	Accomplishments	✓

BIBLE	**Biblical Principles**
	• God takes care of us.
	• God is pleased when we forgive others.
	
	Leading Ideas
	• God took care of Joseph in prison.
	• Joseph forgave his brothers.
	
	Books
	• Bible (KJ)
	• Webster's 1828 *Dictionary*
	
	Supplies
	• Notebook page to include:
	  · the title "Joseph" for the student to write or trace
	  · a space for the student to draw and color a picture of Joseph
	
	BAR
	• *Early Reader's Bible*, 50–65
	• NPRG
		Introduce the memory verse. "For if ye forgive men their trespasses, your heavenly Father will also forgive you." Matthew 6:14
		• **Read** aloud and discuss the memory verse.
		• **Define** unfamiliar vocabulary.
		• **Practice** daily the memory verse with the student for his recitation on Friday.
		Guide the student to the Biblical Principle from the Leading Idea.
		• **Tell** briefly the story of Joseph.
		
		• **Discuss** the following:
		  · Reasons why Joseph's brother's hated him
		  · What his brothers did to him
		
		· How God was with Joseph in Egypt, Genesis 39:23
		· How God helped Joseph in prison
		· Joseph's forgiveness of his brothers and how they responded to it
		· How pleased God is when we forgive those who hurt us
		· How you feel when you are forgiven
		• **Encourage** the student to forgive those who have hurt him.
		
		Notebook Work
		Distribute the prepared notebook page for the student to write or trace the title and to draw and color a picture of Joseph with his brothers.
		
		BAR
		"God Takes Care of Joseph"
		"Joseph Forgives His Brothers"
		(See Weekly Routines for Reading and English.)
			Listen as the teacher reads aloud and discusses the memory verse.
			
			• **Discuss** unfamiliar vocabulary.
			• **Practice** and learn the memory verse for recitation on Friday.
			
			Listen as the teacher tells the story of Joseph.
			Reason orally and answer questions about the Leading Idea:
			• **Why** did Joseph's brothers hate him?
			• **What** did Joseph's brothers do to him?
			
			• **Explain** how God was with Joseph in Egypt.
			• How did God help Joseph in prison?
			• How did Joseph's brothers respond to his forgiveness of them?
			• How does God feel when we forgive those who hurt us?
			• How do you feel when you are forgiven?
			
			Notebook Work
			Write or trace the title on the notebook page and draw and color a picture of Joseph with his brothers.
			
			BAR
			(See Weekly Routines for Reading and English.)
				• To learn and recite the memory verse
				• To learn new vocabulary
				• To learn God takes care of us
				• To learn God is pleased when we forgive others
				• To complete and file notebook work	

The Noah Plan Lessons Kindergarten © 2003 • Foundation for American Christian Education

111

Quarter Two

TEACHING PLAN

Week Six

	Preparation	Lesson	Student Work	Accomplishments	✓
LITERATURE	**Biblical Principles** • God's Principle of Individuality • Unity with Diversity **Leading Idea** Every poem is an expression of an individual's life, his gifts, and his faith. **Books** • Bible (KJ) • NPLG, 8–9 • Christmas stories **Supplies** • Notebook page for the student to illustrate the Christmas story OR • A photocopied picture of the Christmas story for the student to color • Colored pencils	**Review** the Biblical Principles and Leading Idea. **Read** aloud the Christmas Story from the Scriptures, in poetry, and in other works of literature. **Lead** the student to reason about the author's individual perspective and literary style in each selection. *Notebook Work* **Instruct** the student to illustrate the Christmas story or photocopy a picture for him to color.	**Participate** in a review of the Biblical Principles and Leading Idea. **Listen** as the teacher reads aloud the Christmas Story from the Scriptures, in poetry, and in other works of literature. **Reason** and discuss the author's individual perspective and literary style in each of the selections. *Notebook Work* **Draw** a picture of the Christmas story or color one that the teacher photocopied.	• To listen to the Christmas story from the Scriptures, poetry, and other works of literature • To identify the author's style • To complete and file notebook work	

112   The Noah Plan Lessons Kindergarten © 2003 • Foundation for American Christian Education

Week Six   **Quarter Two**

TEACHING PLAN

Preparation	Lesson	Student Work	Accomplishments	✓
Biblical Principle God launches events through individuals He has providentially called and prepared.	**Discuss** the Biblical Principle and the Leading Idea. **Review** the Apostle Paul's character by answering leading questions about how he changed as a result of his conversion.	**Participate** in a discussion of the Biblical Principle and Leading Idea. **Review** the Apostle Paul's character by answering leading questions about how he changed as a result of his conversion.	• To become acquainted with Apostle Paul and his contributions to the westward movement of Christianity	
Leading Idea The Gospel goes westward with Paul.	**Discuss** Paul's "Macedonian Vision," and its effect on history. (The Gospel goes westward to Europe. Acts 16:9–10) • Paul found his first European convert in Lydia. Acts 16:14–15 • The first New Testament church began in Lydia's home.	**Discuss** Paul's "Macedonian Vision" and its effect on history. **Listen** as the teacher reads aloud Acts 16:14–15 and discusses the first New Testament church in Lydia's home.	• To become acquainted with the character of the first century church • To complete and file notebook work	
Books • Bible (KJ) • NPH&GG, 8–9, 70–71 • CHOC I, 16–17 • NPSDS, Providential History, Links	**Discuss** the character of the first century church in an age appropriate manner. • They were "mini-republics" which were self-governing groups. • They took care of their members. • They helped other churches in need.	**Discuss** the character of the first century church. • They were "mini-republics" which were self-governing groups. • They took care of their members. • They helped other churches in need.		
Supplies • Christian history timeline for classroom display (The Noah Plan Wall Timeline, F.A.C.E.) • Simple outline map of continents around the Mediterranean Sea: Asia, Europe, Africa • Overhead projector (optional) • Colored pencils	**Discuss** Paul's travels and locate key places on the classroom map. *Notebook Work* **Distribute** the simple outline map of the continents around the Mediterranean Sea: Asia, Europe, and Africa. • **Place** a cross near Antioch and one near Rome. • **Instruct** the student to color the crosses and complete the map according to the map standard taught in geography class. (The teacher can model the map standard on an overhead projector.)	**Listen** as the teacher discusses Paul's travels and locates key places on the classroom map. *Notebook Work* **Follow** the instructions from your teacher to complete the map work. • **Place** a cross near Antioch and one near Rome. • **Color** the crosses and complete the map according to the map standard taught in geography class.		

HISTORY

The Noah Plan Lessons Kindergarten © 2003 • Foundation for American Christian Education   113

Week Six   **Quarter Two**

TEACHING PLAN

	Preparation	Lesson	Student Work	Accomplishments	✓

GEOGRAPHY

Preparation

Biblical Principle
God created each continent distinct to fit His purpose and His plan. Psalm 115:16

Leading Idea
The nature and character of God are revealed in the continent of Europe.

Books
- Bible (KJ)
- NPH&GG, 148–49, 236–237

Supplies
- Notebook page to include:
  - the title "Europe's Individuality" for the student to write or trace
  - a space to glue pictures of Europe
  - Simple outline map of Europe (Use maps from NPH&GG, 236–237 as a guide.)
- Overhead projector if available
- Map standard
- Colored pencils

Lesson

Review the Biblical Principle and the Leading Idea.

Notebook Work
Provide a simple outline map of Europe.
Model on an overhead projector and instruct the student to follow the map standard for physical maps. (See NPH&GG, 148–149.)
Distribute the prepared notebook page for the student to write or trace the title and to glue the pictures of Europe saved from last week's lesson.

OR

Save these pictures for a group project in the fourth quarter.

Student Work

Participate in a discussion of the Biblical Principle and Leading Idea.

Notebook Work
Color the map of Europe according to the map standard for physical maps.

Write or trace the title on the notebook page and glue the Europe pictures saved from last week's lesson onto the page.

OR

Save these pictures for a group project in the fourth quarter.

Europe

Accomplishments
- To recognize Europe on a world map
- To apply the map standard to a physical map
- To complete and file notebook work

114   The Noah Plan Lessons Kindergarten © 2003 • Foundation for American Christian Education

Week Six   Quarter Two

TEACHING PLAN

Preparation	Lesson	Student Work	Accomplishments	✓
Biblical Principle "Or speak to the earth, and it shall teach thee . . . ." Job 12:8. **Leading Idea** Fossils testify of God's Creation. **Books** • Bible (KJ) • Webster's 1828 *Dictionary* • Science books (Library) **Supplies** • Pictures of different kinds of fossils • Sand, soil, pebbles • Jar • Water • Magazines to cut pictures of fossils • Notebook page to include: • the title "Fossils" for the student to write or trace • a space for the student to glue pictures of fossils	**Guide** the student to the Biblical Principle from the Leading Idea by reading aloud and discussing Job 12:8. • **Introduce** and define fossils as the remains or imprints of plants and animals. • **Discuss** how fossils are formed when plants and animals are buried quickly by sediments. • **Explain** fossils are mostly found in sedimentary rock. • **Demonstrate** the settling of various particles to make sedimentary rock. 1. Pour small amounts of sand, soil, and pebbles into a quart size jar. 2. Fill the jar with water and screw on the cap. 3. Shake the jar and watch what happens. 4. Let the jar stay untouched for several days and see how the particles settle to the bottom of the jar. 5. Discuss how animal and plant remains can be found in the settled particles. • **Discuss** how it is possible for shells to be found in rock on top of mountains (Noah's flood). • **Discuss** the different kinds of fossils: petrified, print, molds, whole specimens. • **Present** visual examples of fossils. • **Reason** and relate how fossils testify of God's Creation. • **Engage** the student in an activity that would show how a fossil print is made. 1. Mix plaster of Paris according to the directions. 2. Pour the plaster over a leaf that it in an aluminum pan. 3. Remove the leaf from the plaster and note the imprint. 4. Let the student paint the imprint. • **Visit** a museum to view fossils. *Notebook Work* **Distribute** the prepared notebook page for the student to write or trace the title and to glue pictures of fossils	**Listen** as the teacher reads aloud and discusses Job 12:8. **Listen** as the teacher defines fossil. **Listen** as the teacher discusses and explains how and where fossils are formed. **Participate** in a demonstration on how fossils are formed. **Listen** as the teacher discusses how it is possible for shells to be found in rock on top of mountains (Noah's flood). **Listen** and observe as the teacher introduces the different types of fossils through visuals. **Reason** and relate orally how fossils testify of God's Creation. **Participate** in an activity as you follow the teacher's directions that would show how a fossil print is made. **Visit** a museum with your teacher to view fossils. *Notebook Work* **Write** or trace the title on the notebook page and glue the pictures of fossils.	• To learn new vocabulary • To learn how fossils are formed • To make fossil prints • To testify of God's Creation through the knowledge of fossils • To observe and participate in a demonstration • To complete and fill notebook work	

SCIENCE

The Noah Plan Lessons Kindergarten © 2003 • Foundation for American Christian Education   115

Week Seven

TEACHING PLAN

Quarter Two

	Preparation	Lesson	Student Work	Accomplishments	✓
BIBLE	**Biblical Principle** Disobedience brings consequences. **Leading Idea** God punished a king who disobeyed Him. **Books** • Bible (KJV) • Webster's 1828 *Dictionary* **Supplies** • Notebook page to include: • the title "Pharaoh and Moses" for the student to write or trace • a space for the student to draw and color a picture of Pharaoh and Moses **BAR** • *Early Reader's Bible*, 82–89 • NPRG	**Introduce** the memory verse: ". . . the face of the Lord is against them that do evil." 1 Peter 3:12b • **Read** aloud and discuss the memory verse. • **Define** unfamiliar vocabulary. • **Practice** daily the memory verse with the student for his recitation on Friday. **Guide** the student to the Biblical Principle from the Leading Idea. • **Tell** the story of Moses and Pharaoh. • **Discuss** the consequences to Egypt because Pharaoh refused to free the Israelites. • **Discuss** how God feels when we say no to Him. • **Identify** the plagues that came upon Egypt. • **Discuss** the last plague that caused Pharaoh to let God's people go free. *Notebook Work* **Distribute** the prepared notebook page for the student to write or trace the title and to draw and color the picture of Pharaoh and Moses. **BAR** "A King Who Said No" (See Weekly Routines for Reading and English.)	**Listen** as the teacher reads aloud and discusses the memory verse. • **Discuss** unfamiliar vocabulary. • **Practice** and learn the memory verse for recitation on Friday. **Listen** as the teacher tells the story of Pharaoh and Moses. **Reason** orally and answer questions about the Leading Idea: • What were the consequences to Egypt because Pharaoh refused to free the Israelites? • How does God feel when we say no to Him? • What were the plagues that came upon Egypt? • What was the last plaque that caused Pharaoh to set God's people free? *Notebook Work* **Write** or trace the title on the notebook page and draw and color a picture of Pharaoh and Moses. **BAR** (See Weekly Routines for Reading and English.)	• To learn and recite the memory verse • To learn new vocabulary • To understand disobedience brings consequences • To complete and file notebook work	

116   The Noah Plan Lessons Kindergarten © 2003 • Foundation for American Christian Education

Week Seven

Quarter Two

TEACHING PLAN

	Preparation	Lesson	Student Work	Accomplishments	✓
LITERATURE	**Biblical Principle** The individuality of a character can be seen through his actions or choices. **Leading Idea** Our actions have consequences. **Books** • Bible (KJ) • NPLG, 8–9, 36, 135–138 • Beatrix Potter biography (Library) • Animal tales written by Beatrix Potter **Supplies** • Prepared notebook pages for the study of the classic • Large illustrations of Beatrix Potter characters and story settings • Colored pencils	**Discuss** the Biblical Principle and the Leading Idea. **Introduce** the individuality and contributions of Beatrix Potter by presenting key events in her childhood and by discussing her life as an author, an artist, and a naturalist. **Review** the literary elements of a classic. **Discuss** the definition of a moral. **Continue** to read aloud the classic animal tales of Beatrix Potter using NPLG, 36 to guide lesson planning. *Notebook Work* Although several of Beatrix Potter's stories will be read aloud and discussed, one book may be developed in the notebook as a record to represent animal tales. **Distribute** the prepared notebook pages for the student to complete and to color. Prepared Notebook pages for the study of the classic to include: • the author's name and picture to color • the title page of the book and picture to color • a page for the student to record the setting • a page for each character and picture to color • a page for the student to record the plot	**Participate** in a discussion of the Biblical Principle and Leading Idea. **Participate** in a discussion about Beatrix Potter's individuality as an author and her contributions to literature. **Name** and review the elements of a classic. **Discuss** the definition of a moral. **Listen** as the teacher reads aloud *The Tale of Peter Rabbit.* • **Identify** the setting. • **Name** and describe the characters. • **Identify** and discuss new vocabulary. • **Discuss** the theme through answering questions. *Notebook Work* **Complete** and color the notebook pages.	• To identify setting, characters and new vocabulary • To learn that our actions have consequences • To complete and file notebook work	

The Noah Plan Lessons Kindergarten © 2003 • Foundation for American Christian Education   117

Week Seven   TEACHING PLAN   Quarter Two

HISTORY

Preparation	Lesson	Student Work	Accomplishments
Biblical Principle God uses individual character to forward His story and His Gospel purpose. **Leading Idea** The early Christians were men and woman of conscience. **Books** • Bible (KJ) • NPH&GG, 8–9, 70 • NPSDS, Providential History, Links • CHOC I, 16–17 **Supplies** • Notebook page to include: • the title "Early Christian Symbols" for the student to write or trace • an outline of a cross or a fish symbol for the student to make a mosaic • 1" or ½" squares of construction paper (values of blue and yellow)	**Introduce** and explain the character and challenges of the early Christians. • They held strong to their Godly beliefs. • They believed religion was voluntary. • They faced death with composure. • They obeyed the laws of the land as long as they did not conflict with the laws of God and violate their conscience. **Show** pictures of the cross and fish as early Christian symbols. • **Discuss** their purpose as a means of identification from one Christian to another. • **Discuss** the ways they represent Christ or the Gospel. *Notebook Work* **Cut** small squares (1" or ½") from construction paper (different values of yellow and blue). **Distribute** the prepared notebook page for the student to write or trace the title and to glue the colored squares on the outline of the cross or fish.	**Listen** to and discuss as the teacher presents background information about the character qualities of early Christians. **View** pictures of the cross and fish as early Christian symbols. • **Discuss** their purpose. • **Discuss** ways they represent Christ or the Gospel. *Notebook Work* **Write** or trace the title on the notebook page and glue the colored squares on the outline of the cross or fish symbol to make a mosaic.	• To appreciate the character of the early Christians • To understand the purpose for the Christian symbols • To recognize various early Christian symbols • To complete and file notebook work

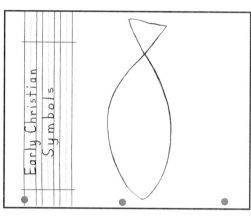

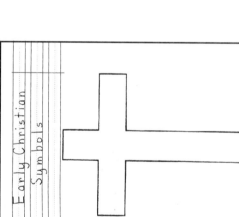

118   The Noah Plan Lessons Kindergarten © 2003 • Foundation for American Christian Education

Week Seven

Quarter Two

TEACHING PLAN

	Preparation	Lesson	Student Work	Accomplishments	✓
GEOGRAPHY	**Biblical Principle** God created each continent distinct to fit His purpose and His plan. Psalm 115:16 **Leading Idea** The nature and character of God are revealed in the continent of North America. **Books** • Bible (KJ) • NPH&GG, 128, 141, 202–206 • T&L, 141–153, 156–157 • CHOC I, 4–5 **Supplies** • World map and globe • Student atlas • Colored pencils • EMBG, Volume 3:3 • Pictures of different regions of North America	**Review** the continents of Asia and Europe by asking the student to locate each of them on the classroom world map, globe, and in the student's atlas. **Ask** the student to recall why Asia is called the "continent of origins or beginnings" and Europe is called the "continent of development." **Guide** the student to the Biblical Principle from the Leading Idea. • **Locate** North America on the classroom world map, globe, and student atlas. • **Introduce** the geographic features that contribute to North America being reserved by God to be the most complete expression of the Christian civilization. • **Present** information about natural resources and climate that contribute to the individuality of North America. • **Display** pictures of various regions in North America (mountains, beaches, plains, etc.). *Notebook Work* **Distribute** EMBG, Volume 3:3 and instruct the student in completing the page.	**Review** Asia and Europe by locating each of them on the classroom world map, globe, and in your atlas. **Recall** and discuss why Asia is called the "continent of origins or beginnings" and Europe is called the "continent of development." **Listen** and observe as the teacher: • **Locates** North America on the classroom world map, globe, and atlas. • **Presents** information about how this continent was reserved by God to be the most complete expression of Christian civilization. • **Identifies** geographic features, natural resources, and climate that contribute to its individuality. **View** pictures of the different regions in North America. *Notebook Work* **Color** and complete the notebook page. North America	• To learn about the location and individuality of North America • To view pictures of North America • To complete and file notebook work	

The Noah Plan Lessons Kindergarten © 2003 • Foundation for American Christian Education

119

Week Seven
Quarter Two

TEACHING PLAN

Preparation	Lesson	Student Work	Accomplishments

Biblical Principles
• God has designed plants to grow according to His laws. Genesis 1:11
• God's Principle of Individuality
• Unity with Diversity
 	
Leading Idea
God has provided the necessary conditions on the Earth for plants to grow.
 	
Books
• Bible (KJ)
• Webster's 1828 *Dictionary*
• Botany books (Library)
 	
Supplies
• Pictures of the different parts of plants
• Small peat or clay pots
• Potting soil
• Bean seeds
• Cards to label the growing conditions of each plant
• Notebook page including:
  • the title "What Plants Need" for the student to write or trace
  • a space for the student to draw and to label plants, flowers, and the things they need to grow—water, sunlight, soil, air
	Introduce botany.
	• **Define** botany as the study of plants and how they grow.
	• **Read** aloud Genesis 1:11 and discuss the Biblical foundation of botany.
	• **Use** visuals to introduce the characteristics of plants:
	  • Their structure—the parts
	  • Their function—what the parts do
	  • Their habits—where and how they grow
	  • Their arrangement (order)—how the parts work together
	
	Discuss how botany reveals:
	• God's Principle of Individuality—Each plant will produce its own kind of seed.
	• Unity with Diversity—All the parts of the plant work together to keep the plant alive.
	
	Introduce the things that plants need in order to grow and discuss what happens to a plant when it is not grown under the right conditions.
	
	Plant with the student bean seeds in five different pots and begin to grow them under a variety of different conditions:
	• With water, air, and sunlight,
	• With water and air, but no sunlight,
	• With sunlight and air, but too much water,
	• With sunlight and air, but no water,
	• With sunlight and water, but no air.
	
	Guide the student to make predictions about which seeds will grow the best.
	
	Guide the student to the Biblical Principles from the Leading Idea by asking:
	• Why do plants need water, air, soil and sunlight in proper amounts to grow?
	
	Notebook Work
	Distribute the prepared notebook page for the student to write or trace the title and to draw and to label plants and flowers and the things they need—sunlight, water (rain), and soil (nutrients/food) and air.
		Listen as the teacher defines botany.
		
		Listen as the teacher reads aloud Genesis 1:11 and discusses the Biblical foundation of botany.
		
		Listen and observe as the teacher introduces the characteristics of plants through the use of visuals.
		
		Reason and relate orally how plants demonstrate the Principles of Individuality and Unity with Diversity.
		
		Listen as the teacher introduces the things that plants need in order to grow.
		
		Reason orally about what happens to a plant that does not have these conditions.
		
		Participate in an experiment as seeds are planted for an experiment.
		
		Make a prediction about which seeds will grow the best.
		
		Reason from the Leading Idea to the Biblical Principle by answering the question:
		• Why do plants need water, air, soil and sunlight in proper amounts to grow?
		
		Notebook Work
		Write or trace the title on the notebook page and follow the teacher's instructions to illustrate the page.
			• To define botany
			• To learn about the Biblical foundation of plants
			• To learn about the characteristics of plants
			• To reason and relate about God's Principles of Individuality and Unity with Diversity in plants
			• To learn the things seeds need in order to grow
			• To plant seeds and make predictions
			• To complete and file notebook work

SCIENCE

The Noah Plan Lessons Kindergarten © 2003 • Foundation for American Christian Education

Week Eight

Quarter Two

TEACHING PLAN

	Preparation	Lesson	Student Work	Accomplishments	✓

BIBLE	**Biblical Principle**
	God gives us courage when we trust Him.
	
	Leading Idea
	David demonstrated his trust in God.
	
	Books
	• Bible (KJ)
	• Webster's 1828 *Dictionary*
	
	Supplies
	• Notebook page to include:
	  · the title "David and Goliath" for the student to write or trace
	  · a space for the student to draw and color a picture of David and Goliath
	
	BAR
	• *Early Reader's Bible*, 162–169
	• NPRG
		Introduce the memory verse: "... Be strong and of a good courage: be not afraid,...for the Lord thy God is with thee...." Joshua 1:9
		• **Read** aloud and discuss the memory verse.
		• **Define** unfamiliar vocabulary.
		• **Practice** daily the memory verse with the student for his recitation on Friday.
		Guide the student to the Biblical Principle from the Leading Idea.
		• **Tell** the story of David and Goliath from the Bible.
		• **Identify** the characters in the story.
		• **Discuss** how David knew God would be with him to face Goliath.
		  · His faith in God was very strong.
		• **Read** aloud 1 Samuel 17:26 and discuss how David saw his situation from God's point of view.
		• **Discuss** the following:
		  · What did Goliath use to fight David?
		  · What did David use to fight Goliath?
		  · How was David's winning the battle a sign of God's power?
		  · How God gives us courage when we trust in Him.
		
		Notebook Work
		Distribute the prepared notebook page for the student to write or trace the title and to draw and color a picture of David and Goliath.
		
		BAR
		"David Is a Brave Boy!"
		(See Weekly Routines for Reading and English.)
			Listen as the teacher reads aloud and discusses the memory verse.
			• **Discuss** unfamiliar vocabulary.
			• **Practice** and learn the memory verse for recitation on Friday.
			
			Listen as the teacher tells the story of David and Goliath.
			• **Identify** the characters in the story.
			• **Discuss** David's faith in God.
			
			Listen as the teacher reads aloud 1 Samuel 17:26 and discusses how David saw his situation from God's point of view.
			• **Identify** the weapon Goliath used to fight David.
			• **Identify** the weapon David used to fight Goliath.
			• **Discuss** how David's winning the battle was a sign of God's power.
			• **Discuss** how God gives us courage when we need it.
			
			Notebook Work
			Write or trace the title on the notebook page and draw and color a picture of David and Goliath.
			
			BAR
			(See Weekly Routines for Reading and English.)
				• To learn and recite the memory verse
				• To learn new vocabulary
				• To put your trust in God
				• To complete and file notebook work	

The Noah Plan Lessons Kindergarten © 2003 • Foundation for American Christian Education

121

Week Eight

Quarter Two

TEACHING PLAN

	Preparation	Lesson	Student Work	Accomplishments	✓
LITERATURE	**Biblical Principle** The individuality of a character can be seen through his actions or choices. **Leading Idea** Our actions have consequences. **Books** • Bible (KJ) • NPLG, 8–9, 36, 135–138 • Animal tales written by Beatrix Potter **Supplies** • Notebook pages for the study of a classic • Large illustrations of Beatrix Potter characters and story settings	**Review** the Biblical Principle and Leading Idea. **Review** *The Tale of Peter Rabbit* and the literary elements identified in the story. **Review** any other stories that have been read together. **Continue** to read aloud, to discuss, and to introduce related activities. (For animal tales written by Beatrix Potter use NPLG, 36 to guide lesson planning.) *Notebook Work* **Continue** to add to the notebook pages of the study begun in Literature Week 7, 117. **Distribute** the prepared notebook pages for the student to complete and to color. Prepared Notebook pages for the study of the classic to include: • the author's name and picture to color • the title page of the book and picture to color • a page for the student to record the setting • a page for each character and picture to color • a page for the student to record the plot	**Participate** in a review of the Biblical Principle and Leading Idea. **Participate** in an oral review of the Beatrix Potter stories that have been read and discussed in previous lessons. **Continue** to listen as the teacher reads aloud selected animal tales written by Beatrix Potter. **Participate** in discussions as you identify the setting, characters, new vocabulary, and theme. *Notebook Work* **Continue** to add to the notebook pages of the study.	• To identify setting, characters and new vocabulary • To complete and file notebook work	

122   The Noah Plan Lessons Kindergarten © 2003 • Foundation for American Christian Education

Week Eight

Quarter Two

TEACHING PLAN

	Preparation	Lesson	Student Work	Accomplishments	✓
HISTORY	**Biblical Principle** God's Word gives life. **Leading Idea** Liberty for the individual is proportionate with his ability to read the Holy Bible in his own language. **Books** • Bible (KJ) • NPH&GG, 8–9, 71, 78, & Appendix 340 for additional books on the Bible in English and the Reformation Period • NPSDS, Providential History, Links • CHOC I, 38–41 **Supplies** • Christian history timeline (student) • Christian history timeline for classroom display (The Noah Plan Wall Timeline, F.A.C.E.) • Colored pencils	**Review** early Christian symbols (the cross and fish) by asking the student to name them and recall some of the ways that they represent Christ or the Gospel. **Introduce** the Bible in English as the fifth link on the Christian history timeline. **Discuss** the Biblical Principle and the Leading Idea. (Remember that you are just planting the seeds of liberty. You do this by carrying on a conversation with the student.) **Locate** with the student the fifth link on the classroom Christian history timeline. **Introduce** the Magna Charta in an age appropriate manner. • It was the first paper written to protect the rights of the individual. • It put limits on the power of the ruler. • It reflected our English heritage's love for liberty and laws based on God's Word. • It is a part of the American system of government. **Read** aloud and discuss selections from the Magna Charta: • No trial without a jury. • No taxation without representation • No man can take another's property from him without his consent. **Discuss** how it reflected a love of liberty based on God's Word. **Discuss** why it is important to Americans today. • The liberties established by the Magna Charta became a part of our American government. *Notebook Work* **Instruct** the student to find the fifth link and color the representative picture on his individual timeline.	**Review** early Christian symbols (the cross and fish) by naming them and recalling some of the ways that they represent Christ or the Gospel. **Participate** in a discussion of the Biblical Principle and Leading Idea. **Locate** the fifth link on the classroom Christian history timeline. **Listen** as the teacher presents information about the Magna Charta and the Englishman's love of liberty based on God's Word. **Restate** in your own words the purpose of the Magna Charta and discuss why it is important to Americans today. *Notebook Work* **Locate** and color the fifth link on the notebook copy of the Christian history timeline.	• To appreciate our English heritage's love of liberty and laws based on God's Word • To restate the purpose of the Magna Charta • To complete and file notebook work	

The Noah Plan Lessons Kindergarten © 2003 • Foundation for American Christian Education

123

Week Eight Quarter Two

TEACHING PLAN

Preparation	Lesson	Student Work	Accomplishments	✓
Biblical Principle God created each continent distinct to fit His purpose and His plan. Psalm 115:16 **Leading Idea** The nature and character of God are revealed in the continent of North America. **Books** • Bible (KJ) • NPH&GG, 128, 141, 202–206 • T&L, 141–153, 156–157 • CHOC I, 4–5 **Supplies** • World map and globe • Student atlas • Pictures of the people of North America • Sources of words, phrases or songs of various groups of North American people	**Continue** to guide the student to the Biblical Principle from the Leading Idea by reviewing the location of North America as well as the unique geographic features, natural resources, and climate that contribute to its individuality. **Present** information about the people who inhabit the countries of North America (culture, customs, foods, languages, etc.). **Display** pictures or artifacts related to North American culture and ask the student to bring items to share. **Prepare** and serve native foods, share interesting customs, play native music, or learn words of a native language.	**Participate** in a review of the Biblical Principle and Leading Idea by reviewing the location of North America, as well as the unique geographic features, natural resources, and climate that contribute to its individuality. **Listen** as the teacher presents information about the culture, customs, and languages of the people who inhabit North America. **View** pictures or artifacts related to North American culture (and/or bring items to share with the class). **Sample** native foods, listen to native music, learn about interesting customs, or learn words of a native language	• To identify North America on a world map, globe, and atlas • To recall unique aspects of North America's geography, natural resources, and climate • To learn about the culture, customs, etc. of the North American people • To view pictures or artifacts related to North American culture • To learn new words or songs • To sample native foods	

GEOGRAPHY

124   The Noah Plan Lessons Kindergarten © 2003 • Foundation for American Christian Education

Quarter Two

TEACHING PLAN

Week Eight

	Preparation	Lesson	Student Work	Accomplishments ✓
SCIENCE	**Biblical Principles** • God's Principle of Individuality • Unity with Diversity **Leading Idea** The parts of plants perform different functions, which contribute to the growth and development of the plant. **Books** • Bible (KJ) • Botany books (Library) • Encyclopedia **Supplies** • Diagram or chart of plants and trees • Potted plants for examination • Root vegetables for tasting • Sweet potato to be rooted • Colored pencils **SCIENCE—** *Notebook pages* (continued on page 126)	**Review** by asking the student to name the characteristics of plants and the things they need in order to grow. **Instruct** the student to observe the bean plants that are being grown under various conditions. **Ask** the student to draw conclusions about the plant's growth or lack of growth. **Identify** the parts of a plant using a diagram, chart, or picture from a book. **Introduce** the concept that each part of a plant has a different function and ask the student to discuss how this illustrates God's Principles of Individuality and Unity with Diversity. **Introduce** the location and the function of roots: • to hold the plant in place • to carry water and food (minerals) from the soil to the plant **Lead** a discussion about how the roots are especially designed by God to carry out their purpose. **Provide** activities to broaden the student's knowledge of roots and their function: • **Remove** a plant from the pot and instruct the student to examine the plant and locate the roots. • **Display** root vegetables and have the student taste them. • **Provide** materials and assistance for the student to root a sweet potato in a jar. **SCIENCE—** *Notebook Work* (continued on page 126)	**Recall** the characteristics of plants and name the things plants need in order to grow. **Observe** the bean plants that are being grown under various conditions. **Draw** conclusions and share your observations. **Name** and locate the parts of a plant as the teacher displays visuals such as charts or diagrams. **Reason** about how the different functions of each part of a plant illustrate the Principles of Individuality and Unity with Diversity. **Listen** as the teacher introduces the location and the function of roots. **Reason** about how roots are especially designed by God for their specific purpose. **Participate** in activities to broaden your understanding of roots and their function: • **Examine** and locate the roots of a plant. • **Sample** some vegetables that are roots. • **Root** a sweet potato in a jar for future observation of root development. **SCIENCE—** *Notebook Work* (continued on page 126)	• To review plant characteristics and the things they need to grow • To observe plants and draw conclusions • To identify plant parts • To reason about how plant parts demonstrate the Biblical Principle Unity with Diversity • To learn the function of roots • To complete and file notebook work

The Noah Plan Lessons Kindergarten © 2003 • Foundation for American Christian Education

125

Week Eight

Quarter Two

TEACHING PLAN

Preparation	Lesson	Student Work	Accomplishments	✓
• Notebook page to include: • the title "God's Principle of Unity with Diversity in Plants" for the student to write or trace • diagrams of a flower and a tree for the student to label the parts • Notebook page to include: • the title "Roots" for the student to write or trace • a space for the student to draw or paste pictures of root vegetables and to color	*Notebook Work* **Distribute** the prepared notebook page for the student to write or trace the title and to label the parts of the diagrams as you model them on the board. **Distribute** the prepared notebook page for the student • to write or trace the title • to draw or paste pictures of root vegetables or to glue pictures of plants and their roots.	*Notebook Work* **Write** or trace the title on the notebook page and label the diagrams as the teacher models the work on the board. **Write** or trace the title on the notebook page, draw or paste pictures of root vegetables or glue pictures of plants and their roots.		

SCIENCE (continued)

126   The Noah Plan Lessons Kindergarten © 2003 • Foundation for American Christian Education

Quarter Two

TEACHING PLAN

Week Nine

	Preparation	Lesson	Student Work	Accomplishments	✓
BIBLE	**Biblical Principle** God answers prayers of those who have faith in Him. **Leading Idea** Daniel prayed to God for help when he was in the lion's den. **Books** • Bible (KJV) • Webster's 1828 *Dictionary* **Supplies** • Notebook page to include: • the title "Daniel and the Lions" for the student to write or trace • a space for the student to draw and color a picture of Daniel and the lions **BAR** • *Early Reader's Bible*, 266–273 • NPRG	**Introduce** the memory verse. "For the eyes of the Lord are over the righteous, and his ears are open unto their prayers. . . ." 1 Peter 3:12a **Read** aloud and discuss the memory verse. • **Define** unfamiliar vocabulary. • **Practice** daily the memory verse with the student for his recitation on Friday. **Guide** the student to the Biblical Principle from the Leading Idea. • **Tell** the story of Daniel and his captivity. • **Discuss** the following: · How did Daniel end up in the lion's den? · What happened to Daniel in the lion's den? · What role did prayer play in keeping Daniel safe? · How was God faithful in Daniel's life? • **Describe** a time when you were afraid and prayed to God. *Notebook Work* **Distribute** the prepared notebook page for the student to write or trace the title and to draw and color a picture of Daniel and the lions. **BAR** "Daniel and the Lion's Den" (See Weekly Routines for Reading and English.)	**Listen** as the teacher reads aloud and discusses the memory verse. • **Discuss** unfamiliar vocabulary. • **Practice** and learn the memory verse for recitation on Friday. **Listen** as the teacher tells the story of Daniel in the lion's den. **Reason** orally and answer questions about the Leading Idea: • How did Daniel end up in the lion's den? • What happened to Daniel in the lion's den? • What did Daniel do in the lion's den? • How was God faithful in Daniel's life? • **Describe** a time when you prayed to God for help. *Notebook Work* **Write** or trace the title on the notebook page and draw and color the picture. **BAR** (See Weekly Routines for Reading and English.)	• To learn and recite the memory verse • To learn new vocabulary • To learn about the importance of prayer • To see the faithfulness of God to man • To complete and file notebook work	

The Noah Plan Lessons Kindergarten © 2003 • Foundation for American Christian Education 127

Week Nine

Quarter Two

TEACHING PLAN

Preparation	Lesson	Student Work	Accomplishments	✓
Biblical Principle The individuality of a character can be seen through his actions or choices.	**Review** the Biblical Principle and the Leading Idea.	**Participate** in a review of the Biblical Principle and Leading Idea.	• To identify setting, characters and new vocabulary	
	Review Beatrix Potter animal tales from previous lessons and discuss the literary elements that were identified in the stories.	**Participate** in a review of the Beatrix Potter stories that have been read and discussed in previous lessons.	• To complete and file notebook work	
Leading Idea Our actions have consequences.	**Continue** to read aloud, to discuss, and to introduce related activities. (For animal tales written by Beatrix Potter use NPLG, 36 to guide lesson planning.)	**Continue** to listen as the teacher reads aloud selected animal tales written by Beatrix Potter.		
Books • Bible (KJ) • NPLG, 8–9, 36, 135–138 • Animal tales written by Beatrix Potter		**Participate** in discussions as you identify the setting, the characters, the new vocabulary, and the theme. Participate in related activities as directed by your teacher.		
Supplies • Notebook pages for the study of a classic • Large illustrations of Beatrix Potter • Characters and story settings	*Notebook Work* **Continue** to add to the notebook pages of the study begun in Literature Week 7, 117. **Distribute** the prepared notebook pages for the student to complete and to color. Prepared Notebook pages for the study of the classic to include: • the author's name and picture to color • the title page of the book and picture to color • a page for the student to record the setting • a page for each character and picture to color • a page for the student to record the plot	*Notebook Work* **Continue** to add to the notebook pages of the study of the classic.		
	Additional Suggestions **Plan** a special day or special activities related to these stories: gardening, sewing, fishing, sketching and painting, a tea party.			

LITERATURE

128   The Noah Plan Lessons Kindergarten © 2003 • Foundation for American Christian Education

Quarter Two

TEACHING PLAN

Week Nine

	Preparation	Lesson	Student Work	Accomplishments	✔
HISTORY	**Biblical Principle** God's Word gives life. **Leading Idea** The Bible in the hands of the people brought liberty. **Books** • Bible (KJ) • NPH&GG, 8–9, 71, 78 • NPSDS, Providential History, Links • CHOC I, 28B–36, 47 • T&L, 166–168 **Supplies** • Notebook page to include: • the title "John Wycliffe, Morning Star of the Reformation" for the student to write or trace • a picture of John Wycliffe for the student to color • Colored pencils	**Review** the Magna Charta by asking leading questions about how it reflected a love of liberty based on God's Word. **Introduce** background information about John Wycliffe and why he is called the "morning star of the Reformation." • Born in England • Became a clergyman • Understood each person needs a personal relationship with God • Believed the Bible was meant to be read by every person • Called the "morning star of the Reformation because he was the first to stir up the desire on the part of many to make available the Holy Scriptures in the language of the people • Translated the Bible from Latin into the English language **Discuss** the effect the power God's Word has in the hands of the individual. Acts 26:18 *Notebook Work* **Distribute** the prepared notebook page for the student to write or trace the title and to color the picture of John Wycliffe.	**Review** the Magna Charta by answering leading questions about how it reflected a love of liberty based on God's Word. **Listen** as the teacher presents information about John Wycliffe and why he is called the "morning star of the Reformation." **Reason** orally about the Bible in English and its place on the Christian history timeline by discussing the effect the power of God's Word has when it was in the hands of the individual. *Notebook Work* **Write** or trace the title on the notebook page and color the picture of John Wycliffe	• To review how the Magna Charta reflected a love of liberty based on God's Word • To appreciate Wycliffe's contributions on the Christian history timeline • To complete and file notebook work	

The Noah Plan Lessons Kindergarten © 2003 • Foundation for American Christian Education

129

TEACHING PLAN

Quarter Two

Week Nine

GEOGRAPHY

Preparation	Lesson	Student Work	Accomplishments	✓
Biblical Principle God created each continent distinct to fit His purpose and His plan. Psalm 115:16 **Leading Idea** The nature and character of God are revealed in the continent of North America. **Books** • Bible (KJ) • NPH&GG, 128, 141, 202–206 • T&L, 141–153, 156–157 • CHOC I, 4–5 **Supplies** • North American plants and animals • Old magazines (*National Geographic, Ranger Rick,* etc.) for cutting	**Continue** to guide the student to the Biblical Principle from the Leading Idea by reviewing the unique culture (customs, foods, languages, etc.) of North America. **Present** information about the plants and animals that are native to North America. **Display** pictures of the plants and animals that are native to North America. *Notebook Work* **Instruct** the student to find and cut pictures from magazines pertaining to North America's topography, culture, plants, and animals to be used in next week's lesson. **Instruct** the student to save these pictures in an envelope and put it into the pocket of his geography notebook.	**Review** by recalling unique aspects of the culture of various groups of people who live in North America. **Listen** as the teacher presents information about plants and animals that are native to North America. **View** pictures of some of the plants and animals that are native to North America. *Notebook Work* **Cut** pictures related to the topography, people, plants and animals of North America. • **Put** the pictures into an envelope. • **Place** the envelope into the pocket of your geography notebook.	• To recall unique aspects of North American culture • To learn about plants and animals native to North America • To view pictures of North American plants and animals • To complete and file notebook work	

Quarter Two

Week Nine

TEACHING PLAN

	Preparation	Lesson	Student Work	Accomplishments	✓

SCIENCE	**Biblical Principles**
	• God's Principle of Individuality
	• Unity with Diversity
	
	Leading Idea
	The parts of plants perform different functions, which contribute to the growth and development of the plant.
	
	Books
	• Bible (KJ)
	• Botany books (Library)
	• Encyclopedia
	
	Supplies
	• Diagram or chart of plants or trees
	• Potted plant for examination
	• Celery or carnations
	• Clear glasses
	• Food coloring and water
	• Notebook page to include:
	  • the title "Stem" for the student to write or trace
	  • a space for the student to draw a picture of a stalk of celery or a carnation to color
	• Colored pencils
		Review the Biblical Principles and the Leading Idea.
		
		Review roots by asking the student to recall their location and function and to name some root vegetables.
		
		Introduce the location and the function of the stem (or trunk):
		• to hold up the leaves and flowers
		• to carry water and food to the rest of the plant or tree
		Lead a discussion about how the stem (or trunk) is especially designed by God to carry out its purpose and relate it to the Principles of Individuality and Unity with Diversity.
		
		Provide activities to broaden the student's knowledge of stems (or trunks) and their function:
		• **Instruct** the student to locate and to examine the stem of a potted plant.
		
		• **Take** the student on a nature walk and instruct him to find the stems (or trunks) on trees, bushes, vines, and other plants.
		• **Instruct** the student to examine a stalk of celery that has been cut in half and locate the tubes that carry the water.
		• **Place** two freshly cut pieces of celery in jars of water and add a different color of food coloring to each one (blue & red work well); leave them overnight and observe what happens.
		• **Instruct** the student to make predictions about what will happen and draw conclusions after the experiment is complete.
		
		Notebook Work
		Distribute the prepared page for the student to write or trace the title and draw a picture of a stalk of celery or a carnation to color after the experiment is complete.
			Participate in a review of the Biblical Principles and Leading Idea.
			Recall the location and function of roots and name some root vegetables.
			Listen as the teacher presents the location and function of the stem (or trunk).
			
			Reason about how the stem (or trunk) is especially designed by God to carry out its specific purpose and relate to the Principles of Individuality and Unity with Diversity.
			Participate in activities to broaden your understanding of stems (or trunks) and their function:
			• **Locate** and examine the stem of a potted plant.
			• **Take** a nature walk and locate the stem (or trunk) on different types of plants.
			• **Examine** a stalk of celery that has been cut in half and locate the tubes that carry the water.
			• **Watch** as the teacher places celery stalks (or carnations) in glasses in which food coloring has been added.
			• **Make** predictions about what will happen and draw conclusions after the experiment is complete.
			
			Notebook Work
			Write or trace the title on the notebook page and draw a picture of a stalk of celery or a carnation and color the picture.
				• To restate the function of roots
				• To locate the stem of a plant
				• To make predictions
				• To draw conclusions
				• To complete and file notebook work	

The Noah Plan Lessons Kindergarten © 2003 • Foundation for American Christian Education

131

Quarter Three

All that I am, or hope to be
I owe to my angel mother.

> —Abraham Lincoln

The philosophy of the schoolroom in one generation will be the philosophy of government in the next.

> —Abraham Lincoln

Gareth R.

Zoology

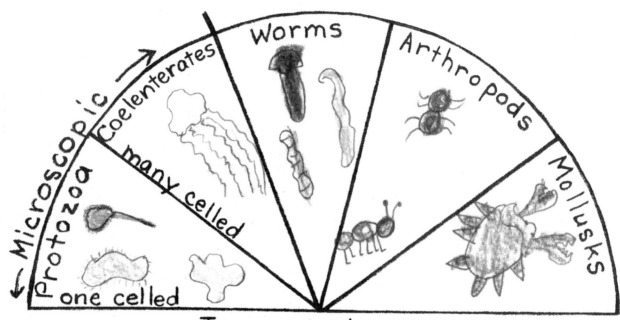
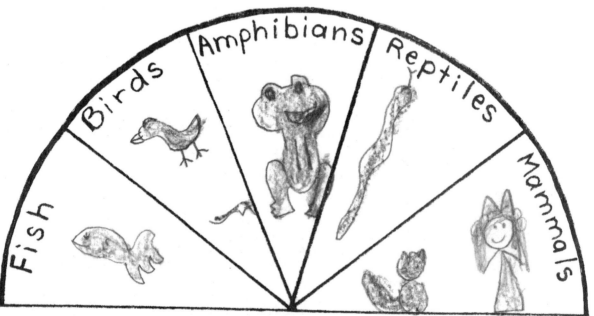

E. D.

Quarter Three Planning Sheet for Teaching Mathematics by Components

Teacher: Mr. Ricciardi   Grade Level: K

"Eye hath not seen nor ear heard, neither have entered into the heart of man, the things which God hath prepared for them that love him." 1 Corinthians 2:9

Week	Foundations	Numbers	Numeration/Notation	Measurement	Operations	Problem Solving	Summary of Principles
1 RSL 43–45	AHCC–Job AP–matching APU–partners CSP–notating GPI–even/odd numbers CFG–naming quantities	Even numbers Odd numbers Place value Quantities 1s, 10s, 100s	Reading abacus entries Recording entries Writing numbers	Rectangle Square Time	Addition Subtraction	Abacus entries Engineering Game Matching Practicing Rhyming Visualizing	The principles and leading ideas of mathematics are demonstrated in the lessons, and are continually clarified for the children as the year progresses. **Governmental Principles** *God's Principle of Individuality* (GPI) Mathematics measures 'how much.' Each number is a unique quantity. *Christian Self-Government* (CSG) Operations (+, −, ×, ÷) govern mathematics. *Christian Character* (AHCC) Mathematics demonstrates God's character. It is systematic, unchangeable, and orderly like God. *"Conscience...Sacred Property"* (CSP) Mathematics enables the individual to Biblically care for property. *Christian Form of Government* (CFG) Quantity is represented in various ways. *Local Self-Government* (LSG) Christ's government is planted into the heart of the student as the student deals with the operations (government) and processes of mathematics. *American Political Union* (APU) Numbers of like kind only may be added. **Subject Principles** *Associative Principle* (AP), NPMG, 104 *Distributive Principle* (DP), NPMG, 104 *Commutative Principle* (CP), NPMG, 104, 113 See **Sample Math Guide/Right-Start Coordination, Lessons, & Annual Schedule**, 269–281.
2 RSL 46–47	AHCC–Job APU–days/weeks AP–matching CSP–notating DP–partitioning GPI–quantities CFG–representation	Even numbers Odd numbers Place value	Reading abacus entries Recording numbers Writing equations	Time	Addition Subtraction	Abacus entries Completing equations Drawing Game Partitioning Practicing	
3 RSL 47–48	AHCC–Job CSP–notating GPI–even/odd	Quantities 1–10 Even numbers Odd numbers Place value	Reading numbers Writing numbers		Addition Multiplication by 10s Subtraction	Abacus entries Completing equations Games	
4 RSL 48–49	AHCC–Job APU–groups GPI–quantities CFG–representation	Place value Quantities 1s, 10s, 100s	Reading abacus entries Writing numbers	Money	Addition Division Multiplication by 10s Subtraction	Abacus entries Completing hundreds chart Constructing with place value cards Money problem	
5 RSL 49–50	AHCC–Job APU–associating AP–matching DP–partitioning GPI–quantities CFG–representation	Place value	Reading abacus entries Writing equations		Addition Multiplication by 2s, 10s Division	Abacus entries Completing equations Constructing Determining quantities Drawing Partitioning Practicing Word problems	
6 RSL 51–52	AHCC–Job CSP–notating DP–partitioning GPI–quantity CFG–graphing	Quantities	Reading numbers Writing equations Writing numbers		Add 1 to 2-digit numbers Multiplication by 2s, 10s Subtraction	Completing equations Determining quantity Graphing Partitioning Practicing Visualizing Word problems	
7 RSL 52–53	AHCC–Job APU–grouping CP–order CSG–patterning DP–partitioning GPI–even/odd numbers CFG–graphing	Even numbers Odd numbers	Reading abacus entries Writing equations Writing numbers		Add 2 to 2-digit numbers Multiplication by 5s Subtraction	Abacus entries Completing equations Determining quantities Graphing Partitioning Patterning Practicing Visualizing	
8 RSL 54–55	AP–matching CP–order DP–part/whole circle GPI–even/odd numbers	Even numbers Odd numbers Place value Quantities 1s, 10s	Reading abacus entries		Addition Combining 1s, 10s Multiplication Subtraction	Abacus entries Completing equations Determining quantities Games Graphing Making calculator entries Making place value entries Matching Practicing	
9 RSL 56–58	CSG–patterning GPI–even/odd numbers DP–partitioning CFG–naming quantities traditionally	Even/odd numbers Ordinal numbers Place value Quantities 1–50	Reading abacus entries Reading equations Traditional numbers Vocabulary Horizontal equations		Addition Multiplication by 5s, 10s Subtraction	Abacus entries Calculator entries Completing equations Constructing 10s & 1s Determining quantity Games Partitioning Patterning Practicing Visualizing Word problems	

The Noah Plan Lessons Kindergarten © 2003 • Foundation for American Christian Education

Quarter Three—Weekly Routines for Reading and English

COMPONENT	Monday	Tuesday	Wednesday	Thursday	Friday
FOUNDATIONS	**Teach** the appreciation of the written Word of God throughout the quarter: God wrote a book to commu-	nicate Himself to us, using language, spelling, and sentences.			
ORTHOGRAPHY Phonemic Awareness Instruction	**Teach** "Suggested Kindergarten Schedule," *Phonemic Awareness in Young Children*, 137–141. **Continue** to vary the repeated activities and increase complexity so that even the most advanced student	will continue to feel interested and challenged. **Reinforce** the mastery of phonograms 1–54 with oral review procedures, *Writing Road to Reading*, 39–40.		**Reproduce** the black line master to use in planning and monitoring visits and revisits to the various activities, *Phonemic Awareness in Young Children*, 142–43.	
Penmanship	**Continue** to master letter formation as phonograms are reviewed.		**Continue** to practice capital letter formation, *The Writing Road to Reading*, 29–30.	**Reinforce** letter formation as phonograms are dictated.	
Spelling	**Reinforce** the mastery of phonograms 1–54 with written review procedures, *Writing Road to Reading*, 41–42. **Mix** and test between 8 and 16 phonograms. **Continue** the Extended Ayers List, *The Writing Road to Reading*, 252–262. **Refer** to Scope and Sequence objectives in *The Writing Road to Reading*, 444. **Administer** the Morrison-McCall Spelling Scale Test to determine the student's progress at the beginning of the quarter, *Spalding Spelling Assessment Manual*, 19. **See** "Spelling Assessment Procedures" in *Spalding Spelling Assessment Manual*, 7–13. **Assign** homework: Write first five words 3x and use in oral sentences.		**Continue** *Spelling Dictation Procedure* with the next five words, *The Writing Road to Reading*, 48–53. **Read** spelling words orally. **Elicit** oral sentences from student. **Write** sentences from oral discussion on the chalkboard. (Student copies and may illustrate.) **Assign** homework: Write five words 3x and use in oral sentences.	**Continue** to review previously learned phonograms by decoding (reading) and encoding (writing). **Continue** *Spelling Dictation Procedure.* **Write** the week's words in a practice test. **Assign** homework: Study for test.	**Continue** to review previously learned phonograms by decoding (reading) and encoding (writing). **Test** spelling words at the end of the week; do not require the markings for test, *Writing Road to Reading*, 85.
COMPOSITION	**Practice** good verbal syntax using words correctly in sentences in conversation and discussion. **Write** statements together then independently. This activity should be done several times a week in any subject.	**Write** a group paragraph on the board after discussing the idea or topic (pre-writing), thinking of a topic sentence together (drafting), and forming good supporting	sentences (revising). This exercise should be done several times throughout the quarter, NPEG, 244–245.		

Quarter Three—Weekly Routines for Reading and English (continued)

Component	Monday	Tuesday	Wednesday	Thursday	Friday
Syntax	Continue teaching the sentence by identifying the subjects and verbs as naming and action words, NPEG, 142–47. Teach the verb as the action word in the sentence by	the word that shows action in the sentence. Teach the subject as the 'doer' of the action. Practice until the student can identify the verb and the subject. Encourage the use of complete sentences in daily speaking and in writing.		Demonstrate the sentence by giving examples of complete thoughts in well-phrased sentences from the literature and Bible. Reinforce the use of simple initial capitalization and end punctuation.	
Etymology	Continue to teach syllables and the ability to identify the syllables of any word, NPRG, 111. Teach precise meanings of words. Show the dictio-		nary and read the definition aloud to impart precise meaning. Continue enjoying words that rhyme, describe, and	many new words from Bible, literature, science, history, and geography. Use daily *Phonemic Awareness in Young Children*, 137–141.	
Reading Phonetic instruction	Practice phonograms using multi-sensory instruction—the Spalding Method. *The Writing Road to Reading*, 6, 39–42.		This practice can be done during the orthography segment.		
Oral Reading	Model fluent reading by reading selected passages aloud simultaneously in a group—choral reading. Provide opportunities for student-adult reading, helping word recognition and providing feedback. Read aloud spelling words from the board and also from the *cahier* (spelling notebook). Introduce partner reading through teacher modeling. The teacher reads aloud as the student follows the text. Then pair		the student with a more fluent reader or pair with a less fluent reader. Another option is to pair students who read at the same level to reread a story for which they have received instruction during a teacher-guided part of the lesson. Assign oral reading homework in supplementary readers (home readers) to be returned daily, NPRG 71. See suggested list of books in NPLK.		Read aloud selected passages from the kindergarten literature curriculum, NPLG, 8–9.
Bible as Reader	Read aloud passages from *The Early Reader's Bible* to correspond to Bible lessons in NPLK. For oral reading methods see NPRG, 66, 97.				
Comprehension	Continue using explicit comprehension instruction as prescribed in "The Reading Lesson," *The Writing Road to Reading*, 121–147. A student who is able to analyze his own thinking, while listening and reading, increases his comprehension and thereby signifi-		cantly improves his performance. During lessons on mental actions students learn how to consciously check their understanding of words, phrases, and sentences, make connections between prior knowledge and the text; and predict the type of writing,		i.e., narrative or informative, *The Comprehension Connection—User's Guide for McCall-Harby* (Spalding Starter Kit for K–2).

Quarter Three
Kindergarten Reading Instruction Supplement

COMPREHENSIVE INSTRUCTION STRATEGIES

PRINCIPLE AND LEADING IDEAS
God gave man the ability to learn to read and to reason:
- *Understanding the process of learning helps my ability to learn.*
- *Reformatting and categorizing information into new forms promotes flexible thinking.*
- *Mastering reading strategies encourages independent learning.*

Fact: Research has shown that instruction in comprehension can help students understand what they read, remember what they read, and communicate with others. Good readers need to have a purpose for reading and they need to be actively involved in the process. Research has shown that instruction in comprehension can help students understand what they read, remember what they read, and communicate with others. (*Put Reading First*, 49)

What are the ways of teaching and learning comprehension? Six strategies have been identified to have a firm scientific basis for improving comprehension.

1. Monitoring comprehension
    a. The student is taught to think about his thinking (metacognition) and take control over his understanding of the text. Before reading he clarifies his understanding by checking words or concepts that are not clear. He previews the text and predicts what may happen.
    b. During reading the student monitors his understanding and adjusts his speed to the difficulty of the text.
    c. After reading he summarizes, checks his understanding, and reformats the information into new forms like lists, outlines, or paraphrases.
2. Using graphic and semantic organizers
    a. Graphic organizers picture concepts and interrelationships between words and ideas. They may be called maps, webs, graphs, charts, frames, or clusters. Semantic organizers are graphic organizers that look somewhat like a spider web. Lines connect a central concept to a variety of related ideas and events. (*Put Reading First*, 50)
    b. Organizers help a student to focus on what he is reading, to visually represent relationships, and to assist in writing a summary of his reading and thinking.
3. Answering questions
    a. Research shows that teacher questioning strongly supports and advances students' learning. In Principle Approach teaching the teacher guides the student's thinking with leading questions calling upon reflective learning.

4. Generating questions
    a. "Teaching students to ask their own questions improves their active processing of text and their comprehension." (*Put Reading First*, 50)
5. Recognizing story structure
    a. "Story structure refers to the way the content and events of a story are organized into a plot." (*Put Reading First*, 50)
    b. Story maps are graphic organizers used to detail the parts of a narrative and the events of the story. In Principle Approach teaching the student also defines the Biblical principle or foundational premise. What is God's word teaching us?
6. Summarizing
    a. Summarizing helps a student to synthesize the important ideas in the text and to remember what he has read.

Why is comprehension important? "Comprehension is the reason for reading. If readers can read the words but do not understand what they are reading they are not really reading." (*Put Reading First*, 48)

When should instruction begin? Instruction begins with parents and teacher reading aloud to a child and guiding his thinking from the beginning, rather than waiting until the child is decoding on his own. Instruction at all grade levels needs to emphasize the idea that reading is a process of making sense out of text, or constructing meaning.

Which methods of instruction are most effective? "Effective comprehension strategy instruction is explicit, or direct." Research shows that explicit teaching techniques are particularly effective for comprehension strategy instruction. In explicit instruction, teachers tell readers why and when they should use strategies, what strategies to use, and how to apply them. The steps of explicit instruction typically include direct explanation, teacher modeling ("thinking aloud"), guided practice, and application. (*Put Reading First*, 53)

- **Direct explanation.** The teacher explains to the student why the strategy helps comprehension and when to apply the strategy.
- **Modeling.** The teacher models, or demonstrates, how to apply the strategy, usually by 'thinking aloud' while reading the text that the students are using.
- **Guided practice.** The teacher guides and assists students as they learn how and when to apply the strategy.
- **Application.** The teacher helps students practice the strategy until they can apply it independently."

"Effective comprehension strategy instruction can be accomplished through cooperative learning." Students working as partners or in small groups with clearly defined tasks help each other to learn and apply comprehension strategies. Teachers monitor the progress of students." (*Ibid.*, 54)

"**Effective instruction helps readers use comprehension strategies flexibly and in combination.** . . . Multiple-strategy instruction teaches students how to use strategies flexibly as they are needed to assist their comprehension (*Ibid.*). In addition to the mental actions strategy there is another multiple-strategy called "reciprocal teaching," the teacher and students work together so that the students learn four comprehension strategies:

- asking questions about the text they are reading
- summarizing parts of the text
- clarifying words and sentences they don't understand
- predicting what might occur next in the text." (*Ibid.*)

What materials are suggested?

Put Reading First: The Research Building Blocks for Teaching Children to Read, September, 2001. Copies available from National Institute for Literacy at ED Pubs, PO Box 1398, Jessup, MD 20794-1398. Phone 1-800-228-8813; Fax 301-430-1244. To download go to the National Institute for Literacy website at www.nifl.gov.

The Writing Road to Reading: The Spalding Method for Teaching Speech, Spelling, Writing, and Reading, 5th Edition, 2003.

The Noah Plan Reading Curriculum Guide, Martha Shirley. San Francisco, F.A.C.E., 1997.

Quarter Three

Week One

TEACHING PLAN

Preparation	Lesson	Student Work	Accomplishments	✓
Biblical Principle God invites us to joyfully enter into His presence.	**Introduce** the memory verse: "Enter into his gates with thanksgiving, and into his courts with praise. . ." Psalm 100:4	**Listen** as the teacher reads aloud and discusses the memory verse.	• To learn and recite the memory verse • To learn new vocabulary • To sing praises to God • To thank God for His goodness • To complete and file notebook work	
Leading Idea Singing and giving thanks are ways to praise God.	• **Define** unfamiliar vocabulary. • **Practice** daily the memory verse with the student for his recitation on Friday.	• **Discuss** unfamiliar vocabulary. • **Practice** and learn the memory verse for recitation on Friday.		
	Guide the student to the Biblical Principle from the Leading Idea by reading aloud Psalm 100 and identifying it as a psalm of praise and thanks to God.	**Listen** as the teacher reads aloud Psalm 100 and identifies it as a psalm of praise and thanks to God.		
Books • Bible (KJ) • Webster's 1828 *Dictionary*	• **Discuss** the following: · People should give thanks to God. · Singing and praising God brings peace and calm to our lives. · God loves to hear our praises. · We can tell God exactly how we feel. · God cares and listens. · Singing and praising God are ways of thanking Him for His goodness.	**Discuss** the following: • People should give thanks to God. • Singing and praising God brings peace and calm to our lives. • God loves to hear our praises. • We can tell God exactly how we feel. • God cares and listens. • Singing praises to God is a way of thanking Him for His goodness.		
Supplies • Notebook page to include: · the title "Thanking God" for the student to write or trace · a space for the student to draw and to color a picture of himself praising God	**Lead** the student in singing a few praise songs. **Ask** the student how he felt after singing praises to God. **Encourage** the student to observe the things around him and to name the things for which he is most thankful.	**Sing** a few praise songs with the teacher. **Discuss** how you felt after singing praises to God. **Look** around you and name the things for which you are most thankful.		
	Notebook Work **Distribute** the prepared notebook page for the student to write or trace the title and to draw and color a picture of himself praising God.	*Notebook Work* **Write** or trace the title and draw and color a picture of yourself praising God.		
BAR—Bible As Reader **Books** • Bible (KJ) • NPRG	**BAR—Bible As Reader** A Psalm of Praise: Psalm 100, KJV (See Weekly Routines for Reading and English.)	**BAR—Bible As Reader** (See Weekly Routines for Reading and English.)		

BIBLE

The Noah Plan Lessons Kindergarten © 2003 • Foundation for American Christian Education

TEACHING PLAN

Week One   Quarter Three

Preparation	Lesson	Student Work	Accomplishments	✓

Biblical Principles
• God's Principle of Individuality
• Unity with Diversity
 	
Leading Idea
Fables and myths are a type of literature that "give insight on the ideas and ideals of many nations."
Rosalie J. Slater
 	
Books
• Bible (KJ)
• Webster's 1828 *Dictionary*
• NPLG, 8–9, 100–103
• A collection of *Aesop's Fables*
 	
Supplies
• Notebook page to include:
  • the title "Aesop's Fables"
  • a picture to color
• Notebook page for each fable studied to include:
  • the title of the fable
  • a picture or space for the student to illustrate the fable
  • the moral of the fable
	Guide the student to the Biblical Principles from the Leading Idea.
	• **Introduce** a brief biography of Aesop, his place on the Christian history timeline, key events in his life, and discuss.
	• **Define** fable and moral.
	• **Lead** a discussion about the oral tradition of folk tales and the fact that animals are the protagonists in these tales. (A protagonist is the leading character in the story about which the action centers.)
	
	• **Read** several fables.
	
	• **Ask** the student to identify the setting and the characters and to state the moral of the lesson in their own words.
	
	Notebook Work
	Distribute the prepared notebook page for the student to write or trace the title "Aesop's Fables" and to color.
	Distribute the prepared notebook page of each fable studied for the student:
	• to write or trace the title
	• to color the picture or illustration
	• to record the moral of fable
		Participate in a discussion of the Biblical Principles and Leading Idea.
		Listen as the teacher presents a brief biography of Aesop and the definition of a fable and moral.
		
		Participate in a discussion about key events in Aesop's life, history during that time period, how oral tradition preserved folk tales through the generations, and why animals are the protagonists in these tales.
		Listen as the teacher reads several fables.
		
		Identify the setting and the characters in each story and be ready to state the moral of the lesson in your own words.
		
		Notebook Work
		Write or trace the title "Aesop's Fables" on the prepared notebook page and color it.
		Write or trace the title for each fable studied.
		• **Color** the picture or draw an illustration for each fable.
		• **Record** the moral for each fable.
		File the notebook page for each illustrated fable behind the title page "Aesop's Fables."
			• To learn new vocabulary—fable and moral
			• To identify setting and characters in fables
			• To state the moral of the story
			• To complete and file notebook work	

LITERATURE

TEACHING PLAN

Week One — Quarter Three

HISTORY

Preparation	Lesson	Student Work	Accomplishments
Biblical Principle "Conscience Is the Most Sacred of All Property."	**Introduce** the Principle "Conscience Is the Most Sacred of All Property."		• To recite the poem "I Am God's Property"
Leading Idea Our conscience is our guide to right and wrong.	• **Review** by having the student recite "I Am God's Property."	**Review** by reciting the poem "I Am God's Property."	• To understand conscience is the most sacred of all property you own
Books • Bible (KJ) • Webster's 1828 *Dictionary* • NPH&GG, 8–9, 68–69 • NPSDS, Providential History, Principles • T&L, 225–232 • CHOC I, 248A, 261	• **Read** aloud and discuss Ephesians 2:10. • **Review** the definition of property. • **Discuss** how each individual is God's property because He made us.	**Listen** as the teacher reads aloud Ephesians 2:10. • **Review** the definition of property. • **Discuss** how each individual is God's property by right of Creation.	• To understand voluntary consent • To complete and file notebook work
	• **Define** internal and external and lead a discussion about property being internal (conscience) and external (toys, clothes, bed, etc.)	**Define** internal and external and identify property being internal and external.	
Supplies • Notebook page to include:	• **Ask** the student leading questions about property. • What does it mean to be God's property? • What has God entrusted into my care? • What are the rights and responsibilities involved? (T&L, 230–32) • How can we be good stewards of our property?	**Answer** leading questions about what it means to be God's property and what rights and responsibilities we have in regard to property. • What does it mean to be God's property? • What has God entrusted into my care? • What are the rights and responsibilities involved? • How can we be good stewards of our property?	
• the title "Conscience Is the Most Sacred of All Property" for the student to write or trace • a copy of the poem "I Am God's Property" • a space for the student to draw a picture	• **Define** conscience. • **Discuss** with the student that our conscience is the most sacred of all property because God gave it to us to help us decide right from wrong. • **Ask** the student to tell how he has been a good steward of his conscience.	**Listen** as the teacher defines conscience and discusses the value and sacredness of our conscience.	
	Introduce voluntary consent. • **Define** voluntary consent. • **Read** aloud Luke 22:42. • **Discuss** how important it is to be obedient to God's will. • **Discuss** how important it is for an individual to give his consent to do what he knows is right and not what is wrong.	**Answer** the question, "How can you be a good steward of your conscience?" **Listen** as the teacher defines voluntary consent. **Listen** as the teacher reads aloud Luke 22:42 and discusses voluntary consent as doing what you know is right, and being obedient to God's will.	
	HISTORY—*Notebook Work* (continued on page 144)	**HISTORY**—*Notebook Work* (continued on page 144)	

The Noah Plan Lessons Kindergarten © 2003 • Foundation for American Christian Education

TEACHING PLAN

Quarter Three

Week One

HISTORY (continued)

Preparation	Lesson	Student Work	Accomplishments	✓
	Notebook Work **Distribute** the prepared notebook page for the student to write or trace the title and to draw a picture of something that demonstrates how he has been a good steward of his conscience underneath the poem.	*Notebook Work* **Write** or trace the title on the notebook page and draw a picture of something that demonstrates how you have been a good steward of your conscience on the notebook page underneath the poem.		

Week One

Quarter Three

TEACHING PLAN

	Preparation	Lesson	Student Work	Accomplishments	✓

GEOGRAPHY	**Biblical Principle**
	God created each continent distinct to fit His purpose and His plan. Psalm 115:16
	
	Leading Idea
	The nature and character of God are revealed in the continent of North America.
	
	Books
	• Bible (KJ)
	• NPH&GG, 128, 148–149, 201–206
	• T&L, 141–153, 156–157
	
	Supplies
	• Notebook page to include:
	  · the title "North America's Individuality" for the student to write or trace
	  · a space to glue pictures of North America
	• Simple outline map of North America (Use maps from NPH&GG, 230–231)
	• Overhead projector if available
	• Map standard
	• Colored pencils
		Continue to guide the student to the Biblical Principle from the Leading Idea.
		• **Review** by naming the plants and animals that are unique to North America.
		<div align="center">OR</div>• **Ask** the student to choose those plants and animals native to North America from assorted pictures.
		Lead the student to identify how the things learned about North America are an example of God's Principle of Individuality.
		
		Notebook Work
		Distribute the prepared outline map of North America for the student to color according to the map standard.
		Model the map standard on an overhead projector, chalkboard, etc.
		Distribute the prepared notebook page for the student to write or trace the title.
		
		Instruct the student to glue onto the notebook page the pictures of North America.
		<div align="center">OR</div>**Save** these pictures for a group project in the fourth quarter.
			Review by recalling plants and animals from memory or by selecting those native to North America from assorted pictures.
			
			Reason and relate about how the things learned about North America are an example of God's Principle of Individuality.
			
			Notebook Work
			Color the map of North America according to the map standard for physical maps.
			
			Distribute the prepared notebook page for the student to write or trace the title.
			Glue the pictures related to North America that were cut and saved from last week onto the prepared notebook page.
			<div align="center">OR</div>**Save** these pictures for a group project in the fourth quarter.
				• To recall unique plants and animals of North America
				• To reason and relate knowledge of North America to God's Principle of Individuality
				• To complete and file notebook work	

The Noah Plan Lessons Kindergarten © 2003 • Foundation for American Christian Education   145

TEACHING PLAN

Week One   Quarter Three

Preparation	Lesson	Student Work	Accomplishments
Biblical Principles • God's Principle of Individuality • Unity with Diversity	**Review** the Biblical Principles and the Leading Idea. **Review** stems by asking the student to recall their location and function.	**Participate** in a review of the Biblical Principles and Leading Idea. **Recall** the location and function of stems.	• To review the function of stems • To locate the leaves on a plant • To make leaf rubbings • To sort leaves • To taste edible leaves • To complete and file notebook work
Leading Idea The parts of plants perform different functions, which contribute to the growth and development of the plant.	**Introduce** the location and the function of the leaves: to make food for the plant. **Lead** a discussion about how different types of leaves illustrate the Principles of Individuality and Unity with Diversity and how leaves are especially designed by God to carry out their purpose.	**Listen** as the teacher presents the location and function of the leaves. **Reason** about how different types of leaves illustrate the Principles of Individuality and Unity with Diversity and how leaves are especially designed by God to carry out their specific purpose.	
Books • Bible (KJ) • Botany books (Library) • Book about leaves (Library) • Encyclopedia **Supplies** • Diagram or chart of plants or trees • A potted plant for examination • Plain paper and crayons for leaf rubbings • Edible leaves for tasting • Prepared notebook page	**Provide** activities to broaden the student's knowledge of leaves and their function. • **Instruct** the student to locate and examine the leaves of a potted plant. • **Take** the student on a leaf-collecting walk and help him to identify different types of leaves. • **Make** leaf rubbings. • **Sort** them by size, color or shape. • **Bring** several types of edible leaves such as lettuce, parsley, cabbage, spinach, watercress, etc. for the student to taste.	**Participate** in activities to broaden your understanding of leaves and their function: • **Locate** and examine the leaves of a potted plant. • **Take** a leaf-collecting walk and identify different types of leaves. • **Make** leaf rubbings • **Sort** the leaves by color, shape, or size. • **Taste** several types of edible leaves.	
	Notebook Work **Distribute** the prepared notebook page for the student to write or trace the title and to add leaf rubbings or samples of real leaves. Prepared notebook page to include: • the title "Leaves" for the student to write or trace • a space for the student to add a leaf rubbing or samples of real leaves	*Notebook Work* **Write** or trace the title on the notebook page and add leaf rubbings or samples of real leaves.	

SCIENCE

146   The Noah Plan Lessons Kindergarten © 2003 • Foundation for American Christian Education

Week Two

Quarter Three

TEACHING PLAN

	Preparation	Lesson	Student Work	Accomplishments	✓
BIBLE	**Biblical Principle** We can trust God to care for us. **Leading Idea** God is a shepherd and a guide for us. **Books** • Bible (KJ) • Webster's 1828 *Dictionary* **Supplies** • Notebook page to include: 　• the title "God, Our Shepherd" for the student to write or trace 　• a space for the student to draw and color a picture of God, our Shepherd **BAR** • Bible (KJ) • NPRG	**Introduce** the memory verse. Psalm 23:1 • **Read** aloud and discuss the memory verse. • **Define** unfamiliar vocabulary. • **Practice** daily the memory verse with the student for his recitation on Friday. **Guide** the student to the Biblical Principle from the Leading Idea by reading aloud Psalm 23 and discussing the following: • God is our Shepherd. • A shepherd takes care of the sheep. • God takes care of us. • We have peace and joy when we allow God, our Shepherd, to guide us. • We can trust God at all times to take care of us. *Notebook Work* **Distribute** the prepared notebook page for the student to write or trace the title and to draw and color the picture of God, our shepherd. **BAR** Psalm 23, "A Psalm of David" (See Weekly Routines for Reading and English.)	**Listen** as the teacher reads aloud and discusses the memory verse. • **Discuss** unfamiliar vocabulary. • **Practice** and learn the memory verse for recitation on Friday. **Listen** as the teacher reads aloud Psalm 23, and discusses the following: • God is our Shepherd. • A shepherd takes care of the sheep. • God takes care of us. • We have peace and joy when we allow God, our shepherd, to guide us. • We can trust God at all times to take care of us. *Notebook Work* **Write** or trace the title on the notebook page and draw and color the picture of God, our Shepherd. **BAR** (See Weekly Routines for Reading and English.)	• To learn and recite the memory verse • To learn new vocabulary • To recognize God is our Shepherd and our guide • To feel the peace and joy that comes from God • To understand that we can trust God to take care of us • To complete and file notebook page	

The Noah Plan Lessons Kindergarten © 2003 • Foundation for American Christian Education　　147

Week Two

TEACHING PLAN

Quarter Three

	Preparation	Lesson	Student Work	Accomplishments	✓

LITERATURE	**Biblical Principles**
	• God's Principle of Individuality
	• Unity with Diversity
	
	Leading Idea
	Fables and myths are a type of literature that "give insight on the ideas and ideals of many nations."
	Rosalie J. Slater
	
	Books
	• Bible (KJ)
	• Webster's 1828 *Dictionary*
	• NPLG, 8–9, 100–103
	• *Uncle Remus Stories*, Joel Harris
	
	Supplies
	• Notebook page to include:
	  • the title "Uncle Remus" for the student to write or trace
	  • a space to draw or paste a picture to color
	• Notebook page for each character to include:
	  • character name for the student to write or trace
	  • a picture or space for the student to illustrate and to color
	• Colored pencils
		Review the Biblical Principles and Leading Idea.
		
		Introduce a brief biography of Joel Chandler Harris as the author of the *Uncle Remus Stories*, and identify:
		• his place on the timeline
		• the historical background of the time period
		• the definition of dialect
		Discuss oral tradition and how it preserved fables and myths.
		
		Discuss how the use of dialect is a reflection of the author's individual style and reinforces the oral tradition that preserved these myths.
		
		Introduce Uncle Remus as the narrator of these tales.
		Read aloud several of the stories.
		
		Instruct the student to identify the setting and the characters.
		Guide the student to reason and to relate by answering questions about the conflict in each story and how it is resolved.
		
		Notebook Work
		Distribute the prepared notebook page for the student to write or trace the title "Uncle Remus" and to color a picture.
		
		Distribute the prepared character pages for the student to write or trace the character's name and to color a picture of the character.
			Participate in a review of the Biblical Principles and Leading Idea.
			Listen as the teacher:
			• Gives biographical information about Joel Chandler Harris
			• Locates his place on the Christian history timeline.
			• Identifies the historical background of the time period.
			• Defines dialect.
			Participate in a review and a discussion about oral tradition and how it preserved fables and myths.
			Observe how the use of dialect is a reflection of the author's individual style and reinforces the idea of oral tradition.
			
			Listen as the teacher introduces Uncle Remus as the narrator of these tales and reads aloud selected Uncle Remus stories.
			
			Discuss the setting and the characters and answer questions about the conflict in each story and how it is resolved.
			
			Notebook Work
			Write or trace the title "Uncle Remus" on the notebook page and illustrate or color a picture on it.
			Write or trace the name of each character on the notebook page and illustrate or color the provided picture.
				• To learn new vocabulary—dialect, tradition
				• Learn about the author, Joel Chandler Harris
				• To identify the setting and characters in *Uncle Remus Stories*
				• To complete and file notebook work	

148   The Noah Plan Lessons Kindergarten © 2003 • Foundation for American Christian Education

Week Two
Quarter Three

TEACHING PLAN

HISTORY

Preparation

Biblical Principle
God launches events through individuals He has providentially called and prepared for His Gospel purpose.

Leading Idea
Christopher Columbus was a man led by Christ.

Books
- Bible (KJ)
- NPH&GG, 8–9, 79, & Appendix 340 for additional books on Columbus
- NPSDS, Providential History, Links
- *America's Providential History*, Beliles and McDowell, 45–46
- Teacher Guide: *Columbus*, F.A.C.E.
- *Columbus*, d'Aulaire

Supplies
- Classroom world map
- Simple map of Italy
- Colored pencils
- Christian history timeline for classroom display (The Noah Plan Wall Timeline, F.A.C.E.)

Lesson

- **Review** the Biblical Principle and Leading Idea.

- **Continue** the study of the Chain of Christianity and its westward move through individuals and nations by introducing Christopher Columbus.
  - **Locate** the sixth link on the classroom Christian history timeline.

- **Discuss** background information about the fifteenth century, the time in which Columbus lived.
  - Only a few people could read.
  - Some thought the world was flat.
  - The ocean was known as the "sea of darkness."

- **Locate** Genoa, Italy (Columbus's birthplace) and the Mediterranean Sea on the classroom world map.

- **Discuss** background information about the geographic individuality of Italy:
  - Shaped like a boot
  - Peninsula (surrounded on three sides by water) extends into the Mediterranean Sea
  - Mountainous
  - Good farm land

- **Read** aloud selected passages from *Columbus*, d'Aulaire. (Teacher Guide: *Christopher Columbus*, F.A.C.E., is a valuable resource for teaching this link.)

Notebook Work

Instruct the student to find the sixth link and color the representative picture on their individual timeline as you point it out on the classroom Christian history timeline. **Distribute** the map of Italy and instruct the student to color the map according to the map standard.

Student Work

- **Participate** in a review of the Biblical Principle and Leading Idea.
- **Locate** the sixth link on the classroom Christian history timeline.

- **Listen** as the teacher discusses background information about the fifteenth century:
  - Only a few people could read.
  - Some thought the world was flat.
  - The ocean was called the "sea of darkness."

- **Locate** Genoa, Italy (Columbus's birthplace) and the Mediterranean Sea on the classroom world map.

- **Listen** as the teacher discusses background information about the geographic individuality of Italy:
  - Shaped like a boot
  - Peninsula (surrounded on three sides by water) extends into the Mediterranean Sea
  - Mountainous
  - Good farm land

- **Listen** as the teacher reads aloud selected passages from *Columbus*, d'Aulaire.

Notebook Work

Locate and color the sixth link on the notebook copy of the Christian history timeline.
Color the map of Italy according to the map standard.

Accomplishments

- To identify Columbus as the sixth link on the Christian history timeline
- To learn about the fifteenth century
- To learn the individuality of Italy
- To complete and file notebook work

The Noah Plan Lessons Kindergarten © 2003 • Foundation for American Christian Education

Week Two

Quarter Three

TEACHING PLAN

Preparation	Lesson	Student Work	Accomplishments	✓
Biblical Principle God created each continent distinct to fit His purpose and His plan. Psalm 115:16	**Guide** the student to the Biblical Principle from the Leading Idea. • **Introduce** the location and geographic features that contribute to South America being called the "continent of vegetation."	**Listen**, observe, and participate in the discussion as the teacher: • **Locates** South America on the classroom world map, globe, and in your atlas.	• To learn about the location and individuality of South America • To visualize South America • To complete and file notebook work	
Leading Idea The nature and character of God are revealed in the continent of South America.	• **Present** information about the natural resources and climate that contribute to the individuality of South America. • **Display** pictures of various regions in South America.	• **Presents** information about why this continent is called the "continent of vegetation." • **Identifies** the geographic features that contribute to its individuality. **View** pictures of different regions in South America.		
Books • Bible (KJ) • NPH&GG, 128, 207–211 • T&L, 141–153, 156–157	*Notebook Work* **Distribute** EMBG, Volume 3:4 and instruct the student in completing the page.	*Notebook Work* **Color** and complete the notebook page.		
Supplies • World map and globe • Student atlas • Colored pencils • Pictures of different regions of South America • EMBG, Volume 3:4				

GEOGRAPHY

150   The Noah Plan Lessons Kindergarten © 2003 • Foundation for American Christian Education

Week Two

Quarter Three

TEACHING PLAN

	Preparation	Lesson	Student Work	Accomplishments	✓

SCIENCE	**Biblical Principles**
	• God's Principle of Individuality
	• Unity with Diversity
	
	Leading Idea
	The parts of plants perform different functions, which contribute to the growth and development of the plant.
	
	Books
	• Bible (KJ)
	• Botany books (Library)
	• Encyclopedia
	
	Supplies
	• Diagram or chart of plants or trees
	• A potted plant for examination
	• Wax or contact paper for preserving pressed flowers
	• Edible flowers such as broccoli or cauliflower
	• Notebook page to include:
	  • the title "Flowers" for the student to write or trace
	  • a space for the student to draw and color a flower
	• Colored pencils
		Review the Biblical Principles and Leading Idea.
		
		Review leaves by asking the student to recall their location and function.
		
		Introduce the function of the flowers: to produce seeds.
		
		Lead a discussion about how the variety of flowers illustrates the Principles of Individuality and Unity with Diversity and how flowers are especially designed by God to carry out their purpose.
		
		Provide activities to broaden the student's knowledge of flowers and their function:
		
		• **Instruct** the student to locate and examine the flowers of a potted plant.
		• **Take** the student on a walk to collect flowers or ask him to bring flowers from home (sort them by color or press them and make collages or glue them on the notebook page).
		• **Bring** edible flowers such as broccoli or cauliflower for the student to taste.
		
		Notebook Work
		Distribute the prepared notebook page for the student to write or trace the title and to draw and color the picture.
			Participate in a review of the Biblical Principles and Leading Idea.
			Recall the location and function of leaves.
			
			Listen as the teacher presents the location and function of the flowers.
			Reason about how different types of flowers illustrate the Principles of Individuality and Unity with Diversity and how flowers are especially designed by God to carry out their specific purpose.
			Participate in activities to broaden your understanding of flowers and their function:
			
			• **Examine** the flowers of a potted plant.
			• **Take** a flower collecting walk or bring a flower from home (sort them by color or press them for a collage or glue to a notebook page).
			• **Taste** edible flowers such as broccoli and cauliflower.
			
			Notebook Work
			Write or trace the title on the notebook page and draw and color a picture of a flower.
				• To restate the function of leaves
				• To locate the flowers on a plant
				• To learn the function of flowers
				• To press flowers
				• To sort flowers
				• To taste edible flowers
				• To complete and file notebook work	

The Noah Plan Lessons Kindergarten © 2003 • Foundation for American Christian Education

TEACHING PLAN

Quarter Three

Week Three

	Preparation	Lesson	Student Work	Accomplishments
BIBLE	**Bible Principle** God helps us to live wisely. **Leading Idea** Proverbs helps us to understand wise sayings. **Books** • Bible (KJ) • Webster's 1828 *Dictionary* **Supplies** • Select a simple Proverb for the student to record. Then, prepare the notebook page accordingly. • Notebook page to include: • the title "A Proverb of Solomon" for the student to write or trace • a space for the student to illustrate the Proverb and color the picture **BAR** • Bible (KJ), Proverbs • NPRG	**Introduce** the memory verse. Proverbs 1:7 • **Read** aloud and discuss the memory verse. • **Define** unfamiliar vocabulary. • **Practice** daily the memory verse with the student for his recitation on Friday. **Guide** the student to the Biblical Principle from the Leading Idea. • **Introduce** the book of Proverbs and discusses the following: · It was written by Solomon, the wisest man who ever lived. · It is a book of wise sayings. · It is a book of answers about every day life. · It is a book that tells us how we should act. • **Read** aloud and discuss selected proverbs the student would understand: · Proverbs 3:5–6 · Proverbs 4:1 · Proverbs 17:22 · Proverbs 23:22 *Notebook Work* **Distribute** the notebook page for the student to write or trace the title and to illustrate the Proverb and color the picture. **BAR** **Select** verses to teach how one chooses wisdom versus foolish behavior. (Suggestion: Solomon's proverbs in Proverbs 10.) (See Weekly Routines for Reading and English.)	**Listen** as the teacher reads aloud and discusses the memory verse. • **Discuss** unfamiliar vocabulary. • **Practice** and learn the memory verse for recitation on Friday. • **Listen** as the teacher introduces the book of Proverbs and discusses the following: · Solomon, the wisest man who ever lived, wrote Proverbs. · It is a book of wise sayings. · It is a book of answers about every day life. · It is a book that tells us how we should act. • **Participate** in a discussion as the teacher reads aloud selected proverbs: · Proverbs 3:5–6 · Proverbs 4:1 · Proverbs 17:22 · Proverbs 23:22 *Notebook Work* **Write** or trace the title and illustrate the Proverb and color the picture. **BAR** (See Weekly Routines for Reading and English.)	• To learn and recite the memory verse • To learn new vocabulary • To obey your parents • To study the scriptures • To be diligent in your work • To help others in your family • To complete and file notebook work

152   The Noah Plan Lessons Kindergarten © 2003 • Foundation for American Christian Education

Week Three

Quarter Three

TEACHING PLAN

	Preparation	Lesson	Student Work	Accomplishments	✓
LITERATURE	**Biblical Principles** • God's Principle of Individuality • Unity with Diversity **Leading Idea** Teaching literature is teaching character and teaching life. **Books** • Bible (KJ) • NPLG, 8–9, 135–138 • *Bambi*, Felix Salten **Supplies** • Chalkboard or charts to model notebook pages • Notebook pages for the study of the classic to include: · the author's name and picture to color · the title of the book and picture to color · a page for the student to record the setting · a page for each character and picture to color · a page for the student to record the plot • Colored pencils	**Discuss** the Biblical Principles and Leading Idea. **Introduce** Felix Salten as the author of *Bambi*. **Give** a brief biography and locate his place on the Christian history timeline. **Review** the elements of a classic. **Discuss** the terms fiction and narrative. **Instruct** the student to create mental images and to mentally review setting, characters, and plot as a chapter or selected passage is read aloud during each lesson. **Lead** a discussion of literary elements by asking the student to use the author's words and descriptions of the setting, the plot, and the characters after you read aloud a selected passage. *Notebook Work* **Establish** the notebook method as a tool for studying a classic by using the chalkboard to model the notebook pages. **Distribute** the prepared notebook pages for the student to complete and color. **Record** simple phrases using the words of the author and have the student copy them on the appropriate page in his notebook.	**Participate** in a discussion of the Biblical Principles and Leading Idea. **Listen** as the teacher introduces Felix Salten and his place on the Christian history timeline. **Participate** in a review of a classic by naming key elements such as setting, characterization, and plot. **Participate** in a discussion of the terms fiction and narrative. **Listen** to the story and identify the setting and the characters in the story as the teacher reads aloud selected passages. **Contribute** to a discussion of literary elements by recalling the author's words and descriptions of the setting, plot, and characters after each selection is read. *Notebook Work* **Complete** and color the notebook pages. **Copy** words and descriptions used by the author on the appropriate notebook page after they are discussed orally and written on the board by the teacher. Setting the middle of the forest in one of those little hidden glades	• To learn new vocabulary—fiction and narrative • To recall the author's words and descriptions of setting, plot and characters • To complete and file notebook work	

The Noah Plan Lessons Kindergarten © 2003 • Foundation for American Christian Education

153

Week Three   **TEACHING PLAN**   Quarter Three

Preparation	Lesson	Student Work	Accomplishments	✓
Biblical Principle God launches events through individuals He has providentially called and prepared for His Gospel purpose. **Leading Idea** Christopher Columbus was a man of faith. **Books** • Bible (KJ) • NPH&GG, 8–9, 79 • NPSDS, Providential History, Links • *America's Providential History*, Beliles and McDowell, 45–46 • *Columbus*, d'Aulaire • Teacher Guide: *Columbus*, F.A.C.E. **Supplies** • Christian history timeline for classroom display (The Noah Plan Wall Timeline, F.A.C.E.) • World map • Prepared notebook page • Picture of the caravel and navigational instruments for the student to color • Colored pencils	**Review** Columbus as the sixth link on the Christian history timeline by asking the student to identify this link on the classroom Christian history timeline and to locate his birthplace on the map or globe. **Give** and discuss background information about Christopher Columbus: • He was born and educated in Genoa, Italy. • He loved the sea. • He had faith in God. • He was influenced by Marco Polo's writings of the Far East. • Prince Henry's School of Navigation prepared and supported Columbus and other sailors. • He was trained as a sailor. • Invention of navigational instruments made traveling safer and more exact enabling Columbus to fulfill God's purpose in his life. • Development of the caravel made for speedy and safer travel for his mission. • He kept logs on his journeys. **Show** pictures of the caravel and navigational instruments. **Read** aloud selected passages from *Columbus*, d'Aulaire. (Teacher Guide: *Christopher Columbus*, F.A.C.E., is a valuable resource for teaching this link.) *Notebook Work* **Distribute** the prepared notebook page for the student to write or trace the title and to color the picture of Columbus. Prepared notebook page to include: • the title "Columbus" for the student to write or trace • a picture of Columbus for the student to color **Distribute** the picture of the caravel and navigational instruments for the student to color.	**Review** Columbus as the sixth link on the Christian history timeline by identifying it on the classroom Christian history timeline and locate his birthplace on a map or globe. **Listen** as the teacher presents background information about Columbus and discusses the key people and events that influenced him. **View** pictures of the caravel and navigational instruments. **Listen** as the teacher reads aloud selected passages from *Columbus*, d'Aulaire. *Notebook Work* **Write** or trace the title on the notebook page and color the picture of Columbus. **Color** the picture of the caravel and the navigational instruments that helped Columbus.	• To learn how God providentially prepared Columbus's discovery of America • To complete and file notebook work	

HISTORY

154   The Noah Plan Lessons Kindergarten © 2003 • Foundation for American Christian Education

Week Three

Quarter Three

TEACHING PLAN

Preparation	Lesson	Student Work	Accomplishments	✓
Biblical Principle God created each continent distinct to fit His purpose and His plan. Psalm 115:16 **Leading Idea** The nature and character of God are revealed in the continent of South America. **Books** • Bible (KJ) • NPH&GG, 128, 207–211 • T&L, 141–153, 156–157 **Supplies** • World map and globe • Student atlas • Pictures or artifacts related to South America • South American words, phrases, or songs	**Guide** the student to the Biblical Principle from the Leading Idea by reviewing the location as well as the unique geographic features, natural resources, and climate that contribute to the individuality of South America. **Present** information about the people who inhabit the countries of South America (culture, customs, languages, etc.). **Display** pictures or artifacts related to South American culture (and/or ask the student to bring items to share). **Prepare** and serve native foods, learn words of a native language, or song.	**Participate** in a review of the location of South America by identifying it on a world map, globe, and in your atlas. **Participate** in a review of the features that contribute to South America's individuality by recalling unique aspects of its geography, natural resources, and climate. **Listen** as the teacher presents information about the culture, customs, and languages of the people who inhabit South America. **View** pictures or artifacts related to South America's culture (and/or bring items to share with the class). **Sample** native foods, learn new words of a native language, or songs. South America	• To locate South America on the map, globe, and atlas • To recall unique aspects of South America's geography, natural resources, and climate • To learn about the culture, customs, etc. of South American people • To view pictures or artifacts related to South American culture • To learn new words or songs • To sample native foods	

GEOGRAPHY

The Noah Plan Lessons Kindergarten © 2003 • Foundation for American Christian Education

TEACHING PLAN

Week Three · **Quarter Three**

	Preparation	Lesson	Student Work	Accomplishments	✓

SCIENCE	**Biblical Principles**
	• God's Principle of Individuality
	• Unity with Diversity
	
	Leading Idea
	The parts of plants perform different functions, which contribute to the growth and development of the plant.
	
	Books
	• Bible (KJ)
	• Botany books (Library)
	• Encyclopedia
	
	Supplies
	• Diagram or chart of plants or trees
	• Different types of seeds
	• Lima bean seeds
	• Notebook page to include:
	  • the title "Seeds" for the student to write or trace
	  • a space for the student to add drawings of plants with visible seeds such as peanuts in the shell, sunflowers, corn on the cob, acorns, etc. or glue different types of seeds to the page
		Review the Biblical Principles and Leading Idea.
		
		Review flowers by asking the student to recall their location and function.
		
		Introduce the function of the seeds: to grow new plants.
		
		Lead a discussion about:
		• How seeds are especially designed by God to carry out their purpose
		• How they illustrate God's Principles of Individuality and Unity with Diversity because a seed will only reproduce the type of plant that it came from
		
		Provide activities to broaden the student's knowledge of seeds and their function:
		• **Supply** several different types of seeds for the student to examine and sort by size, shape, and kind.
		• **Soak** lima bean seeds overnight and open them carefully so that the student can see the baby plants inside.
		• **Supply** different types of edible seeds for the student to taste (sunflower seeds, peanuts in the shell, popcorn, etc.).
		
		Notebook Work
		Distribute the prepared notebook page for the student to write or trace the title and to draw pictures of plants with visible seeds such as acorns, sunflowers, peanuts, corn (on the cob), etc. or to glue samples of seeds to the page.
			Participate in a review of the Biblical Principles and Leading Idea.
			Recall the location and function of flowers.
			
			Listen as the teacher presents the location and function of the seeds.
			Reason about:
			• How seeds are especially designed by God to carry out their specific purpose
			• How they illustrate God's Principles of Individuality and Unity with Diversity in the way they only reproduce the type of plant that they came from
			
			Participate in activities to broaden your understanding of seeds and their function:
			• **Examine** different types of seeds and sort them by size, shape, and kind.
			• **Observe** lima bean seeds that have been soaked overnight.
			• **Taste** several types of edible seeds.
			
			Notebook Work
			Write or trace the title on the notebook page and add drawings of plants with visible seeds such as peanuts in the shell, sunflowers, corn on the cob, acorns, etc. or glue different types of seeds to the page.
				• To restate the function of flowers
				• To sort seeds by size, shape, and kind
				• To taste edible seeds
				• To complete and file notebook work	

Week Four

Quarter Three

TEACHING PLAN

	Preparation	Lesson	Student Work	Accomplishments	✓
BIBLE	**Biblical Principle** We can ask God for wisdom. **Leading Idea** Solomon asked God to make him wise. **Books** • Bible (KJ) • *Webster's 1828 Dictionary* **Supplies** • Notebook page to include: • the title "Solomon" for the student to write or trace • a space for the student to draw and to color a picture of Solomon **BAR** • *Early Reader's Bible,* 178–185 • NPRG	**Introduce** the memory verse. Proverbs 2:6 • **Read** aloud and discuss the memory verse. • **Define** unfamiliar vocabulary. • **Practice** daily the memory verse with the student for his recitation on Friday. **Guide** the student to the Biblical Principle from the Leading Idea by introducing Solomon and discussing: • He was King David's son. • He asked God for wisdom. • He was the wisest man who ever lived. • He wrote most of Proverbs. **Read** aloud and discuss selected passages from the Song of Solomon. **Encourage** the student to ask God for wisdom. *Notebook Work* **Distribute** the prepared notebook page for the student to write or trace the title and to draw and color the picture of Solomon. **BAR** "A Wise King" (See Weekly Routines for Reading and English.)	**Listen** as the teacher reads aloud and discusses the memory verse. • **Discuss** unfamiliar vocabulary. • **Practice** and learn the memory verse for recitation on Friday. **Listen** as the teacher introduces Solomon discusses the following: • He was King David's son. • He asked God for wisdom. • He was the wisest man who ever lived. • He wrote most of Proverbs. **Listen** as the teacher reads from the Song of Solomon and participate in the discussion. *Notebook Work* **Write** or trace the title on the notebook page and draw and color the picture. **BAR** (See Weekly Routines for Reading and English.)	• To learn and recite the memory verse • To learn new vocabulary • To obey your parents and those in authority over you • To ask God for wisdom • To complete and file notebook work	

The Noah Plan Lessons Kindergarten © 2003 • Foundation for American Christian Education   157

Week Four

TEACHING PLAN

Quarter Three

	Preparation	Lesson	Student Work	Accomplishments	✓
LITERATURE	**Biblical Principles** • God's Principle of Individuality • Unity with Diversity **Leading Idea** Teaching literature is teaching character and teaching life. **Books** • Bible (KJ) • NPLG, 8–9, 135–138 • *Bambi*, Felix Salten **Supplies** • Chalkboard or charts to model notebook pages • Colored pencils	**Review** the Biblical Principles and Leading Idea. **Review** aspects of the setting, the characters, and the plot that were discussed in the previous lesson of *Bambi*. **Read** aloud a selected passage during each lesson. **Continue** to lead the student to recall the author's words and descriptions as you discuss the literary elements. *Notebook Work* **Add** author's words and descriptions to model notebook pages on the chalkboard or charts. **Instruct** the student to copy these on the appropriate notebook page. **Continue** to add and color illustrations.	**Participate** in a review of the Biblical Principles and Leading Idea. **Participate** in review of literary elements that were discussed in the previous lesson of *Bambi*. **Listen** as the teacher continues to read a selected passage during the lesson each day. **Contribute** to a discussion by recalling the author's descriptions of setting, plot, and characters. *Notebook Work* **Copy** the author's words and descriptions onto the appropriate notebook pages as the teacher models them on the chalkboard or charts. **Continue** to add and color illustrations.	• To recall the author's words and descriptions of setting, plot, and characters • To complete and file notebook work	

158   The Noah Plan Lessons Kindergarten © 2003 • Foundation for American Christian Education

TEACHING PLAN

Week Four   Quarter Three

HISTORY

Preparation	Lesson	Student Work	Accomplishments
Biblical Principle Faith in God overcomes fear. 1 John 5:4 **Leading Idea** The Gospel sails west with Columbus. **Books** • Bible (KJ) • NPH&GG, 8–9, 79, 182 • NPSDS, Providential History, Links • *America's Providential History*, Beliles and McDowell, 45–46 • *Columbus*, d'Aulaire **Supplies** • *Admiral Christbearer Coloring Book*, William A. Roy, Jr., ARK Foundation • Map of Columbus's first journey (Europe to San Salvador) for the student to color • Colored pencils	**Discuss** the Biblical Principle and Leading Idea. **Review** God's Hand of Providence by asking the student to recall key people and events that influenced Columbus. **Continue** to read aloud selected passages from *Columbus*, by d'Aulaire. • **Discuss** God's call on Columbus's life and his belief that he could take the gospel to China by sailing west. • **Discuss** how Columbus's faith in God overcame the fear of the unknown sea. • **Discuss** Columbus's journeys and discoveries. **Discuss** briefly the Age of Discovery by discussing discoveries made by other explorers and how these discoveries changed the maps that were used in the sixteenth and seventeenth centuries. NPH&GG, 182 *Notebook Work* **Distribute** the prepared map for the student to color according to the map standard.	**Participate** in a review of the Biblical Principle and Leading Idea. **Review** by recalling key people and events that influenced Columbus. **Listen** as the teacher reads aloud *Columbus*, d'Aulaire. • **Discuss** God's call on Columbus's life and his belief that he could reach China by sailing west. • **Discuss** how Columbus's faith in God overcame the fear of the unknown sea. • **Discuss** Columbus's journeys and discoveries. **Listen** as the teacher shares discoveries made by other explorers that changed the maps of the sixteenth and seventeenth centuries. *Notebook Work* **Color** the map of Columbus's first journey according to the map standard.	• To recall key people and events in Columbus's life • To listen to passages about Columbus and his journey • To complete and file notebook work

The Noah Plan Lessons Kindergarten © 2003 • Foundation for American Christian Education

Week Four

Quarter Three

TEACHING PLAN

	Preparation	Lesson	Student Work	Accomplishments	✓
GEOGRAPHY	**Biblical Principle** God created each continent distinct to fit His purpose and His plan. Psalm 115:16 **Leading Idea** The nature and character of God are revealed in the continent of South America. **Books** • Bible (KJ) • NPH&GG, 128, 207–211 • T&L, 141–153, 156–157 **Supplies** • Pictures of South American plants and animals • Old magazines (*National Geographic, Ranger Rick,* etc.) for cutting	**Guide** the student to the Biblical Principle from the Leading Idea by reviewing the unique culture (races, customs, languages, etc.) of South America. **Present** information about the plants and animals that are native to South America. **Display** pictures of the plants and animals that are native to South America. *Notebook Work* **Instruct** the student to find and cut pictures related to South American topography, people, plants, and animal life in nature magazines. **Instruct** the student to save these pictures in an envelope and put it into the pocket of his geography notebook for the next lesson.	**Review** by recalling the unique aspects of the culture (races, customs, languages, etc.) of South America. **Listen** as the teacher presents information about the plants and animals of South America. **View** pictures of some of the plants and animals that are native to South America. *Notebook Work* **Cut** and save pictures related to the topography, people, plants and animal life of South America. • **Put** the pictures into an envelope. • **Place** the envelope into the pocket of your geography notebook.	• To recall unique aspects of South American culture • To learn about plants and animals native to South America • To view pictures of South American plants and animals • To complete and file notebook work	

160   The Noah Plan Lessons Kindergarten © 2003 • Foundation for American Christian Education

Quarter Three

TEACHING PLAN

Week Four

Preparation	Lesson	Student Work	Accomplishments	✓
Biblical Principles • God's Principle of Individuality • Unity with Diversity The heavens declare the glory of God; and the firmament showeth his handiwork. Psalm 19:1 **Leading Idea** The universe is a testimony of God's character and nature. **Books** • Bible (KJ) • Webster's 1828 *Dictionary* • Astronomy books (Library) **Supplies** • Pictures of the universe, the Milky Way Galaxy, the Solar System, and the planets revolving around the Sun • Notebook page to include: • the title "Our Universe" for the student to write or trace the title • a picture of the universe containing the Milky Way Galaxy	**Continue** to study science according to the days of Creation. **Introduce** astronomy. • **Define** astronomy as the study of the universe—Sun, the moon, the planets, the stars, and other bodies in the heavens. • **Lay** the Biblical foundation for astronomy by reading aloud Genesis 1:14–19 and by discussing God created the heavenly bodies on the fourth day of Creation. **Introduce** the Solar System from the universe using visuals. **Guide** the student to the Biblical Principle from Leading Idea by reading aloud Psalm 19:1 and discussing that the universe is a testimony of God's character and nature. **Discuss** the following: • God created the universe. • The universe is a big place where God placed all of His Creation. • Many galaxies (a large group of stars circling around a point) make up the universe. • The Earth is located in the galaxy called the Milky Way (It is called the Milky Way because it looks like spilled milk in the sky.) • Our Solar System is located in the galaxy called the Milky Way. • The Sun is the center of the Solar System. • The Earth and the other planets rotate around the Sun. • **Discuss** distinguishing characteristics of the universe. • **Explain** how God's Principles of Individuality and Unity with Diversity can be seen in the universe. *Notebook Work* **Distribute** the prepared notebook page for the student to write or trace the title and to color the picture.	**Listen** as the teacher introduces and defines astronomy. **Listen** as the teacher lays and discusses the Biblical foundation for astronomy. **Listen** as the teacher reads aloud Psalm 19:1 and participate in a discussion of the universe being a testimony of God's character and nature. **Participate** in a discussion as the teacher introduces the Solar System from the universe using visuals. **Name** some of the distinguishing characteristics of the universe. **Identify** God's Principle of Individuality and Unity with Diversity can be seen in the universe. *Notebook Work* **Write** or trace the title on the notebook page and color the picture.	• To define astronomy • To learn the Biblical foundation for astronomy • To learn about our Solar System from visuals of the universe • To reason and relate about God's Principles of Individuality and Unity with Diversity in the universe • To complete and file notebook work	

SCIENCE

The Noah Plan Lessons Kindergarten © 2003 • Foundation for American Christian Education   161

Week Five

Quarter Three

TEACHING PLAN

	Preparation	Lesson	Student Work	Accomplishments
BIBLE	**Bible Principle** God's house is a place of honor and respect. **Leading idea** Solomon honored God by building a beautiful temple. **Books** • Bible (KJ) • Webster's 1828 *Dictionary* **Supplies** Notebook page to include: • the title "Solomon's Temple" for the student to write or trace • a space for the student to draw and color a picture of Solomon's Temple **BAR** • *Early Reader's Bible*, 187–193 • NPRG	**Introduce** the memory verse. Psalm 26:8 • **Read** aloud and discuss the memory verse. • **Define** unfamiliar vocabulary. • **Practice** daily the memory verse with the student for his recitation on Friday. **Guide** the student to the Biblical Principle from the Leading Idea by discussing the following: • God's house is a place of honor and respect. • Solomon built a great and beautiful temple (house) to worship God. • The temple was built in Jerusalem. • People from far away came to see the temple and worship God. **Discuss** how one should behave in God's house. *Notebook Work* **Distribute** the prepared notebook page for the student to write or trace the title and to draw and color the picture of Solomon's temple. **BAR** "A Beautiful House for God" (See Weekly Routines for Reading and English.)	**Listen** as the teacher reads aloud and discusses the memory verse. • **Discuss** unfamiliar vocabulary. • **Practice** and learn the memory verse for recitation on Friday. **Listen** as the teacher tells you about Solomon building the temple for God and discusses the following: • God's house is a place of honor and respect. • Solomon built a great and beautiful temple (house) to worship God. • The temple was built in Jerusalem. • People from far away came to see the temple and worship God. **Discuss** how you should behave in God's house. *Notebook Work* **Write** or trace the title and draw and color the picture of Solomon's temple. **BAR** (See Weekly Routines for Reading and English	• To learn and recite the memory verse • To learn new vocabulary • To understand the Principle of Stewardship • To complete and file notebook work

The Noah Plan Lessons Kindergarten © 2003 • Foundation for American Christian Education

Week Five

Quarter Three

TEACHING PLAN

	Preparation	Lesson	Student Work	Accomplishments	✓
LITERATURE	**Biblical Principles** • God's Principle of Individuality • Unity with Diversity **Leading Idea** Teaching literature is teaching character and teaching life. **Books** • Bible (KJ) • NPLG, 8–9, 135–138 • *Bambi*, Felix Salten **Supplies** • Chalkboard or charts to model notebook pages • Colored pencils	**Review** the Biblical Principles and Leading Idea. **Review** aspects of the setting, characters, and plot that were covered in previous lessons of *Bambi*. **Read** aloud a selected passage during each lesson. **Continue** to lead the student to recall the author's words and descriptions as you discuss the literary elements. *Notebook Work* **Add** author's words and descriptions to model notebook pages on the chalkboard or charts. **Instruct** the student to copy these on the appropriate notebook page and to continue to add and color illustrations.	**Participate** in a review of the Biblical Principles and Leading Idea. **Participate** in a review of literary elements that were discussed in previous lessons of *Bambi*. **Listen** as the teacher continues to read aloud a selected passage during the lesson each day. **Contribute** to a discussion by recalling the author's descriptions of setting, plot, or characters. *Notebook Work* **Copy** the author's words and descriptions onto the appropriate notebook page as the teacher models them on the chalkboard or charts. **Continue** to add and color illustrations.	• To recall the author's words and descriptions of setting, plot and characters • To complete and file notebook work	

The Noah Plan Lessons Kindergarten © 2003 • Foundation for American Christian Education

163

Week Five

TEACHING PLAN

Quarter Three

	Preparation	Lesson	Student Work	Accomplishments
HISTORY	**Biblical Principle** God uses individual character to carry out His story and His Gospel purposes. Ephesians 2:10	**Guide** the student to the Biblical Principle from the Leading Idea by introducing America's Christian Founding as the seventh link on the Christian history timeline.	**Listen** and observe as the teacher locates the seventh link on the Christian history timeline.	• To learn about America's Christian founding and key individuals in the settling of Jamestown
	Leading Idea God unveils the North American continent for His purpose.	• **Locate** the seventh link on the classroom Christian history timeline. • **Discuss** how God unveils the North American continent for his purposes through the founding of Jamestown, the first permanent English planting.	**Listen** as the teacher introduces how God begins to unveil the North American continent for his purposes through the founding of Jamestown. **Observe** the location of Jamestown as the teacher points it out on the map and globe.	• To learn about the character and contributions of John Smith and Robert Hunt • To complete and file notebook work
	Books • Bible (KJ) • NPH&GG, 8–9, 79, Appendix 340–341 for additional books on America's Christian Founding • T&L, 177–178, 190–194 • CHOC I, 150A–175	• **Locate** Jamestown on the classroom map and globe. • **Present** background information about key individuals such as John Smith and Robert Hunt. • **Lead** a discussion about their character and contributions to the colonization of Jamestown.	**Listen** as the teacher presents background information about key individuals such as John Smith and Robert Hunt. **Participate** in a classroom discussion about the character and contributions of these men.	
	Supplies • Christian history timeline for classroom display (The Noah Plan Wall Timeline, F.A.C.E.) • Picture of the 1607 landing at Cape Henry, Virginia or the original Jamestown fort for the student to color • Colored pencils	*Notebook Work* **Instruct** the student to find the seventh link and color the representative picture on their individual timeline as you point it out on the classroom Christian history timeline. **Distribute** the picture of the 1607 landing at Cape Henry, Virginia or of the original Jamestown fort for the student to color.	*Notebook Work* **Locate** and color the seventh link on the notebook copy of the Christian history timeline as the teacher points it out on the classroom timeline. **Color** the picture of the Cape Henry landing or the Jamestown fort.	

164 The Noah Plan Lessons Kindergarten © 2003 • Foundation for American Christian Education

Quarter Three

TEACHING PLAN

Week Five

GEOGRAPHY

Accomplishments

- To recall unique plants and animals of South America
- To reason and relate knowledge of South America to God's Principle of Individuality
- To complete map of South America
- To complete and file notebook work

Student Work

Participate in a review of the Biblical Principle and Leading Idea by recalling plants and animals native to South America from memory or by selecting them from assorted pictures.

Reason and relate about how the things learned about South America are an example of God's Principle of Individuality.

Notebook Work
Follow the map standard for physical maps and complete a map of South America.

Write or trace the title on the notebook page and glue pictures (cut from magazines last lesson) onto the distributed notebook page.

OR

Save the pictures to be used for a group project in the fourth quarter.

Lesson

Review the Biblical Principle and the Leading Idea.

Review the plants and animals that are unique to South America.

Lead a classroom discussion encouraging students to reason and relate the things they have learned about South America with God's Principle of Individuality.

Notebook Work
Distribute a simple outline map of South America.

Instruct the student to color the map according to the map standard for physical maps.

Distribute notebook page for the student to write or trace the title "South America's Individuality."

Instruct the student to glue pictures of South America on the notebook page.

OR

Save the pictures to be used for a group project in the fourth quarter.

Preparation

Biblical Principle
God created each continent distinct to fit His purpose and His plan. Psalm 115:16

Leading Idea
The nature and character of God are revealed in the continent of South America.

Books
- Bible (KJ)
- NPH&GG, 128, 207–211
- T&L, 141–153,156–157

Supplies
- World map and globe
- Map standard
- Colored pencils
- Notebook page to include:
  · the title "South America's Individuality" for the student to write or trace
  · a space to glue pictures of South America
- Outline map of South America (Use maps in NPH&GG, 234–235 as a guide.)

The Noah Plan Lessons Kindergarten © 2003 • Foundation for American Christian Education

Week Five

Quarter Three

TEACHING PLAN

	Preparation	Lesson	Student Work	Accomplishments	✓

SCIENCE	**Biblical Principle**
	God created the heavenly bodies.
	Genesis 1:14–19
	
	Leading Idea
	The heavenly bodies speak of God's nature and character.
	
	Books
	• Bible (KJ)
	• Webster's 1828 *Dictionary*
	• *Spinning Worlds*, Michael Carroll
	• Astronomy books (Library)
	
	Supplies
	• Pictures of the Sun
	• Pictures of the moon and its phases
	• Notebook page to include:
	  • the title "The Sun and the Moon" for the student to write or trace the title
	  • a space for the student to draw and color a picture of the Sun and the moon
		Discuss the Biblical Principle and the Leading Idea.
		
		Read aloud and discuss 1 Corinthians 15:41.
		
		Discuss the individuality of the Sun.
		• It is the center of the Solar System.
		• Its gravitational pull holds the heavenly bodies in space.
		• It is a star—a ball of burning gases.
		• It is the closest star to the Earth.
		• All the planets revolve around it.
		• It provides heat and light for Earth.
		• It provides light for plants to make food for us and oxygen for us to breathe.
		• It determines weather and climate.
		Present visual examples of the Sun.
		Explain how God's Principles of Individuality and Unity with Diversity can be seen in the distinguishing characteristics of the Sun.
		
		Read aloud and discuss *Spinning Worlds*, "The Sun."
		
		SCIENCE—
		Lesson & Notebook Work
		(continued on page 167)
			Participate in a discussion of the Biblical Principle and Leading Idea.
			
			Listen as the teacher reads aloud 1 Corinthians 15:41 and participate in the discussion.
			
			Participate s in a discussion of the individuality of the Sun.
			
			View pictures of the Sun.
			Reason and relate orally how the Sun demonstrates God's Principles of Individuality and Unity with Diversity.
			Listen as the teacher reads aloud from *Spinning Worlds*, "The Sun."
			
			SCIENCE—
			Student & Notebook Work
			(continued on page 167)
				• To learn about the Sun
				• To learn about the moon
				• To reason and relate about God's Principles of Individuality and Unity with Diversity as seen in the Sun and moon
				• To complete and file notebook work	

166   The Noah Plan Lessons Kindergarten © 2003 • Foundation for American Christian Education

Week Five   Quarter Three

TEACHING PLAN

Preparation	Lesson	Student Work	Accomplishments	✓
	Read aloud and discuss Genesis 1:16. **Discuss** the individuality of the moon. • It is a lifeless place with no air or water. • It has mountains, plains, and craters (large holes). • It has no light of its own. It gets its light from the Sun. • The ocean tides are affected by the moon. • It is Earth's closest neighbor. **Discuss** and present visual examples of the moon's phases. **Explain** how God's Principles of Individuality and Unity with Diversity can be seen in the distinguishing characteristics of the moon. **Read** aloud from *Spinning Worlds*, "Earth and the Moon." **Encourage** the student to observe, if possible, at various times the night sky to see the different phases of the moon. *Notebook Work* **Distribute** the prepared notebook page for the student to write or trace the title and to draw and color a picture of the Sun and the moon.	**Listen** as the teacher reads aloud Genesis 1:16 and participate in a discussion on the individuality of the moon. **Discuss** the moon's phases with the teacher. **View** pictures of the moon's shapes. **Reason** and relate orally how the moon demonstrates God's Principle of Individuality and Unity with Diversity. **Listen** as the teacher reads aloud from *Spinning Worlds*, "Earth and the Moon." **Observe** at various times the night sky to see the different phases of the moon. *Notebook Work* **Distribute** the prepared notebook page for the student to write or trace the title and to draw and color a picture of the Sun and the moon.		

SCIENCE (continued)

The Noah Plan Lessons Kindergarten © 2003 • Foundation for American Christian Education   167

Week Six

TEACHING PLAN

Quarter Three

	Preparation	Lesson	Student Work	Accomplishments	✓
BIBLE	**Biblical Principle** God cares for His people. **Leading Idea** God provided food for Elijah and for the widow. **Books** • Bible (KJ) • Webster's 1828 Dictionary **Supplies** • Notebook page to include: • the title "Elijah" for the student to write or trace • a space for the student to draw and color a picture of Elijah and the raven or Elijah and the widow **BAR** • Early Reader's Bible, 194–209 • NPRG	**Introduce** the memory verse. Psalm 37:25 • **Read** aloud and discuss the memory verse. • **Define** unfamiliar vocabulary. • **Practice** daily the memory verse with the student for his recitation on Friday. **Guide** the student to the Biblical Principle from the Leading Idea. • **Discuss** the following: · How God used ravens to feed Elijah · How God used a poor widow and her son to provide food for Elijah · How God blessed the widow with food for life because she was obedient to God's request • **Discuss** how much God cares for His people. • **Discuss** how God blesses those who help others. *Notebook Work* **Distribute** the prepared notebook page for the student to write or trace the title and to draw and color a picture of Elijah and the raven or Elijah and the widow. **BAR** "Birds with Food for a Man" "Elijah Helps a Family" (See Weekly Routines for Reading and English.)	**Listen** as the teacher reads aloud and discusses the memory verse. • **Discuss** unfamiliar vocabulary. • **Practice** and learn the memory verse for recitation on Friday. **Listen** as the teacher tells the story of Elijah and the widow. • **Discuss** the following: · How God used ravens to feed Elijah · How God used a poor widow and her son to provide food for Elijah · How God blessed the widow with food for life because she was obedient to God's request • **Discuss** how much God cares for His people. • **Discuss** how God blesses those who help others. *Notebook Work* **Write** or trace the title on the notebook page and draw and color a picture of Elijah and the raven or Elijah and the widow. **BAR** (See Weekly Routines for Reading and English.)	• To learn and recite the memory verse • To learn new vocabulary • To help people who need you • To complete and file notebook work	

168   The Noah Plan Lessons Kindergarten © 2003 • Foundation for American Christian Education

Week Six

Quarter Three

TEACHING PLAN

Preparation	Lesson	Student Work	Accomplishments	✓
Biblical Principles • God's Principle of Individuality • Unity with Diversity **Leading Idea** Teaching literature is teaching character and teaching life. **Books** • Bible (KJ) • NPLG, 8–9, 135–138 • *Bambi*, Felix Salten **Supplies** • Chalkboard or charts to model notebook pages • Colored pencils	**Review** the Biblical Principles and Leading Idea. **Review** aspects of the setting, characters, and plot that were covered in previous lessons of *Bambi*. **Read** aloud a selected passage during each lesson. **Continue** to lead the student to recall the author's words and descriptions as you discuss the literary elements. *Notebook Work* **Add** the author's words and descriptions to model notebook pages on the chalkboard or charts. **Instruct** the student to copy these on the appropriate notebook page, and to add and color illustrations.	**Participate** in a review of the Biblical Principles and Leading Idea. **Participate** in a review of literary elements that were discussed in previous lessons of *Bambi*. **Listen** as the teacher continues to read aloud a selected passage during the lesson each day. **Contribute** to discussions by recalling the author's descriptions of setting, plot, and characters. *Notebook Work* **Copy** the author's words and descriptions onto the appropriate notebook page as the teacher models them on the chalkboard or charts. **Add** and color illustrations.	• To recall the author's words and descriptions of setting, plot and characters • To complete and file notebook work	

LITERATURE

The Noah Plan Lessons Kindergarten © 2003 • Foundation for American Christian Education   169

Week Six — **TEACHING PLAN** — Quarter Three

HISTORY

Preparation	Lesson	Student Work	Accomplishments

Biblical Principle
God uses individual character to carry out His story and His Gospel purposes.
Ephesians 2:10
 	
Leading Idea
Pocahontas was used as an instrument of God to help the people of Jamestown.
 	
Books
• Bible (KJ)
• NPH&GG, 8–9, 79
• CHOC I, 158
 	
Supplies
• Notebook page to include:
  • the title "America's Christian Founding at Jamestown" for the student to write or trace
  • a space to draw a picture
• Pictures, charts, or artifacts of life in Jamestown
• *A Children's Color Book of Jamestown in Virginia*, The Dietz Press
	Review by asking the student to recall some of the contributions made by key individuals such as John Smith and Robert Hunt to the unveiling of North America through the founding of Jamestown.
	
	Present background information about some of the challenges that faced the settlers and the relationship that the settlers had with the Powhatan Indians.
	Guide the student to the Biblical Principle from the Leading Idea.
	• **Discuss** how Pocahontas was used as an instrument of God to preserve the struggling settlement of Jamestown.
	• **Lead** an oral discussion:
	  • How did God use Pocahontas's captivity to bring about her conversion?
	  • How did God providentially prepare her to help the colony of Jamestown succeed?
	  • What were some of her contributions?
	
	Display pictures, charts, or artifacts depicting the Jamestown fort, daily life, etc.
	
	Notebook Work
	Distribute the prepared notebook page.
	• **Instruct** the student to write or trace the title.
	• **Instruct** the student to draw a picture of the fort, some aspect of life in Jamestown, or an event that demonstrates God's providence in the settling of Jamestown.
		Review by recalling some of the contributions made by key individuals such as John Smith and Robert Hunt to the unveiling of North America through the founding of Jamestown.
		
		Listen as the teacher presents information about some of the challenges that the settlers faced, their relationship with the Powhatan Indians, and how Pocahontas was used as an instrument of God to preserve the settlement of Jamestown.
		Reason orally about:
		• How did God use the captivity of Pocahontas to bring about her conversion?
		• How was she providentially prepared by God to assist the Jamestown settlement to succeed?
		• What were some of her contributions?
		
		View pictures or artifacts of the Jamestown fort or the daily life of Indians and settlers.
		
		Notebook Work
		Write or trace the title on the notebook page.
		Draw a picture of the Jamestown fort, some aspect of daily life in Jamestown, or an event that demonstrates God's providence in the founding of Jamestown on the notebook page.
			• To recall contributions made by John Smith and Robert Hunt to the founding of Jamestown
			• To learn about the settlers' challenges, their relationship with the Indians, and how Pocahontas was used by God
			• To reason about Pocahontas's life and contributions
			• To complete and file notebook work

170   The Noah Plan Lessons Kindergarten © 2003 • Foundation for American Christian Education

Week Six

Quarter Three

TEACHING PLAN

	Preparation	Lesson	Student Work	Accomplishments	✓

GEOGRAPHY	**Biblical Principle**
	God created each continent distinct to fit His purpose and His plan. Psalm 115:16
	
	Leading Idea
	The nature and character of God are revealed in the continent of Antarctica.
	
	Books
	• Bible (KJ)
	• NPH&GG, 128, 223–225
	• T&L, 141–153, 156–157
	
	Supplies
	• World map and globe
	• Student atlas
	• Colored pencils
	• Pictures of Antarctica
	• EMBG, Volume 3:9
		Guide the student to the Biblical Principle from the Leading Idea.
		• **Locate** Antarctica on the classroom world map and globe.
		• **Introduce** the geographic features that contribute to Antarctica's being called the "continent of hidden resources."
		  • Mountains beneath the snow
		  • Frozen at all times
		  • Covered with ice and snow
		  • Surrounded by the stormiest seas in the world
		  • All of it not yet explored due to its largeness and desolation
		• **Present** information about the natural resources, and climate that contribute to the individuality of Antarctica.
		  • No trees, mostly mosses and lichens
		  • Invertebrate mites and ticks
		  • Contains 90% of the world's fresh water (land ice)
		  • Coldest of the seven continents
		  • True desert due to lack of precipitation
		  • Fierce winds
		  • No sunshine for six months of the year
		• **Display** pictures of various regions of Antarctica.
		
		Notebook Work
		Distribute EMBG, Volume 3:9 and instruct the student in completing the page.
			Listen and observe as the teacher:
			• **Locates** Antarctica on the classroom world map and globe.
			• **Introduces** the geographic features that contribute to Antarctica's being called the "continent of hidden resources."
			
			View pictures of different regions in Antarctica.
			
			Notebook Work
			Color and complete the notebook page.
				• To learn about the location and individuality of Antarctica
				• To view pictures of Antarctica
				• To complete and file notebook work	

The Noah Plan Lessons Kindergarten © 2003 • Foundation for American Christian Education   171

TEACHING PLAN

Quarter Three

Week Six

Preparation	Lesson	Student Work	Accomplishments

Biblical Principles
• God's Principle of Individuality
• Unity with Diversity
• God created the heavenly bodies. Genesis 1:14–19
 	
Leading Idea
The heavenly bodies speak of God's nature and character.
 	
Books
• Bible (KJ)
• Webster's 1828 *Dictionary*
• NPH&GG, 165
• *Spinning Worlds*, Michael Carroll
• Astronomy books (Library)
 	
Supplies
• Pictures of the nine planets
• Notebook page to include:
  • the title "Nine Planets" for the student to write or trace
  • a space for the student to draw and color the nine planets in order from the Sun
	Review the Biblical Principle and Leading Idea.
	Introduce the nine planets.
	• **Read** aloud and discuss Genesis 1:14–19.
	
	• **Discuss** there are nine planets in the Solar System.
	  • A planet is a heavenly body that travels around the Sun.
	  • All the planets have no life accept for the planet Earth.
	  • There are four planets close to the Sun—the inner planets.
	  • There are five planets farther away from the Sun—the outer planets.
	• **Name** and describe the nature of these four inner planets in order from the Sun—Mercury, Venus, Earth, and Mars:
	  • Called Earth-like planets
	  • Solid bodies of rock and metal
	  • About the same size of the Earth
	  • Closest to the Sun
	• **Name** and describe the nature and character of the five outer planets in order from the Sun—Jupiter, Saturn, Uranus, Pluto, and Neptune:
	  • Composed of gases
	  • Larger than Earth
	• **Introduce** the characteristics of each individual planet by reading aloud from *Spinning Worlds* and by showing the pictures associated with each planet.
	
	• **Explain** how God's Principles of Individuality and Unity with Diversity can be seen in the planets.
	
	Notebook Work
	Distribute the prepared notebook page for the student to write or trace the title and to draw and color the pictures of the nine planets in order from the Sun.
		Participate in a review of the Biblical Principle and Leading Idea.
		Listen as the teacher reads aloud and discusses Genesis 1:14–19.
		Participate in a discussion about the characteristics of a planet.
		
		Listen as the teacher names and describes the nature of the four inner planets.
		
		Listen as the teacher names and describes the nature of the five outer planets.
		
		Listen and observe as the teacher introduces the characteristics of the nine planets through reading from *Spinning Worlds* and through the use of the pictures in the book.
		Reason and relate orally how planets demonstrate the Principles of Individuality and Unity with Diversity.
		
		Notebook Work
		Write or trace the title on the notebook page.
		Add a picture of the Sun in the far left corner of the page. Draw the nine planets in order from the Sun.
			• To learn the Biblical foundation for planets
			• To learn the nature of a planet
			• To learn the names of the nine planets
			• To learn the characteristics of each of the nine planets
			• To complete and file notebook work

SCIENCE

172   The Noah Plan Lessons Kindergarten © 2003 • Foundation for American Christian Education

Quarter Three

Week Seven

TEACHING PLAN

	Preparation	Lesson	Student Work	Accomplishments	✔
BIBLE	**Biblical Principle** God calls each one to serve Him in different ways. **Leading Idea** A woman helped Elijah do his work. **Books** • Bible (KJ) • Webster's 1828 Dictionary **Supplies** • Notebook page to include: • the title "Elijah's New Room" for the student to write or trace • a space for the student to draw and color a picture of Elijah and his new room **BAR** • *Early Reader's Bible*, 210–217 • NPRG	**Introduce** the memory verse. 1 Peter 4:9 • **Read** aloud and discuss the memory verse. • **Define** unfamiliar vocabulary. • **Practice** daily the memory verse with the student for his recitation on Friday. **Guide** the student to the Biblical Principle from the Leading Idea. • **Tell** the story of Elijah and the Shunammite woman. 2 Kings 4:8 • **Discuss** the following: • God equips us with different talents to help others and to serve Him. • The Shunammite woman built a room onto her house so Elijah could have a place to rest when traveling. • God can use people, young and old, to help Him. *Notebook Work* **Distribute** the prepared notebook page for the student to write or trace the title and to draw and color the picture of Elijah and his new room. **BAR** "A New Room" (See Weekly Routines for Reading and English.)	**Listen** as the teacher reads aloud and discusses the memory verse. • **Discuss** unfamiliar vocabulary. • **Practice** and learn the memory verse for recitation on Friday. **Listen** as the teacher tells the story of Elijah and the Shunammite woman. • **Discuss** the following: • God equips us with different talents to help others and to serve Him. • The Shunammite woman built a room onto her house so Elijah could have a place to rest when traveling. • God can use people, young and old, to help Him. *Notebook Work* **Write** or trace the title on the notebook page and draw and color a picture of Elijah and his new room. **BAR** (See Weekly Routines for Reading and English.)	• To learn and recite the memory verse • To learn new vocabulary • To recognize each individual has a special gift to use to serve God • To complete and file notebook work	

The Noah Plan Lessons Kindergarten © 2003 • Foundation for American Christian Education

Week Seven
TEACHING PLAN
Quarter Three

LITERATURE

Preparation	Lesson	Student Work	Accomplishments	✓
Biblical Principle God looks on the heart of a man or woman. 1 Samuel 16:7	**Discuss** the Biblical Principle and the Leading Idea.	**Participate** in a discussion of the Biblical Principle and Leading Idea.	• To learn the definition of biography	
Leading Idea The study of a biography is the study of the internal character of an individual.	**Introduce** Ingri and Edgar Parin d'Aulaire as the authors of the biography *Abraham Lincoln*. **Define** biography as the history of the life and character of a person.	**Listen** as the teacher introduces the distinctive qualities of a biography and the authors of the biography, *Abraham Lincoln*.	• To name Abraham Lincoln's influences and character qualities	
	Identify the geographic setting on a simple map and discuss the historical setting of America's frontier during the 1800s.	**Locate** the geographic setting on the map and listen as the teacher presents characteristics of frontier life in America during the 1800s.	• To complete and file notebook work	
Books • Bible (KJ) • Webster's 1828 *Dictionary* • NPLG, 8–9, 129–132 • *Abraham Lincoln*, d'Aulaire	**Read** aloud a section of *Abraham Lincoln* during each daily lesson.	**Listen** as a section of *Abraham Lincoln* is read aloud during each lesson.		
	• **Lead** a discussion about the influences in Abraham's life such as a loving mother who read the Bible to him when he was a young man.	**Participate** in a discussion about the influences that helped to shape Abraham Lincoln's life.		
Supplies • Pictures of Abraham Lincoln from childhood to adulthood • Simple United States map • Notebook pages for the study of a biography to include: · the title page with the name of the book and authors for the student to write or trace and a space for a picture of Lincoln · a T-chart to record the internal and external qualities of Lincoln's character	• **Ask** leading questions about the ways that Abraham Lincoln exemplified Biblical Principles of character in this narrative.	**Answer** the teacher's questions about the ways that Abraham Lincoln exemplified Biblical Principles of character in this narrative.		
	Notebook Work **Distribute** the prepared notebook page for the student to write or trace the title and the authors, and glue a picture of Lincoln on the page. **Model** a T-chart on the board using the author's descriptions of Lincoln's internal and external character qualities for the student to record.	*Notebook Work* **Write** or trace the title and the authors on the notebook page, and glue a picture of Lincoln on the page. **Copy** the descriptions of Lincoln's internal and external character qualities onto the T-chart after the teacher writes them on the chalkboard.		

Abraham Lincoln's
Character

Internal	External
honest	very thin
loved Bible	very tall
trusted God	

174 The Noah Plan Lessons Kindergarten © 2003 • Foundation for American Christian Education

Week Seven

TEACHING PLAN

Quarter Three

Preparation	Lesson	Student Work	Accomplishments	✓
Biblical Principle The Christian Principle of Self-Government **Leading Idea** The Pilgrims are a model of Christian Self-Government. **Books** • Bible (KJ) • NPH&GG, 68–69, 284–291, Appendix 340–341 for age appropriate books on the Pilgrims • NPSDS, Providential History, Links • T&L, 69–72, 177–179, 184–209 • CHOC I, 24–28, 148–150, 176–240 **Supplies** • World map and globe • Student atlas • *Plimoth Plantation Day Packet* (PPDP), F.A.C.E. • Map of Plimoth Plantation (PPDP, 19) • God's World Publications • Prepared notebook page • Pictures of English life in 1600s • Colored pencils	**Introduce** the Christian Principle of Self-Government and the impact that individual/local self-government has on national government. (Review History Qtr. 1, Week 1—Christian Self-government in the classroom, NPLK, 29): • **Define** Christian Self-Government. (When you accept Jesus as your Lord and Savior, you allow Him to govern you. He tells you how to act. Therefore, Christian Self-Government is allowing Jesus to govern your life. • **Discuss** the application of Christian Self-Government in the classroom. (T&L, 186–188) **Present** background information and/or read excerpts from an age appropriate historical account about the life of the Pilgrims in England, their move to Holland, and their reasons for wanting to establish a colony in the New World. **Locate** England, Holland, and Cape Cod on the classroom world map, globe, and student atlas. **Display** pictures of English life in the 1600s to include dress, country and city life, modes of transportation, etc. **Ask** the student to make comparisons with life today. **Lead** an oral discussion about the Pilgrim's desire to propagate the Gospel and how their study of the scripture motivated them to establish local self-government in the Plymouth Colony. *Notebook Work* **Distribute** the prepared notebook page for the student to write or trace the title and to color some aspect of the Pilgrim's life. Notebook page to include: • the title "The Pilgrims, a Model of Christian Self-Government" for the student to write or trace • a picture of some aspect of the Pilgrim's life for the student to color	**Listen** as the teacher introduces the Christian Principle of Self-Government and the impact that individual/local self-government has on national government. • **Apply** the definition of Christian Self-Government to your life. • **Apply** Christian Self-Government to the classroom. **Listen** as the teacher presents background information about the Pilgrims and the geographic setting in which their story takes place. **Locate** England, Holland, and Cape Cod on the classroom world map, globe, and atlas. **View** pictures of seventeenth century English life and compare what is seen with the way we live today. **Participate** in a classroom discussion about the Pilgrims, their desire to propagate the Gospel, and what motivated them to establish local self-government in the Plymouth Colony. *Notebook Work* **Write** or trace the title on the notebook page and color the picture of some aspect of the Pilgrim's life.	• To learn about the Christian Principle of Self-Government and the Pilgrims • To view pictures of seventeenth century English life and make comparisons with life today • To discuss the Pilgrim's desire to propagate the gospel and establish local self-government in the Plymouth Colony • To complete and file notebook work	

HISTORY

The Noah Plan Lessons Kindergarten © 2003 • Foundation for American Christian Education

Week Seven

TEACHING PLAN

Quarter Three

Preparation	Lesson	Student Work	Accomplishments	✓
Biblical Principle God created each continent distinct to fit His purpose and His plan. Psalm 115:16 **Leading Idea** The nature and character of God are revealed in the continent of Antarctica. **Books** • Bible (KJ) • NPH&GG, 128, 223–225 • T&L, 141–153, 156–157 • Antarctica articles, *Journal of F.A.C.E.*, Volume I **Supplies** • World map and globe • Pictures of plants and animals that are native to Antarctica • Old magazines (*National Geographic*, *Ranger Rick*, etc.) for cutting • Student atlas	**Continue** to guide the student to the Biblical Principle from the Leading Idea by reviewing the location as well as the unique geographic features, natural resources, and climate that contribute to the individuality of Antarctica. **Present** information about the plants and animals that are native to Antarctica. **Display** pictures of the plants and animals that are native to Antarctica. *Notebook Work* **Instruct** the student to find pictures related to the topography, plant, and animal life of Antarctica in magazines to cut. **Instruct** the student to save these pictures in an envelope in the pocket of his geography notebook for the next week's lesson.	**Review** the location of Antarctica by identifying it on the classroom world map, globe, and in your atlas. **Review** the features that contribute to Antarctica's individuality by recalling unique aspects of its geography, natural resources, and climate. **Listen** as the teacher presents information about the plants and animals found there. **View** pictures of some of the plants and animals that are native to Antarctica. *Notebook Work* **Cut** pictures of the topography, plant, or animal life of Antarctica. **Save** the pictures in an envelope in the pocket of your geography notebook for next week's lesson. Antarctica	• To locate Antarctica on the classroom world map, globe, and atlas • To recall unique aspects of Antarctica's geography, natural resources, and climate • To learn about the plants and animals native to Antarctica • To view pictures of plants and animals found in Antarctica • To complete and file notebook work	

GEOGRAPHY

The Noah Plan Lessons Kindergarten © 2003 • Foundation for American Christian Education

Week Seven   **Quarter Three**

TEACHING PLAN

Preparation	Lesson	Student Work	Accomplishments	✓
Biblical Principles • God's Principle of Individuality • Unity with Diversity **Leading Idea** God maintains the identity and individuality of everything that He created. **Books** • Bible (KJ) • Webster's 1828 *Dictionary* • T&L, 113 • Zoology books (Library) • Encyclopedia **Supplies** • Picture cards to represent various animals • Colored pencils • Prepared notebook page *Optional* • Notebook page to include a T-chart with the titles "Vertebrate" on the left side and "Invertebrate" on the right side for the student to write or trace	**Continue** to teach science through the days of Creation. **Introduce** zoology as the study of animals created on the fifth and sixth days of Creation. **Read** aloud Genesis 1:20–25 and discuss the Biblical foundation of zoology. **Define** and discuss the differences between vertebrate and invertebrate animals **Ask** the student to name the differences between vertebrate and invertebrate animals. **Play** classification game with cards—separating the vertebrates from the invertebrates. **Guide** the student to the Biblical Principles from the Leading Idea by discussing how God's Principles of Individuality and Unity with Diversity are seen in zoology. *Notebook Work* **Distribute** the prepared notebook page for the student to write or trace the title and to color the pictures. Prepared notebook page to include: • the title "Zoology" for the student to write or trace • pictures of vertebrates and invertebrates for the student to color *Optional* **Distribute** the prepared notebook page for the student to write or trace the titles and write the notes contrasting vertebrate and invertebrate animals on the board for the student to record.	**Listen** as the teacher defines zoology created on the fifth and sixth days of Creation. **Listen** as the teacher reads aloud Genesis 1:20–25 and discusses the Biblical foundation of zoology. **Listen** as the teacher defines and discusses vertebrates and invertebrates. **Name** the major differences between vertebrate and invertebrate animals. **Classify** animals as vertebrates or invertebrates (classification/sorting game). **Discuss** how God's Principles of Individuality and Unity with Diversity are seen in zoology. *Notebook Work* **Write** or trace the title on the notebook page and color the pictures. *Optional* **Write** or trace the title on the notebook page and record the notes modeled on the board by the teacher.	• To learn the definition of zoology • To compare and contrast vertebrates and invertebrates • To relate the Biblical Principles to zoology • To play a classification game • To complete and file notebook work	

SCIENCE

The Noah Plan Lessons Kindergarten © 2003 • Foundation for American Christian Education   177

Week Eight **TEACHING PLAN** **Quarter Three**

	Preparation	Lesson	Student Work	Accomplishments	✔
BIBLE	**Biblical Principle** When we love others we are being obedient to God. **Leading Idea** Jonah learned to care about all people. **Books** • Bible (KJ) • Webster's 1828 *Dictionary* **Supplies** • Notebook page to include: • the title "Jonah" for the student to write or trace • a space for the student to draw and color a picture of Jonah **BAR** • *Early Reader's Bible*, 274–281 • NPRG	**Introduce** the memory verse. 1 John 4:7 • **Read** aloud and discuss the memory verse. • **Define** unfamiliar vocabulary. • **Practice** daily the memory verse with the student for his recitation on Friday. **Guide** the student to the Biblical Principle from the Leading Idea. • **Tell** the story of Jonah. • **Discuss** the following: • Why did Jonah run away? • Why did God send a big storm? • What did Jonah tell the sailors to do to make the storm stop? • How did God save Jonah from drowning? • What did Jonah do in the belly of the whale? • How did Jonah respond to God's second request to go to Nineveh? • How did Jonah feel about going to Nineveh? • Why do you think Jonah felt this way? • **Discuss** when we love others we are being obedient to God. *Notebook Work* **Distribute** the prepared notebook page for the student to write or trace the title and to draw and color a picture of Jonah. **BAR** "Jonah Learns to Obey" (See Weekly Routines for Reading and English.)	**Listen** as the teacher reads aloud and discusses the memory verse. • **Discuss** unfamiliar vocabulary. • **Practice** and learn the memory verse for recitation on Friday. • **Listen** as the teacher tells the story of Jonah. • **Discuss** the following: • Why did Jonah run away? • Why did God send a big storm? • What did Jonah tell the sailors to do to make the storm stop? • How did God save Jonah from drowning? • What did Jonah do in the belly of the whale? • How did Jonah respond to God's second request to go to Nineveh? • How did Jonah feel about going to Ninevah? • Why do you think Jonah felt this way? • **Discuss** how important it is to care about all people. *Notebook Work* **Write** or trace the title on the notebook page and draw and color a picture of Jonah. **BAR** (See Weekly Routines for Reading and English.)	• To learn and recite the memory verse • To learn new vocabulary • To learn to care about all people • To learn to be obedient to God's Word • To complete and file notebook work	

178   The Noah Plan Lessons Kindergarten © 2003 • Foundation for American Christian Education

Week Eight

Quarter Three

TEACHING PLAN

	Preparation	Lesson	Student Work	Accomplishments	✓
LITERATURE	**Biblical Principle** God looks on the heart of a man or woman. 1 Samuel 16:7 **Leading Idea** The study of a biography is the study of the internal character of an individual. **Books** • Bible (KJ) • NPLG, 8–9, 129–132 • *Abraham Lincoln,* d'Aulaire	**Review** the Biblical Principle and the Leading Idea. **Review** the geographical and historical setting, characters, and the descriptions of Abraham Lincoln's character that were covered in the previous selections of d'Aulaire's biography of Abraham Lincoln. **Finish** the biography, *Abraham Lincoln,* by reading a passage each day. **Lead** a discussion about the Hand of Providence in America and Lincoln's contributions to liberty. **Present** information about the Civil War, the Gettysburg Address, and the Emancipation Proclamation. *Notebook Work* **Assist** the student to complete the notebook record of Lincoln's character by writing the author's descriptions in the appropriate column (internal or external) on the chalkboard.	**Participate** in a review of the Biblical Principle and Leading Idea. **Review** the setting and the characters by recalling the author's descriptions that were covered in previous lessons. **Listen** as the teacher concludes the biography, *Abraham Lincoln,* by reading aloud a passage each day. **Contribute** to a discussion about Lincoln's place on the chain of Christianity by recalling his contributions to liberty in America's history. *Notebook Work* **Complete** the notebook record of Lincoln's character by copying the author's descriptions in the appropriate column (internal or external) after they are identified and discussed.	• To name Abraham Lincoln's influences and character qualities • To complete and file notebook work	

The Noah Plan Lessons Kindergarten © 2003 • Foundation for American Christian Education

Week Eight

Quarter Three

TEACHING PLAN

HISTORY

Preparation	Lesson	Student Work	Accomplishments	✓
Biblical Principle God launches events through individuals He has providentially called and prepared. Judges 6:14 **Leading Idea** The strength of a nation resides in the character of its people. **Books** • Bible (KJ) • NPH&GG, 8–9, 247 • NPSDS, Providential History, Links • T&L, 177–179 • CHOC I, 24–27, 176–240 **Supplies** • World map or globe • *Plimoth Plantation Day Packet*, F.A.C.E. • *The Plimoth Plantation Coloring Book*, Carolyn Freeman Travers, Plimoth Plantation, 1963 • Colored pencils	**Discuss** the Biblical Principle and the Leading Idea. **Review** by asking the student to recall reasons for why the Pilgrims wanted to establish a new colony. **Present** background information about: • The Pilgrim's voyage on the *Mayflower* • The circumstances that led them to write the *Mayflower Compact* • The challenges that faced them in the New World • Their relationship with the Indians **Give** the student a deeper understanding of how God providentially prepares key individuals to fulfill His purpose and plan by: • Highlighting Governor Bradford's life as a young English boy • Reading selected passages from his journal, *Of Plimoth Plantation* (found in CHOC I). *Notebook Work* **Distribute** a picture of some aspect of the Pilgrim's life (dress, key events, key individuals, etc.) for the student to color.	**Participate** in a discussion of the Biblical Principle and Leading Idea. **Recall** some of the reasons for why the Pilgrims wanted to establish a new colony. **Listen** as the teacher presents information about: • The Pilgrim's voyage on the *Mayflower* • The *Mayflower Compact* • The challenges that faced the Pilgrims in the New World • The relationship between the Indians and the Pilgrims in the Plymouth Colony **Learn** about the childhood and providential preparation of William Bradford, the first governor of the Plymouth Colony. *Notebook Work* **Color** the picture of some aspect of the Pilgrim life's (dress, key events, key individuals, etc.).	• To recall reasons why the Pilgrims wanted to establish a new colony • To learn about God's Hand of Providence in the lives of the Pilgrims and the Plymouth Colony • To complete and file notebook work	

180   The Noah Plan Lessons Kindergarten © 2003 • Foundation for American Christian Education

Week Eight

Quarter Three

TEACHING PLAN

GEOGRAPHY

Preparation	Lesson	Student Work	Accomplishments	✓

Biblical Principle
God created each continent distinct to fit His purpose and His plan. Psalm 115:16
 	
Leading Idea
The nature and character of God are revealed in the continent of Antarctica.
 	
Books
• Bible (KJ)
• NPH&GG, 128,240
• T&L, 141–153, 156–157
• Antarctica articles, *Journal of F.A.C.E.*, Volume I
 	
Supplies
• World map and globe
• Map standard
• Colored pencils
• Outline map of Antarctica (Use map from NPH&GG, 240 as a guide.)
• Notebook page to include:
  • the title "Antarctica's Individuality" for the student to write or trace
  • a space for the student to glue pictures of Antarctica
	Continue to guide the student to the Biblical Principle from the Leading Idea by reviewing the plants and animals that are unique to Antarctica.
	
	Lead a classroom discussion encouraging the student to reason and relate the things he has learned about Antarctica with God's Principle of Individuality.
	
	Notebook Work
	Prepare and distribute a simple outline map of Antarctica. **Instruct** the student to color the map according to the map standard for physical maps.
	Distribute a notebook page for the student to write or trace the title "Antarctica's Individuality" and glue pictures from last week's lesson onto this page.
	
	OR
	
	Save the pictures to be used for a group project in the fourth quarter.
		Review by recalling the unique plants and animals of Antarctica from memory or by selecting them from assorted pictures.
		Reason and relate about how the things learned about Antarctica are an example of God's Principle of Individuality.
		
		Notebook Work
		Follow the map standard for physical maps and complete the map of Antarctica.
		Write or trace the title on the notebook page.
		Glue pictures (cut from magazines last lesson) onto the distributed title notebook page.
		
		OR
		
		Save the pictures to be used for a group project in the fourth quarter.
			• To recall unique plants and animals of Antarctica
			• To reason and relate knowledge of Antarctica to God's Principle of Individuality
			• To complete and file notebook work	

The Noah Plan Lessons Kindergarten © 2003 • Foundation for American Christian Education

Week Eight

Quarter Three

TEACHING PLAN

SCIENCE

Preparation	Lesson	Student Work	Accomplishments	✓

Biblical Principles
• God's Principle of Individuality
• Unity with Diversity
 	
Leading Idea
All animals are an expression of God's character and nature.
 	
Books
• Bible (KJ)
• T&L, 156
• Zoology books (Library)
• Encyclopedia
 	
Supplies
• Pictures or live specimens of worms
• Notebook page to include:
  • the title "Worms" for the student to write or trace
  • a picture or space for the student to illustrate and color
• Colored pencils
	Review the definitions for zoology, vertebrate, and invertebrate.
	Review the major differences between vertebrate and invertebrate animals and discuss how these differences illustrate God's Principles of Individuality and Unity with Diversity.
	
	Introduce invertebrates by focusing on worms.
	
	Present visuals or live specimens of worms and discuss distinguishing characteristics.
	Explain how God's Principle of Individuality and Unity with Diversity can be seen in the animal kingdom through the distinguishing characteristics of major animal groups and individual animals.
	
	Notebook Work
	Distribute the prepared notebook page for the student to write or trace the title and to color the picture.
		Review the definitions of zoology, vertebrate and invertebrate.
		Review the major differences between vertebrate and invertebrate animals.
		Relate the differences between vertebrate and invertebrate animals to God's Principles of Individuality and Unity with Diversity.
		
		Listen as your teacher introduces and presents visual examples of worms.
		Observe and discuss the distinguishing characteristics of worms.
		Relate these characteristics to God's Principles of Individuality and Unity with Diversity as seen in major groups of the animal kingdom.
		
		Notebook Work
		Write or trace the title on the notebook page and color the picture.
			• To review the definitions of zoology, vertebrate, and invertebrate
			• To review differences between vertebrates and invertebrates and relate to Biblical Principles
			• To view pictures or live specimens of worms
			• To name distinguishing features of worms
			• To draw or color pictures of worms on zoology title page
			• To introduce the major animal groups
			• To complete and file notebook work	

182   The Noah Plan Lessons Kindergarten © 2003 • Foundation for American Christian Education

Quarter Three

TEACHING PLAN

Week Nine

	Preparation	Lesson	Student Work	Accomplishments	✓
BIBLE	**Biblical Principle** God directs our worship. **Leading Idea** Solomon built the temple by following God's direction. **Books** • Bible (KJ) • Webster's 1828 *Dictionary* **Supplies** • A simplified diagram of Solomon's temple to include: · the title "Solomon's Temple" for the student to write or trace the title · a picture of the inside of the temple for the student to color **BAR** Map Work	**Introduce** the memory verse. John 4:24 • **Read** aloud and discuss the memory verse. • **Define** unfamiliar vocabulary. • **Practice** daily the memory verse with the student for his recitation on Friday. **Guide** the student to the Biblical Principle from the Leading Idea. • **Tell** the student Solomon built the temple by following God's directions. • **Discuss** the following: · The different types of material used to build the temple · How many people it took to build the temple · How many years it took to build the temple · How the temple was built to worship God • **Discuss** how good things come to us when we follow God's direction. • **Define** worship and discuss how God directs our worship. **Show** the wall diagram of the temple and discuss the following: • the priests function • the instruments • the tabernacle • the music • the dance *Notebook Work* **Distribute** the prepared diagram of the temple for the student to write or trace title and to color the picture. **BAR** Map work: Diagram of the temple worship—priests, instruments, tabernacle, music, and dance (See Weekly Routines for Reading and English.)	**Listen** as the teacher reads aloud and discusses the memory verse. • **Discuss** unfamiliar vocabulary. • **Practice** and learn the memory verse for recitation on Friday. **Listen** as the teacher tells the story of how Solomon built the temple by following God's directions. **Participate** in discussing the following: • The different types of material used to build the temple • How many people it took to build the temple • How many years it took to build the temple • How the temple was built to worship God **Discuss** how good things come to us when we follow God's direction. **Define** worship and discuss how God directs our worship. **View** the wall diagram of the temple and discuss the following: • the priests function • the instruments • the tabernacle • the music • the dance *Notebook Work* **Write** or trace the title on the notebook page and color the picture of the temple. **BAR** (See Weekly Routines for Reading and English.)	• To learn and recite the memory verse • To learn new vocabulary • To recognize good things come when we follow God's direction • To learn about the temple of Solomon • To complete and file notebook work	

The Noah Plan Lessons Kindergarten © 2003 • Foundation for American Christian Education

Week Nine | **TEACHING PLAN** | Quarter Three

Preparation	Lesson	Student Work	Accomplishments
Biblical Principles • God's Principle of Individuality • Unity with Diversity **Leading Idea** Every poem is an expression of an individual's life, his gifts, and his faith. **Books** • Bible (KJ) • NPLG, 8–9, 108–123 • *A Child's Garden of Verses*, Robert Louis Stevenson **Supplies** • Notebook page to include: • the poet's name to write or trace • the words to a selected piece of his poetry • a picture of Stevenson to color or a space to illustrate the poem • Colored pencils	**Review** the Biblical Principle and the Leading Idea. **Introduce** the poet Robert Louis Stevenson by presenting a brief biography and discussing his place on the Chain of Christianity. **Instruct** the student to identify literary elements such as rhythm, alliteration, and rhyme as you read several selections of his poetry from *A Child's Garden of Verses*. **Lead** a discussion about his poetic style. *Notebook Work* **Distribute** the prepared notebook page for the student to write or trace the title and to color.	**Participate** in a review of the Biblical Principle and Leading Idea. **Listen** as the teacher presents a biographical background for Robert Louis Stevenson. **Participate** in a discussion about his place on the Chain of Christianity. **Identify** literary elements such as rhythm, alliteration, and rhyme as the teacher reads several selections from *A Child's Garden of Verses*. **Discuss** his poetic style. *Notebook Work* **Write** or trace the title and color the picture. Robert Louis Stevenson HAPPY THOUGHT The world is so full of a number of things, I'm sure we should all be as happy as kings. *—Robert Louis Stevenson*	• To learn about the individuality of the poet Robert Louis Stevenson • To identify literary elements in selected poems by Robert Louis Stevenson • To complete and file notebook work

LITERATURE

184   The Noah Plan Lessons Kindergarten © 2003 • Foundation for American Christian Education

Week Nine

Quarter Three

TEACHING PLAN

	Preparation	Lesson	Student Work	Accomplishments	✔
HISTORY	**Biblical Principle** God uses individuals to forward His Gospel and His plan. Ephesians 2:10 **Leading Idea** Squanto was prepared by God to preserve the Pilgrims. **Books** • Bible (KJ) • *Squanto: Friend of the Pilgrims*, Clyde Robert Bulla, Scholastic Inc. **Supplies** • Picture of Squanto for the student to color • Colored pencils	**Discuss** the Biblical Principle and the Leading Idea. **Teach** Squanto and his contributions by reading aloud selections from *Squanto: Friend of the Pilgrims.* *Notebook Work* **Distribute** the picture of Squanto for the student to color.	**Participate** in a discussion of the Biblical Principle and Leading Idea. **Listen** as the teacher reads aloud selections from the book *Squanto: Friend of the Pilgrims* and discusses his contributions. *Notebook Work* **Color** the picture of Squanto.	• To learn about the contributions of Squanto • To appreciate Squanto • To complete and file notebook work	

The Noah Plan Lessons Kindergarten © 2003 • Foundation for American Christian Education

TEACHING PLAN

Week Nine — Quarter Three

GEOGRAPHY

Preparation	Lesson	Student Work	Accomplishments
Biblical Principle God created each continent distinct to fit His purpose and His plan. Psalm 115:16 **Leading Idea** The nature and character of God are revealed in the continent of Australia. **Books** • Bible (KJ) • NPH&GG, 128, 219–222 • T&L, 141–153, 156–157 **Supplies** • World map and globe • Student atlas • Colored pencils • Pictures of Australia • EMBG, Volume 3:8	• **Guide** the student to the Biblical Principle from the Leading Idea. • **Locate** Australia on the classroom world map and globe. • **Introduce** geographic features that contribute to Australia's being called the "continent of antiquity." • **Present** information about the natural resources and climate that contribute to the individuality of Australia. • **Display** pictures of various regions in Australia. *Notebook Work* **Distribute** EMBG, Volume 3:8 and instruct the student in completing the page.	• **Listen** and observe as the teacher: • **Locates** Australia on the classroom world map and globe. • **Presents** information about why this continent is called the "continent of antiquity." • **Introduces** geographic features that contribute to its individuality. **View** pictures of different regions in Australia. *Notebook Work* **Color** and complete the notebook page distributed by the teacher. 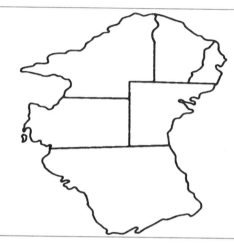 Australia	• To learn about the location and individuality of Australia • To view pictures of Australia • To complete and file notebook work

Week Nine
Quarter Three

TEACHING PLAN

SCIENCE

Preparation	Lesson	Student Work	Accomplishments	✓

Biblical Principles
• God's Principle of Individuality
• Unity with Diversity
 	
Leading Idea
All animals are an expression of God's character and nature.
 	
Books
• Bible (KJ)
• Zoology books (Library)
• Encyclopedia
 	
Supplies
• Pictures or live specimens of arthropods
• Notebook page to include:
  • the title "Arthropods" for the student to write or trace
  • a picture or space for the student to illustrate and color
• Colored pencils
	Review the Biblical Principles and Leading Idea.
	
	Review the individuality of worms.
	
	Introduce and provide information about arthropods.
	
	Present visuals or live specimens of arthropods and discuss distinguishing characteristics.
	• **Discuss** distinguishing features.
	• **Relate** to God's Principle of Individuality and Unity with Diversity as seen in major groups of the animal kingdom.
	
	Notebook Work
	Distribute the prepared notebook page for the student to write or trace the title and to color the picture of arthropods.
		Participate in a discussion of the Biblical Principles and Leading Idea.
		Review worms by naming distinguishing characteristics that illustrate their individuality.
		
		Observe and discuss the individuality of arthropods.
		
		Relate these characteristics to God's Principles of Individuality and Unity with Diversity as seen in major groups of the animal kingdom.
		
		Notebook Work
		Write or trace the title on the notebook page and color the picture of arthropods.
			• To review the characteristics of worms
			• To view pictures or live specimens of arthropods
			• To name distinguishing features of arthropods
			• To complete and file notebook work	

The Noah Plan Lessons Kindergarten © 2003 • Foundation for American Christian Education   187

Quarter Four

How sweet and endearing is the name of home! What music in that sacred sound! . . . Who could wish to leave home and wander forth in the world to meet its tempest and its storms? Without a mother's watchful care and a sister's tender love? Not one. . . . Then give me a place at home, a seat at my father's fireside, where all is so happy and free."
—(An early school composition by Laura Ingall's Mother)

Gareth R.

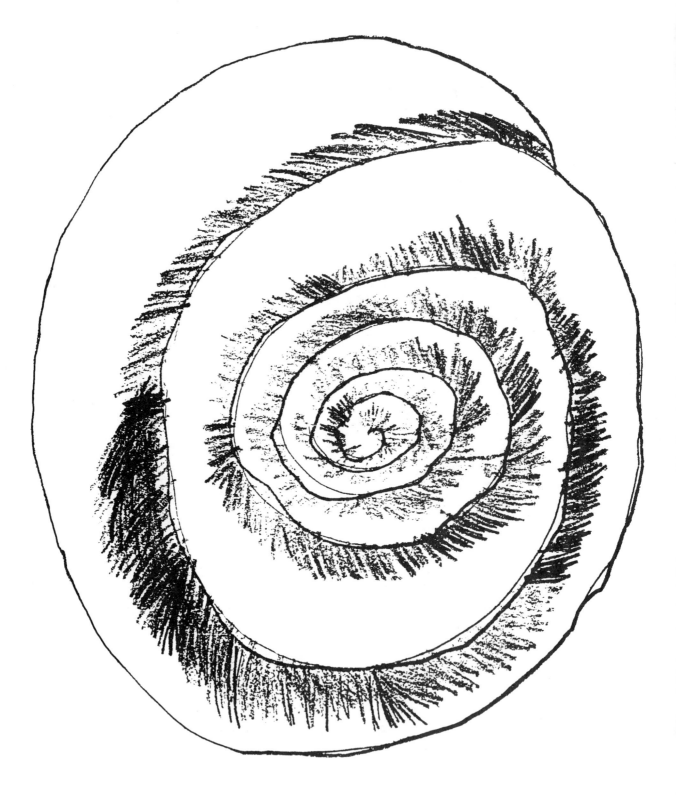

Joshua P.

Quarter Four Planning Sheet for Teaching Mathematics by Components

Teacher: Mr. Ricciardi   Grade Level: K

"Eye hath not seen nor ear heard, neither have entered into the heart of man, the things which God hath prepared for them that love him." 1 Corinthians 2:9

Week	Foundations	Numbers	Numeration/Notation	Measurement	Operations	Problem Solving
1 RSL 58–61	CSG–patterning, CSP–notating, DP–partitioning, GPI–arranging, CFG–traditional quantities	Consecutive numbers, Place value, Teens 11 to 19	Journaling, Naming 11 and 12, Reading abacus entries, Reading numbers, Traditional names 11–19, Vocabulary	Clock	Add 2-digit quantities, Addition, Multiplication by 2s, 5s, 10s, Subtraction	Abacus entries, Constructing number booklet, Partitioning, Patterning, Practicing
2 RSL 61–64	CP–adding 1 to a number, CSP–notating, GPI–arranging, CFG–representation	Place value, Quantities 1–100	Reading abacus entries, Reading about time, Vocabulary, Writing and reading the clock	Clock–numbers around the clock, length of an hour, hands on a clock, o'clock positions	Addition, "+1 more" strategy, Multiplication by 2s, 5s	Abacus entries, Arranging, Games, Practicing
3 RSL 64–67	AP–matching, GPI–order, CFG–representation	Quantities 1–30	Reading abacus entries, Vocabulary	Clock, Distance, Geoboard, Parallel lines, Rectangle	Addition, Multiplication by 2s, 5s	Abacus entries, Constructing, Matching, Practicing
4 RSL 68–70	CSG–discuss, assess, CSP–notating, GPI–comparing, CFG–charting	Even numbers, Odd numbers, Place value, Quantities 1–100	Reading abacus entries, Recording results, Vocabulary	Clock–hour, minute, Linear measure, Rectangle, Square, Triangle	Addition, Multiplication by 2s, 5s, 10s	Abacus entries, Analyzing, Comparing, Matching, Practicing
5 RSL 70–72	CSG–estimating, CSP–forming an opinion, GPI–quantities, CFG–comparing	Odd numbers, Quantities 1–100	Reading abacus entries, Reading water levels, Vocabulary	Clock, Dozen, Rectangle, Square, Volume and weight	Addition, Multiplication by 5s, 10s	Abacus entries, Comparing, Determining quantity, Estimating
6 RSL 73–75	APU–assembling, AP–matching, DP–partitioning, GPI–comparing, CFG–naming	Fractions 1/2 to 1/16	Naming unit fractions, Vocabulary, Reading abacus entries	Clock–quarter hour, Dozen, Money, Octagon	Addition, Division, Multiplication–by 5s, 10s	Abacus entries, Arranging, Comparing, Constructing, Engineering, Folding, Matching
7 RSL 76–77	CFG–modeling, GPI–quantities	Even numbers	Vocabulary	Circle, Clock, Cone, Cylinder, Rectangle, Sphere	Addition, Division	Modeling, Story problems
8 RSL Work Sheets	CFG–notating, GPI–quantities, CFG–representation	Fractions	Halves, Reading abacus entries, Writing equations	Octagon, Pentagon, Semi-circle, Trapezoid	Addition	Abacus entries, Completing equations, Finding halves
9 AFLM	The governmental and subject principles reinforced					

Activities for Learning™ reinforces the components taught during the entire school year this week.

Summary of Principles

The principles and leading ideas of mathematics are demonstrated in the lessons, and are continually clarified for the children as the year progresses.

Governmental Principles

God's Principle of Individuality (GPI) Mathematics measures 'how much.' Each number is a unique quantity.

Christian Self-Government (CSG) Operations (+, -, x, ÷) govern mathematics.

Christian Character (AHCC) Mathematics demonstrates God's character. It is systematic, unchangeable, and orderly like God.

"Conscience...Sacred Property" (CSP) Mathematics enables the individual to Biblically care for property.

Christian Form of Government (CFG) Quantity is represented in various ways.

Local Self-Government (LSG) Christ's government is planted into the heart of the student as the student deals with the operations (government) and processes of mathematics.

American Political Union (APU) Numbers of like kind only may be added.

Subject Principles

Associative Principle (AP), NPMG, 104

Distributive Principle (DP). NPMG, 104, 113

Commutative Principle (CP), NPMG, 104

See **Sample Math Guide/Right-Start Coordination, Lessons, & Annual Schedule**, 269–281.

Quarter Four—Weekly Routines for Reading and English

COMPONENT	Monday	Tuesday	Wednesday	Thursday	Friday
FOUNDATIONS	**Teach** England and France on the Chain of Christianity. God used English to take the Bible to America and	the entire world, NPEG, 47, 56, 60, 77.			
ORTHOGRAPHY Phonemic Awareness Instruction	**Teach** Kindergarten schedule, *Phonemic Awareness in Young Children*, 137–141. **Use** the black line master in for a visual check of how often each activity is practiced, *Phonemic*		*Awareness in Young Children*, 142–143. **Continue** your day-to-day monitoring of your student to guide when to offer new activities and when to revisit or modify old ones.		
Penmanship	**Continue** to master letter formation as phonograms are reviewed.	**Continue** to master letter formation as phonograms	**Continue** to practice capital letter formation, *The Writing Road to Reading*, 29–30.	**Reinforce** letter formation as phonograms are dictated.	
Spelling	**Reinforce** the mastery of phonograms 1–54 with written review procedures, *Writing Road to Reading*, 41–42. **Mix** and test between 8 and 16 phonograms. **Continue** the Extended Ayers List, *The Writing Road to Reading*, 252–262. **Refer** to Scope and Sequence objectives in *The Writing Road to Reading*, 444. **Administer** the Morrison-McCall Spelling Scale Test to determine the student's progress at the beginning of the quarter, *Spalding Spelling Assessment Manual*, 19. **See** "Spelling Assessment Procedures" in *Spalding Spelling Assessment Manual*, 7–13. **Assign** homework: Write first five words 3x and use in an oral sentence.		**Continue** *Spelling Dictation Procedure* with the next five words, *The Writing Road to Reading*, 48–53. **Read** spelling words orally. **Elicit** oral sentences from student. **Write** sentences from oral discussion on the chalkboard. (Student copies and may illustrate.) **Assign** homework: Write five words 3x and use in an oral sentence.	**Continue** to review previously learned phonograms by decoding (reading) and encoding (writing). **Continue** *Spelling Dictation Procedure*. **Write** the week's words in a practice test. **Assign** homework: Study for test.	**Continue** to review previously learned phonograms by decoding (reading) and encoding (writing). **Test** spelling words at the end of the week; do not require the markings for test, *Writing Road to Reading*, 85.
COMPOSITION	**Teach** simple initial and end punctuation. **Continue** writing group paragraphs to learn paragraph form.	**Write** sentences daily. **Write** a simple paragraph independently by spring.		**Introduce** simple initial capitalization and end punctuation.	

Quarter Four—Weekly Routines for Reading and English (continued)

COMPONENT	Monday	Tuesday	Wednesday	Thursday	Friday
SYNTAX	**Continue** teaching the sentence by identifying the subjects and verbs as naming and action word and giving the student opportunity to identify these parts daily in the context of the whole sentence, NPEG, 142–147.	**Encourage** the use of complete sentences in daily speaking and in writing. **Demonstrate** the sentence and paragraph by giving examples of complete thoughts in well-phrased sen-		tences from the literature and Bible. **Reinforce** simple initial capitalization and end punctuation.	
ETYMOLOGY	**Continue** to teach syllables and the ability to identify the syllables of any word, NPRG, 111. **Teach** precise meanings of words. Show the dictionary		and read the definition aloud to impart precise meaning. **Continue** enjoying words that rhyme, describe, and many new words from Bible, literature, science,	history, and geography. **Use** daily *Phonemic Awareness in Young Children*, 137–141.	
READING Phonetic instruction	**Practice** phonograms using multi-sensory instruction—the Spalding Method, *The Writing Road to*		*Reading*, 6, 39–42. This practice can be done during the orthography segments.		
Oral Reading	**Model** fluent reading by reading selected passages aloud simultaneously in a group—choral reading. **Introduce** *reader's theatre* activity to promote cooperative interaction with peers and provide fluency practice. Student reads from scripts that have been derived from Bible or literature passages that are rich in dialogue. Student plays a character that speaks lines or a narrator who shares necessary background information. **Continue** partner-reading activities. The teacher reads aloud as the student follows the text. Pair the student with a more fluent reader or pair with a less fluent reader. Another option is to pair students who read at the same level to reread a story		for which they they have received instruction during a teacher-guided part of the lesson. **Continue** to present opportunities for student to become a fluent reader—provide models of fluent reading, repeated readings with guidance, and offer books at his independent level of reading ability. **Read** aloud spelling words from the board and also from the cahier (spelling notebook). **Assign** oral reading homework in supplementary readers (home readers) to be returned daily, NPRG, 71.	**Read** aloud selected passages from the kindergarten literature curriculum, NPLG, 8–9.	
Bible as Reader	**Read** passages from *The Early Reader's Bible* selected to correspond to Bible lessons in *Noah Plan Lessons Kindergarten* (NPLK) A majority of the students will be able to read with assistance or independently, NPRG, 66–67, 96–97.		**Read** passages from *The Early Reader's Bible* selected to correspond to Bible lessons in the *Noah Plan Lessons Kindergarten* (NPLK).		
Comprehension	**Provide** opportunities for independent practice identifying characters, settings, plots, point of view, theme and Biblical principle, *The Writing Road to Reading*, 121–147.		**Guide** the student as he explains the author's purpose, and the elements in paragraphs. **Confirm** the student's consciously using mental actions—checking comprehension, making connections with prior knowledge, making predictions, reformat-	ting/categorizing information and mentally summarizing, *The Writing Road to Reading*, 121–147. **Use** the "Reading Skills Chart" to guide quarterly planning and to set goals, NPRG, 19.	

The Noah Plan Lessons Kindergarten © 2003 • Foundation for American Christian Education

Quarter Four
Kindergarten Reading Instruction Supplement

FLUENCY INSTRUCTION

PRINCIPLE AND LEADING IDEAS
Conscience Is the Most Sacred of All Property:
- *Individual sounds (phonemes) make up spoken language.*
- *The sounds of speech (phonemes) are distinct from their meaning.*

The Principle of Christian Self-Government:
- *There is order in language, in sentences, and in words.*
- *Rules of propriety govern the way language works.*
- *My command of English helps me be self-governed in all areas of my life.*

Fact: Repeated and monitored oral reading improves reading fluency and overall reading achievement.

What are the ways of teaching and learning fluency? Activities for repeated oral reading practice include student-adult reading, choral reading, tape-assisted reading, partner reading and readers' theatre. (*Put Reading First*, 27–29)

- Student-adult reading. The student reads one-on-one with an adult. The adult reads first, providing a model of fluent reading. Then the student reads and rereads with the adult helping with word recognition until the reading is fluent. This usually takes three to four re-readings.
- Choral reading. Students read as a group with an adult leader. First fluent reading is modeled and then students read along, as they are able. The rereading may be spaced over different days to allow the student to read the text independently.
- Tape-assisted reading. The student reads along with a taped recording or as an echo to an audio-taped model. Again, the reading continues until the student can read without the tape.
- Partner reading.
  - The teacher reads the new passage to the class while the students read the passage silently. She may note new words and concepts in the passage.
  - The students work in pairs and take turns reading the passage to each other.
  - One of the pair takes the role of "student" and reads the passage orally. The "teacher" listens while looking at the words in the story. Both are getting practice with the story.
  - Reverse roles.
  - Read the story a total of four times. Partnering can be with a more fluent partner or a partner of equal ability.

- Readers' theatre. Students read from scripts that have been developed from their reading book, preferably those rich in dialogue. No costumes are used, rather students portray the character with their voice. There is opportunity for many repeated readings as the students rehearse for the performance.

Why is fluency important? "More fluent readers focus their attention on making connections among ideas in a text and between these ideas and their background knowledge." (*Put Reading First,* 22) **They are able to focus on comprehension**. "Fluent readers recognize words and comprehend at the same time. Less fluent readers, however, must focus their attention on figuring out the words, leaving them little attention for understanding the text." (*Put Reading First,* 22)

When should instruction begin?
Instruction should begin when the student is asked to read orally material he has not practiced and makes more than ten percent recognition errors. A second consideration is if the student does not read with expression and lastly if the student's comprehension is poor.

Which methods of instruction are most effective?
A teacher or parent can help his student or child by first modeling fluent reading and then having the student or child reread the text on his own. A second help is have the student repeatedly read passages aloud as you offer guidance. (*Put Reading First,* 26) The reading passages should be at the student's independent reading level and between 50–200 words in length. Use a variety of reading material. Choose stories found in the students' basal readers, Bible readers, or library books. Poetry is also recommended because of the rhythm, rhyme, and meaning, making practice easy and fun.

Research recommends that each passage be read about four times. The number four seems appropriate since the Bible gives us four readings of the life of Christ in Matthew, Mark, Luke, and John.

What materials are suggested?

The Writing Road to Reading: The Spalding Method for Teaching Speech, Spelling, Writing, and Reading, 5th Edition, 2003.

Put Reading First: The Research Building Blocks for Teaching Children to Read, September, 2001. Copies available from National Institute for Literacy at ED Pubs, PO Box 1398, Jessup, MD 20794-1398. Phone 1-800-228-8813; Fax 301-430-1244. To download go to the National Institute for Literacy website at www.nifl.gov.

The Noah Plan Reading Curriculum Guide, Martha Shirley. San Francisco: F.A.C.E., 1997.

Week One   **TEACHING PLAN**   Quarter Four

Preparation	Lesson	Student Work	Accomplishments	✓
Biblical Principle God instructs us to remember what Jesus has done for us.	**Introduce** the memory verse: "This is that bread which came down from heaven . . . he that eateth of this bread shall live forever." John 6:58 • **Read** aloud and discuss the memory verse. • **Define** unfamiliar vocabulary. • **Practice** daily the memory verse with the student for his recitation on Friday.	**Listen** as the teacher reads aloud and discusses the memory verse. ● **Discuss** unfamiliar vocabulary. ● **Practice** and learn the memory verse for recitation on Friday.	• To learn and recite the memory verse • To learn new vocabulary • To understand the significance of the Last Supper • To complete and file notebook work	
Leading Idea Jesus used the Last Supper to help his disciples to remember Him.	**Guide** the student to the Biblical Principle from the Leading Idea. • **Read** aloud Matthew 26:26–28 and discuss the following: • The reason this was going to be the Last Supper with Jesus and his disciples • The breaking of the bread and the drinking of the wine • Jesus' description of the bread • Jesus' description of the wine	**Listen** as the teacher reads aloud Matthew 26:26–28. ● **Reason** orally and answer questions about the Leading Idea: • Why was this going to be the Last Supper with Jesus and his disciples? • What did Jesus do that was very special during this Last Supper? • How did Jesus describe the bread? • How did Jesus describe the wine?		
Books • Bible (KJ) • Webster's 1828 *Dictionary*	• **Explain** to the student that Jesus used the Last Supper to help his disciples to remember Him.	● **Listen** as the teacher explains why Jesus used the Last Supper to help his disciples to remember Him.		
Supplies • Notebook page to include: • the title "The Last Supper" for the student to write or trace • a space for the student to draw and to color a picture of the Last Supper	• **Tell** the student that Christians all over the world take bread and wine in remembrance of Jesus and His death for our sins. This event is called Communion.	● **Listen** as the teacher explains the event called Communion.		
	Notebook Work **Distribute** the prepared notebook page for the student to write or trace the title and to draw and color a picture of the Last Supper.	*Notebook Work* **Write** or trace the title and draw and color the picture of the Last Supper.		
BAR—Bible As Reader Books • *Early Reader's Bible*, 442–450 • Bible (KJ), Matthew 26:26–28 • NPRG	**BAR—Bible As Reader** "Supper with Jesus" "The Lord's Supper," Matthew 26:26–28 (See Weekly Routines for Reading and English.)	**BAR—Bible As Reader** (See Weekly Routines for Reading and English.)		

196   The Noah Plan Lessons Kindergarten © 2003 • Foundation for American Christian Education

TEACHING PLAN

Quarter Four

Week One

LITERATURE

Preparation	Lesson	Student Work	Accomplishments	✓
Biblical Principle God looks on the heart of a man or woman. 1 Samuel 16:7 **Leading Idea** The study of an autobiography is the study of the internal character of an individual. **Books** • *Little House in the Big Woods*, Laura Ingalls Wilder • Bible (KJ) • NPLG, 8–9, 129–132, 134–138 • Teacher Guide: "Pilgrim-Pioneer Character Moving Westward," Rosalie J. Slater, F.A.C.E. • Biography of Laura Ingalls Wilder • Books about frontier life **Supplies** • Classroom map of America • Pictures of frontier life • Prepared notebook page • Tapes of frontier music • Samples of frontier foods • Student atlas • Colored pencils	**Read** aloud 1 Samuel 16:7 and discuss the Biblical Principle and Leading Idea. **Review** the definition and characteristics of a biography. **Introduce** autobiography. • It is a style of literature. • It is a biography of one's life written by himself. **Compare** similarities and differences of a biography and autobiography. **Begin** reading aloud *Little House in the Big Woods* focusing on God's Principles of Individuality and Unity with Diversity in America. **Introduce** the author, Laura Ingalls Wilder. • Her individuality and life as a "pioneer girl." • Her purpose for writing the book. **Present** the individuality of frontier life. • **Locate** Wisconsin on the classroom map of America and in the student's atlas. • **Display** and discuss pictures of transportation and houses. • **Discuss** the character of the people. • **Present** pictures of frontier clothing. • **Listen** to frontier music. • **Provide** samples of food that represent the historical and geographical setting. *Notebook Work* **Distribute** the prepared notebook page for the student to write or trace the title and name of the author and to color the picture. Prepared notebook page to include: • the title of the book and author's name to write or trace • a picture of the author to color	**Listen** as the teacher reads aloud 1 Samuel 16:7 and participate in the discussion. **Participate** in a review of the definition and characteristics of a biography. **Listen** as the teacher introduces autobiography. **Participate** in a discussion of the differences and similarities of a biography and autobiography. **Listen** as the teacher lays the foundation for the study of *Little House in the Big Woods* with a focus on God's Principles of Individuality and Unity with Diversity in America. **Learn** about Laura Ingalls Wilder: • Her individuality and life as a "pioneer girl" • Her purpose for writing the book **Gain** a better understanding of the individuality of frontier life: • **Locate** Wisconsin on the classroom map of America and in your atlas. • **View** and discuss pictures of the homes and transportation. • **Learn** about the character of the people. • **View** pictures of clothing. • **Listen** to music. • **Sample** food that is representative of the historical and geographical setting. *Notebook Work* **Write** or trace the title and name of the author and color the picture.	• To compare biography and autobiography • To view a map and pictures of the frontier • To learn about frontier life • To listen to frontier music • To sample historical foods • To complete and file notebook work	

The Noah Plan Lessons Kindergarten © 2003 • Foundation for American Christian Education

Week One **TEACHING PLAN** Quarter Four

Preparation	Lesson	Student Work	Accomplishments
Biblical Principle The Principle of America's Heritage of Christian Character **Leading Idea** Pressures in life cause growth. **Books** • Bible (KJ) • Webster's 1828 *Dictionary* • NPH&GG, 8–9, 68 • NPSDS, Providential History, Links • T&L, 73–75, 122–124, 210–224 • CHOC I, 24–27, 148–150, 176–240 • *George Washington*, d'Aulaire **Supplies** • Notebook page that represents the T-chart to contrast the trials and tribulations and faith and steadfastness (T&L, 216–219)	**Review** the Pilgrim story by asking the student to recall key events that motivated the Pilgrims to come to the New World. **Introduce** the Principle of America's Heritage of Christian Character. **Define** the terms faith and steadfastness in an age appropriate manner. **Lead** a discussion about how the Pilgrims demonstrated faith and steadfastness and other qualities of Christian character through their trials and tribulations. **Discuss** how the Pilgrims were people who loved God and His Word. **Guide** the student to relate ways he should or has demonstrated Christian character qualities in difficult situations. **Create** a T-chart on the blackboard. (Use T&L, 216–219 as a guide to record some of the examples given by the student about how the Pilgrims responded to trials and tribulations.) **Discuss** the importance of remembering your Christian heritage. (It reminds you how important you are to God.) *Notebook Work* **Provide** a notebook page for the student that is similar to the chart done on the board. The student may fill in the examples listed or may illustrate examples filled in by the teacher.	**Review** the Pilgrim story by recalling key events that motivated the Pilgrims to come to the New World and the challenges that they faced. **Listen** as the teacher introduces the Principle of America's Heritage of Christian Character and defines faith and steadfastness. **Participate** in a discussion about how the Pilgrims demonstrated faith and steadfastness through their trials and tribulations. **Participate** in a discussion of how the Pilgrims were people who loved God and His Word. **Relate** how you have or should have demonstrated Christian character qualities in difficult situations in your own life. **Contribute** to a corporate chart about Christian character by giving examples of how the Pilgrims responded to trials and tribulations. **Discuss** the importance of remembering your Christian heritage and how important you are to God. *Notebook Work* **Record** some of the examples that were listed on the corporate chart of how the Pilgrims demonstrated faith and steadfastness or illustrate the examples recorded by the teacher.	• To recall key events that motivated the Pilgrims to come to the New World • To learn about America's Heritage of Christian Character • To discuss examples of faith and steadfastness demonstrated by the Pilgrims • To relate Christian character qualities to the child's personal life • To contribute examples of Pilgrim faith and steadfastness to a classroom chart • To record or illustrate examples of Pilgrim faith and steadfastness • To complete and file notebook work

The Pilgrims

Trials	Faith
Poverty	Trusted God
Dangers	Showed courage
Difficulties	Patient

HISTORY

198 The Noah Plan Lessons Kindergarten © 2003 • Foundation for American Christian Education

Quarter Four

TEACHING PLAN

Week One

Preparation	Lesson	Student Work	Accomplishments
Biblical Principle God created each continent distinct to fit His purpose and His plan. Psalm 115:16 **Leading Idea** The nature and character of God are revealed in the continent of Australia. **Books** • Bible (KJ) • NPH&GG, 128, 219–222 • T&L, 141–153, 156–157 **Supplies** • World map and globe • Student atlas • Pictures or artifacts related to Australia • Australian words, phrases, or songs	**Continue** to guide the student to the Biblical Principle from the Leading Idea by reviewing the location as well as the unique geographic features, natural resources, and climate that contribute to the individuality of Australia. **Present** information about the people who inhabit Australia (culture, customs, languages, etc.). **Display** pictures or artifacts related to Australian culture (and/or ask the student to bring items to share). **Prepare** and serve native foods or learn words of a native language or song.	**Review** the location of Australia by identifying it on the classroom world map, globe, and atlas. **Review** the features that contribute to Australia's individuality by recalling unique aspects of its geography, natural resources, and climate. **Listen** as the teacher presents information about the culture, customs, and languages of the people who inhabit Australia. **View** pictures or artifacts related to Australia's culture (and/or bring items to share with the class). **Sample** native foods, listen to music or learn words of a native language.	• To locate Australia on the classroom world map, globe, and atlas • To recall unique aspects of Australia's geography, natural resources, and climate • To learn about the culture, customs, etc. of Australian people • To view pictures of Australian culture • To learn new words or a song • To sample native foods

GEOGRAPHY

The Noah Plan Lessons Kindergarten © 2003 • Foundation for American Christian Education

TEACHING PLAN

Quarter Four

Week One

SCIENCE

Preparation	Lesson	Student Work	Accomplishments
Biblical Principles • God's Principle of Individuality • Unity with Diversity **Leading Idea** All animals are an expression of God's character and nature **Books** • Bible (KJ) • Encyclopedia • Zoology books (Library) • Encyclopedia **Supplies** • Pictures or live specimens of birds • Notebook page to include: • the title "Birds" for the student to write or trace • a picture or space for the student to illustrate and color • Colored pencils *Optional* • Different types of bird nests, eggs, feathers, etc. • Fertile eggs • Incubator	**Review** the Biblical Principles and Leading Idea. **Review** arthropods. • **Ask** the student to give examples of different types of arthropods. • **Ask** the student to name some of their individual characteristics. **Introduce** and provide information about birds. • **Provide** opportunities for the student to observe this group of animals through nature study outdoors, live or preserved specimens in the classroom, pictures, etc. • **Discuss** observations with the student. • **Ask** the student to relate God's Principles of Individuality and Unity with Diversity to what he observed in birds. *Optional* **Display** and/or ask the student to collect different types of bird nests, eggs, feathers, etc. **Incubate** eggs. *Notebook Work* **Distribute** the prepared notebook page for the student to write or trace the title and to color the picture.	**Participate** in a review of the Biblical Principles and Leading Idea. **Recall** the names of different types of arthropods and give examples of their unique features. **Listen** as the teacher introduces birds and participate in a discussion about their unique characteristics. **Observe** birds presented in pictures, in live or preserved specimens, or through outdoor nature study. **Participate** in a discussion relating Biblical Principles to observations of birds. *Optional* **Collect** and display different types of bird nests, eggs, feathers, etc. **Incubate** eggs. *Notebook Work* **Write** or trace the title on the notebook page and color the picture.	• To name identifying features of arthropods • To make and record observations about birds • To relate Biblical Principles to the study of birds • To complete and file notebook work

The Noah Plan Lessons Kindergarten © 2003 • Foundation for American Christian Education

Quarter Four

Week Two

TEACHING PLAN

Preparation	Lesson	Student Work	Accomplishments	✓

Biblical Principle We should tell others about Jesus.	**Introduce** the memory verse. Matthew 28:19
	• **Read** aloud and discuss the memory verse.
	• **Define** unfamiliar vocabulary.
	• **Practice** daily the memory verse with the student for his recitation on Friday.
	
	Guide the student to the Biblical Principle from the Leading Idea.
	• **Read** aloud Matthew 28:16–20 and discuss Jesus' parting words to the disciples.
	  · Jesus has all authority on Earth and in heaven.
	  · They must go and make disciples of all nations.
	  · They are to baptize and teach others to obey Jesus' commandments.
	  · Jesus will be with us to the very end.
	
	• **Share** ways you can spread the good news of Jesus.
	
	Notebook Work
	Distribute the prepared notebook page for the student to write or trace the title and to draw and color the picture of Jesus' last visit with His disciples.
	
	BAR
	"Telling Others about Jesus"
	(See Weekly Routines for Reading and English.)
		Listen as the teacher reads aloud and discusses the memory verse.
		• **Discuss** unfamiliar vocabulary.
		• **Practice** and learn the memory verse for recitation on Friday.
		
		Listen as the teacher reads aloud Matthew 28:16–20.
		• **Discuss** the following:
		  · Jesus' parting words to the disciples.
		  · Jesus has all authority on Earth and in heaven.
		  · They must go and make disciples of all nations.
		  · They are to baptize and teach others to obey Jesus' commandments.
		  · Jesus will be with us to the very end.
		
		• **Share** ways you can spread the good news of Jesus.
		
		Notebook Work
		Write or trace the title on the notebook page and draw and color the picture of Jesus' last visit with His disciples.
		
		BAR
		(See Weekly Routines for Reading and English.)
			• To learn and recite the memory verse
			• To learn new vocabulary
			• To tell others about the good news
			• To complete and file notebook page	

Leading Idea Jesus instructed His disciples to spread the good news.				
Books • Bible (KJ) • Webster's 1828 *Dictionary*				

Supplies
• Notebook page to include:
  · the title "Jesus' Last Visit" for the student to write or trace
  · a space for the student to draw and color a picture of Jesus' last visit with His disciples				

BAR **Books** • *Early Reader's Bible*, 466–473 • NPRG				

BIBLE

The Noah Plan Lessons Kindergarten © 2003 • Foundation for American Christian Education   201

Week Two — **TEACHING PLAN** — **Quarter Four**

Preparation	Lesson	Student Work	Accomplishments	✓
Biblical Principle God uses individual character to forward His Gospel. **Leading Idea** Christianity goes westward in America. **Books** • Bible (KJ) • Webster's 1828 *Dictionary* • NPLG, 8–9, 129–132, 134–138 • *Little House in the Big Woods*, Laura Ingalls Wilder • Teacher Guide: "Pilgrim-Pioneer Character Moving Westward," Slater, F.A.C.E. **Supplies** • Map of America • Pictures of frontier life • Prepared notebook pages • Tapes of frontier music • Colored pencils	**Review** the Biblical Principle and the Leading Idea. **Review** the characteristics of frontier life using pictures, music, geographic location, etc. **Emphasize** the elements of a classic identifying setting, characters, and plot as you read aloud *Little House in the Big Woods*. **Define** and discuss new vocabulary as it is encountered. *Notebook Work* **Distribute** the prepared notebook pages for the student to complete and color. Prepared notebook pages for the study of the classic to include: • a page to record the setting • a page for each character and picture to color • a page to record the plot • a page to record the vocabulary **Record** simple phrases using the words of the author and have the student copy them on the appropriate page in his notebook. This is done daily after a section of the book is read and discussed or every other day, alternating reading and notebook work.	**Participate** in a review of the Biblical Principle and Leading Idea. **Recall** the characteristics of frontier life as the teacher reviews, displays pictures, plays music, etc. **Listen** for descriptions of the setting, the characters, and the plot as the teacher reads aloud the book. **Identify** and discuss new vocabulary as it is encountered. *Notebook Work* **Complete** and color the notebook pages. **Copy** words and descriptions used by the author on the appropriate notebook page after they are discussed orally and written on the board by the teacher.	• To review maps, pictures, and characteristics of frontier life • To identify elements of the classic as the book is read • To complete and file notebook work	

Plot
Chapter 1. Preparing for winter in the Little House.
Chapter 2. The season of winter, its activities and the feelings in the family

Week Two

Quarter Four

TEACHING PLAN

	Preparation	Lesson	Student Work	Accomplishments	✓
HISTORY	**Biblical Principle** The Principle of America's Heritage of Christian Character **Leading Idea** The founding fathers and mothers of America practiced Christian Self-Government and established Christian civil government in the New World. **Books** • Bible (KJ) • NPH&GG, 8–9, 54, 79, Appendix 341 for additional books on American Christian Republic • NPSDS, Providential History, Links • T&L, 73–75, 210–223, 240–249 • Biographies and age appropriate books about Christian patriots (See Appendix in NPH&GG, 341–342.) **Supplies** • Christian history timeline for classroom display (The Noah Plan Wall Timeline, F.A.C.E.) • Pictures of patriots introduced in the lesson • Colored pencils	**Guide** the student to the Biblical Principle from the Leading Idea. • **Introduce** the American Christian Republic Link as the eighth link on the Christian history timeline. • **Define** the word republic in an age appropriate manner. (The people elect representatives. Example: A student is elected to perform classroom chores.) • **Explain** the Biblical foundation of our government for aspects such as representation and separation of powers. • **Present** information about the Christian character that was demonstrated and the contributions that were made by selected patriots during the founding and constitutional eras of our nation. · Samuel Adams—united the colonists by his Letters of Correspondence. · Thomas Jefferson—writer of the *Declaration of Independence.* · John Adams—served as the first Vice President and Second President of the United States. · Abigail Adams—wife of our second President of the United States of America; mother of our sixth President, John Quincy Adams. · Benjamin Franklin—initiated prayer for the Constitutional Convention. **Lead** a discussion about what distinguished America as the most complete expression of Christianity in civil government: Examples: • All men created equal. • Men have rights given by God that can not be taken away, etc. *Notebook Work* **Instruct** the student to find the eighth link and color the representative picture on his individual Christian history timeline as you point it out on the classroom timeline.	**Listen** as the teacher introduces the American Christian Republic Link and locates this link on the classroom Christian history timeline. **Listen** as the teacher: • Defines the word republic • Explains the Biblical foundation of our government for representation and separation of powers • Presents information about the Christian character demonstrated by the founding fathers and mothers • Presents contributions made by patriots of the founding and constitutional eras of our nation. **Participate** in a discussion about what distinguished America as the most complete expression of Christianity in civil government. *Notebook Work* **Locate** and color the eighth link on the notebook copy of the Christian history timeline as the teacher points it out on the classroom Christian history timeline.	• To identify the American Christian Republic Link on the Christian history timeline • To learn about the Christian character and contributions of the patriots • To learn the Biblical foundation for several aspects of American government • To complete and file notebook work	

The Noah Plan Lessons Kindergarten © 2003 • Foundation for American Christian Education

Week Two

TEACHING PLAN

Quarter Four

Preparation	Lesson	Student Work	Accomplishments	✓
Biblical Principle God created each continent distinct to fit His purpose and His plan. Psalm 115:16 **Leading Idea** The nature and character of God are revealed in the continent of Australia. **Books** • Bible (KJ) • NPH&GG, 128, 219–222 • T&L, 141–153, 156–157 **Supplies** • Pictures of Australian plants and animals • Old magazines (*National Geographic, Ranger Rick,* etc.) for cutting	**Continue** to guide the student to the Biblical Principle from the Leading Idea by reviewing the unique culture (races, customs, languages, etc.) of Australia. **Present** information about the plants and animals that are native to Australia. **Display** pictures of the plants and animals that are native to Australia. *Notebook Work* **Instruct** the student to find pictures related to the topography, plant, and animal life of Australia in magazines to cut. **Instruct** the student to save these pictures in an envelope in the pocket of his geography notebook for the next week's lesson.	**Review** by recalling unique aspects of the culture of various groups of people who live in Australia. **Listen** as the teacher presents information about the plants and animals of Australia. **View** pictures of some of the plants and animals that are native to Australia. *Notebook Work* **Cut** pictures of the topography, plant, and animal life of Australia. **Save** the pictures in an envelope in the pocket of your geography notebook for next week's lesson.	• To recall unique aspects of Australian culture • To learn about plants and animals native to Australia • To view pictures of Australian plants and animals • To complete and file notebook work	

GEOGRAPHY

204   The Noah Plan Lessons Kindergarten © 2003 • Foundation for American Christian Education

Week Two — TEACHING PLAN — Quarter Four

SCIENCE

Preparation

Biblical Principles
- God's Principle of Individuality
- Unity with Diversity

Leading Idea
All animals are an expression of God's character and nature

Books
- Bible (KJ)
- Encyclopedia
- Zoology books (Library)

Supplies
- Pictures or live specimens of mammals
- Notebook page to include:
  - the title "Mammals" for the student to write or trace
  - a picture or space for the student to illustrate and color

Lesson

Review the Biblical Principles and Leading Idea.

Review birds.
- **Ask** the student to give examples of different types of birds.
- **Ask** the student to name some of their individual characteristics.

Introduce and provide information about mammals.

- **Provide** opportunities for the student to observe this group of animals through nature study outdoors, live or preserved specimens in the classroom (limit the use of preserved mammals as this may disturb the child), pictures, etc.
- **Discuss** observations with the student.

- **Ask** the student to relate God's Principles of Individuality and Unity with Diversity to what he observed in mammals.

Discuss taking care of an animal (in the classroom/home).

Optional
Take a field study trip to a zoo or dairy.

Notebook Work
Distribute the prepared notebook page for the student to write or trace the title and to color the picture.

Student Work

Participate in a review of the Biblical Principles and Leading Idea. **Recall** the names of different types of birds and give examples of their unique features.

Listen as the teacher introduces mammals and participate in a discussion about their characteristics.

Observe mammals presented in pictures, live specimens, or through outdoor nature study.

Discuss your observations with the teacher.

Participate in a discussion relating Biblical Principles to observations of mammals.

Discuss taking care of an animal (in the classroom/home).

Optional
Visit a zoo or dairy.

Notebook Work
Write or trace the title on the notebook page and color the picture.

Accomplishments

- To name identifying features of birds
- To make and record observations about mammals
- To learn the proper care of an animal
- To relate Biblical Principles to the study of mammals
- To complete and file notebook work

The Noah Plan Lessons Kindergarten © 2003 • Foundation for American Christian Education   205

Week Three

TEACHING PLAN

Quarter Four

	Preparation	Lesson	Student Work	Accomplishments	✓
BIBLE	**Bible Principle** God leads us in the way He wants us to go. **Leading Idea** God directed Philip to take the Gospel to people who wanted to hear His Word. **Books** • Bible (KJ) • Webster's 1828 Dictionary **Supplies** Notebook page to include: • the title "Philip and the Gospel" for the student to write or trace the title • a space for the student to draw and to color the picture of Philip preaching the Gospel **BAR** **Books** • Early Reader's Bible, 474–82 • NPRG	**Introduce** the memory verse. Proverbs 16:9 • **Read** aloud and discuss the memory verse. • **Define** unfamiliar vocabulary. • **Practice** daily the memory verse with the student for his recitation on Friday. **Guide** the student to the Biblical Principle from the Leading Idea. • **Introduce** the twelve apostles, as Jesus' helpers and give a brief description of each. • **Read** aloud John 1:43–46 and introduce Phillip: · One of the twelve apostles · Loyal and earnest · Third to join Jesus along with his brothers, Andrew and Peter · Fisherman by trade • **Tell** the story of Philip and the Ethiopian and discuss how God leads us in the way He wants us to go. (Acts 8:26–40) *Notebook Work* **Distribute** the prepared notebook page for the student to write or trace the title and to draw and color the picture of Philip preaching the Gospel. **BAR** "A Man Hears about Jesus" (See Weekly Routines for Reading and English.)	**Listen** as the teacher reads aloud and discusses the memory verse. • **Discuss** unfamiliar vocabulary. • **Practice** and learn the memory verse for recitation on Friday. **Listen** as the teacher introduces the twelve apostles and gives a brief description of each. **Read** aloud John 1:43–46 and introduce Phillip: · One of the twelve apostles · Loyal and earnest · Third to join Jesus along with his brothers, Andrew and Peter · Fisherman by trade **Listen** to the story of Philip and the Ethiopian and participate in the discussion of how God leads us in the way He wants us to go. *Notebook Work* **Write** or trace the title and draw and color the picture of Philip preaching the Gospel. **BAR** (See Weekly Routines for Reading and English.)	• To learn and recite the memory verse • To learn new vocabulary • To learn to listen to God's Word for direction • To talk to others about the good news of Jesus • To complete and file notebook work	

206   The Noah Plan Lessons Kindergarten © 2003 • Foundation for American Christian Education

Week Three

Quarter Four

TEACHING PLAN

Preparation	Lesson	Student Work	Accomplishments	✓
Biblical Principle God uses individual character to forward His Gospel. **Leading Idea** Christianity goes westward in America. **Books** • Bible (KJ) • NPLG, 8–9, 129–132, 134–138 • *Little House in the Big Woods*, Laura Ingalls Wilder • Teacher Guide: "Pilgrim-Pioneer Character Moving Westward," Slater, F.A.C.E. **Supplies** • Notebook pages for the study of the classic to include: • a page to record the setting • a page for each character and picture to color • a page to record the plot • a page to record the vocabulary	**Review** the Biblical Principle and Leading Idea. **Read** aloud a chapter or section from *Little House in the Big Woods* daily. • **Continue** to discuss literary elements as they are described in the story. **Introduce** and discuss the leading idea: The westward movement of Christianity in America. *Notebook Work* **Write** names, definitions, and descriptions of setting; characters; plot; and vocabulary under the correct heading on your model (blackboard or chart) as they are discussed. **Instruct** the student to copy them onto the correct notebook page.	**Participate** in a review of the Biblical Principle and Leading Idea. **Listen** as the teacher reads aloud a chapter or section from *Little House in the Big Woods* daily. • **Continue** to identify and to discuss the author's descriptions of literary elements. **Participate** in a discussion of the leading idea: The westward movement of Christianity in America. *Notebook Work* **Copy** names, definitions, and descriptions of setting; characters; plot; and vocabulary onto the designated notebook page for each literary element. **Follow** the model the teacher writes on the board or chart.	• To identify literary elements through the author's descriptions • To complete and file notebook work	

LITERATURE

The Noah Plan Lessons Kindergarten © 2003 • Foundation for American Christian Education

207

Week Three

TEACHING PLAN

Quarter Four ✓

Preparation	Lesson	Student Work	Accomplishments
Biblical Principle The Principle of America's Heritage of Christian Character **Leading Idea** It is in the home where the foundations of Christian character are laid. **Books** • Bible (KJ) • *George Washington,* d'Aulaire • Books about George Washington (See Appendix in NPH&GG, 341–342.) • Washington's *Rules of Civility and Decent Behavior,* in *George Washington: Character and Influence of One Man,* 144–148, A2–3, FACE **Supplies** • Pictures of George Washington • Pictures and artifacts related to colonial life • Prepared notebook page • Colored pencils	**Discuss** the Biblical Principle and Leading Idea. **Review** the patriots discussed in the last lesson by asking the student to recall some of the Christian character qualities they demonstrated and by linking the patriot to the contribution he or she made to our country. **Introduce** George Washington as a patriot and "father of our country" by giving the student an overview of his character and the contributions he made to the founding of our country. **Present** a character study of George Washington by providing background information about: • His childhood and his life as a young adult • God's providence and protection in his early life. • How God prepared him for leadership. **Read** several of the "Rules of Civility" that Washington was taught as a child. **Lead** a classroom discussion about these rules and ask the student to relate whether these rules are relevant today. **Ask** the student to reason and relate orally about how some of the difficulties Washington faced helped to shape his character. **Display** pictures or artifacts pertaining to colonial life in America. *Notebook Work* **Distribute** the prepared notebook page for the student to write or trace the title and color the picture of Washington. Prepared notebook page to include: • the title "George Washington, Father of Our Country" for the student to write or trace • a picture of George Washington for the student to color	**Participate** in the discussion of the Biblical Principle and Leading Idea. **Review** the patriots discussed in the last lesson by recalling some of their Christian character qualities and by connecting each patriot to the contribution he or she made to our country. **Listen** as the teacher introduces George Washington, patriot and "father of our country," his character, and the contributions that he made to the founding of our country. **Listen** as the teacher presents background about Washington's childhood, young adult life, God's providence and protection in his early life, and his preparation for leadership. **Listen** as the teacher reads aloud several of the "Rules of Civility." **Participate** in a discussion about the "Rules of Civility" that Washington was taught as a young boy and relate whether they are relevant today. **Reason** and relate orally about the difficulties in Washington's early life and how they helped to shape his character. **View** pictures or artifacts pertaining to colonial life. *Notebook Work* **Write** or trace the title on the notebook page and color the picture of Washington.	• To recall Christian character qualities and contributions of the patriots • To learn about George Washington's childhood and young adult life • To reason and relate about *Washington's Rules of Civility and Decent Behavior* • To recall examples of God's providence and protection in Washington's life • To learn about how God prepared Washington for leadership • To reason and relate about the influences that helped to shape Washington's character • To complete and file notebook work

HISTORY

208   The Noah Plan Lessons Kindergarten © 2003 • Foundation for American Christian Education

Week Three

TEACHING PLAN

Quarter Four

Preparation	Lesson	Student Work	Accomplishments	✓
Biblical Principle God created each continent distinct to fit His purpose and His plan. Psalm 115:16	**Continue** to guide the student to the Biblical Principle from the Leading Idea by reviewing the plants and animals that are unique to Australia.	**Review** by recalling the plants and animals of Australia from memory or by selecting from assorted pictures.	• To recall unique animals and plants of Australia • To complete and file notebook work	
Leading Idea The nature and character of God are revealed in the continent of Australia.	**Lead** a discussion encouraging the student to reason and relate the things they have learned about Australia with God's Principle of Individuality.	**Reason** and relate about how the things learned about Australia are an example of God's Principle of Individuality.		
Books • Bible (KJ) • NPH&GG, 128, 219–222 • T&L, 141–153, 156–157	*Notebook Work* **Distribute** the prepared outline map of Australia and instruct the student to color the map according to the map standard for physical maps. **Distribute** the prepared notebook page for the student to write or trace the title and to glue the pictures from last week's less onto this page.	*Notebook Work* **Follow** the map standard for physical maps and complete the map of Australia. **Write** or trace the title on the notebook page and glue the pictures of Australia (cut from magazines in last week's lesson) onto the page.		
Supplies • World map and globe • Map standard • Colored pencils • Simplified outline map of Australia (Use maps from NPH&GG, 238–239 as a guide.) • Notebook page to include: • the title "Australia's Individuality" for the student to write or trace • a space for the student to glue pictures of Australia	OR **Save** the pictures to be used for a group project in the fourth quarter.	OR **Save** the pictures to be used for a group project in the fourth quarter.		

GEOGRAPHY

The Noah Plan Lessons Kindergarten © 2003 • Foundation for American Christian Education

Week Three

Quarter Four

TEACHING PLAN

Preparation	Lesson	Student Work	Accomplishments	✓
Biblical Principles • God's Principle of Individuality • Unity with Diversity **Leading Idea** All animals are an expression of God's character and nature **Books** • Bible (KJ) • Zoology books (Library) **Supplies** • Large piece of paper for mural (bulletin board paper works well) • Nature magazines for animal pictures • Cards with pictures of various animals *Optional* • Notebook page with columns labeled for the way animals move (walk/run, hop, fly, swim)	**Review** the Biblical Principles and Leading Idea. **Review** all animals with student by asking him to recall what he has observed about various animal groups and to relate this to God's Principle of Individuality and Unity with Diversity. **Classify** animals according to various body coverings by creating a large mural with four boxes or quadrants: scales, feathers, skin, and hair/fur. **Instruct** and assist the student to cut pictures from nature magazines and glue them under the appropriate heading. **Classify** animals according to how they move by grouping or matching animal cards according to whether the animal hops, jumps, walks, runs, flies, swims, etc. *Notebook Work (Optional)* **Distribute** the prepared notebook page. • **Instruct** the student to write the names of animals (or draw pictures of animals) under the column labeled for the way the animal moves. • **Model** this for the student on the board.	**Participate** in a review of the Biblical Principles and Leading Idea. **Participate** in a discussion about how the various animal groups and unique characteristics of different types of animals illustrate God's Principle of Individuality and Unity with Diversity. **Contribute** to a mural on which animals are classified by different types of body coverings. **Cut** pictures of animals from nature magazines and place them in the appropriate quadrant according to whether they are covered with scales, feathers, skin, or fur/hair. **Participate** in a classification or a matching game by grouping pictures of animals according to how they move. *Notebook Work (Optional)* **Complete** a notebook page that represents God's Principle of Individuality and Unity with Diversity by writing names or by drawing pictures of animals in different columns according to how they move.	• To identify the body coverings of animals • To place pictures on mural • To identify how an animal moves • To classify/match animal pictures • To complete and file notebook work	

SCIENCE

210   The Noah Plan Lessons Kindergarten © 2003 • Foundation for American Christian Education

Week Four   **TEACHING PLAN**   Quarter Four

Preparation	Lesson	Student Work	Accomplishments	✓

BIBLE

Preparation

Biblical Principle
God wants us to follow Him.

Leading Idea
Saul decided to follow Jesus.

Books
- Bible (KJ)
- Webster's 1828 *Dictionary*

Supplies
- Notebook page to include:
  - the title "Saul Meets Jesus" for the student to write or trace
  - a space for the student to draw and to color a picture of Saul meeting Jesus

BAR
Books
- *Early Reader's Bible*, 482–490
- NPRG

Lesson

Introduce the memory verse:
"The Lord is . . . not willing that any should perish, but that all should come to repentance." 2 Peter 3:9
- **Read** aloud and discuss the memory verse.
- **Define** unfamiliar vocabulary.
- **Practice** daily the memory verse with the student for his recitation on Friday.

Guide the student to the Biblical Principle from the Leading Idea.
- **Introduce** Saul:
  - Born in Tarsus
  - Roman citizen
  - Hated the Christians
  - Persecuted the Christians
- **Tell** the story of Saul's conversion. Acts 9:1–19
- **Discuss** the following:
  - Saul hated Jesus.
  - Saul hated Jesus' friends.
  - Saul did not want people to follow Jesus.
  - Saul changed his mind about Jesus and His followers.
  - Saul's name changed to Paul due to a heart change.

- **Reason** from the story:
  - God loves us very much.
  - God forgives those who repent of their sins.
  - God wants us to follow Him.
  - God wants us to share His Word with others.

Notebook Work
Distribute the prepared notebook page for the student to write or trace the title and to draw and color the picture of Saul meeting Jesus.

BAR
"Brighter Than the Sun"
(See Weekly Routines for Reading and English.)

Student Work

Listen as the teacher reads aloud and participate in a discussion of the memory verse.
- **Discuss** unfamiliar vocabulary.
- **Practice** and learn the memory verse for recitation on Friday.

Listen as the teacher introduces Saul:
- Born in Tarsus
- Roman citizen
- Hated the Christians
- Persecuted the Christians
- The story of Saul's conversion.
Discuss the following:
- Why did Saul hate Jesus?
- Why did Saul hate Jesus' friends?
- Why did Saul not want people to follow Jesus?
- What made Saul change his mind about Jesus and His followers?
- Why Saul's name was changed to Paul.
Reason from the story:
- God loves us very much.
- God forgives those who repent of their sins.
- God wants us to follow Him.
- God wants us to share His Word with others.

Notebook Work
Write or trace the title on the notebook page and draw and color the picture.

BAR
(See Weekly Routines for Reading and English.)

Accomplishments
- To learn and recite the memory verse
- To learn new vocabulary
- To decide to follow Jesus
- To complete and file notebook work

The Noah Plan Lessons Kindergarten © 2003 • Foundation for American Christian Education

Week Four   **Quarter Four**

TEACHING PLAN

	Preparation	Lesson	Student Work	Accomplishments	✔
LITERATURE	**Biblical Principle** God uses individual character to forward His Gospel. **Leading Idea** Christianity goes westward in America. **Books** • Bible (KJ) • NPLG, 8–9, 129–132, 134–138 • *Little House in the Big Woods*, Laura Ingalls Wilder • Teacher Guide: "Pilgrim-Pioneer Character Moving Westward," Slater, F.A.C.E. **Supplies** • Notebook pages for the study of the classic to include: • a page to record the setting • a page for each character and picture to color • a page to record the plot • a page to record the vocabulary	**Review** the Biblical Principle and Leading Idea. **Read** aloud a chapter or section from *Little House in the Big Woods* daily. • **Continue** to discuss literary elements as they are described in the story. **Introduce** and discuss the leading idea, America was built upon: • three spheres of government (home, church, and civil government) • the Christian character qualities of the people • the influence of the Christian character of the people on town growth *Notebook Work* **Write** names, definitions, and descriptions of setting, characters, plot, and vocabulary under the correct heading on your model (blackboard or chart) as they are discussed in class. **Instruct** the student to copy them onto the correct notebook page.	**Participate** in a review of the Biblical Principle and Leading Idea. **Listen** as the teacher reads aloud a chapter or section from *Little House in the Big Woods* daily. • **Continue** to identify and discuss the author's descriptions of literary elements. **Participate** in a discussion of the leading idea: America was built upon the three spheres of government, the Christian character qualities of the people, and the influence of their character on town growth. *Notebook Work* **Copy** names, definitions, and descriptions of setting, characters, plot, and vocabulary onto the designated notebook page for each literary element. **Follow** the model the teacher writes on the board or chart.	• To identify literary elements through the author's descriptions • To complete and file notebook work	

212   The Noah Plan Lessons Kindergarten © 2003 • Foundation for American Christian Education

Week Four

Quarter Four

TEACHING PLAN

	Preparation	Lesson	Student Work	Accomplishments	✓

HISTORY	**Biblical Principle**
	The Principle of America's Heritage of Christian Character
	
	Leading Idea
	God provides and protects those He calls to carry out His plan.
	
	Books
	• Bible (KJ)
	• NPH&GG, 8–9
	• *George Washington: The Character and Influence of One Man*, Verna Hall, F.A.C.E.
	
	Supplies
	• Notebook page to include:
	  • the title "George Washington:" for the student to write or trace
	  • a picture of George Washington for the student to color
	• Colored pencils
		Discuss the Biblical Principle and Leading Idea.
		
		Review George Washington's character as a child and young adult and ask the student to recall examples of God's providence and protection during that period in his life.
		
		Give background information about the American Revolution and George Washington's involvement:
		• The causes of the American Revolution
		• How George Washington was used by God to lead America to independence and establish a new nation
		• How George Washington represented the character of the republic
		
		Read the quote as it pertains to George Washington: "First in war, first in peace, and first in the hearts of his countrymen."
		Lead a discussion by asking the student to reason and relate how this quote refers to Washington's character and leadership during and after the American Revolution.
		
		Notebook Work
		Distribute the prepared notebook page for the student to write or trace the title and color the picture.
			Participate in the discussion of the Biblical Principle and Leading Idea.
			Review George Washington's character as a child and young adult and recall examples of God's providence and protection during that period in his life.
			
			Listen as the teacher gives background information about the American Revolution and George Washington's involvement:
			• The causes of the American Revolution
			• How George Washington was used by God to lead America to independence and establish a new nation
			• How George Washington represented the character of the republic
			
			Listen as the teacher reads and participate in a discussion about the quote: "First in war, first in peace, and first in the hearts of his countrymen" and how it relates to Washington's character and leadership during and after the American Revolution.
			
			Notebook Work
			Write or trace the title on the notebook page and color the picture.
				• To recall examples of God's providence and protection of George Washington as a child and young adult
				• To learn about the causes for the American Revolution
				• To learn how Washington was used by God during the American Revolution
				• To learn how Washington represented the character of the republic
				• To reason and relate orally about the quote "First in war, first in peace, and first in the hearts of his countrymen"
				• To complete and file notebook work	

The Noah Plan Lessons Kindergarten © 2003 • Foundation for American Christian Education   213

Week Four

Quarter Four

TEACHING PLAN

GEOGRAPHY	Preparation	Lesson	Student Work	Accomplishments	✓
	Biblical Principle God created each continent distinct to fit His purpose and His plan. Psalm 115:16	**Locate** Africa on the world map, globe, and in the student's atlas.	**Listen** and observe as the teacher:	• To learn about the location and individuality of Africa	
		Introduce the location and geographic features that contribute to Africa being called the "continent of animal life."	• **Locates** Africa on the classroom world map, globe, and in your atlas.	• To view pictures of Africa	
	Leading Idea The nature and character of God are revealed in the continent of Africa.	**Present** information about the natural resources and climate that contribute to the individuality of Africa.	• **Introduces** the geographic features that contribute to its individuality.	• To complete and file notebook work	
			• **Presents** information about why this continent is called the "continent of animal life."		
		Display pictures of various regions of Africa.	**View** pictures of different regions in Africa.		
	Books • Bible (KJ) • NPH&GG, 128, 194–200 • T&L, 141–153, 156–157	*Notebook Work* **Distribute** EMBG, Volume 3:7 and instruct the student in completing the page.	*Notebook Work* **Color** and complete the notebook page.		
	Supplies • World map and globe • Student atlas • Colored pencils • Pictures of Africa • EMBG, Volume 3:7				

214   The Noah Plan Lessons Kindergarten © 2003 • Foundation for American Christian Education

Week Four

Quarter Four

TEACHING PLAN

	Preparation	Lesson	Student Work	Accomplishments ✓

SCIENCE	**Biblical Principles**
	• God's Principle of Individuality
	• Unity with Diversity
	
	Leading Idea
	God is the Master Designer who created man in his image and equipped him to live in this world.
	
	Books
	• Bible (KJ)
	• Encyclopedia
	• *Learning about My Body*, The Evan-Moor Corp.
	• *My First Body Book*, Chris and Melanie Rice
	• *What's Inside? My Body*, Angela Royston
	• *Me and My Body*, David Evans and Claudette Williams
	• *The Skeleton Inside You*, Phillip Balestrino
	
	Supplies
	• Poster of the body with body parts labeled for display
	• Large picture of the skeletal system
	• An x-ray (optional)
	• Animal bones (optional)
	• Prepared notebook pages
		Continue to teach science according to the days of Creation.
		
		Discuss the Biblical Principles and Leading Idea.
		
		Introduce human anatomy and physiology.
		• **Define** human anatomy and physiology as the study of the body and how it works.
		• **Lay** the Biblical foundation for human anatomy by reading aloud Genesis 1:26–27 and Psalm 139:13–14 and by discussing:
		  • Man was created on the sixth day of Creation separate and distinct from animals.
		  • Man was created in the image of God.
		  • Man is fearfully and wonderfully made.
		Identify on the classroom poster the external body parts.
		
		Discuss how God's Principles of Individuality and Unity with Diversity can be seen in the way the body parts work together. (Example: The skeletal system and the muscular system, each with their individual and unique function, work together to help the individual stand and move.)
		Introduce the skeletal system.
		• **Present** its unique characteristics.
		• **Use** visuals such as charts, pictures in books about the body, a sample x-ray, animal bones, etc.
		• **Name** and locate various bones.
		• **Match** pictures of a particular bone to the correct part of the body.
		• **Discuss** God's Principles of Individuality and Unity with Diversity as they relate to how God formed the skeletal system for a special purpose in the body. (It supports the body and protects the organs.)
		
		SCIENCE—
		Notebook Work
		(continued on page 216)
			Listen as the teacher defines human anatomy and physiology.
			Participate in a discussion of the Biblical Principles and Leading Idea.
			
			Listen as the teacher reads aloud the scriptures that support the Biblical foundation and discusses man was created separate and distinct from animals and in the image of God.
			
			Identify on the classroom poster the external body parts.
			Discuss how God's Principles of Individuality and Unity with Diversity to the way body systems work together but function differently.
			
			Listen and observe as the teacher presents unique characteristics and displays visuals related to the skeletal system.
			Locate various bones in the body and match pictures of bones to their proper location.
			Discuss how God's Principles of Individuality and Unity with Diversity relate to the skeletal system and its unique function in the body.
			
			SCIENCE—
			Student Notebook Work
			(continued on page 216)
				• To recognize God as the Master Designer
				• To praise and worship God for His marvelous Creation
				• To locate external body parts
				• To learn about your body and its functions
				• To learn how God's Principles of Individuality and Unity with Diversity relate to the skeletal system
				• To complete and file notebook work

The Noah Plan Lessons Kindergarten © 2003 • Foundation for American Christian Education

TEACHING PLAN

Quarter Four

Week Four

SCIENCE (continued)

Preparation	Lesson	Student Work	Accomplishments	✓
	Notebook Work **Distribute** the prepared notebook page for the student to write or trace the title and draw a self-portrait. Prepared notebook page to include: • the title "Human Anatomy" for the student to write or trace • a space for the student to draw a self-portrait **Distribute** the prepared notebook page for the student to write or trace the title and to label the major bones as you model it on a large chart or overhead projector. Prepared notebook page to include: • the title "Skeletal System" for the student to write or trace • a picture of the skeletal system for the student to label some of the major bones	*Notebook Work* **Write** or trace the title on the notebook page and draw a self-portrait. **Write** or trace the title on the notebook page and label the major bones.		

216   The Noah Plan Lessons Kindergarten © 2003 • Foundation for American Christian Education

Quarter Four

TEACHING PLAN

Week Five

	Preparation	Lesson	Student Work	Accomplishments
BIBLE	**Bible Principle** We should praise God at all times. **Leading idea** Paul sang about Jesus even when he was in prison. **Books** • Bible (KJ) • Webster's 1828 *Dictionary* **Supplies** Notebook page to include: • the title "Paul and Silas in Prison" for the student to write or trace • a space for the student to draw and color a picture of Paul and Silas in prison **BAR** **Books** • *Early Reader's Bible*, 490–497 • NPRG	**Introduce** the memory verse. Psalm 34:1 • **Read** aloud and discuss the memory verse. • **Define** unfamiliar vocabulary. • **Practice** daily the memory verse with the student for his recitation on Friday. **Guide** the student to the Biblical Principle from the Leading Idea. • **Read** aloud the story of Paul and Silas in prison. Acts 16:22–34 • **Discuss** the following about Paul and Silas: · They were put into prison for preaching the Gospel. · They were beaten and whipped in prison. · They were put in chains. · In spite of it all, they prayed and sang praises to God. · There was a great earthquake that freed them of their chains. · They did not run away. · Their example made the jailors come to know Jesus as their Savior. *Notebook Work* **Distribute** the prepared notebook page for the student to write or trace the title and to draw and color the picture of Paul and Silas in prison. **BAR** "Singing in Jail" (See Weekly Routines for Reading and English.)	**Listen** as the teacher reads aloud and participate in a discussion the memory verse. • **Discuss** unfamiliar vocabulary. • **Practice** and learn the memory verse for recitation on Friday. **Listen** as the teacher reads aloud the story of Paul and Silas in prison. Acts 16:22–34 • **Discuss** the following about Paul and Silas: · Why were Paul and Silas put into prison? · How were treated in prison? · How did they handle their situation in prison? · What happened in the prison? · What did the jailor do? • **Discuss** how Paul and Silas's behavior in prison changed the lives of others. *Notebook Work* **Write** or trace the title and draw and color the picture of Paul and Silas in prison. **BAR** (See Weekly Routines for Reading and English.)	• To learn and recite the memory verse • To learn new vocabulary • To pray and sing praises to God all the time • To trust God to help in times of trouble • To complete and file notebook work

The Noah Plan Lessons Kindergarten © 2003 • Foundation for American Christian Education

217

Week Five

Quarter Four

TEACHING PLAN

Preparation	Lesson	Student Work	Accomplishments	✓

Biblical Principle
God uses individual character to forward His Gospel.
 	
Leading Idea
Christianity goes westward in America.
 	
Books
• Bible (KJ)
• NPLG, 8–9, 129–132, 134–138
• *Little House in the Big Woods*, Laura Ingalls Wilder
• Teacher Guide: "Pilgrim-Pioneer Character Moving Westward," Slater, F.A.C.E.
 	
Supplies
• Notebook pages for the study of the classic to include:
  • a page to record the setting
  • a page for each character and picture to color
  • a page to record the plot
  • a page to record the vocabulary
	Review the Biblical Principle and Leading Idea.
	
	Read aloud a chapter or section from *Little House in the Big Woods* daily.
	
	• **Continue** to discuss literary elements as they are described in the story.
	
	Introduce and discuss the leading idea: Family love and affection are the building blocks of America.
	
	Notebook Work
	Write names, definitions, and descriptions of setting, characters, plot, and vocabulary under the correct heading on your model (blackboard or chart) as they are discussed in class.
	
	Instruct the student to copy them onto the correct notebook page.
		Participate in a review of the Biblical Principle and Leading Idea.
		
		Listen as the teacher reads aloud a chapter or section from *Little House in the Big Woods* daily.
		
		• **Continue** to identify and to discuss the author's descriptions of literary elements.
		
		Participate in a discussion of the leading idea: Family love and affection are the building blocks of America.
		
		Notebook Work
		Copy names, definitions, and descriptions of setting, characters, plot, and vocabulary onto the designated notebook page for each literary element (follow the model that the teacher writes on the board or chart).
			• To identify literary elements through the author's descriptions
			
			• To complete and file notebook work	

LITERATURE

218   The Noah Plan Lessons Kindergarten © 2003 • Foundation for American Christian Education

TEACHING PLAN

Quarter Four

Week Five

HISTORY

Preparation	Lesson	Student Work	Accomplishments
Biblical Principle Principle of Representation **Leading Idea** The *Declaration of Independence* and the *United States Constitution* represent documents of liberty and law in the United States. **Books** • Bible (KJ) • NPH&GG, 8–9, 249–269 • CHOC I, 346B **Supplies** • Copy of the *Declaration of Independence* and the *U.S. Constitution* • Notebook page to include: 　• a T-chart with the titles "Governing Rules" on the left and "Biblical Principles" on the right 　• written rules from the classroom constitution under the title "Governing Rules" • Whiteboard or chalkboard	**Guide** the student to the Biblical Principle from the Leading Idea by introducing the *Declaration of Independence* and the *United States Constitution* as Christian documents of liberty and law in the United States. **Present** background information about the purpose for each, highlight important aspects of their content, and review the character of the men involved in writing these documents in an age appropriate manner. **Create** a T-chart with the titles: "Governing Rule" on the left and "Biblical Principle" on the right. • **Copy** rules from your classroom constitution under the left heading. (Keep it simple.) • **Ask** the student to identify/suggest a Biblical Principle represented by that rule. • **Record** the response under the right heading. Example: "I speak kindly to others" (Governing Rules); "Love your neighbor" (Biblical Principles). *Notebook Work* **Distribute** the prepared notebook page and assist the student in recording the Biblical Principles as you model it on the board.	**Listen** as the teacher introduces the *Declaration of Independence* and the *U. S. Constitution* as Christian documents of liberty and law in the United States. **Learn** about the purpose for each document, the important aspects of their content, and review the character of the men who were involved in writing these documents. **Contribute** to a corporate T-chart by suggesting Biblical Principles that relate to rules included in the classroom constitution. *Notebook Work* **Record** the Biblical Principles on the notebook page related to rules from the classroom constitution as the teacher writes them on the board.	• To learn about the *Declaration of Independence* and the *U.S. Constitution* • To review classroom rules and Biblical Principles • To complete and file notebook work

The Noah Plan Lessons Kindergarten © 2003 • Foundation for American Christian Education

Week Five

Quarter Four

TEACHING PLAN

	Preparation	Lesson	Student Work	Accomplishments	✓
GEOGRAPHY	**Biblical Principle** God created each continent distinct to fit His purpose and His plan. Psalm 115:16 **Leading Idea** The nature and character of God are revealed in the continent of Africa. **Books** • Bible (KJ) • NPH&GG, 128, 194–200 • T&L, 141–153, 156–157 **Supplies** • World map and globe • Student atlas • Pictures of artifacts related to Africa • African words,	**Continue** to guide the student to the Biblical Principle from the Leading Idea by reviewing the location as well as the unique geographic features, natural resources, and climate that contribute to the individuality of Africa. **Present** information about the people who inhabit the countries of Africa (culture, customs, languages, etc.). **Display** pictures or artifacts related to African culture (and/or ask the student to bring items to share). **Prepare** and serve native foods or learn words of a native language or song.	**Review** the location of Africa by identifying it on the classroom world map, globe, and in your atlas. **Review** the features that contribute to Africa's individuality by recalling unique aspects of its geography, natural resources, and climate. **Listen** as the teacher presents information about the culture, customs, and languages of the people who inhabit Africa. **View** pictures or artifacts related to Africa's culture (and/or bring items to share with the class). **Sample** native foods, listen to music, or learn words of a native language.	• To locate Africa on the classroom world map, globe, and atlas • To recall unique aspects of Africa's geography, natural resources, and climate • To learn about the culture, customs, etc. of African people • To view pictures or artifacts related to African culture • To learn new words or songs • To sample native foods	

220   The Noah Plan Lessons Kindergarten © 2003 • Foundation for American Christian Education

Quarter Four

TEACHING PLAN

Week Five

SCIENCE

Preparation	Lesson	Student Work	Accomplishments
Biblical Principles • God's Principle of Individuality • Unity with Diversity **Leading Idea** God is the Master Designer who created man in his image and equipped him to live in this world. **Books** • Bible (KJ) • Webster's 1828 Dictionary • Learning about My Body, The Evan-Moor Corp. • My First Body Book, Chris and Melanie Rice • What's Inside? My Body, Angela Royston • Me and My Body, David Evans and Claudette Williams **Supplies** • Large picture of the muscular system or overhead projector • Prepared notebook page	**Review** the Biblical Principles and Leading Idea. **Review** by questioning the unique characteristics and function of the skeletal system and by asking the student to find a particular bone on a chart or diagram. **Introduce** the muscular system. • **Present** its unique characteristics. • **Use** visuals such as charts, pictures, etc. • **Discuss** the function of muscles. (They enable you to move.) • **Identify** God's Principles of Individuality and Unity with Diversity seen in the different types of muscles (especially voluntary and involuntary). • **Discuss** the stewardship needed to keep muscles functioning properly. **Provide** concrete experience with the function of the muscular system by leading movement activities such as performing various exercises and identifying the muscles used, tightening and relaxing various muscles, smiling, etc. *Notebook Work* **Distribute** the prepared notebook page for the student to write or trace the title and to label various types of muscles as you model it on a large chart or overhead projector. Prepared notebook page to include: • the title "Muscular System" for the student to write or trace • a picture of the muscular system for the student to label various types of muscles	**Participate** in a review of the Biblical Principles and Leading Idea. **Review** the unique characteristics and function of the skeletal system and locate particular bones on a chart or diagram. **Listen** and observe as the teacher presents unique characteristics and displays visuals and discusses the function of the muscular system. **Reason** and relate by discussing God's Principles of Individuality and Unity with Diversity that are seen in the muscular system in the way that different types of muscles perform different jobs. **Listen** as the teacher discusses the proper stewardship that is needed to keep muscles functioning properly. **Participate** in movement activities related to the muscular system. *Notebook Work* **Write** or trace the title on the notebook page and label various types of muscles.	• To recognize God as the Master Designer • To praise and worship God for His marvelous Creation • To learn about your body and its functions in order to have dominion over it • To be a good steward of your body in order to efficiently serve God • To learn about God's Principles of Individuality and Unity with Diversity in the muscular system • To complete and file notebook work

The Noah Plan Lessons Kindergarten © 2003 • Foundation for American Christian Education

221

Week Six

TEACHING PLAN

Quarter Four

	Preparation	Lesson	Student Work	Accomplishments	✓
BIBLE	**Biblical Principle** God gives us courage to tell others about Him. **Leading Idea** Be like Paul, a brave helper to Jesus. **Books** • Bible (KJ) • Webster's 1828 Dictionary **Supplies** Notebook page to include: • the title "Paul's Shipwreck" for the student to write or trace • a space for the student to draw and color a picture of Paul's shipwreck **BAR** **Books** • Early Reader's Bible, 498–506 • NPRG	**Introduce** the memory verse. Philippians 4:13 • **Read** aloud and discuss the memory verse. • **Define** unfamiliar vocabulary. • **Practice** daily the memory verse with the student for his recitation on Friday. **Guide** the student to the Biblical Principle from the Leading Idea. • **Tell** the story of Paul's shipwreck. Acts 27:9–44 • **Discuss** the following: · What the sailors did during the storm. · What Paul told the sailors. · What Paul did to calm the fears of the sailors. · What God did to show His care and protection over them. • **Discuss** how we can help others who are afraid? *Notebook Work* **Distribute** the prepared notebook page for the student to write or trace the title and to draw and color a picture of Paul's shipwreck. **BAR** "Paul Is a Brave Helper" (See Weekly Routines for Reading and English.)	**Listen** as the teacher reads aloud and participate in a discussion of the memory verse. • **Discuss** unfamiliar vocabulary. • **Practice** and learn the memory verse for recitation on Friday. **Listen** as the teacher tells the story of Paul's shipwreck. Acts 27:9–44 • **Discuss** the following: · What did the sailors do during the storm? · What did Paul tell the sailors to help calm their fears? · What did Paul do to calm the fears of the sailors? · What did God do to show His care and protection over them? • **Discuss** how you can help others who are afraid. *Notebook Work* **Write** or trace the title on the notebook page and draw and color a picture of Paul's shipwreck. **BAR** (See Weekly Routines for Reading and English.)	• To learn and recite the memory verse • To learn new vocabulary • To trust God to help in times of trouble • To help people who are afraid • To complete and file notebook work	

222 The Noah Plan Lessons Kindergarten © 2003 • Foundation for American Christian Education

Quarter Four

Week Six

TEACHING PLAN

Preparation	Lesson	Student Work	Accomplishments	✓
Biblical Principle God uses individual character to forward His Gospel.	**Review** the Biblical Principle and Leading Idea.	**Participate** in a review of the Biblical Principle and Leading Idea.	• To identify literary elements through the author's descriptions	
Leading Idea Christianity goes westward in America.	**Read** aloud a chapter or section from *Little House in the Big Woods* daily.	**Listen** as the teacher reads aloud a chapter or section from *Little House in the Big Woods* daily.	• To complete and file notebook work	
	• **Continue** to discuss literary elements as they are described in the story.	• **Continue** to identify and to discuss the author's descriptions of literary elements.		
Books • Bible (KJ) • NPLG, 8–9, 129–132, 134–138 • *Little House in the Big Woods*, Laura Ingalls Wilder • Teacher Guide: "Pilgrim-Pioneer Character Moving Westward," Slater, F.A.C.E.	**Introduce** and discuss the leading idea: A pioneer requires a courageous, self-reliant, frugal, and self-governing spirit.	**Participate** in a discussion of the leading idea: A pioneer requires a courageous, self-reliant, frugal, and self-governing spirit.		
	Notebook Work **Write** names, definitions, and descriptions of setting; characters; plot; and vocabulary under the correct heading on your model (blackboard or chart) as they are discussed in class.	*Notebook Work* **Copy** names, definitions, and descriptions of setting; characters; plot; and vocabulary onto the designated notebook page (follow the model the teacher writes on the board or chart).		
	Instruct the student to copy them onto the correct note-book page.			
Supplies • Notebook pages for the study of the classic to include: • a page to record the setting • a page for each character and picture to color • a page to record the plot • a page to record the vocabulary	*Special Day Celebration:* "Pioneer Day" (See resources on conducting "Pioneer Day," NPLK, 264–67.)			

LITERATURE

The Noah Plan Lessons Kindergarten © 2003 • Foundation for American Christian Education

Week Six

TEACHING PLAN

Quarter Four

HISTORY

Preparation	Lesson	Student Work	Accomplishments	✓
Biblical Principle "Go ye therefore and teach all nations. . . ." Matthew 28:19	**Discuss** the Biblical Principle and Leading Idea.	**Discuss** the Biblical Principle and Leading Idea.	• To identify the ninth link on the Christian history timeline	
Leading Idea The Chain of Christianity moves westward as America grows and expands westward.	**Introduce** Expansion and Erosion as the ninth link on the classroom Christian history timeline.	**Listen** as the teacher introduces Erosion and Expansion as the ninth link and locates this link on the classroom Christian history timeline.	• To review pioneer character and frontier life by relating knowledge from the literature study of *Little House in the Big Woods*	
Books • Bible (KJ) • Webster's 1828 *Dictionary* • NPH&GG, 8–9, Appendix 342 for additional books on Expansion and Erosion • NPSDS, Providential History, Links • T&L, 280–301 • *Rudiments of America's Christian History and Government*, FACE, 4–10	**Review** what has been learned about the pioneer period through the literature study of *Little House in the Big Woods* by asking the student questions about pioneer character, frontier life, etc.

Present information about Noah Webster's character and the importance of the "blue-backed speller" in American education as the pioneers moved westward.

Lead a classroom discussion about how the Bible and the "blue-backed speller" enabled Americans to teach their children as the American frontier expanded. | **Review** what was learned in the literature study of *Little House in the Big Woods* about the pioneer period by answering questions about pioneer character, frontier life, etc.

Listen as the teacher presents information about Noah Webster's character and the importance of his "blue-backed speller" in American education as the pioneers moved westward.

Participate in a discussion about how the Bible and the "blue-backed speller" were used by the pioneers to teach their children. | • To learn about Noah Webster and his contribution to American Christian education

• To complete and file notebook work | |
| **Supplies** • Christian history timeline for classroom display (The Noah Plan Wall Timeline, F.A.C.E.) • Colored pencils | *Notebook Work* **Instruct** the student to find the ninth link and color the representative picture on his individual Christian history timeline as you point it out on the classroom timeline. | *Notebook Work* **Locate** and color the ninth link on the notebook copy of the Christian history timeline as the teacher points it out on the classroom timeline. | | |

224   The Noah Plan Lessons Kindergarten © 2003 • Foundation for American Christian Education

Quarter Four

TEACHING PLAN

Week Six

	Preparation	Lesson	Student Work	Accomplishments	✓
GEOGRAPHY	**Biblical Principle** God created each continent distinct to fit His purpose and His plan. Psalm 115:16 **Leading Idea** The nature and character of God are revealed in the continent of Africa. **Books** • Bible (KJ) • NPH&GG, 128, 194–200 • T&L, 141–153, 156–157 **Supplies** • Pictures of African plants and animals • Old magazines (*National Geographic, Ranger Rick*, etc.) for cutting	**Continue** to guide the student to the Biblical Principle from the Leading Idea by reviewing the unique culture (races, customs, languages, etc.) of Africa. **Present** information about the plants and animals that are native to Africa. **Display** pictures of the plants and animals that are native to Africa. *Notebook Work* **Instruct** the student to find pictures related to the topography, plant, and animal life of Africa in magazines to cut. **Instruct** the student to save these pictures in an envelope in the pocket of his geography notebook for the next week's lesson.	**Review** by recalling unique aspects of the culture of various groups of people who live in Africa. **Listen** as the teacher presents information about the plants and animals of Africa. **View** pictures of some of the plants and animals that are native to Africa. *Notebook Work* **Cut** pictures of the topography, plant, and animal life of Africa. **Save** the pictures in an envelope in the pocket of your geography notebook for next week's lesson.	• To recall unique aspects of African culture • To learn about plants and animals native to Africa • To view pictures of African plants and animals • To complete and file notebook work	

The Noah Plan Lessons Kindergarten © 2003 • Foundation for American Christian Education

225

Week Six

TEACHING PLAN

Quarter Four

Preparation	Lesson	Student Work	Accomplishments
Biblical Principles • God's Principle of Individuality • Unity with Diversity **Leading Idea** God is the Master Designer who created man in his image and equipped him to live in this world. **Books** • Bible (KJ) • Encyclopedia • *Learning about My Body*, The Evan-Moor Corp. • *My First Body Book*, Chris and Melanie Rice • *What's Inside? My Body*, Angela Royston • *Me and My Body*, David Evans and Claudette Williams **Supplies** • Large picture of the circulatory system or overhead projector • A stethoscope • Prepared notebook page	**Review** the Biblical Principles and Leading Idea. **Review** by questioning the unique characteristics and function of the muscular system and by using visuals such as books and charts. **Introduce** the circulatory system. • **Present** information and visuals (charts or pictures) pertaining to the circulatory system and its major organ, the heart. • **Locate** the heart on a chart or diagram. • **Continue** to relate the unique function of the circulatory system in the body to God's Principles of Individuality and Unity with Diversity. • **Provide** concrete experiences to help the student better understand the unique function of the circulatory system through the following activities: · **Locate** the veins in the hand and wrist. · **Find** the pulse on the wrist and neck. · **Listen** to the heartbeat before and after exercise with a stethoscope. *Notebook Work* **Distribute** the prepared notebook page for the student to write or trace the title and to label the various parts of the circulatory system as you model it on the large picture or overhead projector. Notebook page to include: • the title "The Circulatory System" for the student to write or trace • a picture of the circulatory system for the student to label	**Participate** in a review of the Biblical Principles and Leading Idea. **Discuss** and review the unique characteristics and function of muscles. **Listen** as the teacher presents unique characteristics and visuals related to the circulatory system. **Locate** the heart on a chart or diagram. **Reason** and relate orally how the circulatory system demonstrates God's Principles of Individuality and Unity with Diversity. **Participate** in concrete activities related to the circulatory system: • **Find** the veins in the hand and wrist. • **Find** the pulse in the wrist and neck. • **Listen** to the heartbeat with a stethoscope. *Notebook Work* **Write** or trace the title on the notebook page and label various parts of the circulatory system.	• To review the purpose of the muscular system • To recognize God as the Master Designer • To praise and worship God for His marvelous Creation • To learn about your body and its functions in order to have dominion over it • To be a good steward of your body in order to efficiently serve God • To learn about God's Principles of Individuality and Unity with Diversity in the circulatory system • To participate in activities related to the circulatory system • To find the veins in the hand • To locate the heart on a chart • To listen to the heartbeat with a stethoscope • To complete and file notebook work

SCIENCE

226   The Noah Plan Lessons Kindergarten © 2003 • Foundation for American Christian Education

Quarter Four

TEACHING PLAN

Week Seven

	Preparation	Lesson	Student Work	Accomplishments	✓
BIBLE	**Biblical Principle** God desires that we should help others to serve Him. **Leading Idea** Paul helped Onesimus. **Books** • Bible (KJ) • Webster's 1828 *Dictionary* **Supplies** Notebook page to include: • the title "Paul and Onesimus" for the student to write or trace • a space for the student to draw and color a picture of Paul and Onesimus **BAR** **Books** • *Early Reader's Bible*, 506–512 • NPRG	**Introduce** the memory verse. ". . . Inasmuch as ye have done it unto one of the least of these my brethren, ye have done it unto me." Matthew 25:40 • **Read** aloud and discuss the memory verse. • **Define** unfamiliar vocabulary. • **Practice** daily the memory verse with the student for his recitation on Friday. **Guide** the student to the Biblical Principle from the Leading Idea. • **Read** aloud the story of Onesimus. (The book of Philemon) • **Discuss** the following: · Onesimus running away and taking things from Philemon · Meeting Paul and becoming a Christian · Paul asking Philemon to forgive Onesimus and taking him back · Onesimus's changed attitude • **Discuss** ways to help others *Notebook Work* **Distribute** the prepared notebook page for the student to write or trace the title and to draw and color the picture of Paul and Onesimus. **BAR** "Helping a Friend" (See Weekly Routines for Reading and English.)	**Listen** as the teacher reads aloud and discusses the memory verse. • **Discuss** unfamiliar vocabulary. • **Practice** and learn the memory verse for recitation on Friday. **Listen** as the teacher reads aloud the story of Onesimus. (The book of Philemon) • **Discuss** the following: · Why did Onesimus run away? · What did Onesimus take with him? · What happened to Onesimus when he meets Paul? · What did Paul ask Philemon to do? · How can you help others? *Notebook Work* **Write** or trace the title and draw and color the picture of Paul and Onesimus. **BAR** (See Weekly Routines for Reading and English.)	• To learn and recite the memory verse • To learn new vocabulary • To help others come to Jesus • To forgive those who have trespassed against us • To complete and file notebook work	

The Noah Plan Lessons Kindergarten © 2003 • Foundation for American Christian Education

Week Seven

TEACHING PLAN

Quarter Four

	Preparation	Lesson	Student Work	Accomplishments	✓

LITERATURE	**Biblical Principle**
	All truth is God's truth.
	
	Leading Idea
	"Next to the Bible, Shakespeare offers our children the richest and most lasting experience with language and literature." Rosalie Slater
	
	Books
	• Bible (KJ)
	• Webster's 1828 *Dictionary*
	• NPLG, 8–9, 148–171, 190
	• Biography of William Shakespeare
	
	Supplies
	• Notebook page to include:
	  · the title "Shake-speare, Bard of the Bible" for the student to write or trace
	  · a picture of Shake-speare to color
	• Notebook page to include:
	  · the title "Globe Theater" for the student to write or trace
	  · a picture of the Globe Theater to color
	• Colored pencils
		Discuss the Biblical Principle and the Leading Idea.
		
		Introduce Shakespeare by presenting his biographical background.
		
		Lead a discussion about why Shakespeare is referred to as the "Bard of the Bible."
		
		Define drama and discuss how it differs from other types of literature.
		
		Explain the contribution of drama on the Chain of Christianity.
		
		Present a large picture of the Globe Theater and give background information about the Elizabethan theater.
		
		Define tragedy and comedy and discuss the differences between these two types of drama.
		
		Notebook Work
		Distribute the prepared notebook pages for the student to write or trace the titles and to color the pictures.
			Participate in a discussion of the Biblical Principle and Leading Idea.
			
			Listen as the teacher presents biographical information about Shakespeare.
			
			Participate in a discussion about why Shakespeare is referred to as the "Bard of the Bible."
			
			Gain an awareness of what drama is and how it differs from other literary types.
			
			Understand the contribution of drama on the Chain of Christianity.
			
			View a picture of the Globe Theater and listen as the teacher presents unique characteristics of Elizabethan theater.
			
			Discuss the differences between comedy and tragedy in drama.
			
			Notebook Work
			Write or trace the titles on the notebook pages and color the pictures.
				• To reflect upon the principle and leading idea
				• To learn about William Shakespeare
				• To be aware of the individuality of the literary types of literature
				• To overcome difficult language by familiarity and study
				• To complete and file notebook work	

228   The Noah Plan Lessons Kindergarten © 2003 • Foundation for American Christian Education

Quarter Four

TEACHING PLAN

Week Seven

	Preparation	Lesson	Student Work	Accomplishments	✓
HISTORY	**Biblical Principles** • God looks for individuals whose hearts are turned toward Him. 2 Chronicles 16:9 • The Principle of Representation **Leading Ideas** • God has a unique purpose and place on the Chain of Christianity for each one of us. • The Liberty Bell and the American flag are symbols of our nation's courage, liberty, and loyalty. **Books** • Bible (KJ) • Webster's 1828 *Dictionary* • NPH&GG, 8–9, 79, Appendix 342 for additional books on the Restoration Link • NPSDS, Providential History, Links • CHOC 1, 371 • Books on the American flag and Liberty Bell **Supplies** • Liberty Bell picture • American flag • Prepared notebook pages #1 and #2 • Colored pencils	**Discuss** the Biblical Principles and Leading Idea. **Introduce** the tenth link Restoration, My Place in God's Providence and locate this link on the classroom Christian history timeline. **Lead** a discussion by: • Reviewing the meaning of "providence." • Asking the student to reason and relate about why God made each one of us special. • Identifying the responsibility of a child of God and as an American in Christ, His Story. **Define** the word symbol and ask the student to give examples of symbols he knows. **Present** the American flag and the Liberty Bell as national symbols of America and give background information about the origin and significance of these two symbols of liberty. *Notebook Work* **Distribute** the prepared notebook page #1 for the student to write or trace the title and color the picture of the Liberty Bell. Notebook page #1 to include: • the title "The Liberty Bell Proclaimed Liberty" for the student to write or trace • a picture of the Liberty Bell for the student to color **Distribute** the prepared notebook page #2 for the student to write or trace the title and to color the picture of the American flag. Notebook page #2 to include: • the title "Our American Flag" for the student to write or trace • a picture of the American flag for the student to color	**Participate** in a discussion of the Biblical Principles and Leading Idea. **Observe** as the teacher introduces Restoration, My Place in God's Providence and locates this link on the classroom timeline. **Participate** in a discussion by: • Reviewing the definition of providence. • Relating how you are special. • Identifying your responsibilities as a child of God and an American in Christ, His Story. **Relate** examples of symbols after the teacher defines and explains the word. **Listen** as the teacher introduces and gives background information about the origin and significance of the American flag and the Liberty Bell. *Notebook Work* **Write** or trace the title on notebook page #1 and color the picture. **Write** or trace the title on notebook page #2 and color the picture.	• To identify the tenth link on the timeline • To discuss Providence as it relates to the individual today • To relate examples of symbols • To learn about the origin and significance of two national symbols • To complete and file notebook work	

The Noah Plan Lessons Kindergarten © 2003 • Foundation for American Christian Education

TEACHING PLAN

Week Seven Quarter Four

GEOGRAPHY

Preparation	Lesson	Student Work	Accomplishments

Biblical Principle
God created each continent distinct to fit His purpose and His plan. Psalm 115:16
 	
Leading Idea
The nature and character of God are revealed in the continent of Africa.
 	
Books
• Bible (KJ)
• NPH&GG, 128, 194–200
• T&L, 141–153, 156–157
 	
Supplies
• World map and globe
• Map standard
• Colored pencils
• Simplified outline map of Africa (Use maps from NPH&GG, 228–229 as a guide.)
• Notebook page to include:
  · the title "Africa's Individuality" for the student to write or trace
  · a space for the student to glue pictures of Africa
	Continue to guide the student to the Biblical Principle from the Leading Idea by reviewing the plants and animals that are unique to Africa.
	Lead a discussion encouraging the student to reason and relate the things they have learned about Africa with God's Principle of Individuality.
	
	Notebook Work
	Distribute the prepared outline map of Africa and instruct the student to color the map according to the map standard for physical maps.
	Distribute a prepared notebook page for the student to write or trace the title and to glue the pictures from last week's lesson onto this page.
	
	OR
	
	Save the pictures to be used for a group project in the fourth quarter.
		Review by recalling the plants and animals of Africa from memory or by selecting from assorted pictures. **Reason** and relate about how the things learned about Africa are an example of God's Principle of Individuality.
		
		Notebook Work
		Follow the map standard for physical maps and complete map of Africa.
		Write or trace the title on the notebook page and glue pictures of Africa (cut from magazines in last week's lesson) onto the page.
		
		OR
		
		Save the pictures to be used for a group project in the fourth quarter.
		
		Africa
			• To recall unique animals and plants of Africa
			• To complete and file notebook work

230 The Noah Plan Lessons Kindergarten © 2003 • Foundation for American Christian Education

TEACHING PLAN

Quarter Four

Week Seven

SCIENCE

Preparation	Lesson	Student Work	Accomplishments

Biblical Principles
• God's Principle of Individuality
• Unity with Diversity
 	
Leading Idea
God is the Master Designer who created man in his image and equipped him to live in this world.
 	
Books
• Bible (KJ)
• Encyclopedia
• *Learning about My Body*, The Evan-Moor Corp.
• *My First Body Book*, Chris & Melanie Rice
• *What's Inside? My Body*, Angela Royston
• *Me and My Body*, David Evans and Claudette Williams
 	
Supplies
• Large picture of the respiratory system or overhead projector
• Notebook page to include:
  • the title "The Respiratory System" for the student to write or trace
  • a picture of the respiratory system for the student to label
	Review the Biblical Principles and Leading Idea.
	
	Review by questioning the unique characteristics and function of the circulatory system and by using visuals such as books and charts.
	
	Introduce the respiratory system.
	• **Present** information and visuals (charts or pictures) pertaining to the respiratory system and its major organ, the lungs.
	• **Locate** the lungs on a chart or diagram.
	
	• **Discuss** the unique function and characteristics of the lungs and respiratory system and continue to reinforce how this is an example of God's Principles of Individuality and Unity with Diversity.
	• **Provide** concrete activities to help the student better understand the unique function of the respiratory system.
	• **Blow** up a balloon to illustrate what happens to the lungs when you inhale.
	• **Instruct** the student to hold his rib cage as he breathes in and out in order to feel his lungs get larger and smaller.
	
	Notebook Work
	Distribute the prepared notebook page for the student to write or trace the title and to label various parts of the respiratory system as you model it on the large picture or overhead projector.
		Participate in a review of the Biblical Principles and Leading Idea.
		Contribute to a classroom review of the circulatory system by answering questions about its function and unique characteristics.
		Listen as the teacher presents unique characteristics and visuals related to the respiratory system.
		Locate the lungs on a chart or diagram.
		
		Reason and relate orally through a classroom discussion of how the respiratory system demonstrates God's Principles of Individuality and Unity with Diversity.
		Participate in activities related to the respiratory system such as inhaling and exhaling deeply to feel the air flow or holding the rib cage when breathing to feel the lungs get larger and smaller.
		
		Notebook Work
		Write or trace the title on the notebook page and label various parts of the respiratory system.
			• To review the purpose of the circulatory system
			• To recognize God as the Master Designer
			• To praise and worship God for His marvelous Creation
			• To learn about your body and its functions in order to have dominion over it
			• To be good stewards of it in order to efficiently serve God
			• To learn about God's Principles of Individuality and Unity with Diversity in the respiratory system
			• To participate in activities related to the respiratory system
			• To complete and file notebook work

The Noah Plan Lessons Kindergarten © 2003 • Foundation for American Christian Education

Week Eight   **TEACHING PLAN**   Quarter Four   ✓

Preparation	Lesson	Student Work	Accomplishments

Biblical Principle
God asks us to give Him our Best.
 	
Leading Idea
Christ, the Lamb was the perfect sacrifice for our sins.
 	
Books
• Bible (KJ)
• Webster's 1828 *Dictionary*
 	
Supplies
Notebook page to include:
• the title "The Lamb of God" for the student to write or trace
• a space for the student to draw and color a picture of Jesus
	Introduce the memory verse.
	". . . Behold the Lamb of God, which taketh away the sin of the world." John 1:29
	• **Read** aloud and discuss the memory verse.
	• **Define** unfamiliar vocabulary.
	• **Practice** daily the memory verse with the student for his recitation on Friday.
	Guide the student to the Biblical Principle from the Leading Idea.
	Define lamb and discuss:
	• A young sheep in Bible times used for:
	  • Food—2 Samuel 12:4
	  • Clothing—Proverbs 27:26
	  • Trade—Ezra 7:17
	  • Tribute—2 Kings 3:4
	  • Covenants—Genesis 21:28–30
	  • Sacrifices—Exodus 12:5
	• God's people are called lambs—Isaiah 5:17.
	Read aloud an age appropriate book about Jesus as the Lamb of God or read aloud John 1:29–34.
	• **Discuss** the following:
	  • John the Baptist calling Jesus the Lamb of God
	  • Jesus' sacrifice for us
	  • Jesus as the perfect sacrifice for our sins
	
	Encourage the student to share the ways Jesus has changed him.
	
	Notebook Work
	Distribute the prepared notebook page for the student to write or trace the title and to draw and color a picture of Jesus as the Lamb of God.
	
	BAR
	Use an age appropriate book about Jesus as the Lamb of God.
	(See Weekly Routines for Reading and English.)
		Listen as the teacher reads aloud and discusses the memory verse.
		
		• **Discuss** unfamiliar vocabulary.
		• **Practice** and learn the memory verse for recitation on Friday.
		Listen as the teacher defines lamb and discusses the usage of a lamb in Bible times:
		• A young sheep used for:
		  • Food—2 Samuel 12:4
		  • Clothing—Proverbs 27:26
		  • Trade—Ezra 7:17
		  • Tribute—2 Kings 3:4
		  • Covenants—Genesis 21:28–30
		  • Sacrifices—Exodus 12:5
		• God's people are called lambs–Is. 5:17.
		Listen to and participate in a discussion as the teacher reads aloud a book about Jesus as the Lamb of God or John 1:29–34 and discusses the following:
		• John the Baptist calling Jesus the Lamb of God
		• Jesus' sacrifice for us
		• Jesus as the perfect sacrifice for our sins
		
		Share ways Jesus has changed you.
		
		Notebook Work
		Write or trace the title on the notebook page and draw and color a picture of Jesus as the perfect lamb of God.
		
		BAR
		(See Weekly Routines for Reading and English.)
			• To learn and recite the memory verse
			• To learn new vocabulary
			• To love and appreciate the sacrifice Jesus made for mankind
			• To complete and file notebook work

BAR Books • Use an age appropriate book about Jesus as the Lamb of God. • NPRG			

BIBLE

232   The Noah Plan Lessons Kindergarten © 2003 • Foundation for American Christian Education

Week Eight

Quarter Four

TEACHING PLAN

	Preparation	Lesson	Student Work	Accomplishments	✓
LITERATURE	**Biblical Principle** All truth is God's truth. **Leading Idea** "Next to the Bible, Shakespeare offers our children the richest and most lasting experience with language and literature." Rosalie J. Slater **Books** • Bible (KJ) • NPLG, 8–9, 148–171, 190 • *Tales from Shakespeare*, Charles & Mary Lamb **Supplies** • Notebook pages for the student to color: · Setting of the story · Main characters	**Review** the Biblical Principle and the Leading Idea. **Review** key events in Shakespeare's life and information about the Globe Theater. **Introduce** *As You Like It.* • **Identify** it as a comedy. • **Give** background information about the setting, characters, and plot. **Read** aloud *As You Like It* from Charles and Mary Lamb's *Tales from Shakespeare* (a section each day.) **Discuss** literary elements as they are encountered in daily reading. **Discuss** Shakespeare's use of Biblical themes in his writing. *Notebook Work* **Distribute** the prepared notebook pages for the student to color and file.	**Participate** in a review of the Biblical Principle and Leading Idea. **Recall** key events of Shakespeare's life and characteristics of the Globe Theater. **Listen** as the teacher presents background information about the setting, the characters, and the plot and begins to read aloud *As You Like It* from Charles and Mary Lamb's *Tales from Shakespeare.* **Participate** in a discussion about the literary elements encountered in each daily reading. **Participate** in a discussion about Shakespeare's use of Biblical themes in his writing. *Notebook Work* **Color** the notebook pages and file them behind the notebook pages of Shakespeare and the Globe Theater.	• To overcome the difficult language by familiarity and study • To recognize Shakespeare's use of Biblical themes • To complete and file notebook work	

The Noah Plan Lessons Kindergarten © 2003 • Foundation for American Christian Education   233

Week Eight TEACHING PLAN Quarter Four

HISTORY

Preparation

Biblical Principle
The Principle of Representation

Leading Idea
The American Bald Eagle, Statue of Liberty, and the Seal of the President of the United States are symbols of our nation's strength, freedom, and our Christian form of government.

Books
- Bible (KJ)
- NPH&GG, 8–9, 270–273
- *Our National Symbols*, Linda Carlson Johnson
- Books about the American Bald Eagle, the Statue of Liberty, and the Seal of the President

Supplies
- A picture and/or replica of the American Bald Eagle
- A picture and/or replica of the Statue of Liberty
- Pictures of the first six presidents and the Seal of the President (the seal is found on the dollar bill)
- Prepared notebook page
- Colored pencils

Lesson

Discuss the Biblical Principle and Leading Idea.

Review the Liberty Bell and the American flag by asking the student to recall aspects of each one that make it a symbol of our country.

Introduce the American Bald Eagle and the Statue of Liberty as additional symbols of our nation.
- **Present** information about the origin and significance of these two national symbols.

Name the first six presidents of the United States.

- **Display** pictures of the first six presidents and a picture of the Seal of the President of the United States.
- **Point out** that the Seal of the President of the United States is found on the dollar bill.
- **Lead** a discussion about the items that appear on the seal, what they represent, and what the Latin words *"E Pluribus Unum"* mean to Americans.

Notebook Work
Distribute the prepared notebook page for the student to write or trace the title and color the pictures. Notebook page to include:
- the title "Symbols of the United States" for the student to write or trace,
- a picture of the American Bald Eagle, the Statue of Liberty, and the Seal of the President of the United States of America for the student to color. (Separate pages can be prepared for each symbol.)

Student Work

Participate in a discussion of the Biblical Principle and Leading Idea.
Review the Liberty Bell and American flag by recalling aspects of each that make it a symbol of our country.

Listen as the teacher introduces the American Bald Eagle and the Statue of Liberty as national symbols, and presents background information about the origin and significance of these two symbols.

Listen as the teacher names the first six presidents of the United States.
- **View** pictures of the first six presidents and a picture of the Seal of the President of the United States (on the back of a dollar bill).
- **Participate** in a discussion about what the items on the Seal of the President represent and what the Latin words *"E Pluribus Unum"* mean to Americans.

Notebook Work
Write or trace the title on the notebook page and color the pictures.

Accomplishments

- To recall aspects of the American flag and Liberty Bell that symbolize our nation
- To learn about the origin and significance of the national symbols
- To view a picture of the Seal of the President of the United States and pictures of the first six presidents
- To discuss the symbolism of the items in the Seal of the President
- To complete and file notebook work

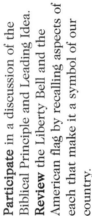

234 The Noah Plan Lessons Kindergarten © 2003 • Foundation for American Christian Education

Week Eight

Quarter Four

TEACHING PLAN

Preparation	Lesson	Student Work	Accomplishments	✓
Biblical Principle Weather and climate are under Divine control. 1 Samuel 12:16–19 **Leading Idea** Climate is not the same as weather. **Books** • Bible (KJ) • NPH&GG, 128, 167 **Supplies** • Map of world divided into climate zones, and labeled with the equator, North Pole, and South Pole. (Use map from NPH&GG, 167 as a guide.) • Colored pencils • Overhead projector if available	**Discuss** the Biblical Principle and Leading Idea. **Read** aloud 1 Samuel 12:16–19 and discuss climate and weather being under Divine control. **Introduce** the difference between climate and weather. • Climate refers to the general weather conditions of a region throughout the years. • Weather changes from day to day. It may be hot one day and cold the next. **Discuss** the benefits of knowing the climate of an area and the daily weather: • It helps people to know how to dress. • It helps farmers to know what kind of crops to plant. • It helps us to know what kind of houses to build. • It tells us what kind of animals and plants will inhabit an area. *Notebook Work* **Distribute** the prepared map of the world. **Teach**, model, and instruct the student to color the frigid areas blue, the torrid area red, and the temperate areas green. 	**Participate** in a discussion of the Biblical Principle and Leading Idea. **Listen** as the teacher reads aloud 1 Samuel 12:16–19 and discusses that climate and weather are under Divine control. **Listen** as the teacher defines climate and weather and discusses the difference between them. **Reason** and relate the benefits of knowing the climate and weather of an area. *Notebook Work* **Follow** the teachers instructions on coloring the distributed climate map: • Frigid areas are blue. • Torrid areas are red. • Temperate areas are green.	• To learn God controls the climate and weather • To learn the difference between climate and weather • To complete and file notebook work	

GEOGRAPHY

The Noah Plan Lessons Kindergarten © 2003 • Foundation for American Christian Education

Week Eight

Quarter Four

TEACHING PLAN

Preparation	Lesson	Student Work	Accomplishments	✓
Biblical Principles • God's Principle of Individuality • Unity with Diversity **Leading Idea** God is the Master Designer who created man in his image and equipped him to live in this world. **Books** • Bible (KJ) • *Learning about My Body*, The Evan-Moor Corp. • *My First Body Book*, Chris and Melanie Rice • *What's Inside? My Body*, Angela Royston • *Me and My Body*, David Evans and Claudette Williams **Supplies** • Large simplified picture of the digestive system or overhead projector • Glass of water and sugar • Blender and bits of food • Prepared notebook page	**Review** the Biblical Principles and Leading Idea. **Review** by questioning the unique characteristics and function of the respiratory system and by using visuals such as books and charts. **Introduce** the digestive system. • **Present** information and visuals (charts or pictures) pertaining to the digestive system. • **Discuss** the importance and unique function of the digestive system and how this illustrates God's Principles of Individuality and Unity with Diversity. • **Provide** concrete experiences that help the student to better understand the process of digestion. • **Dissolve** sugar in a glass of water. • **Blend** bits of food in a blender, etc. *Notebook Work* **Distribute** the prepared notebook page for the student to write or trace the title and to label various parts of the digestive system as you model on a chart or overhead projector. Notebook page to include: • the title "The Digestive System" for the student to write or trace • a picture of the digestive system for the student to label various parts	**Participate** in a review of the Biblical Principles and Leading Idea. **Contribute** to a review of the respiratory system by answering questions about its function and unique characteristics. **Listen** as the teacher presents unique characteristics and visuals related to the digestive system. **Reason** orally through a discussion of the importance and unique function of the digestive system and how this demonstrates God's Principles of Individuality and Unity with Diversity. **Observe** as experiments related to the digestive system are performed and relate this information to facts about the digestive system. *Notebook Work* **Write** or trace the title on the notebook page and label the various parts of the digestive system.	• To review the purpose of the respiratory system • To recognize God as the Master Designer • To praise and worship God for His marvelous Creation • To learn about your body and its functions in order to have dominion over it • To learn about God's Principles of Individuality and Unity with Diversity in the digestive system • To observe experiments related to the digestive system • To complete and file notebook work	

SCIENCE

236   The Noah Plan Lessons Kindergarten © 2003 • Foundation for American Christian Education

Week Nine   TEACHING PLAN   Quarter Four

Preparation	Lesson	Student Work	Accomplishments	✓
Biblical Principle God promises that Jesus will return. **Leading Idea** God told John to tell others that Jesus would return. **Books** • Bible (KJ) • Webster's 1828 *Dictionary* **Supplies** Notebook page to include: • the title "Jesus is King" for the student to write or trace the title • a space to draw and color a picture of Jesus as King **BAR Books** • Bible (KJ), Book of Revelation • Suggestion: May use the *Young Reader's Bible*, 430–435 used in the first grade. May use other applicable story book or the Bible that the teacher reads to the student.	**Introduce** the memory verse. "Behold, he cometh with the clouds; and every eye shall see him. . . ." Revelations 1:7 • **Read** aloud and discuss the memory verse. • **Define** unfamiliar vocabulary. • **Practice** daily the memory verse with the student for his recitation on Friday. **Guide** the student to the Biblical Principle from the Leading Idea. • **Tell** the story of John from Revelation. • **Discuss** the following: • The reason John is put into prison • The visions Jesus gave John • The directions Jesus gave John • The description of heaven Jesus gave John • The last message Jesus gave to John *Notebook Work* **Distribute** the prepared notebook page for the student to write or trace title and to color the picture of Jesus as King. **BAR** "Come Quickly Lord" (See Weekly Routines for Reading and English.)	**Listen** as the teacher reads aloud and discusses the memory verse. • **Discuss** unfamiliar vocabulary. • **Practice** and learn the memory verse for recitation on Friday. **Listen** as the teacher tells the story of John from the book of Revelation. **Discuss** the following: • Why was John put in jail? • What visions did God show John? • What directions did Jesus give to John? • How did Jesus describe heaven? • What did Jesus say about his return to Earth? *Notebook Work* **Write** or trace the title on the notebook page and color the picture of Jesus as King. **BAR** (See Weekly Routines for Reading and English.)	• To learn and recite the memory verse • To learn new vocabulary • To do our best until Jesus comes again • To complete and file notebook work	

BIBLE

The Noah Plan Lessons Kindergarten © 2003 • Foundation for American Christian Education   237

Week Nine   **TEACHING PLAN**   Quarter Four

	Preparation	Lesson	Student Work	Accomplishments	✓
LITERATURE	**Biblical Principle** All truth is God's truth. **Leading Idea** "Next to the Bible, Shakespeare offers our children the richest and most lasting experience with language and literature." Rosalie J. Slater **Books** • Bible (KJ) • NPLG, 8–9, 148–171, 190 • *Tales from Shakespeare*, Charles & Mary Lamb **Supplies** • Notebook pages for the student to color: · Setting of the story · Main characters • Colored pencils	**Review** the Biblical Principle and the Leading Idea. **Review** what has been read and discussed in previous lessons. **Read** aloud the remainder of the play in *Tales from Shakespeare* by Charles and Mary Lamb. **Lead** a discussion about whether or not the characters demonstrate Biblical character qualities in their actions (*i.e.,* brotherly love, honesty, etc.) *Notebook Work* **Distribute** the prepared notebook pages for the student to color.	**Participate** in a review of the Biblical Principle and Leading Idea. **Recall** the setting of the play and the names of characters that have been introduced in previous reading. **Listen** as the teacher continues to read aloud the play. **Analyze** the actions of the characters against the Biblical model of character and name the ways that the characters do or do not exhibit this Biblical standard of behavior. *Notebook Work* **Color** notebook pages and file them behind the notebook pages of Shakespeare and the Globe Theater.	• To cultivate a love for language from the writings of Shakespeare • To discern between good and evil character qualities • To complete and file notebook work	

238   The Noah Plan Lessons Kindergarten © 2003 • Foundation for American Christian Education

Week Nine — Quarter Four

TEACHING PLAN

HISTORY

Preparation	Lesson	Student Work	Accomplishments
Biblical Principle "And ye shall know the truth, and the truth shall make you free." John 8:32 **Leading Idea** Liberty begins internally, but it must have its external expression. **Books** • NPH&GG, 8–9, 294–301 • *Our National Symbols*, Linda Carlson Johnson **Supplies** • Words to patriotic poems • Words and music to patriotic songs	**Discuss** the Biblical Principle and the Leading Idea. **Define** liberty. **Read** aloud and discuss the scriptures Leviticus 25:10 and 2 Corinthians 3:17 pertaining to liberty. **Prepare** for Liberty Day. • **Practice** reciting the Pledge of Allegiance and flag etiquette. • **Practice** singing the national anthem. **Celebrate** Liberty Day using suggestions included in the NPH&GG, 294–301 or by reading and memorizing patriotic poems and songs which could be presented to parents or other guests.	**Participate** in a discussion of the Biblical Principle and Leading Idea. **Listen** as the teacher defines liberty. **Listen** as the teacher reads aloud and discusses the scripture verses pertaining to liberty: • Leviticus 25:10 • 2 Corinthians 3:17 **Practice** for Liberty Day. • **Practice** reciting the Pledge of Allegiance, and flag etiquette. • **Practice** singing the national anthem. **Celebrate** Liberty Day by participating in a special program or by memorizing and presenting patriotic poems and songs to parents or other guests.	• To pledge allegiance to the American flag • To sing the national anthem • To celebrate Liberty Day

The Noah Plan Lessons Kindergarten © 2003 • Foundation for American Christian Education

Week Nine

Quarter Four

TEACHING PLAN

Preparation	Lesson	Student Work	Accomplishments	✓
Biblical Principle "Write the vision and make it plain upon tables, that he may run that readeth it." Habakkuk 2:2	**Discuss** the Biblical Principle and the Leading Idea.	**Participate** in a discussion of the Biblical Principle and Leading Idea.	• To express God's Principle of Individuality as it pertains to the continents by displaying pictures on a bulletin board	
	Construct a bulletin board.			
Leading Idea Bulletin boards are a means of communication and individual expression.	• **Cover** it with blue paper. • **Make** a transparency of a world map to be projected on the bulletin board. • **Outline** and label each continent. • **Instruct** the student to cover each continent with pictures that relate to that continent's unique individuality. **Instruct** the student to use the pictures saved in the envelope for this project.	**Contribute** to a bulletin board project by gluing the saved pictures that relate to the unique individuality of each continent on the map drawn by the teacher.		
Books • Bible (KJ)				
Supplies • World map or globe				

GEOGRAPHY

240 The Noah Plan Lessons Kindergarten © 2003 • Foundation for American Christian Education

Week Nine

TEACHING PLAN

Quarter Four

Preparation	Lesson	Student Work	Accomplishments	✓
SCIENCE				

Biblical Principles
• God's Principle of Individuality
• Unity with Diversity
 	
Leading Idea
God is the Master Designer who created man in his image and equipped him to live in this world.
 	
Books
• Bible (KJ)
• Encyclopedia
• *Learning about My Body*, The Evan-Moor Corp.
• *My First Body Book*, Chris and Melanie Rice
• *What's Inside? My Body*, Angela Royston
• *Me and My Body*, David Evans and Claudette Williams
• *My Five Senses*, Aliki Brandenberg
 	
Supplies
• Objects to use or matching game (by shape or color)
• Objects to use for hearing activity (to make various sounds)
• Prepared notebook page
• Visuals of good health habits or proper nutrition
	Review the Biblical Principles and Leading Idea.
	
	Review by questioning the unique characteristics and function of the digestive system and by using visuals such as books and charts.
	
	Introduce the nervous system.
	• **Present** information and visuals (charts or pictures) pertaining to the nervous system and its major organ, the brain.
	• **Locate** the brain on a chart or diagram.
	• **Name** the five senses and the part of the body related to each sense. (Tell how each one sends a different message to the brain.)
	• **Locate** the organ used for each of the five senses on a chart or diagram.
	• **Discuss** the following:
	  • How the unique function of the nervous system and the importance of the brain (controls the body and acts as the center of thinking) illustrates God's Principle of Individuality
	  • How the five senses demonstrate Unity with Diversity.
	• **Provide** concrete experiences:
	  • **Use sight**—match objects by shape and color.
	  • **Use hearing**—make a sound with a chosen object while the student is blindfolded and ask the student to find that object in a group of items.
	  • **Use touch**—identify or match items by touch alone
	  • **Use smell**—identify or match smells while blindfolded.
	  • **Use taste**—identify various foods as salty, sour, sweet, or bitter while nose is pinched and eyes are closed.
	
	SCIENCE—
	Lesson & Notebook Work
	(continued on page 242)
		Participate in a review of the Biblical Principles and Leading Idea.
		Contribute to a review of the digestive system by answering questions about its function and unique characteristics.
		Listen as the teacher presents unique characteristics and visuals related to the nervous system.
		Locate the brain on a chart or diagram.
		
		Locate the organ used for each of the five senses as the teacher names them and discusses their function.
		Reason orally through a classroom discussion about:
		• The importance of the brain
		• The unique function of the nervous system and the five senses
		• How these demonstrate God's Principles of Individuality and Unity with Diversity
		Participate in activities related to the five senses.
		
		SCIENCE—
		Student & Notebook Work
		(continued on page 242)
			• To review the purpose of the digestive system
			• To recognize God as the Master Designer
			• To praise and worship God for His marvelous Creation
			• To learn about your body and its functions in order to have dominion over it
			• To learn about God's Principles of Individuality and Unity with Diversity in the nervous system
			• To locate the brain on the chart
			• To participate in experiments involving the five senses
			• To learn good health habits and proper stewardship of our bodies
			• To complete and file notebook work	

The Noah Plan Lessons Kindergarten © 2003 • Foundation for American Christian Education

Week Nine   Quarter Four

TEACHING PLAN

Preparation	Lesson	Student Work	Accomplishments	✓
	Discuss the good health habits and nutrition necessary for the proper stewardship (care) of our bodies. • **Include** topics such as tooth care, personal hygiene, and exercise. • **Introduce** the food pyramid and discuss what we need to eat in order to be healthy. *Notebook Work* **Distribute** the prepared notebook page for the student to write or trace the title and to label various parts of the nervous system. Notebook page to include: • the title" The Nervous System" for the student to write or trace • a picture of the nervous system for the student to label various parts	**Discuss** the good health habits and nutrition necessary for the proper stewardship (care) of our bodies. • **Include** topics such as tooth care, personal hygiene, and exercise. • **Introduce** the food pyramid and discuss what we need to eat in order to be healthy. *Notebook Work* **Write** or trace the title on the notebook page and label the various parts of the nervous system.		

SCIENCE (continued)

242   The Noah Plan Lessons Kindergarten © 2003 • Foundation for American Christian Education

Supplemental Information

OVERVIEWS OF KINDERGARTEN SUBJECTS FOR STUDENT NOTEBOOKS 245

CULTIVATING THE LOVE OF LEARNING IN KINDERGARTEN 258

    Winnie-the-Pooh Tea Party 258

    Beatrix Potter Day 259

    Grandparents' Day 263

    Pioneer Day/*Little House in the Big Woods* Day 264

    The Kindergarten Field Studies 268

KINDERGARTEN MATHEMATICS 269

SAMPLE TEACHER LESSON PLANS AND ACTUAL STUDENT WORK

    Bible as a Reader and English Lessons 282

RESOURCES

    Alphabetical List of Books and Publishers 295

    Ordering Information 297

Jenny C.

The Overviews of Kindergarten Subjects for Student Notebooks

Overviewing the subject gives a sense of dominion—a view over the subject. Instead of endless facts that pour forth like unstrung pearls, the overview gives the subject wholeness, identity, and a place on the great Chain of Christianity. The overview unifies the subject for the grade level by presenting its principles, its leading ideas, the sequence of its presentation, and its purposes and goals. A copy of the overview is placed in the front of the student notebook after the title page and reviewed frequently to provide the student with the whole view of the year's work in the subject. It should be referred to as each new unit is introduced to show the student his progress through the subject and to remind him of the whole purpose of his study.

Prepare thy work without,
and make it fit for thyself in the field;
and afterward build thine house.
—Proverbs 24:27

For which of you, intending to build a tower,
sitteth not down first, and counteth the cost,
whether he have sufficient to finish it?
—Luke 14:28

Kindergarten
MATHEMATICS OVERVIEW

For the invisible things of him from the creation of the world are clearly seen, being understood by the things that are made, even his eternal power and Godhead; . . .
(Romans 1:20)

Principles:
God's Principle of Individuality

Principle of Representation

Commutative Principle of Addition

Associative Principle of Addition

Principle of Symmetry

Principle of Place Value

Purposes:
Reveal God and His divine nature and character through mathematics.

Identify and demonstrate the principles governing mathematics.

Reason from principles of mathematics and apply them to problem solving.

Teach the place of mathematics on the Chain of Christianity moving westward.

Form the character of the American Christian mathematician.

CONTENT:
The following concepts will be taught and reviewed throughout the school year.

Foundations:
Biblical Foundations

Men on the Chain of Christianity

Tools of Mathematics

Numbers:
Counting objects and arranging in groups of tens

Skip-counting by twos to 30, by fives to 100, by tens to 100

Counting with cardinal and ordinal numbers

Recognition of quantities 1 to 100 and representing them on the abacus

Place value—10 ones is 1 ten, 10 tens is 1 hundred

Knowledge of even and odd numbers

Division of objects into halves and fourths

Numeration and Notation:
Reading and writing numbers 1 to 100

Reading and writing addition equations

Learning about graphs

Measurement:
Monetary—recognition, value, and name of the penny, nickel, dime

Time—knowing days of the week, months of the year, time to the hour and half-hour

Linear—determining length with nonstandard measure

Geometry—knowing the mathematical names of the triangle, rectangle, and circle, parallel and perpendicular lines, and patterning

Operations:
Addition—combining parts to form a whole, partitioning, number combinations

Subtraction—understanding subtraction as a missing addend and separating a whole

Problem Solving:
Solving addition problems

Solving missing addend problems

Solving subtraction problems

Kindergarten
ENGLISH GRAMMAR & COMPOSITION OVERVIEW

... let every man be swift to hear, slow to speak, slow to wrath:
(James 1:19)

Purpose:

Learning the English language is a particular gift from God for communication. Mastery of our native language is the basis of all enterprise and learning and the vehicle for propagating the Gospel in every sphere of life.

Principle:

God's Principle of Individuality is seen in the sounds, spellings, words, and writings of English and in the individual expression through writing and speaking.

Requirements and Practice:

The elements of English are taught through the *Writing Road to Reading* with beginning phonetics, speaking, penmanship, reading, and spelling.

A notebook is kept for filing English and literature papers.

Literature and poetry inspire the love of language and present an excellent and enjoyable model of expression.

CONTENT:

I. **Biblical Foundation and Providential History of the English Language**

   Learning that language is a gift from God and appreciating the written Word of God

   Learning about England and France on the Chain of Christianity

   Understanding that the purpose of language is to communicate ideas

II. **Orthography**

   The "beginning to read" stages of learning: English is taught as a system of sounds based on reasoning and reflective processes.

III. **Etymology**

   Identifying syllables

   Learning about the dictionary

   Enjoying all kinds of words—rhyming, descriptive, important words from literature, science, history, geography, and Bible

   Learning the precise meaning of words

   Using words in story-telling and poems

IV. **Syntax**

   Introducing the structure of the English language and its parts wholistically

   Practicing the sentence as a whole thought in speaking and writing

   Subjects and verbs as naming and action words

   Simple punctuation and capitalization

V. **Prosody**

   Using correct pronunciation and diction for clear articulation

   Expanding listening skills through reading aloud and appreciating the excellence of language in poetry and literature

   Memorization and presentation of poems and scripture

   The study of children's literature

VI. **Composition**

   Inventing and combining ideas by asking questions, using words in sentences, describing with detail, noticing and observing, and participating in a group paragraph

   Clothing ideas with words by speaking always in sentences, practicing correct verbal syntax, using verbs, and describing words by invention

   Putting words in order by writing sentences as statements, practicing verbal syntax, and learning to write a paragraph with a topic sentence

   Committing words to paper by beginning sentences with a capital letter and ending with a period; learning to indent

   Writing sentences from literature, science, geography, Bible, and writing a simple paragraph daily by spring

Kindergarten
READING OVERVIEW

For thou wilt light my candle: the LORD my God will enlighten my darkness.
(Psalm 18:28)

Purposes:

Cultivate enlightened learners through reading the word of God—The Bible.

Inspire and equip students with a lifelong love of reading, especially of reading the Bible, literary classics, and poetry.

Unify all elements of language learning from phonetics to literature, composition, grammar, spelling, penmanship, listening and speaking.

Lay the foundation of reading skills in an order and sequence that produce mastery of language and literacy.

Establish the habits of study and scholarship.

Build into the lives of students the foundation stones of Christian character and the truths of the Bible for the practice of Christian liberty.

Principles:

Principle of Individuality

Principle of Representation

Unity with Diversity

Student Performance Goals:

Awareness of the sounds (phonemes) that make up spoken words—phonemic awareness

Auditory and visual discrimination of letter-sound associations

A sense of directionality in writing and reading

Development of oral language and listening skills by listening to a variety of literary forms, recognizing rhythm and rhyme, and following one-step and two-step directions

A speaking vocabulary that enables ideas to be expressed clearly

Development of basic phonetic principles as introduced in *The Writing Road to Reading*™

Usage of a variety of strategies while practicing early reading skills—decoding, fluency, vocabulary, and text comprehension

Memorization of scripture verses and poems

Reading with instruction *The Early Reader's Bible* and other readers

Identification of passages as narratives or informatives

Comprehension and retelling of stories, sequences events, and identification of main ideas

Writing complete sentences in shared writing activity

248   The Noah Plan Lessons Kindergarten © 2003 • Foundation for American Christian Education

Kindergarten
BIBLE OVERVIEW

...from a child thou has known the holy scriptures, which are able to make thee wise unto salvation through faith which is in Christ Jesus.
(II Timothy 3:15)

Purposes:
Inspire a love for the Word of God.

Enlighten the mind of each child to the knowledge of God through His written word.

Lead the child to salvation through Christ.

Establish the authority and infallibility of the Word of God.

Teach God's providence in the lives of Biblical characters.

Principle:
God's Principle of Individuality

Content:

First Quarter:
I. **The Immediacy of Jesus Christ:**

Nine weeks are spent on chosen aspects from the Gospels revealing Christ's ministry among men from the prophecy of His coming to His commissioning of His disciples and His ascension to the right hand of God.
  A. Birth of Jesus
  B. Jesus as a youth growing in stature and wisdom
  C. Baptism of Jesus
  D. "The Parable of the Talents"
  E. "The Parable of the Good Samaritan"
  F. "The Parable of the Lost Sheep"
  G. The Resurrection
  H. Map Work: The Holy Land at the time of Christ

Second Quarter:
II. **The Old Testament History:**

This nine-week period starts with beginnings—the beginnings of Creation, of man, of sin, of the promise of a Savior, of a people. It reveals to us a God who is merciful and forgiving, who seeks to convict His children of the necessity of obeying His Law in order to maintain righteous lives. This study covers the history of Israel—from its formation, through the captivity, until the return to rebuild Jerusalem.
  A. Creation
  B. Noah and the flood
  C. Abraham and the Hebrew nation
  D. The story of Pharaoh and Moses
  E. David and Goliath
  F. Daniel

Third Quarter:
III. **The Literature and Wisdom of the Bible:**

This nine-week period covers the words of the prophets and the glorious knowledge of God's Wisdom books. The prophets are taught as civil and religious reformers, as well as foretellers of some future events in His Story.
  A. Selection of favorite Psalms
  B. Memorize Psalm 100
  C. Map Work
  D. Worship—priests, instruments, tabernacle, temple, music, dance

Fourth Quarter:
IV. **The New Testament History:**

This quarter focuses on the New Testament study of the church and the first century Christian in the epistles and the Book of Revelation. These faithful servants of Christ endeavored to forward His Story by taking the outreach of the Gospel to all nations.
  A. The twelve Apostles preach the Gospel
  B. The conversion of Saul
  C. Selection of passages from Epistles
  D. "The Lamb of God" in the book of Revelation

The Noah Plan Lessons Kindergarten © 2003 • Foundation for American Christian Education

Kindergarten
LITERATURE OVERVIEW

Finally, brethren, whatsoever things are true, whatsoever things are honest, whatsoever things are just, whatsoever things are pure, whatsoever things are lovely, whatsoever things are of good report; if there be any virtue, and if there be any praise, think on these things.
(Philippians 4:8)

Purposes:

Inspire the highest standard of the English language.

Exercise the God-given gift of communication.

Cultivate and refine language skills.

Establish the Bible as the greatest literary masterpiece.

Instill a lifetime love and enjoyment of classic literature.

Principles:

God's Principle of Individuality

Christian Character

"Conscience Is the Most Sacred of All Property."

Christian Self-Government

First Quarter:

I. **Introduction to Literature:** Definition and qualities of literature

II. **The Literature of the Bible:** Introduction to the Book of Psalms, reading of a selection of Psalms, and memorization of Psalm 100 (KJV)

III. **Lullabies from around the World:** Reading and singing lullabies and memorization of "All through the Night"

IV. **Children's Poets and Poetry:** Definition and discussion of poetry, the poetry of Christina Rossetti, and memorization of "Holy Innocents"

V. **Fairy Tales:** The qualities of a fairy tale, the conflict between good and evil, reading and discussing a selection of fairy tales

Second Quarter:

I. **Mother Goose and Other Nursery Rhymes:** Rhymes and rhythms of Mother Goose and their humor, wit, and nonsense

II. **Children's Classics—*Winnie-the-Pooh*:** The study of an animal tale, the individuality of the author, A. A. Milne, introduction to the elements of the classic, reading of the classic, and Special Day, "Winnie-the-Pooh Tea Party."

III. **Children's Poets and Poetry:**

  A. Henry Wadsworth Longfellow: his life, his place on the Chain of Christianity, and his poems

  B. Isaac Watts: his life, his contributions on the Chain of Christianity, and poetry from *Divine Songs in English Language for the Use of Children* (1715)

  C. Reading of the Christmas Story from the Scriptures and a variety of Christmas poetry

IV. **Children's Classics—*The Tale of Peter Rabbit*:** The individuality and contributions of Beatrix Potter and reading of *The Tale of Peter Rabbit*

Third Quarter:

I. **Fables and Myths:** Fables and myths as a type of literature, reading of *Aesop's Fables*, and reading of *Uncle Remus* by Joel Chandler Harris

II. **Children's Classics—*Bambi*:** The individuality of the author, Felix Salten; the reading of *Bambi*; learning the Notebook Approach

III. **Biography—*Abraham Lincoln*:** Biography as a type of literature; the authors: Ingri and Edgar Parin d'Aulaire; and the life and influences in young Abraham's childhood

IV. **The Children's Poets and Poetry:** Robert Louis Stevenson, his life, and place on the Chain of Christianity and reading of selections from *A Child's Garden of Verses*

Fourth Quarter:

I. **Individuality of Nations in Literature—*Little House in the Big Woods*:** Autobiography as a type of literature; the individuality and contributions of the author, Laura Ingalls Wilder; America's individuality on the frontier; and Special Day Celebration: "*Little House* Day"

II. **William Shakespeare—*As You Like It*:** William Shakespeare—Bard of the Bible; drama as a type of literature; drama on the Chain of Christianity; reading of *As You Like It* from Lamb's *Tales from Shakespeare*

250   The Noah Plan Lessons Kindergarten © 2003 • Foundation for American Christian Education

Kindergarten
History Overview

For God has allowed us to know the secret of His plan, and it is this: He purposed long ago in His sovereign will that all human history should be consummated in Christ.
(Ephesians 1:9–10, Phillips)

Purpose:
Identify the Christian idea of man as it appears gradually in government, traveling westward with the Gospel to America, for the complete expression of religious and civil liberty in the American Christian constitutional republic.

Principles:
God's Principle of Individuality

"Conscience Is the Most Sacred of All Property."

The Christian Principle of Self-government

The Principle of America's Heritage of Christian Character

Content:

First Quarter:
I. Introduction to History
  A. Definition of history as Christ, His Story
  B. Biblical foundation of history
  C. Introduction to the Providential view of history

II. Introduction to the Chain of Christianity and its westward move of the Gospel and liberty through individuals and nations
  A. God's Principle of Individuality
  B. Creation Link: God as Creator

Second Quarter:
I. The Chain of Christianity and its westward move of the Gospel and liberty through individuals and nations
  A. Moses and the Law Link: Moses as the deliverer of the Israelites from Egypt, lawgiver, and historian
  B. Jesus Christ—Focal Point of History: his birth, his individuality, his Gospel
  C. Paul and the Christian Church Link: his individuality, his giftings, and the movement of the Gospel westward
  D. The Bible in English Link: John Wycliffe, "Morning Star of the Reformation"

II. Celebration of "Plimoth Plantation Day"

Third Quarter:
I. Introduction to the Principle, "Conscience Is the Most Sacred of All Property"—James Madison
  A. Knowing right from wrong: "Conscience is that little spark of celestial fire that tells me right from wrong." —George Washington
  B. Voluntary consent, yielding my will: *"Not my will, but Thine be done."* (Luke 22:42)
  C. Stewardship of my property—external and internal

II. The Chain of Christianity and its westward move of the Gospel and liberty through individuals and nations
  A. Columbus Link: his individuality, his giftings, and his preparation as "Christ-Bearer to the New World"
  B. Christian Founding—Pilgrims, Patriots, & Pastors: God's unveiling of the North American continent for His purposes
  C. Introduction to the Christian Principle of Self-government
  D. The first Christian Constitutional Republic

Fourth Quarter:
I. Introduction to the Principle of America's Heritage of Christian Character

II. The Chain of Christianity and its westward move of the Gospel and liberty through individuals and nations
  A. American Christian Republic Link: Founding fathers and mothers of American Christian character and government establish Christian civil government—"Liberty for all!"; George Washington's individuality as a patriot and father of his country; The Christian documents of liberty in America: the *Declaration of Independence* and the *United States Constitution*
  B. Expansion and Erosion: Studied in the literature curriculum
  C. Restoration Link: My Place in History
  D. Symbols of Liberty in America

III. Celebrate "Liberty Day"

The Noah Plan Lessons Kindergarten © 2003 • Foundation for American Christian Education

Kindergarten
GEOGRAPHY OVERVIEW

*And God called the dry land Earth;
and the gathering together of the waters called he Seas. . . .*
(Genesis 1:10)

*Thou madest him to have dominion over the works of thy hands;
Thou has put all things under his feet.*
(Psalm 8:6)

Each continent has, therefore, a well-defined individuality,
which fits it for an especial function.
—Guyot, *Christian History*, 4

Purpose:

The purpose of teaching geography in kindergarten is to begin to give the student a sense of dominion over his world. He will begin to use globes, maps, and an atlas. He will begin to recognize each continent and see God's purpose for that continent. He will be able to identify God's Principle of Individuality and see that principle in the creation of the world.

Principles:

God's Principle of Individuality—geographically

The Principle of Property—Genesis 1:28

First Quarter:

I. Introduction to Geography

II. The individuality of the Earth in its universal setting

Second Quarter:

I. Asia: Continent of History / Origins

II. Europe: Continent of History / Development

III. North America: Continent of History / Christian Civil Government

Third Quarter:

I. North America: Continent of History / Christian Civil Government continued

II. South America: Continent of Nature / Vegetation

III. Antarctica: Continent of Nature / Hidden Resources

IV. Australia: Continent of Nature / Antiquity

Fourth Quarter:

I. Australia: Continent of Nature / Antiquity continued

II. Africa: Continent of Nature / Animal life

III. Atmosphere of the Earth: Climate and weather

Kindergarten
SCIENCE OVERVIEW

In the beginning God created the heaven and the earth.
(Genesis 1:1)

Purposes:

Celebrate the knowledge of God in His creation.

Discover scriptural principles in creation by observing and reasoning.

Principles:

God's Principle of Individuality

Principle of Order

Unity with Diversity

First Quarter:

I. **Introduction to science:** definition, Biblical foundation, overview of science

II. **Introduction to human anatomy and physiology:** definition, Biblical foundation, God's Principles identified through the study of the body systems

Second Quarter:

I. **Human anatomy and physiology continued:** proper stewardship of our bodies—exercise, hygiene, healthy foods, rest

II. **Introduction to meteorology:** definition, Biblical foundation, weather, characteristics and purpose of the seasons, effect of seasons on plants and animals

III. **Introduction to zoology:** definition, Biblical foundation, distinguishing characteristics of invertebrates and vertebrates

Third Quarter:

I. **Zoology continued:** invertebrates and vertebrates

II. **Introduction to ecology:** definition of ecology, Biblical foundation, conservation of natural resources

Fourth Quarter:

I. **Introduction to botany:** definition of botany, Biblical foundation, characteristics of plants-structure, function, habits, and arrangement, what plants need in order to grow

The Noah Plan Lessons Kindergarten © 2003 • Foundation for American Christian Education   253

Kindergarten
FRENCH OVERVIEW

*Let your speech be always with grace, seasoned with salt,
that you may know how ye ought to answer every man.*
(Colossians 4:6)

Purposes:

Begin to broaden the worldview of the student by identifying through French the value and significance of other cultures.

Cultivate an appreciation of the diversity of God's creation through the individuality of the French language and people.

Establish in the minds of the student the pattern of language learning and to develop an aptitude for all future language study.

Begin in the early years to lay the groundwork for future mastery of the French language, which will provide the student with a useful tool for communication, for possible research in science or medicine, and for enjoying the rich realms of French literature.

Principles:

Language is a gift from God to man, for the purpose of communication.

Each language, including French, has its own structure and individuality.

Foreign language learning is most effective when begun in early childhood.

First Quarter:

The French sound system; France on the globe; Alphabet; Songs; Basic vocabulary for greetings; Notebook pages; French names; General geographical features of France; Classroom directions

Second Quarter:

Nursery rhymes; Songs; Counting 1–10; Three well-known Paris monuments; Christmas in France; Individuality of France—customs and culture; Basic vocabulary for classroom objects; Montrez-moi game; Qu'est-ce que c'est? game; Notebook pages

Third Quarter:

La famille vocabulary; the family in France; Vocabulary—les couleurs; Notebook pages; Songs: "Ainsi font, font, font," and "Fais Dodo"

Fourth Quarter:

Simple phrases and sentence; Cæsar and Gaul—origin of France; Joan of Arc; Songs: "Sur le pont d'Avignon," "Alouette;" Body vocabulary; General review of songs and games; Complete notebook pages; Nursery rhymes in French

Kindergarten
ART OVERVIEW

The heavens declare the glory of God; and the firmament sheweth his handywork.
(Psalms 19:1)

Purpose:

Develop the knowledge of God's character in Creation through the visual arts.

Teach the Biblical principles of art and build Christian character through their applied use.

Instill a love for art history, the visual record of the Gospel, through a study of the individual lives of master artists.

Develop the disciplined use of each child's God-given talent to produce visual art for the glory of God.

Draw from every child his fullest potential in creative expression, thereby building self-esteem.

Develop a lifetime habit of good stewardship of time, talent, and tools.

Develop and sharpen observation and problem-solving skills.

Explore a wide variety of art media with an emphasis on the fine arts.

Content:

I. Art Practice
  A. Introduction to God's elements of design through the study of creation
  B. Introduction to drawing
  C. Introduction to painting
  D. Introduction to pastels

II. Crafts
  A. Leaf rubbings
  B. Paper cutting
  C. Clay
  D. Printing
  E. Mixed media projects

III. Art "His" Story
  A. Looking at the whole of art history with an art timeline from a Christian perspective
  B. Early Christian Art
  C. Individual artists and their masterpieces:
   1. Fra Angelico (1400–1458)
   2. Michelangelo (1475–1564)
   3. Albrecht Dürer (1471–1528)
   4. John J. Audubon (1785–1851)
   5. Claude Monet (1840–1926)
   6. Walt Disney (1901–1966)
   7. Your students (Twenty-first Century)

IV. Special Days
  A. Field trip to an art museum
  B. School art show
  C. Association of Christian Schools International (ACSI) Art Show or other group sponsored art shows

Kindergarten
MUSIC OVERVIEW

I will sing unto the Lord as long as I live:
I will sing praise to my God while I have my being.
(Psalm 104:33)

Purpose:

Enable and equip the student to enjoy and to respond to quality music.

Participate in music-making as technical abilities and understanding increase.

Actively participate in music activities of some sort throughout the student's lifetime.

Principles Taught:

God's Principle of Individuality—sounds, instruments, and rhythm

Christian Self-Government—deportment

Unity with Diversity—conducted choral singing; conducted instrumentals

Content:

Through a variety of activities, the kindergarten student will experience many facets of music. He will grow throughout the year in all of the following areas:

Singing:

- Building a repertoire of a variety of songs
- Matching pitch; recognizing higher and lower pitch
- Using good posture to sing unison songs
- Using our four different voices: singing, speaking, shouting, whispering

Moving:

- Moving to singing games
- Learning sign language
- Moving rhythmically
- Echoing rhythmic patterns

Playing and Understanding Instruments:

- Playing rhythm and accompaniment instruments
- Learning about instruments of the orchestra

Appreciation:

- Listening to different styles of music
- Learning music and/or dances from historical periods studied in literature and/or history
- Developing listening skills

Hearing:

- Distinguishing among high, low, and middle musical sounds
- Distinguishing between soft and loud musical sounds
- Distinguishing among various tempos

Music Writing and Theory:

- Knowing the part of a note
- Drawing notes
- Understanding that different kinds of notes are held for different amounts of time
- Recognizing the staff as the "home" of notes

Kindergarten
PHYSICAL EDUCATION OVERVIEW

*What? Know ye not that your body is the temple of the Holy Ghost which is in you,
which ye have of God, and ye are not your own?
For ye are bought with a price: therefore glorify God in your body,
and in your spirit, which are God's.*
(I Corinthians 6:19–20)

Purposes:

Develop and strengthen the child in both body and spirit through conditioning.

Participate in the physical, mental, emotional, and spiritual activities that develop strength, speed, skill, endurance, coordination, and cooperation.

Principles:

God's Principle of Individuality

Man as God's Property

Man as Sacred Property

Content:

I. Internal Objectives

   A. Developing listening skills

   B. Developing respect for teachers and fellow students

   C. Learning good sportsmanship—Matthew 7:12

   D. Developing confidence and self-esteem, always focusing on the positive points

   E. Developing a good attitude—II Timothy 2:5

   F. Learning to follow directions

   G. Developing self-control and learning to be self-governed—Colossians 3:24–25

   H. Developing cooperation with others

II. External Objectives

   A. Developing skill and coordination

   B. Gaining a general knowledge of the rules of games and sports

   C. Developing an interest in playing these sports competitively later in life

   D. Learning to exercise—to learn the benefits both physically, mentally, and spiritually

   E. Developing endurance

   F. Developing physical strength

   G. Strengthening the weaknesses—further develop strong points

   H. Developing good health habits—I Corinthians 3:16–17

   I. Learning to play with others safely—Proverbs 4:11–13

   J. Showing an overall improvement from September to June

Throughout the year, we will play games such as dodge ball, relay races, and running distances. We will also work on skills with the ball (catching, dribbling, passing), jump rope, and hula-hoop.

In the first quarter we will learn competitive games and rules. These games will be kickball, volleyball, soccer, and football.

In the second quarter, we will continue with kickball, soccer, football, and add basketball.

In the third quarter we will continue with basketball and soccer.

In the fourth quarter we will continue with soccer and kickball and introduce "T" ball.

We will review rules during each sport.

Cultivating the Love of Learning in Kindergarten

The key to enjoying learning is in imparting a love-of-learning spirit in the classroom—*philomathy*. (philomath, *n.* A lover of learning.)

The variety and elevation of our curriculum inspire many special programs, presentations, projects, and field study tours. The degree to which the student is actively involved in the subject determines how much he enjoys it. Each teacher develops his enrichment and traditions that foster excitement in learning.

The Notebook Method instills a sense of property that inspires students to excel. It gives a tangible, visible, lasting reward for labor. Through its use students develop an interest in learning and a commitment to achievement.

Special Days

Special days are a Biblical tradition that is first recorded in Genesis. They are memorial days set aside to commemorate an event or truth. Memorials established by men are Jacob's stone (Genesis 28:18–22), Altar at Jordan (Joshua 22:9–16), and Feast of Purim (Esther 9:28.) and those established by God are Passover (Exodus 12:14) and The Lord's Supper (Luke 22:19). In imitation of the Biblical model to commemorate any particular truth, a special day serves to enhance the truth being studied in the mind and heart of the learner. See NPH&GG, 284–301 for suggestions on how to conduct special days.

Winnie-the-Pooh Day

November ____

Dear Parents,

To culminate our *Winnie-the-Pooh* study we will view the *Winnie-the-Pooh* movie and have a special lunch on Friday, _____.

In order to assist with this special day, we are asking each family to contribute one of the following for the students and guests:

1. Mr. Owl Fruit Kabobs
2. Piglet Blankets (pigs in a blanket)
3. Pooh's Honey Buns (monkey bread)
4. Christopher Robin's Egg Salad (egg salad sandwiches)
5. Tigger Stripes (celery with peanut butter)
6. Honey Pot Punch (mix lemonade, pineapple, juice, and honey to taste)
7. Honey and Peanut Butter Pooh Sandwiches
8. Hard Boiled Robin Eggs (dyed blue)
9. *Winnie-the-Pooh* cups and napkins.

Sincerely,
Sheree Beale

Return the bottom portion with your selection by _____ .

My child, _____ , will bring item number _____ to share.

Parent Signature _____

Beatrix Potter Day

Purposes & Celebrating the Day

March _____

Dear Parents,

Every year, the StoneBridge kindergarten students spend several weeks studying the life of Beatrix Potter and reading several of the classic animal tales that she wrote. This study, which is part of the literature curriculum, focuses on how the individuality of the animal characters can be seen in their actions and in the choices that they make. The children quickly see the connection between the choices of the characters and the consequences that they face. They relate these actions and situations to their own lives and begin to understand that actions have consequences, either for good or evil. They also begin to have an appreciation for the author and her unique individuality.

Beatrix Potter was a naturalist, artist, and story teller who had a great affection and respect for God's creatures. Her respect and affection for animals can be seen in the hundreds of sketches and nature studies that she made throughout her life. Her character qualities of diligence and perseverance directly influenced the publication of her books and our ability to enjoy these classic tales today.

As a culmination of this literature study, the kindergarten classes celebrate "Beatrix Potter Day." This year, it will be celebrated on March ____ with center activities such as Jeremy Fisher's Fishing Pond, The Tailor of Gloucester's Shop, Mr. McGregor's Garden, Mrs. Tiggy Winkle's Wash Center, Hunca Munca's Kitchen, and Beatrix Potter's Schoolroom. The morning will end with a tea party which includes butterfly sandwiches, carrot raisin salad, chamomile tea, and blackberry tea.

In-depth studies of classic literature and authors give, even very young students, a greater appreciation for language and the creative abilities that God has placed within each one of us.

Sincerely,

Sheree Beale

Sample Invitation

Organization

Parental help is needed to make this day a special time.

1. Prepare and distribute the Invitation to the parents and other guests.
2. Man the centers—three helpers for Kitchen, two for each other center.
3. Baked items (to serve ____ persons), two people for each item:
   Nut bread (2 loaves)   Carrot cookies
4. Loan or purchase supplies (save all receipts):
   - Paper goods
     Napkins   Plates (30 Beatrix Potter, 20 pastel)
     Doilies   Napkins
   - Gardening supplies
     Square or round, clay, plastic, or peat 3" or 4" pots   Potting soil
   - Ingredients for Hunca Munca Kitchen
   - Fabric and yarn for Tailor Shop
   - Miscellaneous
     Small plastic wading pool   Cutting boards & knives   Doll or small baby clothes
     Iron & ironing boards   Measuring cups   Serving plates
                                                                (optional, story characters)
5. Prepare items for centers:
   - *Cut felt or tab board waistcoats and yarn for sewing.*
   - *Cut name tags for center grouping and rotation.*
   - *Trace Peter Rabbit on watercolor paper using a light box.*
6. Set up and serve Tea Party—two helpers
7. Clean up committee—classroom and activity centers

Sample Activities Centers

Prepare six centers with different activities to experience. The students will be put into groups of not more than 6. The groups will rotate through these stations spending approximately 20 minutes at each activity (see schedule).

Mr. MacGregor's Garden
Materials needed:

Seeds	Watering can	Pictures of plant growth
Pots	Markers and sticks	Pictures of parts of a plant
Soil	Magnifying glass	Sequencing cards
Crayons		

Activities (approximately 5 minutes each):
Discuss seeds.
    Examine and compare several seeds (use a magnifying glass).
    Sequence plant growth (using cards).
    Name parts of a plant.
Color a marker top and glue it to the stick.
    (Write the child's name and kind of seed planted on it.)
Choose a seed, plant it, and water it.

Mr. Jeremy Fisher's Fishing Pond

Materials needed:

Bucket with sand or soil
Rubber fishing worms
Small plastic shovels

Fishing poles with magnets
Fish with magnetic tips
Small swimming pool or wash tub

Optional: galoshes
mackintosh
(raincoat)

Activities:

Dig for worms—place them in a bucket.
Fish for plastic fish.
Try on mackintosh and galoshes if time allows.

Mrs. Tiggy Winkle's Wash Day

Materials needed:

Wash boards
Wash tub
Clothes pins
Cloth napkins

Detergent (mild)
Drying rack
Clothesline

Irons and ironing boards
Doll or small baby clothes
Small basket

Activities:

Wash doll clothes in tub using wash boards.
Hang clothes on clothesline or rack.
Iron cloth napkins, fold them, and place them in the basket.

The Tailor of Gloucester's Shop

Materials needed:

Sewing notions:

Needles	Pattern
Thimble	Fabric samples
Thread	Plastic needles

Yarn
Waistcoats cut from felt (one coat, front and back,
  per student)
Pictures that sequence the progression of making
  an article of clothing from start to finish

Activities:

Examine some of the tools that a tailor would use.
Discuss what a tailor does—what he makes.
Stitch a waistcoat cut from felt.
  (Pre-thread the needle and tie the yarn to the first hole of the waistcoat.)

Beatrix Potter's Schoolroom—Watercolor Lesson

Materials needed:

Brushes
Watercolor paint

Palettes for mixing paint
Water jars

Pictures of Peter Rabbit
  on watercolor paper

Activities:

The children will paint Peter Rabbit and draw a carrot to be placed in Peter Rabbit's hand.

The Noah Plan Lessons Kindergarten © 2003 • Foundation for American Christian Education

Hunca Munca's Kitchen

Materials needed:

2 small mixing bowls	Forks	Recipes for dishes to be prepared
1 medium mixing bowl	Vegetable peeler	Ingredients for each recipe
1 large mixing bowl	Grater	Knives (paring and butter)
Mixing spoons	Rotary blender	Measuring cups and spoons

Activities:

Each group will prepare one of the recipes provided, to be served at the Tea Party.
   (See *The Peter Rabbit and Friends Cook Book,* Naia Bray-Moffatt or *Peter Rabbit's Natural Foods Cookbook,* Arnold Dobrin, F. Warne & Co. [out-of-print], or make up your own recipes.)
Some simple foods that children can prepare are:
   Celery with cream cheese and raisins on top
   Sandwiches with sliced cucumbers, cream cheese, and dill
   Sandwiches with tuna mixed with salad dressing & lettuce
   Banana and peanut butter sandwiches
   Egg salad sandwiches

Sample Beatrix Potter Day Center Rotations

Center ╲ Time	8:45 – 9:05	9:05 –9:25	9:25 –9:45	9:45 –10:00	10:00 –10:20	10:20 –10:40	10:40 –11:00
Mr. MacGregor's Garden	1	2	3	S	4	5	6
Jeremy Fisher's Fishing Pond	2	3	4	N	5	6	1
Mrs. Tiggy Winkle's Wash Day	3	4	5	A	6	1	2
The Tailor of Gloucestor's Shop	4	5	6	C	1	2	3
Beatrix Potter's Schoolroom	5	6	1	K	2	3	4
Hunca Munca's Kitchen	6	1	2	S	3	4	5

Grandparents' Day

October _____

Dear Parents,

As you are aware, Grandparents' Day is Thursday, October __. We are preparing a short presentation based on some of the things we have studied in Bible, history, and literature. We will sing and do movements to a couple of nursery rhymes as well as present the highlights of our history study focusing on "God's Principle of Individuality." Please review the poem "Starting with Me" with your child to support our classroom practice. Some of the children have volunteered or have been chosen to present portions of our study of creation or individuality. These parts are listed below. If your child has an individual part, please help him to review it each day so that he will feel comfortable sharing it on Grandparents' Day. Please feel free to call me at home if you have any questions.

Sincerely,
Sheree Beale

Creation

ALL:	"In the beginning, God created the heaven and the earth." Genesis 1:1
Darian & Gareth:	On the first day of creation, God created light and separated it from the darkness.
Isaac & Victoria:	On the second day of creation, God separated the waters above from the waters below.
Logan & Ryan:	On the third day of creation, God separated the land from the water and He created plants of every kind.
Natalie & Rachel:	On the fourth day of creation, God made the sun to govern the day and the moon and stars to govern the night.
Allie & Adam:	On the fifth day of creation, God created the birds of the air and the fish of the sea.
Madison & Maddie:	On the sixth day of creation, God created animals and man.
Johnny & Jack:	On the seventh day of creation, God rested. This day is the Sabbath and it is a holy day.
ALL:	"And God saw every thing that he had made, and, behold, it was very good." Genesis 1:31

History

ALL:	**"Starting with Me"** God made me special Like no one else you see God made me a witness To His diversity
Isaac, Jack, Logan:	God's Principle of Individuality can be seen in nature in the diversity of seashells. This means that there are many different kinds of shells.
Natalie, Madison, Allie:	God's Principle of Individuality can be seen in the design of leaves. We can tell what kind of tree a leaf came from by its design.
Adam, Darian, Gareth:	God's Principle of Individuality can be seen in the distinct breeds of dogs.
Ryan, Victoria, Rachel:	God's Principle of Individuality can be seen in the symmetry of a snowflake. All snowflakes have six points, *but* no two snowflakes are just alike.

The Noah Plan Lessons Kindergarten © 2003 • Foundation for American Christian Education

Kindergarten
Reflections

I liked Pioneer Day.
It was fun. One of
my favorite things
was butter making.
We shook whipped
cream and it turned
into butter. Then we
spread it on the crackers
and ate it. I also
made a neck lace. We
took a hammer and we

hammered designs
onto the leather.
Then we put it in our
Pioneer bag. Pioneer Day
showed all of us what
it was like in the
"olden" days.
Moriah T.

Pioneer Day

Purposes

To culminate the study of the key classic, *Little House in the Big Woods,* and to understand our own history as it pertains to one particular family in the American mid-western frontier

To represent a chronicle of American Christian pioneer life and character

To appreciate the Pilgrim-pioneer character moving westward as it is weaved throughout the curriculum

To appreciate the musical contribution to the period of American life and character

To teach the Biblical principle, "God's Principle of Individuality" and to build Christian character through its applied use

To strengthen and celebrate the Christian virtues which our students are taught in the Bible, history, and literature curricula

Celebrating the Day

Pioneer Day is an all-day event. It affords the students the opportunity for dressing in the American fashion of the time period, eating foods representative of this period of American life, and enjoying crafts, art, and music. The classroom is transformed into the individuality of America of the nineteenth century.

The classroom is transformed into the "little house" representing the sights and sounds of pioneer life. Classroom bulletin boards depict pictures of pioneer life. Music from this time-period is played to add to the ambiance of the classroom.

Organization

Parental help is needed to make this day a special time. The day's activities are divided into four committees:
1. Set up committee—decorates classroom, prepares name-tags, and schedule of events and rotation
2. Activities committee—prepares and assists in activity stations
3. Lunch committee—prepares picnic lunch and serves food

    Suggestions for a picnic lunch are:

Applesauce	Corn bread	Lemonade/apple juice
Baked beans	Fruit and nuts	Ice
Chicken nuggets	Popcorn (for snack)	Ice cream (for dessert)

4. Clean up committee—classroom and activity stations

Sample Activities Stations

Prepare six stations with different activities to experience. The students will be put into groups of not more than 6. The groups will rotate through these stations spending approximately 20 minutes at each activity.

Laundry Station

This center allows the students to experience the washing and drying of clothes as depicted in the nineteenth century. Each student will have the opportunity to wash clothes on a washboard and the drying of clothes on a clothesline.

Items needed:

Buckets	Paint brushes	Doll or baby clothes for washing
Metal wash tubs	Clothes pins	Rope for clothesline
Washboards	Water	Hoops

Quilting Station

This center introduces the students to the importance of quilting and the usefulness of quilts. It gives the students the opportunity to view different quilt patterns through books or actual quilts. It allows the students to view the demonstration of different sewing techniques. Each student will begin to sew his or her own sampler.

Items needed:

Batting	Quilt pattern	Needles
Hoops	Bottom layer	Thread

Butter Making Station

This center introduces the students to old-fashioned butter making. The process for butter making is explained and demonstrated. Each student will have the opportunity to make his or her own butter.

Items needed:

Crackers	Jars	Poster to illustrate butter-making
Salt	Napkins	Heavy whipping cream

Bread-making Station

This center introduces making bread from scratch. The students will see the process wheat goes through, as it becomes ready to make bread. The students will help mix the dough. They will have the opportunity to handle and knead the dough.

Items needed:

Bowls	Books/visual tools to illustrate
Baggies	the process for bread-making
Ingredients for dough	One slice of prepared bread for each student

Leather Embossing Station

This center allows the students to discover the uses of leather through the use of visuals. The students will each make a leather pendant by choosing a pattern and using the correct tools to stamp and mark the leather.

Items needed:

Bowls of water	Leather tools for embossing
Leather	Leather lace

Tin Punching Station

This center introduces the students to the art of tin punching and enables them to see the decorative uses of this craft. The students will pick a pattern and be invited to punch a tin circle. Adult supervision is crucial.

Items needed:

Hammers	Yarn	Original designs for copying
Nails	Wooden boards	Various copies of patterns to punch
Tape	Orange juice lids	

Pioneer Day
Sample Schedule of Events and Rotation

  8:30– 8:45 Name Tags Assigned

  8:45– 9:00 Devotions/Pledges

  9:00– 9:10 Individual Pictures /Group Pictures

  9:10– 9:30 **1st Activity Station**

  9:30– 9:35 Rotate to 2nd Activity Station

  9:35– 9:55 **2nd Activity Station**

  9:55–10:15 Snack/Restroom Break

10:15–10:35 **3rd Activity Station**

10:35–10:40 Rotate to 4th Activity Station

10:40–11:00 **4th Activity Station**

11:00–11:05 Rotate to 5th Station

11:05–11:25 **5th Activity Station**

11:25–12:15 Lunch/Restroom Break

12:15–12:35 **6th Activity Station**

12:35– 1:00 Pioneer Music, Games, and Dance or P.E.

  1:00– 2:30 Movie—*Little House in the Big Woods*

  2:30– 3:00 Clean up

Field Studies

The purpose of the field study trip is to enrich the student's classroom learning, relate history and science to his own life, and to deepen the student's love of history for a lifetime of study. By taking notes and sketching his own experiences, he will begin a habit of recording that will inspire him throughout his life.

Suggested Trips

The kindergarten class visits Bergy's Dairy in relation to their study of zoology. They feed calves, observe cows being milked, and sample freshly made ice cream.

The kindergarten class visits the art museum to enrich the student's learning experiences. The director can conduct two different tours. Students may go on a "safari hunt" to find different *animals* in the paintings, in relation to their study of zoology. Alternately, students may be asked to find *shapes* and *colors* in the paintings, which apply to art, math, and science. For additional information see SAG, 84–85.

The Teacher's Responsibilities:

The teacher is responsible to prearrange the tour by calling the site and speaking with the educational director or historic interpreter. By explaining the focus of the curriculum to be covered by the trip, the director can make the tour applicable to the kindergarten students.

The teacher will also need to explain to the students that the guide may have a secular viewpoint and what their response should be.

The students will need to be trained in Christian manners. They will be expected to be courteous and respectful. They should be taught that they are ambassadors and, as such, represent their families, their school, and Jesus Christ.

The teacher will want to show appreciation by writing a thank you note to the educational director.

Distribute a prepared notebook page about the tour for students to illustrate and file in their notebooks.

The Students' Responsibilities

The students are to be attentive to the guide by listening and asking questions.

The students are required to demonstrate his Christian self-government and thereby show themselves to be a good 'ambassador' for Christ.

Upon returning to class, the students will illustrate a prepared notebook page with a sketch of what they enjoyed most and file it in their notebooks.

Kindergarten Mathematics

Assessment in Mathematics

In the mathematics classroom paper and pencil tests may give a fair assessment of rote learning, but they generally do not give accurate information on how well children understand concepts. Oftentimes children guess the correct answers beyond their level of understanding, especially on multiple choice tests. How children solve problems on these tests remains a mystery.

Another way to assess children's knowledge is to observe them in an informal situation, such as during a game. The Corners Game is an ideal way to assess children on several topics. By sitting in on a game with three or four children for 10–15 minutes you can determine how well the players know the facts that total 50, 10, and 15, what strategies they use when they are unsure, and how well they understand tens and ones when they do their scoring.

Social skills can also be assessed. How willing the child is in helping (not giving answers to) another child, how the child handles mistakes, and how diligently the child uses the time between turns to plan ahead, all are apparent during a Corners Game.

—Joan Cotter
RightStart Mathematics, First Grade
Activities for Learning, 121

Kindergarten
Reflections

I enjoyed math class. We used our mathcubes to make patterns and shapes. My pattern was orange and red. A pattern keeps going. The tiles were fun too. We used them to help us add numbers. We also sorted them by colors. We entered stairsteps on our abacus. We learned a

poem as we counted and made the stairsteps. I learned that numbers are different. We see God's Principle of Individuality in math.

James T.

Steps to Guide the Kindergarten Teacher toward Integrating *RightStart* with *The Noah Plan Mathematics Curriculum Guide*

Review Related Skill or Concept
- Reflect upon and review previous principles studied.

Research
- Use the *RightStart Mathematics Kindergarten Notebook* manual to locate the particular lessons to be taught.
- Read the objectives, goals, and purposes provided within the manual with the intent of understanding the vocabulary.
- See The Language of Mathematics Chart as it pertains to the components of mathematics. This process helps uncover the principles of the lesson. (NPLK, 273)

Reason
- From the research, extrapolate the Christian, governmental, or mathematical principles demonstrated in the lesson. Therefore, the teacher makes that which is invisible (principles) visible! This is the "peculiar excellence" of the subject that is unique to mathematics, making it so enjoyable to the student because he is enabled to see principles, whereas in other subjects principles are 'hidden from view.' Use the Quarterly Plan Sheet for Teaching Mathematics by components to record observations. (NPMG, 84)
- Once the principles are identified, develop a leading idea that causes the learner to observe the principles within the lesson. Reason coupled with revelation will inspire the individual toward personal application. For guidance with leading ideas and principles, see NPMG, 82.

Relate
- Refer to, reflect on, and utilize the Biblical methods already incorporated in the lessons so that the student is challenged to internalize his learning and is enabled to give it personal application. (NPMG, 112–117) As one teaches, remember to model the four steps: research, reason, relate, and record. (NPMG, 80–81)
- Require student practice, participation, and presentation by:
  - Asking reason questions
  - Requiring the student to perform various mathematical activities such as calculations, problem solving, tallying, entering quantities on the abacus, and finding given quantities, etc.
  - Summarizing, reviewing, and evaluating
  - Utilizing good practice techniques such as rhyme, taps, games, drawing, abacus entries, etc.

Record
- Record the Biblical, governmental, or mathematical principles observed within the lessons.
- Memorize portions of scripture, nursery rhymes that support mathematical skills and computations.
- Evaluate the student's understanding and application of the principles through games, hands-on activities, memorization, computation, and written evaluation.

Components* for Kindergarten Mathematics Reveal God's Nature and Character

It is the peculiar excellence of mathematics,
that its principles are demonstrable.
—Noah Webster, 1828

This chart is designed with the intent of communicating to the teacher and student that each component of mathematics partially yet uniquely reveals an aspect of God's character and or nature. One's view of teaching and learning mathematics must return to incorporating this understanding to all who are learning this subject. It is what gives life, liberty, and love for the learning of the subject. The source of life, liberty, and love is God. Without an understanding of God's nature and character applied to mathematics, the subject loses much of its internal and eternal meaning and purpose rendering the study of it vain, uninteresting, and void of love and joy.

Mathematics Components*	Demonstrated Godly Character Trait
Foundations (NPMG, 12–13)	I am Alpha and Omega, the beginning and the ending, saith the Lord, which is, and which was, and which is to come, the Almighty. (Revelation 1:8) God is eternal, infinite, and the source of mathematics.
Numbers (NPMG, 12–13)	**Numbers** reveal God's nature and character. • How **great** is our God? • How **large** is He? He is **immense**, **large**, and **infinite**. He concerns Himself with every detail or **fraction** of our life. Simultaneously, He is **boundless** (GPI), **orderly, precise, immutable,** and **unchangeable.** (God's Principle of Individuality)
Numeration & Notation (NPMG, 12–13)	". . . write the vision, and make it plain upon tables, that he may run that readeth it." (Habakkuk 2:2) All are enabled to see the invisible nature of God through the encoding and decoding process. It makes the invisible source of excellence, order, precision, and infinity visible to all! This is the peculiar excellence of mathematics.
Measurement (NPMG, 12–13)	Jesus Christ is the divine standard against which all else is **measured** or **judged.** (Ephesians 4:13)
Operations (NPMG, 12–14)	The operations of mathematics reveal God's ways, methods, and government of all He has created giving unity to the subject by their dependability, order, and rule.
Problem Solving (NPMG, 12, 14)	The secondary purpose of studying mathematics is to help man cooperate and love each other (second New Testament commandment, Matthew 22:39). It serves to solve practical, physical, technological, economic, and scientific problems for His glory and our peaceful existence on earth. (Dominion Mandate—Genesis 1:28)

* These components are charted on the Quarterly Planning Sheet for Teaching Mathematics by Components.

The Language of Mathematics
Vocabulary of the Subject Categorized by Component
(Non-exhaustive)

Words have meaning! Understanding the vocabulary of a subject leads to mastery of the subject. One approach to mastering the subject's vocabulary is to categorize it into the components of the subject. The following chart is an example of categorizing the kindergarten mathematics vocabulary found and used in *RightStart* into its associated component. This process helps one classify the parts of a subject by putting it into an organized form in order to comprehend the whole subject.

Numbers	Numeration & Notation	Measurement	Operations	Problem Solving
Addend Cardinal Eight Even numbers Five Four Fraction Hundreds Nine Odd numbers One Ordinal Place value Remainder Seven Six Sum Teens Three Two Zero	Figures Finger sets Journaling Naming numbers Reading abacus entries Reading numbers Signs Symbols Tallying Tapping Vocabulary Writing equations Writing numbers	Circle Cone Cylinder Diagonal Dozen Ellipse Hexagon Linear measure Money denominations Octagon Parallel lines Patterns Perpendicular Plus Quadrilateral Rectangle Rhombus Square Symmetry Time (clocks) Triangle Weights	Addition Combining Counting Directionality (left/right) Division Less Multiplication Subtraction	Abacus entries Arranging Comparing Constructing Determining quantity Drawing Engineering (building) Estimating Folding Games Graphing Matching Money problems Ordering Partitioning Patterning Reason questions Recitation Review & Practice Rhyming Simplifying Sorting Strategies Subitizing (NPMG, 116) Summarizing Totaling Translating (NPMG, 117) Visualizing

Sample Lesson Plan
Demonstrating How to Integrate RightStart with
The Noah Plan Mathematics Curriculum Guide

Grade: K   **Date**: _____   **Quarter**: 1   **Week**: 2   **Title**: Quantities

Component: Numbers, Numeration, Notation, Operations, Sorting, Matching, Problem Solving

Math Skill(s): Subitizing, Tallying, Ordinal Counting, Directionality

Resources: Bible (KJ); T&L, 65, 69, 77, 98, 119, 125, 225–231; Webster's 1828 *Dictionary*; *RightStart*, Lessons 1–4; NPMG, 18–19, 112–114

Biblical References: Romans 10:17   **Homework**: None

Principle(s) Taught or Demonstrated	• God's Principle of Individuality (GPI)—likenesses or differences • Christian Self-Government (CSG)—consent • "Conscience Is the Most Sacred of All Property" (CSP)—agree or disagree • Representation—tally sticks and fingers
Leading Idea(s)	Quantities are unique, recognizable, infinite, and measure how much.
Goal of the Lesson	• To subitize quantities 1–5 • To learn to tally for quantities 1–5 • To learn how quantities change • To practice ordinal counting • To learn to sort and match
Teacher Presentation: • **Review Related Concept or Skill** • **Vocabulary** • **Instruction and Reasoning** (This portion is already done for you on NPLK, page 19.)	 Teach the nursery rhyme to capture the students attention: "One, Two, Buckle my Shoe" (*RightStart*, Lesson 1) Left, right, number, quantity, infinity, agree, disagree, tally **Refer** to *RightStart*™ Mathematics Kindergarten Lessons 1–4. **Introduce** the purpose and goal of the lesson. • See Objectives—*RightStart* Lessons 1–4. **Review** related skill or concept. • **Use** the nursery rhyme, "One, Two, Buckle my Shoe" to teach the student quantities and numbers. **State** the principles being taught and demonstrated through the lesson in an age appropriate manner. (The emphasized principle for kindergarten is "God's Principle of Individuality.") • **Examine** the vocabulary in *RightStart*, Lessons 1–4 and relate to the Christian, governmental, or mathematical principles as demonstrated below: <table><tr><td>**Vocabulary**</td><td>**Principle**</td></tr><tr><td>Left, right</td><td>Directionality</td></tr><tr><td>Recognize a quantity without counting</td><td>Subitizing</td></tr><tr><td>Tallying</td><td>Representation</td></tr><tr><td>Numbers</td><td>GPI (infinity)</td></tr><tr><td>Disagreeing agreeably</td><td>Conscience / Property and CSG</td></tr></table>

	• **Categorize** the vocabulary by component using the Quarterly Plan Sheet for Teaching Mathematics (NPMG, 84) and consulting the Biblical Teaching Methods (NPMG, 112–117.) • **Conclude** (identify) the Biblical, governmental, or subject principle(s) demonstrated by the vocabulary as shown above. **Require** the student to practice, to participate, and to present. • **Ask** the student reason questions. (This portion is already incorporated into the *RightStart*™ lessons.) • **Require** the student to perform various mathematical activities—sorting, matching, calculating, problem solving, tallying, finding given quantities, making abacus entries. **Summarize**, review, and evaluate. • **Utilize** good practice techniques—rhyming, tapping, drawing, etc.
Student Interaction and Reinforcement	**God's Principle of Individuality**: • **Ask** the student to decide on a number from 1–5 and to make it with his tally sticks. • **Ask** the student to change a given number (2) to another number (3) or (1). • **Ask** the student how he changed the number: by adding or removing one or more tally sticks. (*RightStart*, Lesson 1) **Christian Self-Government and Representation**: *"Faith comes by hearing, and hearing the Word of God"* (Romans 10:17). • **Ask** the student to listen to 3 using taps. • **Tap** various numbers between 1–5 and ask the student to identify them by showing finger sets, saying the words, and showing tally sticks. (*RightStart*, Lessons 3 and 4) **"Conscience Is the Most Sacred of All Property"** • **Place** 3 objects on one tray and 2 on another tray. • **Ask** the student if they agree that there are 3 objects on both trays. It is very important that the student be able to feel comfortable disagreeing with you. • **Add** one more object to the tray with 2 and ask if they agree now that they both have 3 objects. (*RightStart*, Lesson 1)
Lesson Enhancement	• **Show** the student how he can combine the contents of two containers onto a work area. Then, he proceeds to sort the objects and to return them to his original containers. Alternately, where a container has several different types of objects, (for example, different colored counters) the student can sort them into different piles and then can return all the objects to the original container. This activity helps to determine likenesses and differences through sorting—GPI. (*RightStart*, Lesson 2) • **Play** the ordinal counting game. (*RightStart*, Lesson 2) • **Make** triangles and quadrilaterals. (*RightStart*, Lesson, 4)
Evidence of Teaching Success	The student can participate in the mathematical activities that cause mathematical thinking—sorting, matching activities, and ordinal counting game. The student can successfully complete sorting and matching activities. The student can name quantities 1–6.
Evidence of Learning Success	The student can represent quantities correctly using fingers and tally sticks. The student can visualize quantities 1–6 with his eyes closed. The student can recognize quantities without counting. The student demonstrates the ability to discriminate between left and right The student demonstrates the ability to change quantities. The student can detect the number of taps from 1–4.

Sample Annual Teaching Schedule for Mathematics

Week	Monday	Tuesday	Wednesday	Thursday	Friday
Quarter 1					
1	BIBLICAL		FOUNDATIONS*		
2	1	2	3	4	AFLM
3	5	6	7	8	AFLM
4	9	10	10 WS 1	11	AFLM
5	12	13	13 WS 2	14	AFLM
6	15	16	17	18	AFLM
7	18 WS 3-1	19	19 WS 4	20	AFLM
8	21	21 WS 5-1	22	23	AFLM
9	24	25	26	Assessment	Field Trip
Quarter 2					
1	Noah	27	27 WS 6	28	AFLM
2	Noah	29	29	30	AFLM
3	Noah	31	31 WS 7-1	32	AFLM
4	Noah	33	34	35	Special Day
5	Noah	35 WS 8	36	36 WS 9	AFLM
6	Noah	37	37 WS 10-1	38	AFLM
7	Noah	38 WS 11	39	36 WS 12-1	AFLM
8	40	40 WS 12-2	41	41 WS 13	AFLM
9	42	43	43	Assessment	AFLM
Quarter 3					
1	Job	43 WS 14	44	45	AFLM
2	Job	46	46 Game	47	AFLM
3	Job	47 WS 15	48	48	AFLM
4	Job	48 WS 16	49	49	Special Day
5	Job	49 WS 17	50	50 WS 18	AFLM
6	Job	51	51 WS 21	52	AFLM
7	Job	52 WS 20	53	53 WS 21	Field Trip
8	54	54 WS 22-A	55	55 WS 23	AFLM
9	56	57	57 WS 24	58	Assessment
Quarter 4					
1	58 WS 25	59	60	61	AFLM
2	61 WS 28	62	63	64	AFLM
3	64 WS 27	65	66	67	AFLM
4	68	69	70	AFLM	Special Day
5	70 WS 27	71	AFLM	72	AFLM
6	73	AFLM	74	75	AFLM
7	76	77	18 WS 3-2	21 WS 5-2	AFLM
8	31 WS 7-2	37 WS 10-2	54 WS 22-B	Assessment	AFLM
9	AFLM	AFLM	AFLM	AFLM	Liberty Day

Explanation and Key for Using the Schedule

The schedule provided is intended to pace the teacher when using the *Right Start* curriculum. The Biblical foundations, Christian character studies, special days, and field trips are woven into the school year, which are not included in the *RightStart* curriculum. This kindergarten teaching schedule is one example of the various schedules that may be developed.

KEY

AFLM = Activities for Learning
A book enhancing and reinforcing the mathematical skills taught in the *RightStart* lessons. These activities should not be omitted.

WS = *RightStart* reinforcement worksheets.

Noah and Job = Locate these men on the Christian History of Mathematics Timeline (NPMG, 69–70), and study their individual contributions that advanced the Gospel and liberty of the individual. See NPMG, 136 for a model on how to do a character study on "People Who Impacted History."

Assessment = Evaluation of the student's progress. See "Assessment in the 'Kinder' Garden" (NPLK, 13) and comments on mathematics assessment from *RightStart* author, Joan Cotter (NPLK, 269).

Special Day = Applied to literature (Winnie-the-Pooh Tea Party, Pioneer Day); history (Plimoth Plantation Day); math (Noah, Job). See NPH&GG, 93, 284–301 for conducting Special Days.

Field Trip = See NPH&GG, 94–95 for conducting a field study tour.

Liberty Day = It is a celebration on the last day of school which memorializes God's Hand of Providence in the foundation of America. See NPH&GG, 294–301 for conducting Liberty Day.

* See Biblical Foundations Lessons, Days 1–5, NPLK, 277–281.

Biblical Foundations of Mathematics Lesson, Day 1

Grade: K Date: _____ Quarter: 1 Week: 1 Day: 1
Title: The Notebook Method
Component: Foundations Math Skill(s): Organization
Resources: Bible; T&L; Webster's 1828 *Dictionary*; *RightStart*; *The Noah Plan Mathematics Curriculum Guide*
Biblical References: Deuteronomy 16:20; Proverbs 16:11 Homework: None

Principle(s) Taught or Demonstrated	• God's Principle of Individuality—The notebook is a product of the student's creativity and illustrations. • Christian Self-Government—The notebook recording is a discipline. • Conscience/Property—The notebook reflects the internal character of the student in caring for his personal property.
Leading Idea(s)	The notebook method is a tool of reasoning and academic discipline.
Goal of the Lesson	• To make a producer and establish the skills and character of scholarship • To develop independent learning habits • To develop a permanent record of progress and learning for further study and reflection • To develop a self-governing character

Teacher Presentation:
• Review Related Concept or Skill
 	
• Vocabulary
 	
• Instruction and Reasoning
	• See NPSDS, Basic Steps & Notebook chapter for a complete description of the Notebook Method
	• See NPMG, 98–100 for a complete description of the mathematics notebook method and setup.
	
	method, record, permanent
	
	Introduce the purpose and goal of the lesson.
	• **Explain** and discuss the reason for the notebook.
	• **Read** aloud Deuteronomy 16:20 and Proverbs 16:11.
	• **Discuss** God requires man to keep accurate records and measurement.
	Teach the notebook standard of form.
	• **Assist** the student in setting up his notebook. NPMG, 98–100
	• **Distribute** a prepared notebook page to include:
	  • the title "Mathematics" for the student to write or trace
	  • a space for the student to draw a mathematical related picture (for example: an abacus)
	  • the necessary tabs or dividers to separate the student's work
	• **Reinforce** daily the notebook standard of form.
	Instruct on good notebook habits to avoid misfiling papers.
	Ask the student reason questions about the purpose of the notebook.
	Require student participation and presentation.
	• The student presents the finished notebook.
	Summarize, review, and evaluate.

Student Interaction and Reinforcement	**Listen** as the teacher introduces the purpose and goal of the lesson. **Discuss** with the teacher the reason for the notebook. • **Listen** as the teacher reads aloud Deuteronomy 16:20 and Proverbs 16:11. • **Discuss** God requires man to keep accurate records and measurement. **Write** or trace the title on the notebook page and draw a mathematical related picture. • **File** the title page. • **File** the necessary tabs or dividers. **Listen** as the teacher instructs on good notebook habits. **Answer** reason questions about the purpose of the notebook. **Utilize** good notebook methods to avoid misfiling. **Present** the finished notebook for evaluation.
Lesson Enhancement	Color the illustration on the title page.
Evidence of Teaching Success	The student can successfully follow directions and complete the notebook title and notebook tabs. The student can articulate the reason for a notebook. The student can successfully present a completed title page and notebook tabs.
Evidence of Learning Success	The student organized his notebook. The student produced an individual expression of the lesson—the mathematics notebook.

The Noah Plan Lessons Kindergarten © 2003 • Foundation for American Christian Education

Biblical Foundations of Mathematics Lesson, Day 2

Grade: K   **Date:** _____   **Quarter:** 1   **Week:** 1   **Day:** 2

Title: Mathematics and Its Branches

Component: Foundations   **Math Skill(s):** To appreciate mathematics in God's providence

Resources: Bible; T&L; Webster's 1828 *Dictionary;* *RightStart;* *The Noah Plan Mathematics Curriculum Guide*

Biblical References: John 15:5   **Homework:** None

Principle(s) Taught or Demonstrated	God's Principle of Individuality • The whole and its parts • Unity with Diversity • "I am the vine and ye are the branches." John 15:5
Leading Idea(s)	The study of mathematics results in a greater appreciation of the works of God.
Goal of the Lesson	• To introduce mathematics and how to 'think mathematically' NPMG, 106–107 • To understand the subject of mathematics from the whole to its parts—Unity with Diversity

Teacher Presentation:
 	
• **Review Related Concept or Skill**
 	
• **Vocabulary**
 	
• **Instruction and Reasoning**
	
	Read NPMG, 3, 9, 11, and 18–19.
	
	mathematics, arithmetic
	
	Introduce the purpose and goal of the lesson.
	Define mathematics and discuss its related vocabulary in simple terms.
	Guide the student to the Biblical Principle from the Leading Idea.
	• **Read** aloud and discuss John 15:5.
	• **Draw** a tree and five (5) branches on the board to model mathematics and its branches.
	• **Label** the tree accordingly:
	  • Trunk—mathematics
	  • Branches—arithmetic, algebra, geometry, trigonometry, calculus
	Relate mathematics and its branches to problem solving in simple terms. NPMG, 11
	Distribute a prepared notebook page with a tree and five branches for the student to color and file in the notebook.
	Summarize, review, and evaluate.
	Require student participation and presentation.
	• Ask the student reason questions about the lesson.

Student Interaction and Reinforcement	**Listen** as the teacher introduces the purpose and goal of the lesson. **Listen** as the teacher defines mathematics and discusses its related vocabulary. **Listen** to and discuss with the teacher John 15:5. **Observe** as the teacher draws a tree representing mathematics and its branches. **Listen** as the teacher applies mathematics to problem solving. **Color** the tree. **File** the picture of the tree representing mathematics and its branches. **Answer** reason questions about the lesson.
Lesson Enhancement	**Discuss** the body and its many parts.
Evidence of Teaching Success	The student was engaged in the discussions.
Evidence of Learning Success	The student was able to articulate the definition of mathematics and its branches in his own words.

278   The Noah Plan Lessons Kindergarten © 2003 • Foundation for American Christian Education

Biblical Foundations of Mathematics Lesson, Day 3

Grade: K   **Date**: _____   **Quarter**: 1   **Week**: 1   **Day**: 3

Title: Biblical Source and Origin of Mathematics

Component: Foundations   **Math Skill(s)**: Reasoning with the Word of God

Resources: Bible; T&L; Webster's 1828 *Dictionary; RightStart; The Noah Plan Mathematics Curriculum Guide*

Biblical References: Genesis 1:1–3; Psalm 19:1–3; John 1:1–3,14a, 15:5; 1 John 5:7; Hebrews 1:1–3a   **Homework**: None

Principle(s) Taught or Demonstrated	God's Principle of Individuality • In the beginning the God spoke, and by the power of His Word, the universe came into existence. Genesis 1:1–3 • *"I am the vine and ye are the branches."* John 15:5
Leading Idea(s)	Mathematics is an expression of God's character and nature.
Goal of the Lesson	• To reveal God and His divine nature and character through mathematics. • To guide the student in their understanding that mathematics and its branches begins with the living God and the authority of His Word, the Bible.

Teacher Presentation:
 	
• **Review Related Concept or Skill**
 	
• **Vocabulary**
 	
• **Instruction and Reasoning**
	
	Read NPMG, 7–8, 18–19, 47–48, and 52–55.
	
	nature, origin, source
	
	Review the definition of mathematics and its related vocabulary and its branches.
	Introduce the purpose and goal of the lesson.
	• **Define** and discuss the new vocabulary in simple terms.
	• **Guide** the student to the Biblical Principle from the Leading Idea by reading aloud and discussing Genesis 1:1–3; Psalm 19:1–3; John 1:1–3,14a, 15:5; 1 John 5:7; and Hebrews 1:1–3a
	• **Reason** with the student from the Scriptures. See NPMG, 52–55.
	  • God's nature is the origin of mathematics.
	  • Mathematics is not a created thing, but is of God.
	  • Mathematics and its branches stem from the Word of God.
	Draw a tree on the board to model mathematics and its branches stemming from the Word of God.
	Label the tree accordingly:
	• Trunk—mathematics
	• Branches—arithmetic, algebra, geometry, trigonometry, calculus
	• Roots—open-face Bible with John 1:1–3 inscribed in the book
	Distribute a prepared notebook page to represent the above tree for the student to color.
	Summarize and review the lesson.
	Ask the student reason questions about the lesson.

Student Interaction and Reinforcement	**Review** the definition of mathematics, its related vocabulary, and its branches. **Listen** as the teacher introduces the purpose and goal of the lesson. **Discuss** with the teacher the definitions of the new vocabulary. **Listen** to and discuss with the teacher the Scriptures that support the Biblical source and origin of mathematics. **Reason** with the teacher from the supporting Scriptures that mathematics is the very nature and character of God. **Color** the tree. **Participate** in a review and answer reason questions about the lesson.
Lesson Enhancement	**Contribute** to a bulletin board to model mathematics and its branches according to the recorded diagram in your notebook.
Evidence of Teaching Success	The student was engaged in the discussions. The questions asked by the student were indicative of learning.
Evidence of Learning Success	The student was able to reason from the Word of God and articulate the origin of mathematics

The Noah Plan Lessons Kindergarten © 2003 • Foundation for American Christian Education

Biblical Foundations of Mathematics Lesson, Day 4

Grade: K **Date:** _____ **Quarter:** 1 **Week:** 1 **Day:** 4
Title: Math on the Chain of Christianity
Component: Foundations **Math Skill(s):** Sequencing of time visually
Resources: Bible; T&L; Webster's 1828 *Dictionary*; RightStart; *The Noah Plan Mathematics Curriculum Guide*
Biblical References: Genesis 2:8; Psalm 72:8; Acts 16:9–15 **Homework:** None

Principle(s) Taught or Demonstrated	God's Principle of Individuality—God uses the continents and men to accomplish His plan and purposes for mathematics.
Leading Idea(s)	Mathematics advanced the progress of the gospel and liberty for the individual and for nations. NPMG, 8
Goal of the Lesson	• To prepare the subject of mathematics on the Chain of Christianity moving westward • To teach God's Gospel purposes for the subject

Teacher Presentation:
• Review Related Concept or Skill
• Vocabulary
• Instruction and Reasoning
	See NPMG, 64–73—Christian History of Mathematics Timeline.
	
	Chain of Christianity
	
	Discuss the Biblical Principle and Leading Idea by reading aloud Genesis 2:8, Psalm 72:8, & Acts 16:9–15.
	Introduce the purpose and goal of the lesson.
	• **Explain** and discuss the purpose of a Christian history timeline.
	• **Define** and discuss the term Chain of Christianity.
	• **Relate** the history of mathematics on the Chain of Christianity moving westward to the student in simple form. See NPMG, 64–73 for a detailed mathematics timeline.
	  • Asia—the continent where our number system began
	  • Europe—the continent where mathematics developed
	  • America—the continent where mathematics has helped bring liberty for the individual and aided in the spreading of the Gospel
	Distribute a prepared notebook page with the title "Chain of Christianity" for the student to write or trace.
	• **Model** the notes on the board to be written by the student. See NPMG, 163–164.
	• **Instruct** the student to file the notes.
	Summarize, review, and evaluate by asking questions.

Student Interaction and Reinforcement	**Participate** in a discussion of the Biblical Principle and Leading Idea. **Listen** as the teacher introduces the purpose and goal of the lesson. **Discuss** the purpose of the Christian history timeline. **Listen** as the teacher defines and discusses the Chain of Christianity. **Listen** as the teacher relates the history of mathematics on the Chain of Christianity. **Write** or trace the title on the notebook page. • **Record** the notes from the board modeled by the teacher. • **File** the notes in the notebook as instructed by the teacher. **Participate** in a review and answer reason questions about the lesson.
Lesson Enhancement	**Locate** Asia, Europe, and America on the classroom world map, globe, and atlas.
Evidence of Teaching Success	The student was engaged in lesson. The student can successfully present a notebook page.
Evidence of Learning Success	The student can articulate the history of mathematics on the Chain of Christianity.

280 The Noah Plan Lessons Kindergarten © 2003 • Foundation for American Christian Education

Biblical Foundations of Mathematics Lesson, Day 5

Grade: K   **Date:** _____   **Quarter:** 1   **Week:** 1   **Day:** 5

Title: God's Character in Numbers

Component: Foundations   **Math Skill(s):** Reasoning with the Word of God

Resources: Bible; T&L; Webster's 1828 *Dictionary; RightStart; The Noah Plan Mathematics Curriculum Guide*

Biblical References: Genesis 1:31; Psalm 147:5; Hebrews 13:8; Ephesians 3:3   **Homework:** None
Romans 1:19–20; 2 Corinthians 14:40; Malachi 3:6; James 1:17

Principle(s) Taught or Demonstrated	• God is a God of order. Genesis 1:31 • God is infinite. Psalm 147:5 • God does not change. Hebrews 13:8
Leading Idea(s)	Numbers reveal God's character. Romans 1:19–20
Goal of the Lesson	To guide the student in his understanding of God's nature and character through the study of arithmetic.
Teacher Presentation: • **Review Related Concept or Skill** • **Vocabulary** • **Instruction and Reasoning**	**Review** by questioning the student about the previously taught Biblical foundations, definitions, origin, and purpose. reveal, infinite, order **Introduce** the goal and purpose of the lesson. • **Define** and discuss the new vocabulary words using simple terms. • **Read** aloud and discuss with the student the Scriptures that support the definitions: • Reveal—Ephesians 3:3 • Infinite—Psalm 147:5 • Order—1 Corinthians 14:40 **Guide** the student to the Biblical Principle from the Leading Idea by asking reason questions: • What do Hebrews 13:8, Psalm 147:5, and Genesis 1:31 teach us about God? • How do these Scriptures relate to numbers? **Require** student practice, participation, and presentation. • **Ask** the student to describe the largest number he knows and then add one (1) to it. • **Repeat** the process until the student grasps the idea of God's infinite (never-ending) nature. • **Distribute** a prepared notebook page with the title "God's Character in Numbers" for the student to write or trace. • **Model** on the board the notes to be written in the student's notebook. (See NPMG, 163 for a sample student notebook page. Keep the notes simple.) • **Instruct** the student to file the notes. **Summarize**, review, evaluate. • Ask the student reason questions about numbers as a revelation of God's character.
Student Interaction and Reinforcement	**Participate** in a review of the previously taught lesson. **Listen** as the teacher introduces the purpose and goal of the lesson. **Discuss** as the teacher defines and discusses the new vocabulary. **Listen** as the teacher reads aloud and discusses the scripture verses that support the definitions. **Reason** and relate how God's character is never-ending (infinite) as demonstrated by numbers and addition. **Write** or trace the title on the notebook page. **Summarize**, review and evaluate. • Record the notes modeled on the board by the teacher and file in the notebook. **Participate** in a review of the lesson by answering reason questions about numbers.
Lesson Enhancement	**Listen** as the teacher reads aloud other Scriptures to support the goal of the lesson: Malachi 3:6; James 1:17
Evidence of Teaching Success	The student was actively engaged in the lesson. The student made the notebook record.
Evidence of Learning Success	The student can articulate today's lesson in his own words the next school day. The student can answer reason questions successfully.

The Noah Plan Lessons Kindergarten © 2003 • Foundation for American Christian Education

Sample Teacher Lesson Plans
with
Actual Student Work for
Bible as a Reader and English

It is written, That man shall not live by bread alone, but by every word of God.
(Luke 4:4)

Bible as Reader Lesson Plan

Grade: Kindergarten
Title: "Noah Makes a Big Boat"
Teacher: Mrs. Carroll
Biblical References: Genesis 6 and 7

Biblical Principle: Obedience brings blessings.

Leading Idea: Noah obeyed God. God wants us to obey Him.

Teacher Preparation

Books
- *The Early Reader's Bible*
- Webster's 1828 *Dictionary*

Supplies
- Notebook page to include:
  - a space for the student's name
  - the title "I Am Thankful"
  - a space for the student to record the things for which he is most thankful
- Paper, pencil, and crayons

Content/Lesson:

Day One:
- **Read** aloud "Noah Makes a Big Boat," 19–23.
- **Define** and discuss the new vocabulary: care, Noah, family, obey
- **Encourage** the student to use the new vocabulary in his own oral sentences.
- **Identify** and discuss the main characters, setting, and plot in the reading passage.

Day Two:
- **Review** by asking the student to retell the story of "Noah Makes a Big Boat."
- **Ask** the student reason questions pertaining to the story.
  - Who takes care of you?
  - How can you show your thankfulness to your parents?
  - Have you thanked God? Others?
- **Distribute** the prepared notebook page for the student to write his name and to record the things for which he is most thankful.

Day Three:
- **Assist** the student in choral reading of "Noah Makes a Big Boat."
- **Guide** the student to Biblical Principle from the Leading Idea by asking reason questions.
  - What was the result of Noah's obedience to God?
  - How did he show his thankfulness?
  - What might have happened if Noah did not obey God?

Student Work

- **Read**, reflect upon, and discuss, "Noah Makes a Big Boat."
- **Relate** how you will show thankfulness to others.
- **Record** in the notebook the things for which I am most thankful.

Accomplishments

- To read, listen to, and enjoy a story being read aloud
- To discuss and reflect on a Bible story
- To learn new vocabulary
- To integrate reading and writing
- To understand obedience to God brings blessings
- To identify the elements of a narrative
- To complete and file notebook work

The Noah Plan Lessons Kindergarten © 2003 • Foundation for American Christian Education

Bible as Reader Lesson Plan

Grade: Kindergarten
Title: Jonah Learns to Obey
Teachers: Miss Fleshman, Mrs. Shirley
Biblical Reference: Jonah and the Fish, Jonah 1–3

Biblical Principle: When we love God, we choose to obey him.

Leading Idea: Jonah's disobedience had consequences and resulted in punishment.

Teacher Preparation

Books
- *The Early Reader's Bible*
- Show pictures from the *Children's Illustrated Bible*, 174–175.

Supplies
- Mental action strips displayed in a pocket chart—monitoring comprehension, making connections, making predictions, mentally summarizing, and reformatting
- Map showing Nineveh and Jonah's journey
- Sequence chain form

Content/Lesson:

Set the stage and discuss unfamiliar vocabulary—*monitoring comprehension* by checking for understanding, words, phrases, and sentence.
- **Locate** Nineveh and discuss Jonah's roundabout journey.
- **Discuss** the size of a fish that could swallow a man.
- **Read** scripture passages from the Bible book of Jonah to give the outline of the story.
- **Show** pictures from *The Children's Illustrated Bible*, 174–175.

Make connections—*connecting stated information I have already learned.*
- **Connect** with personal storm experiences and fish.
- **Connect** with previous story of Noah, "Noah Makes a Big Boat."
- **Connect** with story of Adam and Eve—"Something Bad, Something Sad."
- **Connect** understanding importance of making decisions to be obedient.

Guide reading—*making predictions* and *mentally summarizing* by using a K–W–L chart. What I know (K), What I want to know (W), What I have learned (L).

K	W	L
A fish swallowed Jonah.	Why did he run away? How did he end up in the fish?	Jonah obeyed and went to Nineveh. The people learned about God.

- **Check** comprehension by having the students sequence the events of the story.
- **Reformat** the story into a sequence chain.
  - God sent a big storm.
  - The big fish swallowed Jonah.
  - Jonah asked God for forgiveness.
  - He obeyed God.
  - He went to Nineveh.
  - Jonah told the people about God.
- **Provide** oral reading practice using partner reading guidelines.

Student Work

Complete the sequence chain form with pictures and sentences.
Engage in partner reading.

Notebook Work
File form.

Accomplishments

- To link information into overarching principles and leading ideas
- To employ mental actions strategy to learn more effectively
- To discuss information with others
- To question themselves about what they know
- To think critically about information as they organize, restructure, and apply what they have learned

Sequence Chain Form (See NPLK, 286)

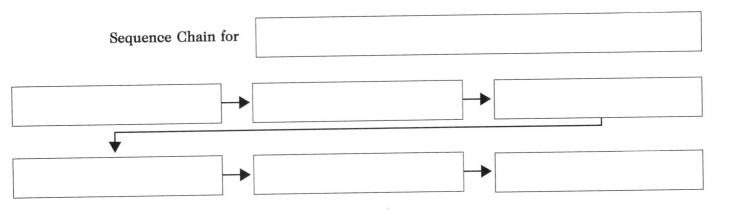

Partner reading: Partner, or paired, reading is an excellent way for students to read independently and grow as readers. In addition, the students can repeat the number of times they read to increase fluency and comprehension. Research has found that repetitive practice, at least four times, especially benefits struggling readers. The following guidelines were adapted from *Reading Essentials* by Regie Routman, Heinemann, 2003.

PARTNER READING GUIDELINES

- Find a place in the room where no one else is right next to you.
- The reader holds the book.
- Sit close enough so both partners can see the words.
- Take turns reading.
- Go back and reread if you don't understand.
- Turn and talk. (Tell your partner what happened. Both partners should talk.)
- Problem solve with your partner. (If one partner doesn't want to read so much, the other partner can read more.)

Sequence Chain for Jonah Obeys

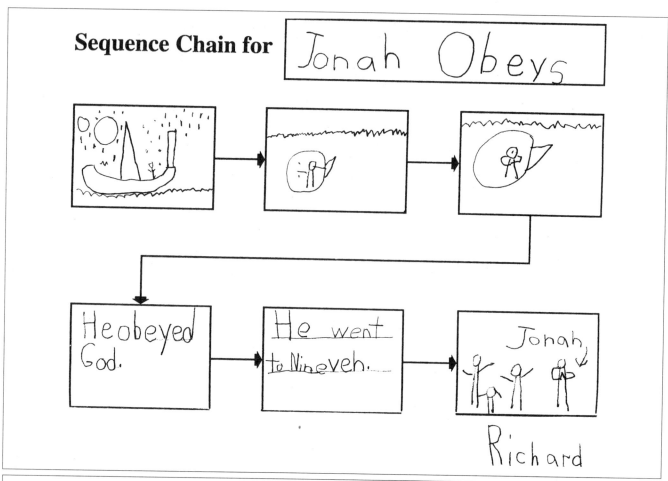

Richard

Sequence Chain for Jonah learns to Obey

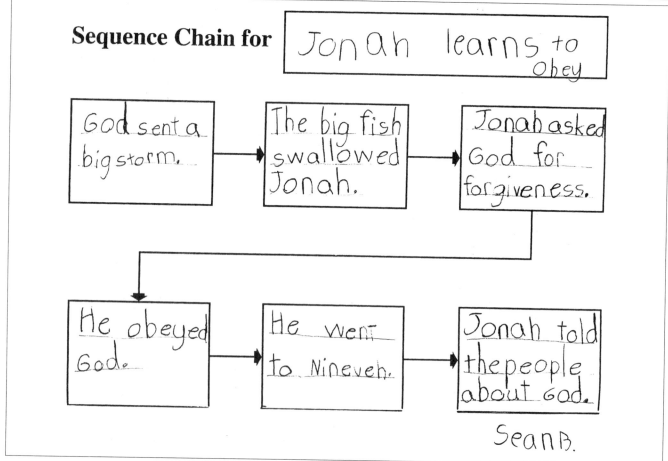

Sean B.

Bible as Reader Lesson Plan

Grade: Kindergarten
Title: "Supper with Jesus," 442–450

Teachers: Mrs. Carroll, Mrs. Shirley
Biblical Reference: Matthew 26

Biblical Principle: God instructs us to remember what Jesus has done for us.

Leading Idea: Jesus used the Last Supper to help his disciples to remember Him.

Teacher Preparation

Books
- *The Early Reader's Bible*, 442–450
- *The Children's Illustrated Bible*, 262–263, 264–265

Supplies
- Mental action strips displayed in a pocket chart—monitoring comprehension, making connections, making predictions, mentally summarizing, and reformatting
- Bread and wine (grape juice) for display
- Map of Holy Land with Jerusalem marked
- Story circle form

Content/Lesson:

Set the stage and discuss unfamiliar vocabulary
- **Show** the picture from, "Preparing for the Passover," *Children's Illustrated Bible*, 262–263.
- **Discuss** the place where the meal was held.
- **Discuss** the meaning of the Passover meal and introduce the vocabulary.
- **Use** the picture, "The Last Supper," *Children's Illustrated Bible*, 264–265.

Guide oral reading
- **Read** page 443 and answer the question, "Where will we eat?"

- **Read** top of page 444 and discuss picture on 445.
- **Ask,** "Why were the friends sad?"
- **Read** page 445.
- **Ask,** "What was Jesus' response?" (His singing)

Check comprehension
- Who was eating together?
- What did Jesus give his friends? Why?
- Who was singing?

Reason and Write
- **Reformat** the main events of the story into a story circle.

Student Work

Engages in discussion led by the teacher.
Reads orally from the Bible text.

Notebook Work
Complete the story circle

Accomplishments

- To link information into overarching principles and leading ideas
- To employ strategies to learn more effectively
- To discuss information with others
- To question themselves about what they know
- To think critically about information as they organize, restructure, and apply what they have learned

The Noah Plan Lessons Kindergarten © 2003 • Foundation for American Christian Education

Employ Strategies to Teach More Effectively

I. Relating the *five mental actions strategy* to "The Lord's Supper," Matthew 26

During the lesson the teacher engages the student's thinking using the five mental actions. The student learns how to consciously check his understanding of words, phrases, and sentences, and make connections between prior knowledge and the text. He summarizes what has been read and then reorganizes the information. In this story, he draws pictures for a story circle to sequence the events.

1. **Monitoring comprehension**—checking for understanding, words, phrases, and sentences
2. **Making connections**—connecting stated information I have already learned
3. **Making predictions**—forecasting, supporting, revising
4. **Mentally summarizing**—confirming or deriving the main idea
5. **Reformatting**—categorizing (reorganizing) information to use or file

II. A second strategy is the K-W-L.

The student analyzes what he knows (K) before reading and asks what he wants to know (W). This second step helps him monitor and regulate comprehension while he is reading. Thirdly, after reading the text, he states what he has learned (L) and draws conclusions and judges his predictions.

(K) I Know >   **(W)** What do I want to know?   **(L)** What have I learned?

Mental Action	Teacher Directs	Student Responds
Monitoring Comprehension	Vocabulary—supper, together, cup, twelve, drank, Jerusalem Discuss the different meanings of *supper* in this story.	Discuss the different meanings of *supper* in this story. Twelve friends refer to disciples.
Making connections	Twelve, connect with the twelve disciples in the life of Jesus from previous stories, "Jesus and the Children," and "Look What Jesus Can Do!" Jerusalem. (Mentioned in previous story, "Jesus on a Donkey.")	See the relationship between Jesus and the disciples.
Making predictions **Revising forecast**	What were the feelings of the disciples after they ate? Why did they meet in Jerusalem? **K**—Jesus had friends-disciples. There was a supper with Jesus. **W**—Where did they eat? Who was eating together? What did He give his friends? Why?	**K**—What do I know? **W**—What do I want to know?
Mentally summarize	**L**—They would eat at a house in Jerusalem.	**(L)** What have I learned?
Reformatting	Fill in a story circle. They met in a house in Jerusalem Jesus and his friends ate together. They did not want Jesus to die. Jesus sang and they were happy.	Draw pictures to tell the story of "The Lord's Supper."

The Noah Plan Lessons Kindergarten © 2003 • Foundation for American Christian Education

III. **A third strategy** is the **"Story Circle."** The Story Circle is a technique to help a student's comprehension, discussion, and summarizing skills. The teacher draws a circle on the board, on an overhead transparency, or on a handout. The circle is divided into the number of parts necessary to tell the story. It can vary according to the age of the student and the complexity of the story—four to eight. It is helpful to number the parts so each student will follow the sequence in the proper direction. The story is read either orally with the teacher or silently. After reading a discussion helps the student focus on the significant events and allows recalling the events in correct sequence. The student then records the main story events on the outside of the circle frame and illustrates the event inside the circle segments.

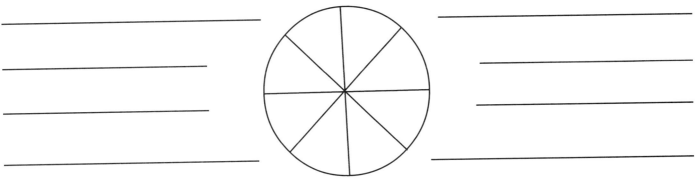

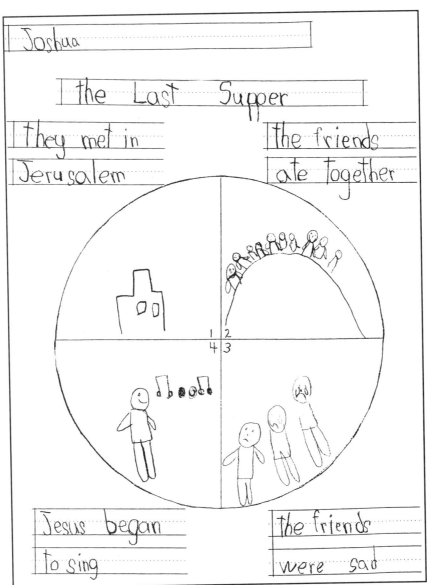

289

Sample English Language Lesson Plan

Grade: Kindergarten   **Quarter:** One   **Component:** Biblical Foundations

Skill Taught: The student will be inspired to understand that language is a gift from God and that the purpose of language is communicating ideas.

Principle: God uses language to bring us into relationship with Him.

Biblical Reference: Luke 4:4 "It is written, That man shall not live by bread alone but by every word of God."

Materials/Resources: Teacher should review NPEG, 49–52, 78.

The Structure of the Lesson

1. **Introduce the purpose and the goal of the lesson.** Language is a delightful gift from God. God gives us language for many reasons—so that we can know God, so that we can relate to each other, so that we can work and learn. One of the reasons God gives us language is just to delight us.

2. **Review related skill or concept.** Define the word 'delight.' Ask the student if he remembers a time when he laughed at funny words or enjoyed rhymes and rhythms in words. Use a nursery rhyme such as "Humpty Dumpty" as an example. Allow the student to offer other examples.

3. **Present new principle and idea with appropriate methodology.** Words and language are gifts that often bring us joy and delight. Language can make pictures in your mind and "feed" your imagination. Choose a selection from your literature to illustrate this idea, or use this quote from Monica Shannon's *Dobry*:

   > When we eat the good bread, we are eating months of sunlight, weeks of rain and snow from the sky, richness out of the earth. We should be great, each of us radiant, full of music, and full of stories. Able to run the way clouds do, able to dance like the snow and the rain.

   Discuss the pictures these words create in the student's imagination. Explain fully the idea of the bread being the result of the sun, rain, and snow. Explain how God feeds us to make us strong internally and externally. Ideas can feed our spirits like bread can feed our bodies. Words used delightfully touch our imaginations. In the Bible, God uses language to give us Truth using many "word pictures." Read and explain Luke 4:4.

4. **Require student practice, participation, and presentation.** Ask student to explain the quote in his own language. How do the clouds 'run.' How do the snow and rain 'dance.' Draw a picture showing how the richness of the earth, sky, sun, rain, and snow give us good bread.

5. **Summarize, review, and evaluate.** God gave us language to communicate with us to inspire us, to teach us, and to delight us. Words can create pictures in our minds that make ideas understandable.

The lesson succeeds when every child relishes language as a delight.

Sample English Language Lesson Plan

Grade: Kindergarten   **Quarter**: Two   **Component**: Biblical Foundation of English

Skill Taught: To appreciate English in God's providence; to place Wycliffe chronologically; to tell a narrative in detail and in order; to record neatly in notebook

Principle: God's Principle of Individuality: the uniqueness of English with its providential purpose and qualities; how God uses individuals to accomplish his will

Biblical Reference: Genesis 1:1,3—the verses that inspired John Wycliffe and the verse that represents Wycliffe's role

Materials/Resources: NPEG, 86. Teacher preparation, NPEG, 49, 60, 77; the Holy Bible; Classroom Timeline; Picture of John Wycliffe, CHOC, 28B

The Structure of the Lesson

1. **Introduce the purpose and the goal of the lesson.** Use the timeline to show that until 1384 the Bible was only in Latin in England. Latin is a foreign language that most people could not read. God used John Wycliffe to give England the first English Bible that people could read and understand for themselves.

2. **Review related skill or concept.** Review England on the globe. Review the chain of Christianity beginning in Asia. Review the uniqueness of English and God's purpose for the English language to propagate the Gospel.

3. **Present new principle and idea with appropriate methodology.** Using "Grandmother Rosalie's Story of John Wycliffe: the Morning Star of the Reformation," NPEG, 86, and a picture of John Wycliffe CHOC, 28B, tell and read the story. Tell the students that Wycliffe's work began the Reformation in England—a time when people turned to the Bible as the source of truth.

4. **Require student practice, participation, and presentation.** Students record in notebooks: "John Wycliffe, Morning Star of the Reformation" and draw his picture. Record the Genesis verses. A line-drawn picture of Wycliffe could be given for color penciling. Students individually retell the story orally remembering as many details as possible.

5. **Summarize, review, and evaluate.** Discuss John Wycliffe as a morning star. Place a large star on the classroom timeline to represent John Wycliffe.

The lesson succeeds when every child:

1. Makes the notebook record

2. Retells the story of John Wycliffe understanding the morning star analogy.

Sample English Language Lesson Plan

Grade: Kindergarten   **Quarter**: Two   **Component**: Syntax

Skill Taught: The student will learn that the sentence is the unit of thinking and language. The sentence expresses a complete thought.

Principle: There is order in language. We speak well when we speak in complete thoughts. The sentence is a complete thought.

Biblical Reference: 2 Corinthians 10:5 ". . . bringing into captivity every thought to the obedience of Christ. . . ."

Materials/Resources: Teacher should review NPEG, 140–148; 151.

The Structure of the Lesson

1. **Introduce the purpose and the goal of the lesson.** Explain that to express a complete thought, the speaker or writer must use a complete sentence. Give many examples of complete thoughts in simple sentences.

2. **Review related skill or concept.** Write a sentence on the board showing a capital initial letter and end punctuation. "My kite flies high in the sky." Explain that this is a sentence because it expresses a complete thought—an action "flies" and a 'doer' of the action—"kite."

3. **Present new principle and idea with appropriate methodology.** This thought can be represented in a diagram that shows the action and the doer of the action:

<u>Kite | flies</u>

4. **Require student practice, participation, and presentation.** Repeat some of the sentences used as examples in step 1. Write them on the board and have the student identify the action and the doer as you diagram.

5. **Summarize, review, and evaluate.** Have the student copy one sentence in the notebook with an accompanying diagram of the action and the doer.

The lesson succeeds when every child makes the notebook record. This exercise will be repeated many times throughout the year until the student understands that every sentence has a verb and a subject.

Sample English Language Lesson Plan

Grade: Kindergarten   **Quarter**: Three   **Component**: Etymology

Skill Taught: The student will hear and identify syllables in familiar words.

Principle: There is order in language. Words have parts called syllables. Each part or syllable is one breath of air.

Biblical Reference: Genesis 2:7 "And the Lord God formed man of the dust of the ground, and breathed into his nostrils the breath of life; and man became a living soul."

Materials/Resources: Teacher should review NPEG, 115–116 and NPRG, 111.

The Structure of the Lesson

1. **Introduce the purpose and the goal of the lesson.** Explain that every word is pronounced by using our breath. Have the student hold his hand an inch from his mouth and say the following word after you: go. Have the student notice the breath against his hand as he says the word 'go.' Explain that words have parts and each part is a syllable that is pronounced with one breath.

2. **Review related skill or concept.** Ask the student to think of other words that have just one breath. Practice feeling the air of the breath against the hand as each word is suggested. When a multiple-syllable word is suggested, have the student notice that the word has more than one breath, therefore more than one syllable.

3. **Present new principle and idea with appropriate methodology.** Words have patterns and parts. Say the word 'go' and clap your hands for one breath or one syllable. Now say the word 'going.' Clap your hands for each breath or syllable. Introduce the words 'do,' 'see,' 'good,' clapping the syllables. Now add a suffix to the words and pronounce them clapping the breaths or syllables; 'doing,' seeing,' 'goodness.' Be sure the student hears the sound and feels the breath thus identifying the syllable.

4. **Require student practice, participation, and presentation.** Ask the student to think of other words that are one syllable and pronounce them with claps. Pause often to offer a multi-syllable word for them to pronounce and clap, identifying more than one syllable.

5. **Summarize, review, and evaluate.** Have student write several one-syllable words in the notebook adding several simple two-syllable words and leaving a space between the syllables.

The lesson succeeds when every child makes the notebook record and can identify syllables by clapping the breaths.

The Noah Plan Lessons Kindergarten © 2003 • Foundation for American Christian Education

Sample English Language Lesson Plan

Grade: Kindergarten   **Quarter**: Four   **Component**: Composition

Skill Taught: To write a paragraph by inventing an idea, clothing it with words, putting it in order and committing it to paper as a group.

Principle: "Conscience Is the Most Sacred of All Property." God gave me a property in my ability to express ideas. I should use my gift of language to serve God's glory and to keep a good conscience.

Biblical Reference: Philippians 4:8—showing the standard for all thinking and thus writing.

Materials/Resources: NPEG, 244–249; the Holy Bible; a sample paragraph from the classic being studied that demonstrates a vivid description.

The Structure of the Lesson

1. **Introduce the purpose and the goal of the lesson.** Read the sample paragraph from the classic, demonstrating to the student its various qualities—imagery, phrases that conjure pictures, apt words, etc. Re-read the paragraph having the student listen again for the qualities presented.

2. **Review related skill or concept.** Tell the student how God uses writing to inspire and direct us; in fact, He gave us the whole Bible in written form. He thinks writing is so important! Inspire the student to know that his education is designed to make him become an excellent writer, like the author just read, so that they can bless others. Read the scripture that sets the standard for writing.

3. **Present new principle and idea with appropriate methodology.** Tell the student that the beginning of all writing is to learn to write effective paragraphs of several sentences. It begins with practicing writing paragraphs as a group on the board together. Give the topic (related to the sample paragraph just read. For instance, if reading *Little House in the Big Woods*, you might choose the paragraph on page 5 that describes winter.) Discuss how well the paragraph makes you see and feel winter. Now the student and teacher will together invent a paragraph about _____, (Choose something the children are experiencing now—like springtime.)

4. **Require student practice, participation, and presentation.** Lead the student in thinking (brainstorming, envisioning, listing, collecting) ideas about springtime. After some discussion and suggestions, lead the student in making a topic sentence. For instance: "Springtime makes everything new." Lead the student in making supporting sentences that complete the picture of the newness spring brings. The teacher might draw a simple line drawing on the board to demonstrate how each idea might fit or not fit into the topic. All suggestions are worthy, and with the teacher's 'editing,' can become supporting sentences. This is an exercise in modeling. The goal is the student understanding that writing has form and order, and steps and sequence.

5. **Summarize, review, and evaluate.** When the supporting sentences are written, lead the student in making a concluding sentence that restates the topic. Read orally together the paragraph with the title. The goal is that the student enjoys and appreciates the effort made to write an effective paragraph. The paragraph should remain on the board and be copied into the notebook the next day after re-reading it together. Writing has permanence and value.

The lesson succeeds when every child:
1. Participates in creating the paragraph inspired by the sample writing shared.
2. A worthy paragraph has been created and recorded.

Alphabetical List of Books and Publishers

Essential books are in bold print.

Ordering information by Publishers is found on NPLK, pages 297–98.

(New editions of out-of-print books or used books may be found using *Books-in-Print* through your local bookstore or library or online through www.amazon.com or www.bookfinder.com.)

A Beka Book, Inc.—Supplementary Readers
- *Basic Phonics Readers Set,* (Twelve small readers for beginners)
- *Big Owl Books,* (A series of four books for advanced students)
- *First Grade Readers,* (Larger books which begin with simple one-vowel word stories)
- *Little Books 1–10,* (Illustrated books that start with vowels sounds, consonants, blends, words, and simple sentences)
- *Little Owl Books,* (Eight small books with controlled vocabulary for beginners)
- *Reading for Fun Enrichment Library,* (Fifty-five books for reading enjoyment)

Abraham Lincoln (d'Aulaire), Doubleday; obtainable through the Foundation for American Christian Education (F.A.C.E.)

Admiral Christbearer Coloring Book, William A. Roy, Jr., ARK Foundation

Aesop's Fables, Henry Holt & Co.

American Dictionary of the English Language, Facsimile 1828 Edition, Foundation for American Christian Education (F.A.C.E.)

America's Providential History, Providence Foundation

Animal tales by Beatrix Potter and biography of Beatrix Potter, (local library)

Astronomy books, (local library)

Bambi, Pocket Books, division of Simon & Schuster, Inc.

Beginning Geography, K–2, The Evan-Moor Corp.:
 Vol. 1, Continents and Oceans;
 Vol. 2, How to Use a Map;
 Vol. 3, Landforms and Bodies of Water.

Botany books and books about leaves, (local library)

Children's Color Book of Jamestown in Virginia, The Dietz Press

Children's Illustrated Bible, Penguin Group, USA; obtainable through F.A.C.E.

Child's Garden of Verses, Chronicle Books LLC; obtainable through F.A.C.E.

Christian History of the American Revolution: Consider and Ponder, Foundation for American Christian Education (F.A.C.E.)

Christian History of the Constitution of the United States of America, Vol. I: Christian Self-Government, Foundation for American Christian Education (F.A.C.E.)

Christmas story book, (local library)

Dickson New Analytical Study Bible, World Bible Publishing; obtainable through F.A.C.E.

Divine and Moral Songs in Easy Language, Cumberland Missionary Society; obtainable through F.A.C.E.

Dogs books, (local library)

Early Reader's Bible, Gold 'n' Honey Books, division of Multnomah Publishers, Inc.; obtainable through F.A.C.E.

Encyclopedia, (local library)

Fairy Tale books, (local library)

Family and the Nation: Biblical Childhood, includes "Christian Idea of the Child," Foundation for American Christian Education (F.A.C.E.)

French Primer; see Mes Premiers Pas de Français

Fun with Snowflakes Stencils, Dover Publications, Inc.

George Washington's *Rules of Civility and Decent Behaviour,* in *George Washington: The Character and Influence of One Man,* Foundation for American Christian Education (F.A.C.E.)

International Bible Dictionary, Zondervan Publishing House

Journal of F.A.C.E., Volume I: Antarctica articles

Learning about My Body, The Evan-Moor Corp.

Little House in the Big Woods, HarperCollins Children's Books; obtainable through F.A.C.E.

Lullaby books, (local library)

Commentary on the Whole Bible, Matthew Henry, Hendrickson Publishers

Me and My Body, Penguin Group, USA

The Noah Plan Lessons Kindergarten © 2003 • Foundation for American Christian Education

Mes Premiers Pas de Français, Foundation for American Christian Education (F.A.C.E.)
Mother Goose and other nursery rhyme books, (local library)
My First Body Book, HarperCollins Children's Books
My Five Senses, Penguin Group USA

Noah Plan English Language Curriculum Guide, Foundation for American Christian Education (F.A.C.E.)
Noah Plan History and Geography Curriculum Guide, Foundation for American Christian Education (F.A.C.E.)
Noah Plan Lessons for Kindergarten, Foundation for American Christian Education (F.A.C.E.)
Noah Plan Literature Curriculum Guide, Foundation for American Christian Education (F.A.C.E.)
Noah Plan Map Makers' Kit, Foundation for American Christian Education (F.A.C.E.)
Noah Plan Mathematics Curriculum Guide, Foundation for American Christian Education (F.A.C.E.)
Noah Plan Program Notebook, Foundation for American Christian Education (F.A.C.E.)
Noah Plan Reading Curriculum Guide, Foundation for American Christian Education, (F.A.C.E.)
Noah Plan Self-Directed Seminar and Principle Approach Methodology, Foundation for American Christian Education (F.A.C.E.)
Noah Plan Wall Timeline, Foundation for American Christian Education (F.A.C.E.)

Our National Symbols, Milbrook Press

Peter Rabbit & Friends Cook Book, or *Peter Rabbit's Natural Foods Cookbook,* F. Warne & Co.
Plimoth Plantation Day Packet, Foundation for American Christian Education (F.A.C.E.)
Pilgrim Plantation Coloring Book, Plimoth Plantation and Mayflower II
Phonemic Awareness in Young Children: A Classroom Curriculum, Paul H. Brooks Publishing Co.; obtainable through F.A.C.E.
Poetry of Christina Rossetti, Henry Wadsworth Longfellow, and Isaac Watts, (library)
Primary Phonics, Educators Publishing Service

RightStart Mathematics: Kindergarten, Activities for Learning
Rudiments of America's Christian History and Government: Student Handbook, Foundation for American Christian Education (F.A.C.E.)

Science books, (local library)
Skeleton inside You, HarperCollins Children's Books
Snowflake Bentley, Houghton Mifflin Company
Spinning Worlds, Michael Carroll; obtainable through F.A.C.E.
Squanto, Friend of the Pilgrims, Scholastic Inc.
Starter Kit, Spalding Education International, 2003, includes:
  • *The Writing Road to Reading*
  • *The Comprehension Connection*
  • *McCall-Harby, Test Lessons in Primary Reading* (K–1ˢᵗ grade)
  • *Student Assessment Manual*
  • *McCall-Harby, Standard Test Lessons in Reading* (Book A–2ⁿᵈ grade)
  • *Spalding Phonogram Sounds*—70 phonograms on CD
  • Spalding paper
  • Purple and white spelling notebook
  • Individual phonogram cards
  • Word Builder Card Set
  • Ruler
  • Red Pencil
  • Book Marker
  • Blue Canvas Tote Bag
StoneBridge Art Guide, Foundation for American Christian Education (F.A.C.E.)

Tale of Peter Rabbit, Frederick Warne & Co.
Tales from Shakespeare (Lamb's), Random House Value Publishing, Inc.; obtainable through F.A.C.E.
Teaching and Learning America's Christian History: The Principle Approach, Foundation for American Christian Education (F.A.C.E.)
Teacher Guide: "Pilgrim-Pioneer Character Moving Westward," Foundation for American Christian Education (F.A.C.E.)
Teacher Guide: "Christopher Columbus, Christbearer to the New World," Foundation for American Christian Education (F.A.C.E.)
3 in 1: (A Picture of God), Concordia Publishing House

Uncle Remus Stories, Random House

Weather books, (local library)
What's inside My Body?, Penguin Group USA
Winnie-the-Pooh, Penguin Putnam, Inc.
Who Lives Here?, Random House (rare, but available)

Zoology books, (local library)

Ordering Information for Kindergarten Lessons Resources

(New editions of out-of-print books or used books may be found using *Books-in-Print* through your local bookstore or library or online through www.amazon.com or www.bookfinder.com)

A Beka Book
P. O. Box 19100
Pensacola, FL 32523-9100
Fax: 1-800-874-3590
Toll-Free: 1-877-223-5226
Website: www.abeka.com

Activities for Learning
(*Information Line*)
21374 York Road
Hutchinson, MN 55350-6748
1-320-587-9146
1-800-593-7030
E-mail: joancott@alabacus.com
Website: www.alabacus.com

Activities for Learning
(*Order Line*)
9120 Highway 1804 SW
Linton, ND 58552
1-888-272-3291
E-mail: order@alabacus.com
Fax: 1-701-336-7828

ARK Foundation
Admiral Christbearer,
William A. Roy, Jr.
1-937-256-2759
www.arky.org

Concordia Publishing House
3558 S. Jefferson Avenue
St. Louis, MO 63118
1-800-325-3040 (Customer Service)
1-314-268-1268 (Concordia Book Store)
E-mail: cphorder@cph.org
Fax: 1-800-490-9889

(The) Dietz Press
930 Winfield Road
Petersburg, VA 23803
1-800-391-6833
1-804-733-0123
E-mail: Owen-dietz@erols.com
Fax: 1-804-733-3514

Dorling Kindersley Publishing, Inc.
(see **Penguin Group USA**)

Dover Publications, Inc.
31 East 2nd Street
Mineola, NY 11501-3582
1-516-294-7000
1-800-223-3130
Fax: 1-516-742-5049
www.dover.com

Educator's Publishing Service
31 Smith Place
Cambridge, MA 02138-1000
1-800-225-5750
Fax: 1-617-547-0412
Website: www.epsbooks.com

(The) Evan-Moor Corp.
18 Lower Ragsdale Drive
Monterey, CA 93940-5746
1-831-649-5901
E-mail: www.evanmoor.com
Fax: 1-800-777-4332

Foundation for American Christian Education (F.A.C.E.)
4225-B Portsmouth Blvd
Chesapeake, VA 23321
1-757-488-6601
1-800-352-3223
E-mail: info@face.net
Fax: 1-757-488-5593
Website: www.face.net

HarperCollins Children's Books
(Division, **HarperCollins Publishers**)
10 East 53rd Street
New York, NY 10022
1-212-246-2058
1-212-207-7000

Hendrickson Publishers
P.O. Box 3473
Peabody, MA 01961-3473
1-800-358-3111
Email: orders@hendrickson.com
24-hr. Fax: 1-978-531-8146

Henry Holt & Co
115 W. 18th Streeet
New York, NY 10011
1-212-886-9200

Houghton Mifflin Company
(**Piper Books Series**)
1900 S. Batavia Avenue
Geneva, IL 60134
Fax: 1-800-733-2098
Toll-Free: 1-800-733-2828

(The) Millbrook Press
PO Box 218
Parnasus, NY 27653
1-888-866-6631
Fax: 1-800-943-9831

Paul H. Brookes Publishing Co.
PO Box 10624
Baltimore, MD 21285-0624
1-800-638-3775
E-mail: www.brookepublishing.com
Fax: 1-410-337-8539

Penguin Group USA
405 Murray Hill Parkway
E. Rutherford, NJ 07073
1-800-526-0275
Fax 1-800-227-9604
Email: customer.service@
us.penguingroup.com

Plimoth Plantation & Mayflower II
PO. Box 1620
Plymouth, MA 02362
1-508-746-1622
Fax 1-508-746-4978

Pocket Books
(Division, **Simon & Schuster Inc.**)

Providence Foundation
442 Westfield Road
P.O. Box 6759
Charlottesville, VA 22901
1-434-978-4535

Random House
400 Hahn Rd.
Westminster, MD 21157
1-800-733-3000
Fax 1-888-204-0336

Scholastic Inc.
557 Broadway
New York, NY 10012
1-212-343-6166
E-mail: custserv@scholastic.com
Toll-Free: 1-877-286-0137

Simon & Schuster Inc.
1230 Avenue of the Americas
New York, NY 10020
1-212-698-7000

Spalding Education International
2814 W Bell Road, Suite 1405
Phoenix, AZ 85053
1-602-866-7801
E-mail: spalding@neta.com
Fax: 1-602-866-7488

William A. Roy, Jr.
(See **ARK Foundation**)

World Bible Publishing
636 S. Oak Street
Iowa Falls, IA 50126
1-641-648-5155 (Information Line)
Fax: 1-641-648-5106
(Order Line-Clifton Book Co.
1-800-228-0939)

Zondervan Publishing House
5300 Patterson Ave SE
Grand Rapids, MI 49530
1-616-698-6900
1-800-226-1122
E-mail: zprod@zondervan.com